MARIE DE ROHAN, DUCHESSE DE CHEVREUSE

(*From a picture painted in Lorraine in 1627, and now in the Versailles Museum*)

The Duchesse De Chevreuse

A LIFE OF INTRIGUE AND ADVENTURE IN THE DAYS OF LOUIS XIII

BY

LOUIS BATIFFOL

ILLUSTRATED

LONDON
WILLIAM HEINEMANN
1913

Copyright

INTRODUCTION

It may appear a somewhat bold undertaking, after the publication of Victor Cousin's highly valued work (*Mme. de Chevreuse*, 1862), to write a life of the Duchesse de Chevreuse. But I have ventured to treat the subject afresh, because it has appeared to me that Victor Cousin was unacquainted with a number of documents which throw a new light on the life-story of Cardinal Richelieu's famous opponent; that he did not, perhaps, extract all the advantage he might have gained from the texts published in the Appendix to his work—texts of which, in some cases, fuller and more extensive copies exist than those of which he has made use; and finally, because, swayed by scruples far removed from those which affect the rights of the historical critic, he thought himself bound to soften down certain of his heroine's regrettable characteristics, and thus render his portrait of her more flattering.

I have taken all these documents in hand again, I have sought out fresh ones, I have made a closer analysis of the feelings of Mme. de Chevreuse. And I believe that I have thus been able to produce a more life-like impression of one of the most representative figures in the aristocracy of the seventeenth century. If the theory that one of the chief elements of history is to be found in the action of individuals—either in solitary instances, and thus ruled by the variations of each person's unstable temperament, or grouped into crowds, and then swayed by the contradictory tides of the collective phenomena produced by "mental contagion"—be a true one, such a psychological study as that I offer here embodies a more exact contribution to the

INTRODUCTION

understanding of a particular period than many a general description, even of the most brilliant kind. And this contribution will be found likewise in the picture drawn of the figures that moved in the circle in which Mme. de Chevreuse lived. I have striven to instil life into these figures—such as Louis XIII and Richelieu, for instance—and to give them their real physiognomies, such as the documents consulted show them to have been, and not transformed, as we find them in novels, and plays, and legend. The links connecting this biography with general history are thus of a quite different nature, enlightening, explanatory. History, which has hitherto been solely occupied with wars, negotiations, institutions, and outlines, economic or philosophic, must now be applied to the revelation of "the life" of past ages, in all its immediate and positive reality. Michelet has given us the expression which best fits this particular form, he calls it "resurrection."

The objection advanced against such "resurrections" is that they are fanciful, or "romantic,"—the truth, in this instance, is at fault, inasmuch as it resembles an imitation of itself! This reproach may be justified when the author, untrammelled by the discipline of science, thinks he must add the suggestions of his own capricious fancy to texts which he considers insufficient. But the duty of the historical critic is, on the contrary, to restrict the part played in his work by conjecture within the severest limits, and to seek out, select, and use his documents in sufficient numbers to enable him, with their help alone, to trace the succession of events, and that in the orderly sequence indispensable to the interest inspired by any literary composition.

The form of this work has not permitted me to indicate the authorities consulted at the foot of each page. I have carefully mentioned, in the course of my narrative, the names of the witnesses on whose testimony I have relied: a list of my references will be found in the Appendix, and

INTRODUCTION

I have endeavoured, by means of a number of fairly explicit quotations, to prove that my descriptions are by no means an exaggeration of contemporary opinion. Whatever symptoms of "imagination" may appear in certain passages of my story, my readers will be forced to admit that it faithfully follows the authorities at my disposal. Even more than "the art of telling a tale," history must be "a method" for the discovery, the criticism, the grouping together, of the texts of bygone days.

L. B.

CONTENTS

CHAP.		PAGE
I	MARIE DE ROHAN: DUCHESSE DE LUYNES	1
II	THE CHEVREUSE MARRIAGE	28
III	BUCKINGHAM	54
IV	THE CHALAIS AFFAIR	86
V	THE EXILE IN LORRAINE: THE PASSION OF CHÂTEAUNEUF	118
VI	THE FLIGHT INTO SPAIN	156
VII	IN ENGLAND: MADAME DE CHEVREUSE AND RICHELIEU	193
VIII	THE DEATH OF LOUIS XIII: THE RETURN OF MADAME DE CHEVREUSE	224
IX	AMIDST THE INTRIGUES OF THE FRONDE	262
X	RETIREMENT AND DEATH	303
	INDEX	337

LIST OF ILLUSTRATIONS

To face page

MARIE DE ROHAN, THE DUCHESSE DE CHEVREUSE
(*From a picture painted in Lorraine in 1627, and now in the Versailles Museum*)
Frontispiece

ANNE OF AUSTRIA   18
(*From a picture by Rubens in the Louvre Museum*)

THE DUKE OF BUCKINGHAM   60
(*From a picture by Rubens in the Pitti Palace, Florence*)

THE DUCHESSE DE CHEVREUSE   108
(*From a painting in the possession of the Duc de Vendôme, and now at Belmont Castle*)

THE CHÂTEAU DE COUZIÈRES, NEAR MONTBAZON IN TOURAINE   156

THE COURT OF CHARLES I OF ENGLAND AT GREENWICH   196
(*From a picture attributed to Janssen in the Royal Collection at Buckingham Palace*)

THE DUC DE CHEVREUSE   218
(*From a contemporary painting in the Museum at Blois*)

THE CHÂTEAU DE DAMPIERRE AT THE BEGINNING OF THE SEVENTEENTH CENTURY   304
(*From an engraving by d'Androuet du Cerceau*)

CHAPTER I

MARIE DE ROHAN : DUCHESSE DE LUYNES

The Duc de Montbazon—Marie de Rohan Montbazon : her childhood, her character—Her marriage to the Duc de Luynes—Anne of Austria—Influence of the Duchess on the Queen—Madame de Luynes disturbs the peace of Louis XIII—Her disgrace—1600-22.

TOWARDS the middle of the nineteenth century there still stood in the city of Paris, at the corner of the Rue de l'Arbre Sec and the Rue de Béthizy, an ancient dwelling, the elegant decorations of which, defaced though they were, proved it to have been the home, in bygone days, of some important family. At the end of a courtyard to which the action of the weather had imparted a shabby and sorry-looking air, there rose a brick-built façade, with stone chain-courses, crowned by a sharply pointed roof; the windows (those on the ground floor were grated) were flanked, on the upper floors, by pilasters adorned with Ionic capitals. The house dated from the Renaissance period. The property, in the sixteenth century, of Antoine du Bourg, Chancellor of France, and let, at a later date, to Admiral de Coligny, who was murdered within its walls on St. Bartholomew's Day, August 24, 1572; it was purchased, in 1617, by a prominent nobleman, Hercule de Rohan, Duc de Montbazon, Peer of France and Grand Veneur to His Majesty. Sauval tells us that M. de Montbazon had the whole edifice repaired and redecorated, that he caused the words "Hôtel de Montbazon" to be set over the door in letters of gold; that within its walls he displayed an excessive luxury. The somewhat moderate proportions of the building, as it

THE DUCHESSE DE CHEVREUSE

appeared before its final demolition in 1853, render any explanation of so sumptuous a manner of life somewhat difficult. In the days of Louis XIV the house was no more than a tavern; previously to that period it had known some palmy days.

This Duc de Montbazon was a great personage, indeed. Born of a family whose records—so one of his forefathers asserts, in a memorandum drawn up in the days of Henri III—covered twelve centuries, which was descended from the earliest kings of Brittany, was allied with "the greatest monarchs in Europe, and all the greatest princes of Christendom," was connected with the royal family, and had succeeded, for over a thousand years, in transmitting "the rank and honour of its original stock and author" by direct male descent, M. de Montbazon, with his great stature, his imposing air, his broad and energetic countenance, was a worthy representative of his race. The third son of Louis de Rohan, Prince de Guéméné, he had become duke on the death of an elder brother, in whose favour King Henri III had erected the estate of Montbazon into a duchy, and had at the same time married that dead brother's young *fiancée*, Madeleine de Lenoncourt.

His contemporaries all agree in asserting his intelligence to have been exceedingly moderate. Especially did they consider him brutal in his habits. Bautru, who wrote a biting libel on him, crammed with stinging taunts, and entitled *Ozonandre or the Coarse Fellow, a Satire*, turned him into utter ridicule, never vouchsafing him any name save "Prince of Louts," or "Prince of Béthizy"—an allusion to his house in the street of that name. To complete the picture, M. de Montbazon, like most great gentlemen of that epoch, had the morals of a horse-trooper. At a later date he was to be accused, when Governor of Paris, of going forth in full dress, and attended by mounted guards, to "plunge into debauchery." During his visits

MARIE DE ROHAN

to Montbazon, his castle on the banks of the Indre, some three leagues from Tours, or his still more frequent stays at the charming Château of Couzières, close by—a residence of which he was particularly fond—he indulged a passion for a certain courtesan of Tours, named Louise Roger, which supplied the whole province with entertainment. As a just retribution, his wife, so we are told, was constantly unfaithful to him.

The important position to which he rose is explained by the fact that to his name, his title, and his brilliant family descent, he added a perfect fidelity to his King, at a period when fidelity was a virtue rare indeed. He had followed the fortunes of Henry of Navarre. Henri IV, when seated on the throne, kept his kindly feeling for him. There was a story current in the family that when the Dauphin, afterwards to become Louis XIII, was born, Montbazon was in the Queen's apartments at Fontainebleau. The King, issuing from the chamber in which Marie de Médicis lay, to present the newly born Prince to his assembled courtiers, caught sight of Montbazon, and laid the infant in his arms, with the words, "Here's a heavy burden! It needs a Hercules to carry it!" M. de Montbazon was with the King when Ravaillac murdered him, in 1610. He continued in the service of Marie de Médicis, and defended her in the civil wars which ensued. He was employed on confidential missions, and zealously performed his duties.

As a reward, honours were showered upon him. He was made the King's Lieutenant in Normandy and his Governor in Picardy; in the year 1619 he was appointed Governor of Paris and the Île de France, and "Grand Veneur" of France shortly afterwards; he was one of the foremost noblemen about the Court.

He married twice. By his first wife, who had been betrothed to his brother, and who died in 1602, after four years of wedded life, at the age of nineteen, he had two

THE DUCHESSE DE CHEVREUSE

children. Twenty-six years later, when he was sixty, he married again. His second wife was "a beauteous damsel," so Souvigny tells us, of eighteen, Marie d'Auverjour de Bretagne, daughter of Charles, Comte de Vertus, whom he carried off from the convent in which the young lady had proposed to take her vows; a magnificent creature, tall and full bosomed, with a white skin and black hair, a nose a trifle thick and lips a little thin, of imposing presence and passionate temperament: the famous Madame de Montbazon of Anne of Austria's Regency.

The elder of the two children by the first marriage was a boy, Louis VII de Rohan, Prince de Guéméné; the younger was a girl, and this girl was Marie-Aimée de Rohan, destined, by her first marriage, to become Duchesse de Luynes, and by her second, Duchesse de Chevreuse. Marie-Aimée de Rohan was born in December, 1600, two years after her brother, who came into the world on August 5, 1598. She was given the name borne, in Henri II's time, by a great aunt, Marie de Rohan-Guéméné, the friend of the Constable de Montmorency. She could not remember her mother, who died when she was only two years old. Her childhood was a neglected one. The education she received was not of a nature to inspire any predisposition to a virtuous life.

If it be true that Madeleine de Lenoncourt had been unfaithful to her husband before she had reached the age of twenty, she thus gave proof of a temperament which in her daughter's case was sufficiently strongly developed. The father was not in a position to counteract so regrettable a tendency by any opposite qualities of his own, and Marie de Rohan, thus affected by a double dose of hereditary inclination, showed symptoms, at an early age, of a fascinating gift of coquetry, and an alarming lightness of behaviour. Brought up in the house of a parent who certainly never thought of giving her good advice, even when he was not actually setting her a bad example, left

MARIE DE ROHAN

to the care of governesses who possessed no authority over her, she had nobody about her to correct any of the dubious tendencies of her nature. Between Couzières, whither she often went, and Paris, which was her real home, she led a life that was little short of being quite independent, a life of pleasure, caprice, and liberty of every kind.

As a comrade she had her brother. In later years they were to go to law; as children the understanding between them was excellent. Short of stature, ugly, with the small grimacing face of a shortsighted creature trying to see things clearly, short irregular features, and twisted at that, Guéméné was far from attractive-looking: somebody declared he looked like a professional "tooth-drawer." But he was exceedingly witty. Everything he said was amusing. Marie de Rohan, who loved to laugh and scoff, got on well with a brother so perfectly suited to her taste: they were never apart. Tallemant des Réaux tells us that people were "astonished that the son and daughter of M. de Montbazon should have so much wit!"

Thus Marie de Rohan grew up, a spoilt child, in an atmosphere of careless gaiety. Such things as principles and prejudices she hardly possessed. Yet she was the true daughter of her century. She was fully conscious of the position occupied by her family, and that to which her father had attained; she knew what was her own due, and was never to forget who she was. But considerations of honour were never to stand in her way. Her religious sentiments, we shall see, were those suitable to a woman of her rank, and they were sincere; but religion was not destined to restrain her actions, any more than honour.

In early girlhood she revealed her possession of the charms which were to have such enduring power. She was pretty, full of refinement and distinction. Her small face, the purest oval, possessed the delicate and aristocratic features peculiar to an ancient and court-bred race. The tempting scarlet lips of her well-modelled mouth offer us some explanation of the passionate adorations she inspired. The wide-open and sensitive nostrils betrayed their owner's inheritance of the maternal temperament. Beneath a smooth forehead and widely opened golden eyelashes, the eyes, above all, drew others to them—eyes that had a certain reserve in them, a mysterious power of penetration, too, youthful, full of life, haunting and spiritual, at once scornful and captivating. Her hair was fair and silky, her figure slight, supple, not over tall, but well proportioned: altogether a very graceful, refined, and feminine being.

Wherever she went Marie de Rohan stirred innumerable hearts to love. Old and young, noblemen, bourgeois, peasants, every man who approached her fell under the charm. She wrote of herself, "I believe I am fated to be the object of the madness of unreasonable men!" It was as though she sent forth some heady perfume that had the gift of disturbing even the staidest heart. For a moment it even overcame Louis XIII and Richelieu. A wondrous power of fascination! Few women of the seventeenth century have wielded so far-reaching and decisive an influence over their contemporaries!

She was quite aware she possessed it, and made no attempt to lessen its power. We shall see her give herself up to her love affairs with a sort of amused and careless indifference. The fact is that she was exceedingly good-natured. And she delighted, besides, in loving and in being loved. It mattered little to her whether the object of her passion were always the same or not: as long as he was in possession, she was faithful to her chosen one. "It was not difficult," said one who knew her well, "to impose any particular lover upon her, but once she had accepted him, she loved him solely and faithfully. She once acknowledged to Mme. de Rhodes and to myself that by some caprice of fortune, as she thought it to be, she had never loved the person best whom she had esteemed the most, except, she added, in the case of her poor Buckingham. In spite of a devotion to her passion, which may be called eternal, though its object was occasionally changed, a whim here and there would turn her thoughts aside. But back she always came, and that with a transport which made her slip appear delightful."

And then Marie de Rohan delighted in fun. Wherever she went she left behind her the fascinating memory of a joyous being. Her cheerfulness vanquished the dreariness of the most gloomy surroundings. "She makes our Court so merry," writes Lord Montague from London, in 1638, to the Commandeur de Souvré, "that you will find it no less pleasing than that of Turin." Her lively conversation, full of quick repartee, proved an activity of mind which was often remarked by Richelieu, whom she drove to despair. Petted wheresoever she chose to go—at Court, to begin with, in the earlier days, before Richelieu's time, at all events; then in Lorraine, where she was treated like a queen; and in London, above all, where the royal family, Charles I and his Queen Henrietta-Maria, could not bear her out of their sight, and where all the English lords vied with one another in offering her proofs of their admiration, Marie de Rohan was everybody's delight. One understands how Fontenay-Mareuil came to write of her, "Nothing was really impossible to a woman of her beauty and her wit."

Was her judgment sound? The numerous letters she has left us, scrawled in an untidy and crabbed hand, do not cast much light on the point. They show us a nature that must have been sincere, self-contained, reserved, somewhat precise and cold, as a rule, in business matters; and never very warm-hearted. Mme. de Chevreuse wrote a "Discourse on Love," which still lies in the manuscript; its text, which is brief enough, is no more than a vague commentary on Montaigne: we learn nothing from it.

THE DUCHESSE DE CHEVREUSE

Our best means of knowing her is to follow her in her intrigues.

"An active and restless mind," says Monglat; "more clearly convicted of factiousness than any lady in the kingdom," declares Retz, Mme. de Chevreuse made intrigue the favourite occupation of her whole life. No other person has excelled her in the art of inventing complications, spreading them abroad, tangling them together, and rendering them so formidable as to end, thanks to her external relations and the personal charm she exercised over sovereigns and statesmen, in creating those political dangers which cost the Cardinal de Richelieu many an anxious thought. The author of a *Mazarinade,* which appeared in the year 1652, "*La Vérité prononçant ses Oracles,*" gives us the following outline of the activities of Mme. de Chevreuse: "Everybody knows she has given the first impulse to many great movements, and has been the moving intelligence of several great designs; the unhappy thing is that not one that is good has been ascribed to her. She is said to be exceedingly busy, but she never sets anything on a sure foundation; she is said to be very clever at tangling the skein of an intrigue, but she never can unravel any. She is said to be very clever at finding her way out of a labyrinth, but never does it without first of all getting herself into another. She is said to be a thorough marplot, and that says everything!" The conclusion the writer draws is that Mme. de Chevreuse was a person of incautious and meddling disposition, and this estimate is fairly justified by facts.

But the author is mistaken on one point—when he ascribes the activity of Mme. de Chevreuse to a regard for her personal interest. St. Simon, too, has said: "Intrigue, obedient to the star of the House of Rohan, served this family's interests." Mme. de Chevreuse was not an interested person. Mme. de Motteville, who saw a great deal of her, thought her rather absent-minded than otherwise,

MARIE DE ROHAN

full of fancies, and ruled by passion rather than by reason. Marie de Rohan was neither selfish nor ambitious. She intrigued her whole life long, but it was to amuse herself, and serve the cause of those she loved. "I have heard her say herself," continues Mme. de Motteville, "that no ambition had ever touched her heart, and that she had followed her own pleasure—that is to say, that she had interested herself in worldly affairs solely out of consideration for the persons who had been dear to her." Retz went still further, saying: "If the Duchesse de Chevreuse had been born into the world in a century when there had been no affairs of state, it would never have entered her head that such things existed." It may well be that in other and calmer times Mme. de Chevreuse might have spent her energies on peaceful and beneficent undertakings. But living as she did at a period when her social position and her relations with royalty enabled her to exercise a certain political influence, and being by her nature "fond of gallantry, lively, bold and enterprising," she was in a position, as La Rochefoucauld tells us, "to use all her charms in the endeavour to ensure the success of her plans": she did attempt it. Unfortunately she harmed all the causes and all the persons she tried to serve. "There was no peace in France," writes Mazarin, "until she had left it." The continuous effort such an existence presupposes makes its insignificant results appear small indeed in proportion.

She had hardly reached her seventeenth year when her father, who was anxious to get her off his hands, cast about for a husband for her. A lucky chance was to bring her a marriage at once brilliant, wealthy, and unexpected.

It was just at this moment—in 1617—that Louis XIII, having put an end to his mother's Regency by the execution of Concini, had taken the reins of government into his own hands. His favourite, at that moment, was Honoré d'Albert, shortly to become Duc de Luynes. M. de

THE DUCHESSE DE CHEVREUSE

Luynes was a young gentleman of modest extraction, from the Comtat Venaissin, who had reached his thirty-ninth year, and owed his somewhat sudden rise in life to the lively attachment with which he had inspired Louis XIII. The King had showered honours upon him. He had carried his affection to the length of desiring to make a marriage between him and his own natural sister, Mlle. de Vendôme. But the lady had refused, not considering M. de Luynes a suitor worthy of her: she had set her mind on marrying the Duc du Maine. Luynes, timid by nature, alarmed by her resistance, and fearing he might draw on himself the enmity of the Vendôme family and of the Duc du Maine, conceived the idea of getting out of his delicate position by marrying somebody else as soon as he could manage it. And then it was that he cast his eyes on Marie de Rohan. She was a most attractive creature. Her family, said to be very rich, was one of the greatest in the kingdom. Louis XIII gave his consent. The Comte de Montguyon was despatched to ask for the young lady's hand. M. de Montbazon had not a moment's hesitation. His private affairs had fallen into confusion. The objection that M. de Luynes came of a family far less illustrious than his own was largely counterbalanced by the prospect of the numberless advantages that should accrue to Marie de Rohan and her kinsfolk from the honour of being allied to the King's favourite. Day by day, the young wife's position would rise higher, as M. de Luynes' favour with the King waxed greater. The father agreed, the daughter made no objection. In those days, and in such great families as those of which I write, difference of age was held to be of no importance.

The marriage contract was discussed. M. de Montbazon promised everything he was asked: a dowry of 200,000 *livres*—the lawyers agreed that he should pay 50,000 *livres* down the night before the wedding, 100,000 more a year later, and the rest in another two years, with

MARIE DE ROHAN

interest on all unpaid sums, and a yearly income of 10,000 livres, as well, to be taken out of the fortune of the bride's mother and grandmother. From the reports of a lawsuit brought by Mme. de Chevreuse against her father, some thirty years later, we learn that M. de Montbazon never paid either the 200,000 *livres* or the promised interest, and that Marie's share of her mother's and grandmother's fortune did not reach the sum of 10,000 *livres* a year. But M. de Luynes was not very particular. And besides, complications of this sort were common enough in great families, in those days. The arrangements for the ceremony were made.

Before it was celebrated, M. de Luynes bestowed a first proof of his own favour on Marie. He himself was not to become a duke and peer till 1619. According to the custom of the Court of France, Mme. de Luynes, being married to a man of no more than gentle birth, had no right to a seat in the Queen's presence, whereas duchesses, and even the daughters of the other branches of the House of Rohan, could claim a *tabouret*. Luynes induced the King to decide that his bride should enjoy the same privilege as that possessed by the other ladies of the Rohan family—that of the *tabouret*, in fact—and that she should preserve it after she became his wife. No protest was raised, and M. de Montbazon was delighted.

There was no grand wedding. On Monday, September 11, in the Queen's apartment in the Louvre, and in the presence of the King and a few of the gentlemen about the Court, the betrothal ceremony was performed and the blessing pronounced, by the Archbishop of Tours, Bertrand d'Eschaux. Two days later, on Wednesday the 13th, the marriage properly so called was celebrated at five o'clock in the morning, in the presence of a small company of witnesses, in the Queen's Chapel at the corner of the old Louvre, on the side looking towards the Pont Neuf. Louis XIII, who had risen at half-past three o'clock in the morning, went to Luynes' chamber to fetch him, and conducted him to the chapel, where the couple were united by that same Archbishop of Tours. In the evening the bridegroom gave a great supper, and then departed with his young wife to the château of Lésigny-en-Brie.

Lésigny-en-Brie, an ancient turreted dwelling, formed part of the spoils snatched from Eleonora Galigaï, the wife of Concini, and Luynes had succeeded in obtaining possession of it only a few weeks previously. He was very much pleased with the property, he was to make great improvements in it, and spend so much money upon it that public opinion was to accuse him of having wasted the treasure of the State in the process. He little dreamt, when he took the new Mme. de Luynes there, that within thirty years, and in the course of civil wars which she would have partly stirred, his house was to be burnt down, with all the papers and correspondence that would have been so precious to the historian!

In Paris M. de Luynes bought his wife the Hôtel de la Vieuville, built by the architect Clément Métézeau in the Street of St. Thomas du Louvre, on the site of the present Place du Carrousel. He paid 175,000 *livres* for it, enlarged and beautified it; in later days it was to become the Hôtel de Chevreuse.

As the wife of M. de Luynes, Marie de Rohan might aspire to an exceptional position at Court. She was appointed Superintendent of the Queen's Household. Thus did Anne of Austria and the future Mme. de Chevreuse—whose lives were to be so closely mingled for well-nigh half a century—first meet, and meet for their own misfortune.

Their age was the same—both were seventeen. Slight, of middle height, with beautiful, rather short-sighted eyes, quantities of fair hair that waved and curled, a fair white skin, a small and "ruddy" mouth, Anne of Austria, so it was said, was "one of the most beautiful women of her century." This, no doubt, was an exaggeration, for her nose was thick, her eyes were a little too big, and her complexion was not satisfactory. But the shape of her face was exquisite, her brow well modelled, her figure charming. In the matter of intelligence she was less well provided; though she was not a fool, her mind lacked flexibility; she said little, and her ideas were few and far between. Indolent and lazy like the Spaniard she was, with enough love of admiration to make her play with fire, if not to expose her to the risk of letting it burn her, she was a child, full of easy and passive carelessness, always ready to laugh, rather superficial, and anything but decided in character. Marie de Rohan, "pretty, roguish, and lively," as Tallemant des Réaux tells us, possessed every quality best calculated to exercise the most detestable influence on the young Queen, whom her impetuous gaiety and passionate eagerness completely led astray.

The first meeting was chilly. Anne of Austria disliked M. de Luynes. She had, so she told the English Ambassador, Lord Herbert of Cherbury, "every possible reason for hating him." She endured the presence of the favourite's wife against her own will, and solely because the King insisted upon it. Similarity of age and sentiment was to bring about an understanding, the understanding was to end in liking, and that was to grow into friendship. Marie de Rohan spent all the resources of her fertile mind on the work of attracting the regard of the princess in whose service she was destined to live. She offered her endless proofs of attention to her wishes, gave suppers for her, took an active part in the ballets in which the sovereign danced; above all, she kept her amused with her merry and frivolous talk. We have some knowledge of the nature of this talk. It was improper beyond all bounds. Mme. de Luynes' education, combined with her own natural predisposition, had given the young wife a strong taste for coarse conversation and coarse stories. At

THE DUCHESSE DE CHEVREUSE

a later period, when Chalais was under trial and cross-examination, he asserted, with some severity, it may be, that "All the said lady's conversation turned on licentious acts, giggling tales, gallantries, and taking God's Name in vain." At the very best, Mme. de Luynes was caught giving the Queen immoral books to read. All these pranks amused Anne of Austria. She was sorry for it afterwards. She told Mme. de Motteville that she "did not then know the danger of living in the society of persons filled with passion and vanity." But by degrees an intimacy sprang up between the Queen and her Superintendent, which was all the closer because Anne of Austria—and she was much blamed for it—somewhat distant and haughty in her treatment of the ruck of her courtiers, admitted those who formed her more immediate circle to a familiarity which was considered excessive.

Favours, grants, dignities, all these things soon proved the Queen's affection for her Superintendent. It was in December, 1618, that Mme. de Luynes had been appointed "Superintendent of the Queen's Household and Purse, and Head of her Council,"—she was just eighteen. Her office carried great prerogatives with it: she gave all the orders within the Queen's apartments, all the officers of the Household made their oaths of fealty to her, she handed the sovereign her napkin at dinner, "held her pincushion, handed her shift, waited on the Queen at table, in her coach, within her lodging,"—all the privileges, in fact, known as "the honours." The Lady of Honour—next in rank to the Superintendent, and who in this case was no other than the Duchesse de Montmorency, widow of the Constable, a respectable lady of fifty—objected to having a child who was not even a Duchess put over her head, made a protest, and retired from Court: she was allowed to go. The Queen was to bestow many another public mark of her affection on Mme. de Luynes.

Sixteen months after her marriage, Marie de Rohan

MARIE DE ROHAN

brought a daughter into the world. Her wish was to betroth her at once to some great personage. Anne of Austria helped her, and together they cast their choice on a Prince of the House of Lorraine, M. de Joyeuse, son of the Duc de Guise. According to the contract, M. de Luynes was to give his daughter 600,000 *livres,* and the Duc de Guise was to endow his son with the property called Joyeuse, and a yearly income of 25,000 *livres.* The King and Queen bestowed a gift of 100,000 *livres* upon the baby betrothed. The child was too young, and the future too uncertain : the marriage was never to become a reality.

On December 25, 1620, Mme. de Luynes bore a son. Anne of Austria watched over her friend the whole night. In the morning all the bells began to ring. Louis XIII, who was at Calais with M. de Luynes, conveyed the fact of his good fortune to the happy father by means of salvos of cannon, fired from the castle of the town. He presented 8000 crowns to the man who brought the news. He gave orders that the christening ceremony should be of the most splendid kind, and granted a sum of 80,000 francs for the purpose. The church in which the rite was performed, and the Hôtel de Luynes, where the subsequent festivities were held, were profusely adorned. There were banquets and comedies and ballets; princes, princesses, courtiers and great lords, came in their crowds. The King stood godfather to the child, Marie de Médicis was his godmother, and the ceremonial was that used for a Dauphin of France. Seldom, indeed, had any married couple been so eminently and publicly favoured—the husband by the King, his partner by the Queen.

Cardinal de Richelieu accuses Mme. de Luynes, in his Memoirs, of having abused this favour by her exercise of a lamentable influence over the Queen's mind. "She was the ruin of the Queen," he says, "whose natural good sense was led astray by her bad example," she took possession of the sovereign's mind, corrupted it, turned the princess

THE DUCHESSE DE CHEVREUSE

away from the King and her duty to him, and sowed dissension between the royal pair!

Under a less severe form, Mme. de Motteville formulates the same accusation. "The Queen's misfortune," she writes, "was that the King did not love her enough, and so she was driven to fill her heart by giving it to ladies who made a bad use of her affection, and who, in her earlier years, instead of encouraging her to seek opportunities of pleasing him, and trying to gain his esteem, separated her from him as much as they could, so as to have her more completely under their own influence." Mme. de Motteville seems to lessen Mme. de Luynes' responsibility by representing it as shared by other members of the Queen's circle. But Richelieu's reproach still holds good, for Mme. de Luynes really was the centre and soul of the whole group.

The group in question was thus composed: Antoinette de Luynes, the Duke's sister, married to a certain Barthélemy du Vernet, and who had been appointed "dame d'atour" to Anne of Austria, a young lady of inconsistent and superficial character; Mlle. de Verneuil, the natural daughter of Henri IV, "as scatter-brained a creature as any about the Court," according to Tallemant des Réaux; and above all, the Princesse de Conti, Louise Marguerite de Lorraine, daughter of that Henri Duc de Guise who had been murdered at Blois, and widow of the Prince de Conti, an extraordinary creature—she had reached the age of forty-four—the looseness of whose conversation and conduct was notorious, who had done much to lead Mme. de Luynes into adventures of a sentimental kind, and had destroyed any remnant of scrupulous feeling she might have preserved. "The Princesse de Conti," wrote Louis de Marcillac to Richelieu, with a pen that was far from merciful (April 29, 1622), "has acted as the go-between in Mme. de Luynes' passing love affairs, which were going on during the Constable's lifetime."

MARIE DE ROHAN

The Court soon found out that thanks to Mme. de Luynes, Anne of Austria's intimate circle was an extremely merry gathering, in which the liveliest kind of remarks were in vogue. Some of these were whispered, with a smile, from ear to ear. The thing grew into a scandal. Well-intentioned persons took fright. Corsini, the Nuncio, relates in one of his letters that he has been approached with a request that he would use his influence with Anne of Austria's confessor, to put a stop to the cause of these reports. "Many of these ladies, and the chief among them," he writes, "live licentiously in the Queen's own presence, and, not imposing any restraint on their tongues nor their conversations, do not restrict their aspirations within the limits of modesty or propriety. I have been given to understand that my office demands that I should find some means of remedying these disadvantages, so that no report of them may reach the King's ears, for this might lead him to believe the mischief greater than it really is. I have been begged to take such action as will show the Queen the danger to which she is exposing herself. And I have resolved to speak of the business to her confessor, using, of course, the greatest caution, for I know how warily one must touch on certain subjects." This intervention bore no fruit. Matters reached such a point that M. de Montbazon himself felt it his duty to warn Louis XIII that his daughter Mme. de Luynes had given the Queen a book entitled *Le Cabinet satyrique, ou recueil parfait des vers piquants et gaillards de ce temps,* a volume full of poetry on dubious subjects. Such a course of education could not fail to produce its effect in the long run on a nature so indolent as Anne of Austria's, and so predisposed already to what she herself called "la galanterie."

"The Queen," writes Mme. de Motteville, "made no difficulty about telling me that in her young days she did not understand why ' la belle conversation '—what is

THE DUCHESSE DE CHEVREUSE

known as 'virtuous gallantry' into which no private attachment enters—could ever be worthy of blame, any more than the ordinary conversation of the Spanish ladies within the palace. In the person of the Duchesse de Luynes she had a favourite who allowed herself to be completely absorbed by these foolish amusements. Through the entertainments she proposed for the Queen's amusement, Mme. de Luynes imbued her, as much as she possibly could, with her own propensities to gallantry and merriment, and made the most grave and important matters serve as food for gaiety and jests." One subject of these jests was love. The gay coterie found amusement in other people's intrigues, and then, by degrees, arrived at the point of finding adorers for Anne of Austria herself.

Young and pretty as she was, the Queen was more than likely to stir passionate attachments. These were provoked, and encouraged, for the sake of the amusement they provided. One of the first was that of the old Duc de Bellegarde, Grand Écuyer to the King, a former comrade of Henri IV, a very courteous gentleman, full of old-fashioned gallantry. Mme. de Luynes and the Princesse de Conti filled him with high hopes, and everybody laughed, Louis XIII leading the way. Malherbe has left us two songs about this love affair. M. de Bellegarde was made to look ridiculous. Another passion might have had more dangerous consequences—that of the Duc de Montmorency, the brilliant and attractive nobleman who was to die on the scaffold at Toulouse, at the age of thirty-seven. He was a fine figure, though he did squint, —both elegant and magnificent. And he fell in love with the Queen. Luckily for that Princess, his heart was also occupied by the fair Marquise de Sablé. Anne of Austria, aware of this fact, made as though she were not conscious of the Duke's attentions to herself. "The Queen," writes Mme. de Motteville again, "did me the honour of telling me she had never seriously considered

ANNE OF AUSTRIA
(*From a picture by Rubens in the Louvre Museum*)

MARIE DE ROHAN

the feeling the Duc de Montmorency may have entertained for her, and she only remarked and accepted what the public voice had reported concerning him as a tribute to her own beauty, being persuaded that his passion for herself had really been very moderate." In reality it did produce some effect upon Anne. Mme. de Luynes and the other persons about the Queen soon proceeded to a far more dangerous experiment, that on the Duke of Buckingham. But, meanwhile, whether with her own will or against it, Mme. de Luynes was to threaten the peace of the royal couple after a very different fashion.

Cold though he was by temperament, and virtuous by principle, Louis XIII was far from being devoid of passion. As early as in the month of June, 1617, his courtiers had observed that the beauty of one of the Queen's maids-of-honour, Mlle. de Maugiron, had not failed to attract his attention. The King was fond of talking to the damsel, and liked to look at her. Anne of Austria took alarm, lost no time about finding a husband for her maid of honour, and married her as far away as possible, in Dauphiné, with a dowry of 10,000 crowns. Louis XIII said nothing at all. In December, 1618, it became evident, to the general surprise, that the King was taking a certain interest in Mme. de Luynes. Was he attracted by the intoxicating spell the young Duchess cast about her? Or was it out of regard for M. de Luynes that he paid so much attention to Marie de Rohan? The Nuncio Bentivoglio asks himself this question in one of his letters, and comes to the conclusion that the matter is in no wise serious or alarming. But the Queen seemed to be aware of the monarch's feelings: they distressed her. In the following year, 1619, the Spanish Ambassador, Giron, noted that Mme. de Luynes appeared to cause some emotion in the King's breast. Louis XIII paid frequent visits to his favourite's wife, held lengthy converse with her, allowed his eyes to dwell upon her for long moments.

THE DUCHESSE DE CHEVREUSE

Anne of Austria, who had noted it too, still held her peace. Was her Superintendent playing some coquettish game? Had she perceived, provoked, the King's emotion? Did she encourage it? The Queen did not believe it. But little by little the monarch's attentions to Mme. de Luynes became more evident. Deeply hurt, Anne of Austria ended by opening her heart to the Spanish Ambassador. The Ambassador communicated the facts confided to him to the Court of Madrid. The Queen, he said, was deeply affected, and avowed herself "the most unhappy woman in the kingdom, the most forsaken and wretched of them all."

The Ambassador tried to calm her fears, assured her she exaggerated the state of things, gave her counsels of prudence. And yet, not over sure himself, he wrote that his suspicions seemed likely to be confirmed. The Nuncio, too, grew anxious: his opinion was that the Queen's sorrow had its foundation not so much in her jealousy, as in her vexation at seeing that the King despised her own charms. After some hesitation, he made up his mind to speak to the King's confessor, Father Arnoux; but the confessor replied that he could answer for the purity of the King's intentions. And yet everybody's testimony agreed. The Venetian Envoy, Contarini, relates that in January, 1621, when the King came back from Calais, after the birth of the Duc de Luynes' son, and arrived at the Louvre, he paid a most hurried visit to his Queen, and then proceeded at once to see the Duchesse de Luynes in her apartment, found her in her bed, and kissed the new-born baby with a "very tender affection." Constantly, after that, Louis XIII was supping with Mme. de Luynes. His courtiers related, as a joke, how, during the siege of Montauban in 1621, the King lived with Luynes in the somewhat small and inconvenient Château of Piquecos, and sent the Queen and her suite to Moissac, from which place she occasionally came to see him, arriving in the

MARIE DE ROHAN

morning and departing again at night. One day, it would seem, the Duchesse, who was in attendance on the Queen, expressed a wish to remain at Piquecos. "But there is no bed!" objected the Queen. "Oh," replied Mme. de Luynes, heedlessly, we are told, "hasn't the King a bed?" Everybody began to talk! Bassompierre tells us in his Journal that the King "had an extreme passion for Mme. la Connétable." In reality the story was to come to a sudden end. Tallemant des Réaux, who had no friendly feeling for Louis XIII, declares the King "never had wit enough" to supplant the Duc de Luynes in his wife's affections. "Yet," he affirms, "everybody would have been delighted if he had done it, and she certainly was worth the trouble it would have given him." But the King, virtuous, timid, and anything but enterprising, would never have dared to try. To state the case more precisely, his feeling for the Luynes, husband and wife, had undergone a change.

In spite of the commonplace letters of condolence indited by Louis XIII on the occasion of the Duke's sudden death, in December, 1621, there can be no doubt that the favourite's demise preceded a fall which all contemporary witnesses coincide in describing as inevitable. Intoxicated by the honours the King had consented to shower upon him, Luynes, now a Duke and Constable of France, had taken on airs of authority which had ended by wearing out his master's patience. The sentiment of affection, more physical than anything else, which the King had felt for his friend, was destined to die out when Luynes himself disappeared from his sight. Once he was dead, Louis XIII felt a sort of spite and bitterness against his former favourite's memory, which had their root partly in his displeasure and partly in his sense of humiliation. The dead man's family, and the Duchess more especially, were destined to suffer from the effects of this angry antipathy.

THE DUCHESSE DE CHEVREUSE

In the main, even if the charms of Mme. de Luynes had, for a moment, stirred the King's passions, he had never felt any esteem for her. Serious-minded and thoughtful as he was, he well knew the nature of the influence she wielded over his Queen, and the manifestation of his consequent displeasure only awaited a favourable moment. Towards the close of the Constable's life the relations between his wife and the Duc de Chevreuse—Prince of Lorraine, and brother of the Princesse de Conti—had assumed a most suspicious appearance. Louis XIII ventured, one day, in a fit of bad temper, to tell Luynes M. de Chevreuse was in love with his wife, and Bassompierre, to whom the King repeated his remark, was surprised by the animosity of the tone in which the monarch added, "I was very glad to avenge myself on her, and cause him discomfort." When Luynes lay on his deathbed at Longuetille near Monheurt, on the banks of the Garonne, he committed his wife and children to the King's kind care, and Louis promised he would never forsake them. But once the Constable was out of sight his master's real sentiments made themselves apparent.

When the King returned to Paris, after the campaign in the course of which Luynes had died, he did not go to see Mme. de Luynes. The young widow was on the brink of her confinement; the King sent her word that she must quit the Louvre, because it was not proper for her to remain there in her condition,—that honour, he declared, being reserved for princesses of the blood royal only. Remonstrances were addressed to him, and as Mme. de Luynes, being Superintendent of the Queen's Household, must necessarily reside in the Louvre, he consented to countermand his order, but forced her to change her apartment, and relegated her to a dark and distant corner of the palace. She bore a daughter. But the King was slow about paying her a visit. "He did not show her any

MARIE DE ROHAN

sign of tenderness," writes the Venetian Ambassador. The Constable's sister, Mme. du Vernet, had already been requested to leave the Louvre. Louis XIII now informed Luynes' brothers that they must not show themselves in future at the Council Board, and that they, too, must disappear from the palace precincts: they obeyed. The persons known as "the Constable's remains," feeling their day was done, went their way in silence. But not so Marie de Rohan!

Startled for a moment by her disgrace, Mme. de Luynes soon regained her courage. One refuge she possessed against the King's wrath—Anne of Austria, whose Superintendent she still was. The young Queen, glad in her heart to see the Constable depart, clung more than ever to her friendship with Mme. de Luynes. She had troubles of her own. Her mother-in-law, Marie de Médicis, who had been reconciled to the King after his favourite's death, had come back, and, with her jealous, domineering, unruly temper, was disturbing the peace of the royal couple. It was to Mme. de Luynes that Anne poured out her sorrows. "The Queen's only consolation," writes Mme. de Motteville, "was the sympathy the Duchesse de Luynes showed her in her troubles." But while she consoled the Queen, she also amused her with the usual diversions of her dissipated circle. There were young gentlemen connected with these. The courtiers began to talk again about the too great freedom of the Queen's circle, and the far from modest conversation that went on around her. Ministers took alarm, and requested the Nuncio to speak to Anne of Austria's confessor once more. "They have asked me," writes the Nuncio, on February 23, 1622, "to convey to the Queen Regnant that certain gentlemen of evil life hold conversations of so licentious a kind with ladies of her court, whose behaviour is no better than theirs, that they exceed all the limits of decency and respect, which might

THE DUCHESSE DE CHEVREUSE

have regrettable results, by exposing the Queen to the ill-natured tongues of persons of good birth and of her people. The desire is that she should get rid of the Princesse de Conti, of Mlle. de Verneuil, of the Constable's widow. I shall endeavour, as dexterously as I may, to use her confessor for this purpose." Louis XIII knew all about it. His anger against the Duchess grew deeper every day. One final incident was to make the storm burst at last.

At that moment—in March, 1622—the Queen had hopes of shortly giving a Dauphin to France. This was not the first time: all her earlier expectations of the kind had been disappointed, to the King's great grief. The most extreme precautions had been recommended to Her Majesty; she was to avoid the smallest imprudence, to take every care of herself. Matters were following their normal course, and the physicians were reckoning on the longed-for success, when the hope of the whole nation was dashed once more, and that by the fault of Mme. de Luynes.

On Monday evening, March 14, 1622, the Princesse de Condé held a reception after supper—"tenir le lit" it was called in those days—in her apartment in the Louvre. The Queen, attended by the Superintendent and by Mlle. de Verneuil, was present at the gathering. The entertainment had been a brilliant one, princesses and court ladies had been there in numbers. Quite late—it was after midnight—Anne of Austria thought of returning to her own apartments. She had to cross the great apartment on the first floor of the Louvre, then used as a hall, or for great banquets, and now known as the Salle Lacaze. At one end of this room stood a low platform, upon which, on days of great ceremony, the King's throne was placed under a dais. Mme. de Luynes was seized with the foolish notion of making the Queen run along, with Mlle. de Verneuil holding one of her arms and the Duchess herself the other. When Anne came to the step of the throne, she stumbled and fell. A sharp pain seized her, she was put

MARIE DE ROHAN

to bed, and two days later, on Wednesday the 16th, the "hopes" had melted into thin air.

There was great distress at Court. Some of the Ambassadors came to present their compliments of condolence. Nothing was said to the King, who departed to Orleans and the South on the following Sunday (Palm Sunday), March the 20th. The Queen's indisposition was attributed to some ordinary cause.

But at Orleans, on the 25th, the King had to be told. He flew into a violent passion, caused by his disappointment as a sovereign and a father, his distress as a husband, his annoyance as a ruler. Punishment was to follow swiftly. One of the Gentlemen of his Bedchamber, M. de la Folaine, was despatched to Paris, bearing three letters: one for Mme. de Luynes, one for Mlle. de Verneuil, and one for the Queen. To Mme. de Luynes the King wrote: "Cousin,—Having come to the conclusion that it is necessary for the good of my service that the Queen's Household shall in future be ordered in a manner different from that which has obtained in it hitherto, I have decided that this cannot be better done than in the form, and by the means, which will be notified to you by the Sieur de la Folaine, whom I depute to express my will to you." This will was that Mme. de Luynes should immediately leave the Court. Mlle. de Verneuil was dismissed likewise, and made over to the charge of the Duchesse d'Angoulême. To the Queen, Louis wrote as follows: "The care which it is my duty to take, to keep good order in your household, has led me to decide on a change which will only bring it greater good, as you will recognize in time. I send La Folaine to explain my will in this matter to you, and beg you will carry it into effect at once, and be as prompt about giving me the satisfaction I expect it to bring me, as I believe you ready to ensure me that I confidently expect from you." Not a word of affection, just a curt note.

These measures, and above all the form in which they

THE DUCHESSE DE CHEVREUSE

were couched, produced an effect which my readers will easily imagine on the Queen and her friends. Anne of Austria was deeply offended. "The Queen," writes Mme. de Motteville, "who knew herself, and felt herself blameless, considered she had not been treated as she deserved. Human pride, always too strong in the heart of the great ones of the earth, made her a lenient judge of her own cause, and feeling Mme. de Luynes' disgrace to be an outrage she herself could hardly endure, she allowed others to perceive that she did not realize, as she ought, that to a virtuous wife a husband's will must be her immutable law." Anne of Austria sent her equerry, M. de Putange, to Orleans with a letter for the King, expressing her deep affliction. She had always, she protested, ordered her household in the proper way. She implored the monarch to tell her of what fault Mme. de Luynes had been guilty, so that she herself might take suitable measures on her own account, and she ended by assuring the King that in any case she would carry out whatever commands he laid upon her.

Louis XIII, already uneasy about his wife's health, grew softer. On March 27, he replied to her letter: "I did not intend, when I ordered my sister De Verneuil and the Connétable de Luynes to reside outside the Louvre, to forbid them to enter it, nor to deprive you of the freedom of seeing them." But that was not to happen often. Anne sent Putange again, and after him M. de Bonneuil, Introducer of Ambassadors, to press her request. Louis grew angry. Then the Queen begged M. de Montbazon to go to the King, who by this time had started for Blois; M. de Montbazon was received with downright rudeness. She sent M. de Verneuil, the Duc de Guise, the Duc de Chevreuse. The King lost his patience. On April 15th he ordered President Jeannin to wait on his Consort and communicate his final decision to her. "I am writing to the Queen," said the monarch, "to

MARIE DE ROHAN

tell her my will, which is that I absolutely will not allow her to see the Connétable de Luynes, except occasionally and rarely. To this end you will hand my letter to her, and I beg you will give her with it your own wise and salutary advice, so that she may conform to my desire in every particular." This was the final warning. Président Jeannin, in the King's name, gave Mme. de Luynes three days. If she had not left the Court at their expiration she would expose herself to the harshest treatment. There was nothing for it but to obey. Anne of Austria bowed her head.

So Mme. de Luynes was driven out! It was reported that her place as Superintendent of the Queen's Household was to be taken from her and bestowed on Mme. de Montmorency. Widowed, without helper or support, since the Queen herself could not defend her, an object of antipathy to the King, who could not bear the sight of her, Marie de Rohan seemed to have risen so high, thanks to her marriage with the Constable de Luynes, only to fall to the lowest depths, in the crash and scandal of her sudden ruin. But she was a woman of resource. She did not mean to capitulate, she meant to fight, and she was to find means to hold her own against the King, and triumph over evil fortune!

CHAPTER II

THE CHEVREUSE MARRIAGE

The Guise Family—The Duc de Chevreuse—His Marriage with Mme. de Luynes—The Duchy of Chevreuse—Dampierre—Return to Court —M. and Mme. de Chevreuse and the King of England—The Marriage of Charles I and Henrietta-Maria—1622-25

EVER since the time, early in the preceding century, when a younger son of the reigning House of Lorraine (then a German country) had settled in France, to push his fortunes there, and, after doing signal service to François the First, had been created Duc de Guise (his family name had been Claude de Lorraine, Duc d'Aumale), the prestige and power of the House of Guise had risen steadily higher, from generation to generation. The eldest of Claude's eight sons and four daughters had been that brilliant Duke François de Guise—a matchless soldier, one of the best leaders of the sixteenth century—murdered near Orleans, by Poltrot de Méré. His younger brothers were the Cardinals of Lorraine and Guise, both of them valued counsellors of the Valois kings. Their sister, Queen of Scotland, was the mother of Mary Stuart, married to King François II of France. So, through Mary Stuart's marriage, this younger branch of a foreign house became related to the royal family; the Guises of the second generation, brothers and uncles of the Queen, already stood higher than any of the greatest families of France. In the third generation they only just missed becoming kings. It was in the memory of all men that towards the year 1620, the son of Duke François, Henri de Guise, the popular hero known as "le Balafré," who had

THE CHEVREUSE MARRIAGE

led the League formed to defend the national religion, at that time imperilled by the weakness of the King, had attained an authority unequalled in the kingdom, and so vigorously maintained the struggle against the sovereign (who was far too much inclined to accept Henri de Navarre, the Huguenot, as his successor), that the question of the wisdom on the part of the States-General, of calling him to the throne, instead of choosing a Protestant King, had been seriously debated. Henri II, in his dread of being dethroned, and even put to death, and his alarm at the all-powerful position the Duke seemed likely to attain, caused him to be murdered at Blois, in 1588.

Of the five children left by the Duc de Guise, the eldest, Charles, was a man of very moderate worth; the second, Louis, had taken orders, was Cardinal de Guise, and Archbishop of Rheims, and considered a man of very dubious morals. The fourth, François, Chevalier de Guise, was to be celebrated during the reign of Louis XIII for his love of fighting duels which were lamentably like assassinations. The daughter was that Princesse de Conti, whose reputation was so compromised. The third son was Claude de Lorraine, who was first Prince de Joinville, and ultimately Duc de Chevreuse.

This Duc de Chevreuse was not entirely devoid of good qualities. We have a pretty picture of him as a child, painted by Leonard Gaultier. The long face, with its high and slightly prominent forehead, reminds us of Henri de Guise. The countenance is refined and distinguished-looking; the lower part well modelled. As a young man, the Prince was attractive, charming, well-bred looking. As time went on, his face altered. War, and the habit of command, gave him a masculine and energetic air. Towards 1622, when he had reached his forty-fifth year, he was a good-looking nobleman, powerful in frame, with large and pronounced features, the appearance natural to an active man. Only the calm eyes and good-natured glance

THE DUCHESSE DE CHEVREUSE

revealed his easy-going nature, ready to accept things as they were, full of careless resignation, touched with a certain naïve simplicity. Gaston d'Orléans used to say to Chalais, "M. le Duc de Chevreuse is faithless, soft, and devoted to his own ease." But he misjudged him. M. de Chevreuse, though possessed of what Tallemant des Réaux calls "a tolerable wit," was somewhat weak-minded and pusillanimous in ordinary life. But on the field of battle, he was extremely brave. He had joined the cause of Henri IV, after that monarch embraced Catholicism, and fought valiantly at his side. Men would quote his exploits during the sieges of La Fère and Amiens, during which last he had saved the life of the Maréchal de Biron, who had been surrounded by the enemy, and had brought him back to safety, covered, himself, with blood and wounds. "As to bravery," says Tallemant des Réaux, "nothing cooler was ever seen." When peace was signed, M. de Chevreuse went and fought against the Turks. When there were no more infidels, Huguenots, or Spaniards for him to run through, he fought duels. A first-class swordsman, he was well-known for his hot-blooded and quarrelsome ways with other men of his own age; Schomberg, Termes, Sommerive, Saint-Luc, Pompignan, all of them fashionable young bloods, and accomplished performers in the Court ballets. Over and over again, Henri IV had been obliged to interfere, and prevent him from going out to fight. As was sure to happen to a man of this character, and crowned with such a reputation, Claude de Lorraine had won endless favours from the tender sex.

By an unlucky chance, he had principally fallen in love with the mistresses of Henri IV—an unfortunate coincidence. First of all with the Comtesse de Moret; that time the King invited him to travel to England, and then sent him into quarantine at the Château of Marchais, the house of his brother, the Duke. Then came the Marquise de Verneil; this time, Chevreuse having only just failed in

THE CHEVREUSE MARRIAGE

killing the Duc de Bellegarde, one fine evening, in the Rue de la Cerisaïe, in the Marais, the King, in a fury, talked about "cutting his throat." Everybody knew the story of Claude de Lorraine's *liaison* with Mme. de Villars, wife of the Governor of the Havre: with Angélique Paulet, a famous singer of that day: and especially with the Maréchale de Fervaques, a widow past her first youth, who, being exceedingly enamoured of him, allowed him to dissipate her fortune on the plea that he had promised to marry her. His love affair with Mme. de Luynes was to be the decisive one of his life.

Marie de Rohan and he had seen a great deal of each other at Court, meeting in the rooms of M. de Chevreuse's sister, the Princesse de Conti. It would have been a surprising thing in that easy going society, if Claude de Lorraine, accustomed as he was to be kindly treated by fair ladies, had not remarked the captivating charm of Mme. de Luynes, and dangled about her skirts. Mme. de Conti, guessing her brother's feelings, made it easy for them to meet. M. de Luynes was still alive. His Duchess, dazzled by the prestige and glory of Claude de Lorraine, and urged on by Mme. de Conti, granted her lover's prayer. We understand what Louis de Marillac meant when he wrote to Richelieu that the Princesse de Conti had been the go-between in the love-affairs that went on in the Constable's lifetime.

Before long, everybody about the Court was aware of the intrigue between Marie de Rohan and M. de Chevreuse. The husband, as usual, was the only person who knew nothing at all. He and M. de Chevreuse continued on the most friendly terms. "I have read M. de Luynes the letter you have written him," writes Rucellaï to Chevreuse, "and have transmitted the protestations of amity and service you make him: he is very much pleased with them, and holds you in dear esteem." Louis XIII, as we have seen, had ended, in a moment of irritation, by making an

THE DUCHESSE DE CHEVREUSE

allusion to his wife's misconduct in the favourite's presence. When Bassompierre ventured to remark to the King, in this connection, "that it was a sin to sow dissension" between a husband and wife, "in this fashion," the monarch replied with a smile, "God will forgive it me, if He chooses!" He knew right well that the secret was no secret at all.

After the death of Luynes, in December, 1621, the two lovers exhibited their passion shamelessly. They were constantly seen together in public. The whole Court rang with it. When Mme. de Luynes fell into disgrace, in April 1622, she realized that her only chance of getting out of her difficulties, and inducing the King to revoke his decision, was to marry M. de Chevreuse.

According to the rules which governed the French Court, a Prince of Lorraine was not a Frenchman; he had no place in the hierarchy of the nobility of the kingdom, and in public ceremonies, as the records had it, "no regard was paid him." At the very most, and as a matter of courtesy, he was granted some special treatment within the apartments of the King and Queen. But if he could succeed in obtaining the title of a French Duke, his position would be totally changed. He would not cease to be a foreigner, as a matter of principle, but once his title had been verified and registered in Parliament, he would be bound by his oath to the King of France, he would be answerable to the jurisdiction of the sovereign courts of the kingdom, entitled to assume the position assigned to persons of his rank in the French aristocracy, and consequently would be, in a certain sense, a native of the country. Persons occupying this situation enjoyed, at one and the same time, the respect paid to their ducal title, and the attentions due to their rank as foreign princes related to a reigning family in Europe. This was the position occupied by the Guise family. They were treated with consideration. And besides, the alarm their political power had inspired

THE CHEVREUSE MARRIAGE

for the past half-century inclined the Kings of France and their ministers to more than a little prudence in their dealings with a family which had come within an ace of dethroning one of the successors of St. Louis. By this time the Guises were related to the Royal Family; the sister of the Duc de Chevreuse, Mme. de Conti, being the King's cousin, and a Princess of the blood royal.

Personally, Claude de Lorraine enjoyed the King's special regard, on account of his fidelity, and the signal services he had rendered to the sovereign. He had taken Marie de Médicis' part in the troublous times of her regency, and that of Louis XIII through all the civil wars arising out of the revolt of the nobles and the Queen-Mother, subsequently to the year 1617. "The diligence you have made in His Majesty's service," so runs a letter from Rucellaï to the Prince, written in 1620, in the King's name, "has exceedingly strengthened the esteem in which your person is held here, and as you are one of the few noblemen who have served the King, and as among those few, your services have been held valuable above all others, you may rest assured that you will be the most privileged henceforward."

To marry M. de Chevreuse meant, therefore, for Mme. de Luynes, to make her entry into a family which would ensure her the enjoyment of all the privileges—legal, moral, and political—its members possessed. It meant being the wife of an important nobleman, to whom profound respect was paid. Nobody would dare to strike at her; she would have the House of Guise, and all its numerous ramifications, a most powerful cabal, behind her. There would be no possibility of driving her from Court. The Princesse de Conti, once she was her sister-in-law, would see to that. Further, such a marriage meant, for Mme. de Luynes, the realization of a splendid dream. She would be allied to the reigning family of a foreign kingdom, related to the King of England, who treated the Duc de Chevreuse

THE DUCHESSE DE CHEVREUSE

as his personal friend. M. de Chevreuse was "that very high and illustrious Prince, Monseigneur Claude de Lorraine, Peer, Grand Chamberlain of France, the King's Governor and Lieutenant-General in Upper and Lower Auvergne." The courtiers called him "Monseigneur," and "Your Highness": Marie de Médicis called him "Nephew": when he went abroad, foreign courts received him with all the honours due to members of quasi-sovereign houses. In London, for instance, he dined in "the King's Bedchamber," a most signal favour! He had his own chamber at the Louvre, just over the King's. He was said to be very rich: he had a pension of 40,000 *livres* a year from the King, who made him presents as well, from time to time, 12,000 and 15,000 *livres* at once! Quite recently, on the death of the Duc du Maine, in 1621, the office of Grand Chamberlain, the second in importance of the "domestic offices of the Crown," had been conferred on him, in proof of the absolute confidence and esteem in which the monarch held him. He enjoyed the highest possible favour.

He had never married. At one time he had wished to espouse Mlle. de Vendôme, the natural daughter of Henri IV, but the Duc du Maine came forward as her suitor, and Chevreuse retired. For a moment he had thought of Mlle. du Maine; the negotiations were carried to a certain point, and then broken off. Mme. de Luynes was not likely to find it difficult to induce him to marry her.

Had the idea already been discussed between them? Mme. de Luynes was to declare it had. M. de Chevreuse will seem to have been unaware of it. It is quite probable that the plan had been talked over, and no final decision reached.

In the course of the three days that followed the summons to retire from Court, of which Jeannin had been the bearer, Marie de Rohan despatched a gentleman, a friend of her own, to M. de Chevreuse. M. de Chevreuse was not in Paris; he had gone on pilgrimage to Notre-Dame de

THE CHEVREUSE MARRIAGE

Liesse, near Laon, with M. de Liancourt, M. de Blainville, MM. Zamet and Fontenay-Mareuil. This gentleman found M. de Chevreuse and explained his errand. Mme. de Luynes made no mystery of the fact that she had been ordered to retire from Court, and that she could devise no other way of escape from her disgrace, save that of marrying the Duc de Chevreuse. She begged the Duke to consent to this union, and inform the King of it, adding that "nobody doubted that, out of consideration for him, His Majesty's order would be cancelled." But haste was urgent, because "if she once left the Louvre, it would be more difficult to put the matter right."

Surprised, M. de Chevreuse hesitated. He began by cross-questioning the messenger as to the reasons of Mme. de Luynes's disgrace. What had happened? Then he consulted his travelling companions. Fontenay-Mareuil, who was present, tells us in his Memoirs that each of them in turn tried to dissuade the Duke. His own position, they urged, would be compromised: he was certain to meet with all sorts of annoyances: after all the benefits the King had bestowed on him, and especially the office of Grand Chamberlain, to which he had just been appointed, he would fail in his duty to His Majesty if he married a person so little liked by him. Convinced by their arguments, M. de Chevreuse told the gentleman he was unable to accede to Mme. de Luynes' proposal.

He went back to Paris, and he went to see Mme. de Luynes. That was a very imprudent thing to do. He had reckoned without her powers of seduction. She cast her toils about him, pleaded with him; he began to weaken. She redoubled her entreaties, he gave in. To make assurance doubly sure, she told him she would write at once to the King to announce their marriage, and solicit his permission, in the usual manner. He had not strength to resist her.

When Louis XIII received Mme. de Luynes' letter, he became furiously angry. His first impulse was to refuse his consent. Those about him dissuaded him. After all, it was suggested, it would be against his conscience to prevent two persons who had notoriously compromised each other, from marrying now. If His Majesty desired to keep Mme. de Luynes away from Court, he would always find means of carrying out his wish: if he preferred to show consideration for M. de Chevreuse, things might be settled quietly, without any open break, and the King's dignity would be safeguarded. Louis XIII allowed himself to be convinced.

But before he had made his decision known, he heard that Mme. de Luynes, without waiting for his answer, had caused her marriage to be celebrated forthwith. Did she fear a refusal from the King? More probably, knowing his weak and irresolute nature, she thought M. de Chevreuse might change his mind. The ceremony was hurriedly performed, in the presence of a few persons only, on the 20th of April, just four months after the death of the Constable de Luynes. "I know not what the consequences will be," wrote Marillac, when he announced the news to Richelieu. There was a chorus of derisive laughter. The King was exceedingly angry. "The King," writes Marillac to Richelieu again, "is deeply offended with the Connétable and M. de Chevreuse, and has conceived a great hatred against them. He says that not one of the relations would sign the marriage contract."

But the thing was done. And what could others do, save endure what they were powerless to prevent? Within a few days, Louis XIII, following the correct formula, sent a letter of congratulation to the newly married couple; the courtiers' compliments were quickly added. There may well have been a touch of irony in all these congratulations. Everybody thought Mme. de Luynes far the most fortunate of the two partners; she was held to acquire "a great deal of glory—widow of the Constable though she

THE CHEVREUSE MARRIAGE

was—by her marriage with a Prince of the House of Lorraine!"

None of the relations, so the King had asserted, would sign the marriage contract. He was to some extent mistaken. This contract is still in existence. On the side of the Duc de Chevreuse, at all events, sixteen of his relations, and these the most important, did append their names to the document: the bridegroom's brother, the Duc de Guise, his uncle, the Duc de Nemours, his cousins, Charles de Gonzague and the Comte d'Harcourt, his aunt, the Dowager Princesse de Condé, his cousin, the Princesse de Condé, his mother, Catherine de Clèves, widow of "le Balafré," besides the Princesse de Conti, the young Duchesse de Guise, and four of his cousins, the Duchesses de Mercœur, de Longueville, d'Elbeuf, and de Vendôme. The abstentions were on Mme. de Luynes' side. Nobody belonging to her would sign, in fact. Even her father, M. de Montbazon, in whose house in the Rue de Béthizy the lawyers prepared the document, empowered a third person to sign for him.

Under the terms of this contract, the newly married persons were to have the independent enjoyment of their respective patrimonies. Marie de Rohan was to pay a sum of 300,000 *livres* into the common purse, and M. de Chevreuse, in return, ensured his widow the possession of a dowry of 10,000 *livres* a year, charged on the income of the Duchy of Chevreuse, and the enjoyment as a residence of the Château de Dampierre, furnished "in a manner fitted to her quality, with its poultry-yards, gardens, and canals." If Mme. de Chevreuse married again, she was to give up Dampierre. The bride and bridegroom made over to each other everything either of them had acquired in the way of fortune, apart from the personal patrimony of each, and it was specifically provided that each was to pay his or her own debts. This precaution was to prove anything but superfluous.

THE DUCHESSE DE CHEVREUSE

Public opinion was somewhat exercised by the fact that Marie de Rohan, who had only received 200,000 *livres* from her father, on the occasion of her first marriage, and even that sum not fully paid, was able to give 300,000 *livres* to M. de Chevreuse. "According to the contract," writes Marillac to Richelieu, on April the 26th, "the bride gives all her fortune, whatever it may be, to the children that may be born of this marriage, to the exclusion of those of her first." The lawsuits of later years were to prove that this donation of 300,000 *livres* was fictitious. Besides, the children of the Connétable de Luynes had their father's fortune. They did not depend on their mother, and were, indeed, to come to her help in hours of difficulty.

In the letters of congratulation addressed by Louis XIII to the newly married couple, he made no reference to his order that Marie de Rohan should leave the Court. Thus it remained uncancelled. There was nothing for it but to wait, and husband and wife retired from Paris till the question should be definitely settled. The marriage took place on the 20th of April, and on the 21st Mme. de Chevreuse carried off her husband to Lésigny-en-Brie. "The happy lovers," writes Marillac, "have gone to praise God for their prosperity in the chapel at Lésigny, and take possession together of the house the dead man prepared for them without ever thinking of it! It is the joke of the whole Court!" Presently M. de Chevreuse took his wife to the Château de Dampierre, there to do her the honours of his Duchy of Chevreuse. And thus did Marie de Rohan enter into possession of the domain on the name of which she was to shed lustre, and of the house she was to love so dearly, and inhabit so long, through so many hours of joy and sorrow!

Once a small and unpretending manor, the Château of Chevreuse, with the property surrounding it, had been erected into a barony in the first place, and then, in 1545, transformed into a Duchy, by King Francis the First, for

THE CHEVREUSE MARRIAGE

the benefit of the Duke and Duchess d'Étampes. Parliament had refused to register the letters of erection on the plea that the manor of Chevreuse lacked the importance requisite for such an honour. It was, in fact, a maxim among the Crown lawyers that the title of Duke, the most important in the country, was not to follow any landed property unless the value of the lands warranted the honour, and unless the income they brought in would permit the owner to make a fine figure at Court. After the Duchesse d'Étampes' time, the Cardinal de Lorraine, brother of the Duc de Guise, bought the place, added to the landed property, and then petitioned Henri II to renew the erection of the barony into a dukedom. To this the King agreed, in 1555. And this time Parliament did register the act. From the Cardinal, the Duchy of Chevreuse passed to his nephew, the Duke Henri, "le Balafré," and after his murder at Blois, to his eldest son, Charles de Guise. Henri IV had often told Duke Charles that if he would make over Chevreuse to one of his brothers, he (the King) would add a peerage to the dukedom. In 1606, Charles handed over the property to his brother Claude de Lorraine, Prince de Joinville. Henri IV forgot his promise, but Louis XIII kept it for him in 1612. Once more Parliament made difficulties. It did not give way until 1627.

A feudal property brought in two kinds of revenue; the income returned by the owner's own personal estates, his private property, which he either let out in farms or farmed himself; and the feudal revenues made up of the dues and rights paid to the feudal lord by the people who lived on the manor lands, or on the fiefs belonging to it. In the sixteenth century, the lordship of Chevreuse included, besides the village of Chevreuse itself, the lands, fiefs, and manors of Maurepas, Damvilliers, Maincourt, and some others. Dampierre did not, at that moment, form part of the property. The whole was a dependency of the diocese

THE DUCHESSE DE CHEVREUSE

of Paris, and the Baron de Chevreuse swore his oath of homage and fealty to the Bishop. The Cardinal de Lorraine enlarged the property by the addition of the manor of Meudon, the lands of Dampierre, the fiefs of Saclay and Cottigny, and thus succeeded in getting together a property that represented an income of some 6000 *livres tournois*.

When Parliament consented, on May 10, 1555, to authorize the erection of Chevreuse into a duchy, a stipulation was made that this sum of 6000 *livres* was only to be accepted provisionally, and on condition that the Duc de Chevreuse should increase it to 10,000 *livres*. In July 1564, the Cardinal de Lorraine obtained letters-patent, issued by Charles IX, whereby the King took the place of the Bishop of Paris, as the immediate over-lord of the lands of Chevreuse. Successive dukes added to the property. Claude de Lorraine was to enlarge its borders so considerably that it was valued towards the middle of the seventeenth century at something like six or seven millions of francs of our money. Marie de Rohan had not been mistaken. M. de Chevreuse did not appear to be a very wealthy man.

A splendid reception was prepared for the new Duchess. The small and ancient village of Chevreuse, peaceful and neat-looking, like all the villages in the Île de France, stood within its hoary walls, even as it stands to this day, at the foot of the Madeleine, and its ancient castle, built in the Middle Ages. People talked of "the town and castle of Chevreuse," the *manants et habitants*. To the lands and fiefs which had composed the Duchy of Chevreuse in the sixteenth century, others had been added—Villepreux and the adjoining parishes, Choisel, at the end of the present park of Dampierre, the Château of Becquencourt; and the private domains of the owner had been increased by the addition of the lands of La Tuilerie, Mousseaux, the Mare aux Bois, and the mills of Tan, the Pont de Beauce, etc.

All the officials who managed the estates: the officers of

THE CHEVREUSE MARRIAGE

justice, a bailiff, who sat at Chevreuse, assisted by a clerk and an official scribe; local justices, sitting in several places, and deciding cases that did not exceed a certain fixed value, against which decisions appeal could be made to the bailiff of Chevreuse, and ultimately to the Parliament of Paris: —for the woods, which were of considerable extent, necessitating the employment of special foresters, to watch and protect the trees, and make them return a profit, there were chief Rangers and chief Foresters—all these came to present their duty to the Duchess.

In her coach, Mme. de Chevreuse visited every village and hamlet. She was shown all her husband's domains. The inhabitants welcomed her with rejoicings. The spot that was to attract her most was the place where she was ultimately to fix her residence, Dampierre, in the pretty valley of the Yvette.

The Château of Dampierre was not in those days the stately edifice we now admire, which was built by Mansard, in 1618. The old house, constructed in the sixteenth century by a Treasurer of France, and embellished by the Cardinal de Lorraine, consisted of a group of low buildings in the style of the Renaissance, with tiled roofs and corner towers, all in red brick with stone courses, set round several courtyards of various sizes. Moats full of water encircled it. The general effect was picturesque; the tall steep roofs, the slender shafted chimneys, the high windows adorned with sculptured stone decorations that stood out against the roofs, imparted a varied and pleasing appearance to the whole pile. For those days, the house was an unpretending one.

From the road, which ran straight across the valley, between a large sheet of water, still there, and the Château, the traveller reached the entrance gate, a steep-roofed pavilion, with three windows. The outer court was small, surrounded by low outbuildings, and beyond them, to the eastern side, lay a larger court, the poultry-yard,

THE DUCHESSE DE CHEVREUSE

with outhouses all round it—a remnant of which still remains in the shape of a large open-raftered hall, entered by a doorway which is not devoid of character. On the right side of the outer court, and behind a drawbridge, was the second entrance of the Château, a one-storied pavilion, with a steep roof in the style of Henri IV. Then came the inner courtyard, very plain, square, the buildings all round it of one story only, except those on the western side, which had another story looking over the water. In the middle of these stood the entrance door of the house, rather low, arched, and without any kind of ornament, and in this central part of the dwelling, on the left, was the great hall, a fine room with open rafters and a tall monumental stone chimney-piece, lighted by six windows. The rest of the house was taken up with living-rooms and servants' quarters.

On the other side of the main building, towards the south, there was a square grass-plot, with flower-beds cut in it, surrounded by a portico, along the outer edge of which a ditch full of water ran. Another lawn of still larger dimensions, also cut up into flower-beds, and bounded by the waters of a canal, completed the garden on the Chevreuse side. There was no park at all. All about the place lay a perpetual succession of woods, cultivated fields, meadow-land, "warrens," and vineyards. The thing that struck one was the quantities of water. People used to say, "the enclosures, gardens, ponds, canals and fountains of Dampierre." In its frame of woodland and greenery, Dampierre was the picture of a delightful rural habitation, an ideal retreat, buried in the solitude and calm of the quiet country.

Madame de Chevreuse took a fancy to the place; she liked the squat homelike dwelling and its view over the great pond; the walk under the stone portico that ran round the flower lawn, and reminded her of the finest houses of the preceding century—Gaillon, for instance—

THE CHEVREUSE MARRIAGE

delighted her. At her instigation, the duke her husband began to take an interest in the place. Not caring to construct another dwelling—he was no house-builder—he made up his mind to enlarge the flower gardens, and create a large park all round them. He it was who made the great park of Dampierre. He followed the methods of an opulent nobleman, to whom the complaints of his humbler neighbours and his own outlay mattered but little. He bought the land he wanted by sheer compulsion, without taking the trouble to do things delicately. He enlarged his borders as far as the parishes of Choisel and Senlis, three-quarters of a league away. He was not the only person who did such things. "He made his park," explains Tallemant, "after the fashion of old d'Angoulême at Grosbois. He simply enclosed everybody else's land!" To quiet the uproar, he promised keys of the park to all the injured persons. But he never gave away one. A "Captain of the Château of Dampierre," aided by "the Steward of the Household of Monseigneur the Duc de Chevreuse, and Forester of that place," was put in charge of the Château, and kept all things in order there.

But great as the delights of Dampierre, its woods and its duchy, might be, the new Duchess had no notion of spending her life there. How did she stand with the King? Could she go back to Court or not? She applied for information to her sister-in-law, the Princesse de Conti.

This lady, as the author, though indirectly, of their marriage, owed it to her brother and her friend to help them out of their uncertainty. Alone and unaided, she might have found some difficulty in doing it; she summoned Bassompierre to her assistance.

Bassompierre, at that time in high favour with Louis XIII, was attending the King on his campaign against the Southern Huguenots. He had the sovereign's ear, and could reckon on being favourably received. Louis delighted in the company of this handsome nobleman,

THE DUCHESSE DE CHEVREUSE

unfailingly gay, jovial, witty, deferential, and devoted to his master. In July of that same year (1622) he was to make him a Marshal of France. Now Bassompierre doted on the Princesse de Conti, whose faithful lover he remained for thirty years. He undertook to perform the commission suggested to him. The attempt to get Mme. de Chevreuse recalled was soon known at Court. The affair was nick-named "the ladies' cabal." Well-informed people doubted its success. "Bassompierre," wrote Marillac to Richelieu, "has nothing to go on except his own cunning and effrontery. The Princess will find his favour will give her no better support than her own legs just after she had lain in. His favour is as slight as her legs were shaky." He was mistaken. Bassompierre had excellent means at his command.

As a matter of fact, the position of M. de Chevreuse was by no means so compromised by his marriage as might have been imagined. He was too powerful for that. Louis XIII, at war with the Huguenots, did not care to provoke a quarrel with his great nobles as well. The memory of the seven or eight years of civil strife they had already waged against him was too present to his mind for his Ministers to fail in advising all necessary caution. The Guise family was one of the most influential in the country; its following was large; its renown would quite probably attract many partisans. All these circumstances had served M. de Chevreuse. His personal favour with the King was still high, and that for reasons which rendered his marriage without the King's leave, to a lady who was in disgrace with the monarch, a fault not so particularly grave as to outweigh his credit. At that very moment, indeed, Louis stood in need of his services, and was making use of them. The Court of France had been trying, for a considerable period, to arrange a marriage between the King's young sister, Henrietta-Maria, and the son of the King of England, who

THE CHEVREUSE MARRIAGE

afterwards became Charles I. There were many difficulties in the way, and the negotiations had been broken off several times. M. de Chevreuse, who was in friendly relations with the King of England, his kinsman, acted as unofficial go-between. The King depended on his help. This was not the moment to fall out with him over a marriage in which he had been the victim of the lady's cunning rather than a deliberate offender against his master's will.

Bassompierre felt his way. Might M. de Chevreuse come and make his bow to the King, who was carrying on his campaign against the Huguenots in Guyenne? A favourable answer was vouchsafed, and a month after his marriage, on May 20, 1622, the Duc de Chevreuse reached the camp before St. Émilion, near Libourne, whither the King had come after the surrender of Royan.

He was well received. Louis XIII seemed to have forgotten all about his marriage, and never mentioned it to him. He showed him just as much favour as before, to such a point, indeed, that on the 27th, M. de Chevreuse was appointed Grand Falconer of France! Everybody concluded Marie de Rohan's business was on the way to a satisfactory settlement. M. de Chevreuse's conduct justified the royal affection for him. Nobody was braver in the field; in June, when the attack on Négrepelisse was delivered, he took command of the forlorn hope—a flying column of attack—and hurled himself, with Bassompierre and Praslin, upon the enemy's defences. He only just escaped with his life. Louis XIII sought his advice, invited him to attend his councils of war, listened to his opinions. It would have been difficult to desire a more established position.

So Chevreuse, having concerted measures with Bassompierre, ventured to speak to the King of his wife, and to ask His Majesty for a word which would permit her to return to Court. The moment he opened his mouth he

THE DUCHESSE DE CHEVREUSE

was snubbed;—Louis XIII was a suspicious man. There was nothing for it but to wait. It was a well-known fact that the Council of Ministers, with the exception of M. de Puisieux, who favoured the Duchess for personal reasons of his own, was strongly opposed to her return. From the 20th of May till the 3rd of July, Chevreuse and Bassompierre carried on a siege, prudent, methodical, gradual. Louis XIII could not well hold out for ever. By the end of the sixth week the petitioners had gained their point. The King consented to allow Mme. de Chevreuse to take up her duties about the Queen. She was to continue in her offices, including that of Superintendent of the Household; but the royal forgiveness was only bestowed out of regard for M. de Chevreuse. "Out of the affection I bear my cousin the Duc de Chevreuse," wrote the King to Anne of Austria, "I am very glad his wife should come back." He was never to lose any opportunity of stating, in the most specific manner, that anything he did for Mme. de Chevreuse was granted solely on her husband's account. The winding up of M. de Luynes' affairs had been a somewhat complicated business (it had been necessary, in fact, to appeal to the King for leave to include moneys belonging to the Constable, and found, after his death, in the Citadel of Amiens, in the sum at the disposal of his heirs), and Louis XIII had facilitated the arrangements, on condition that the money thus secured should be handed over directly to M. de Chevreuse, as an instalment of the 300,000 *livres* the Duchess his wife was bound to pay into the common purse. "Now that it has been explained to me," writes Louis to M. de Luynes' brother, M. de Chaulnes, "that the sums held in common by the Duchesse de Chevreuse and my late cousin the Constable, have been liquidated, it has been my pleasure to inform you that once you have set aside the share of his children in the inheritance of the moneys found in my Citadel of Amiens, belonging to my

THE CHEVREUSE MARRIAGE

said cousin the Constable, you are at liberty to hand over to my cousin the Duc de Chevreuse, without making any difficulty at all, all that he acquires through his marriage. The duties he performs about my person, to my own satisfaction and the benefit of my service, lead me to aid the arrangement of his affairs which he expects thereby." Precarious indeed was the return of Mme. de Chevreuse to Court, as long as the King nourished such feelings concerning her!

Quietly she crept back to Paris, unobtrusively she retook her place in the Queen's circle. From the earliest moments of her reappearance, she was to feel the effect of the King's displeasure.

During the life-time of the Duc de Luynes, the old Duchesse de Montmorency, Anne of Austria's Lady of Honour, had not renewed her protest against the appointment of so young a woman to the post of Superintendent of the Queen's Household; she had been content with absenting herself from Court, and not performing her duties there. Once M. de Luynes was dead, his family fallen into disgrace, and his widow's position sorely shaken, she decided to make a fresh claim. Her stepson, the Duc de Montmorency, took up her quarrel: he set forth that when Mme. de Montmorency had been appointed Lady of Honour, there had been a promise that, to save her dignity, no Superintendent should be appointed at all. The appointment of Mme. de Chevreuse had been a contravention of this undertaking, and ought to be cancelled. Mme. de Chevreuse defended her own cause. Two years earlier, Louis XIII would have imposed silence on Mme. de Montmorency. This time, he affected a desire to do what was just and fair. A commissary was deputed to examine the documents connected with the case, and make his report to the Council, which was to decide the matter.

The verdict was that both ladies were to resign their functions. This decision displeased everybody. "The

THE DUCHESSE DE CHEVREUSE

judgment," wrote Bassompierre, "is the worst they could have come to, seeing it gives offence to both parties." And these parties "two such powerful houses as those of Lorraine and Montmorency!" To calm this emotion, the King promised the Duc de Chevreuse he would make it up to him, and appointed him First Gentleman of his Bedchamber, an office that had remained vacant since the death of the Duc de Luynes. It was the Duke, not the Duchess, who was given the compensation! The office of Superintendent of the Queen's Household was suppressed, and Mme. de Lannoy was appointed Lady of Honour.

Mme. de Chevreuse consoled herself. Though she had no official functions to perform in the Household of Anne of Austria, none the less was she the sovereign's constant companion and friend. She was perpetually in her company, the old intimacy had been resumed, and she herself was still the same merry, lively being, the pet of the Queen's circle. She had contrived, in short, except for the King's personal dislike of her, to save the situation; and her position, in a sense, was even better than it had been before.

Marie de Rohan was no longer the wife of a King's favourite, risen from a comparatively low estate,—risen extremely high, indeed, but exposed to any sudden fall. She was a member of a foreign princely house, she was called "Your Highness," she was far better armed, now, against the "slings and arrows of outrageous fortune!"

An important conjuncture of circumstances was shortly to shed still greater lustre, in the eyes of courtiers and people alike, on the proud position she had regained.

After much difficult negotiation, the marriage of Henrietta-Maria and the Prince of Wales was practically arranged. This union had been earnestly desired by the English Princes. Their letters to M. de Chevreuse prove the fact. They express their writers' gratitude for the

THE CHEVREUSE MARRIAGE

Duke's zeal in promoting the success of the business. In spite of perpetual disappointments, M. de Chevreuse continued to press the advisers of Louis XIII to adhere to a plan conceived by Henri IV, and cherished for years by Marie de Médicis. He kept up constant intercourse with the English Ambassadors, and was in regular correspondence with London. And from London, answers to his letters reached him. King James I's Minister and favourite, who voiced the sentiments of his Master and his Master's son, the Prince of Wales, assured M. de Chevreuse that he possessed his "whole affection," invited him to come over to England, sent him splendid gifts in the meantime, and in April, 1620, despatched three splendid saddle-horses for his acceptance. "Had it not been for my desire to send you some earnest of my passion for your service, I would have awaited your arrival, so that you might choose out of all that I possess that which might be most agreeable to you, to give you pleasure when you ride abroad." And M. de Chevreuse, delighted to have his share in so important an undertaking, put fresh pressure on the Ministers of the French King, urging them not to insist so pertinaciously on the conditions they thought it right to impose, and striving to clear up every misunderstanding. "We know not," wrote King James to him, on July 24, 1624, "which we should value most, the constancy of your affection, or the kindness and sincerity of your contribution in favour of this negotiation, so necessary to Christendom, so fitting for the two crowns, so equally balanced as regards the individuals! And although the certainty we feel takes away all reason for begging you to persevere in your good offices, we cannot refrain from esteeming your mediation, and thanking you for it." The Prince of Wales added the expression of his own gratitude to his father's. "You are my dear friend," he wrote to M. de Chevreuse, "and daily you give me proofs of it. Render me all the good services that the nearness of my blood to yours demands!" If he won

THE DUCHESSE DE CHEVREUSE

Henrietta-Maria for his wife, he was resolved he would accept his bride from no hand but that of M. de Chevreuse; he would request it might be M. de Chevreuse who should conduct his betrothed to meet him. "I shall be more glad to receive that gentle Princess from you, as her conductor, than from any other person in the world." And Chevreuse, touched by the friendship and confidence shown him by the English Prince, answered with fervent expressions of his own devotion. "My blood and my life," he wrote, "are not too poor a thank-offering!"

It was in the autumn of the year 1624 that the marriage, after endless discussion, was finally arranged. The Prince of Wales was to have travelled to France to espouse the Princess, and conduct her back to London. But in the meantime James I died, and the new King, Charles I, could not leave his kingdom. Thus the nuptial ceremony, according to the usual custom, was to be solemnized in Paris, and the King of England to be represented by a person chosen by him, and to whom he delegated power to espouse the French Princess in his name and stead. According to the promise given, the personage thus chosen by Charles I was M. de Chevreuse.

Joyfully M. de Chevreuse accepted the honour. His letter in reply to the King's overflowed with delight. After the ceremony he was to attend the bride to England; Mme. de Chevreuse was to follow. The pomp of the wedding ceremony, performed in the most magnificent surroundings, busying the whole Court, attracting the whole populace, drew every eye upon the happy Duke. Honours, respect, all good things were to be showered on him who, by a diplomatic fiction, was to be assimilated, for the nonce, to the King of England. Mme. de Chevreuse was to have her share in this glory and good fortune.

On the morning of the day fixed for the betrothal ceremony, May 8, 1625, the two Ambassadors Extraordinary from the English Court, the Earls of Carlisle and

THE CHEVREUSE MARRIAGE

Holland, attended by a numerous train of gentlemen, went in solemn procession to fetch M. de Chevreuse from his chamber in the Louvre, and conduct him to the King's Bedchamber, where Louis XIII, surrounded by the Royal Family, the Princes of the Blood, his great nobles, and his Ministers, awaited him. The Duke was dressed in black, with diamond-studded bands, the tags or aiguillettes of which were adorned with precious stones. Henrietta-Maria wore a gown of gold and silver tissue, worked with *fleurs de lis,* and ornamented with pearls. The Chancellor of France read the marriage contract aloud, the terms of the procuration sent to M. de Chevreuse by the King of England were transcribed on to the document, and then the King, Henrietta-Maria, the two Queens, M. de Chevreuse, and the Ambassadors, affixed their signatures. This done, the Cardinal de la Rochefoucauld, Grand Almoner of France, blessed the betrothed pair, the Duc de Chevreuse acting as *fiancé.*

On Sunday, the 11th of May, the marriage was solemnized at Notre-Dame de Paris. The church had been hung, for the occasion, with beautiful tapestries worked with gold and silver threads, belonging to the King. In front of the great door a huge scaffolding had been erected, and covered with hangings. This was connected with the entrance to the cathedral choir by a gently sloping platform, and with the archiepiscopal palace—an ancient edifice, dating from the Middle Ages, which stood on the southern arm of the Seine—by a covered gallery, along which the procession was to pass. At nine o'clock in the morning, Henrietta-Maria was conducted to the Archbishop's palace. At eleven, one of the Queen's coaches, in which the Earls of Carlisle and Holland were seated, carried the Duc de Chevreuse from his house in the Rue St. Thomas du Louvre to the palace, likewise. Meanwhile, all the state authorities were passing into Notre-Dame, and taking up their places there, Members of Parliament

THE DUCHESSE DE CHEVREUSE

in their red robes, judges of the courts, sheriffs, the Mayor of Paris, officials of every order and every jurisdiction. The King, attended by the Court, Princes and Princesses, Dukes, great lords and ladies, all in full dress, was to go and fetch the bride and lead her into church. He never came till half-past four in the afternoon. At five the procession began to move. At its head, after the Grand Master of the King's Household and the Grand Master of the Ceremonies, surrounded by noblemen, and with the Earls of Holland and Carlisle on either side of him, walked the Duc de Chevreuse, magnificently attired in black, with a scarf studded with diamond roses, and a black velvet cap clasped with a diamond badge. After him came the Captain of the Louvre Gate, the Cent-Suisses of the Bodyguard, hautboy players, drummers and trumpeters, the Knights of the Holy Ghost, seven heralds at arms, three Marshals of France, Dukes and Peers, Princes, and then Louis XIII, covered with gold and silver embroideries, and leading Henrietta-Maria by one of her hands, while her other was held by Gaston d'Orléans, and her long train was borne by the Princesses de Condé and de Conti, and the Comtesse de Soissons. The two Queens followed, also in gowns with long trains: Marie de Médicis with an equerry on either side, Anne of Austria between the Duc d'Uzés and the Marquis de Mauny. Then came Mlle. de Montpensier, the Duchesse de Guise, and in her proper place, Marie de Rohan, between two courtiers, her train borne by an equerry. The Dowager of Elbeuf and the reigning Duchess closed the procession. Slowly the array passed on, to the sound of the music, and the clanging of the bells, and the cheers of the assembled crowds. On the scaffolding there was a pause. The King of England being a "Huguenot," his marriage could not take place within the church; it was solemnized on this exterior platform; Louis XIII and Monsieur gave away their sister to M. de

THE CHEVREUSE MARRIAGE

Chevreuse; the Cardinal de la Rochefoucauld pronounced the liturgical prayers appointed for the benediction of the marriage ceremony, and once more the procession moved on into Notre-Dame. When it reached the choir, M. de Chevreuse and the two English Ambassadors made their obeisance to the King, and left the church. Mass was said—late though it was—by the Cardinal de la Rochefoucauld. That over, the Duc de Chevreuse returned, reassumed his office at the entrance to the choir, and the procession wended its way back to the archiepiscopal palace.

In the evening, a splendid banquet was served in the great hall of that same palace, at which Louis XIII was present. On his right sat Marie de Médicis and Anne of Austria; on his left Henrietta-Maria, the Duc de Chevreuse, Holland, Carlisle and Mme. de Chevreuse. According to custom, the greatest lords of the Court served the Royal personages, and the other guests were waited on by noblemen. Paris was illuminated, there were bonfires at all the crossways, the Place de la Grève resounded with the noise of cannon and mortars. In the courtiers' eyes, the splendour of these festivities underlined the exceptional importance of the position attained by M. and Mme. de Chevreuse.

The hand of Fate which had once threatened Marie de Rohan had been turned aside. She was free to take up her old existence. In the Queen's inner circle her impulsive gaiety, her giddy humour, her love of pleasure and adventure might run their course unchecked. Once more she fed Anne of Austria's mind on that in which her own delighted—love and intrigue. And more than that, she was soon to do her best to draw the Queen into a love-affair of the most dangerous kind: within a fortnight of the marriage of Henrietta-Maria, on May 24, 1625, the young and fascinating Duke of Buckingham, the King of England's all-powerful Minister, sent by his Royal Master to conduct the newly married Sovereign of Great Britain to her future home, arrived in Paris.

CHAPTER III

BUCKINGHAM

Love-affairs of Mme. de Chevreuse and the Earl of Holland—Buckingham—His journey to Paris—Buckingham and Anne of Austria—The Amiens episode—Mme. de Chevreuse in England—Richelieu's displeasure—1625

AMONG the various English ambassadors with whom the Duc and the Duchesse de Chevreuse had had dealings in the course of the negotiations connected with the marriage of Henrietta-Maria, their closest intercourse had been with the Earl of Holland. Henry Rich, Lord Kensington, and afterwards Earl of Holland, belonged to the illustrious family of Warwick. He was destined to play his part in the English Revolution, and to die on the scaffold. King James I had sent him into France as early as in the spring of 1624, with orders to hurry on the negotiations, and he had asked to be assisted by the Earl of Carlisle, as second Ambassador Extraordinary.

Still young, with a fine figure and elegant manners, Holland was a very attractive man. Tallemant des Réaux thought his good looks had something "insipid" about them, and La Porte, in his Memoirs, declares that "though he was one of the handsomest men in the world, Holland was effeminate." He was very well received at the Hôtel de Chevreuse.

This house, to which frequent reference will be made in the course of this book, was the dwelling the Duc de Luynes had bought for his young wife in the Rue St. Thomas du Louvre, which he had left to his widow, and which had been sold to the Duc de Chevreuse in March, 1622. A great entrance in the Rue St. Thomas, between

BUCKINGHAM

the Rue du Doyenné and the Rue St. Honoré, adorned with pilasters, statues and trophies, and closed by doors of carved wood, embellished with medallions representing various personages, opened on a square inner courtyard, in the charming style of that earlier half of the sixteenth century, which inherited all the best of the Renaissance work. The architect, Métézeau, had gone for his inspiration to Lescot's work on the Louvre. Between the windows were niches filled with statues, framed by pilasters, surmounted by flat entablatures. Higher up, windows with sculptured stone frontals stood out, breaking the line of the roof. The general effect was distinctly pleasing. A large garden ran westward to the Rue St. Nicaise, where it was closed by a railing. From that side the façade of the house, which consisted of a central building with a raised pavilion on either hand, was very handsome. Set in a quiet quarter between the Louvre and the Tuileries, in the midst of the network of small streets that covered the space now occupied by the Place du Carrousel, the dwelling was considered one of the pleasantest and most luxurious abodes in the city.

The Earl of Holland, who had begun by coming to the house on business connected with the marriage, soon returned, and came more and more often, for a quite different reason. The brilliant beauty of the lady whose merriment enlivened the whole dwelling had produced its effect upon him. His heart became engaged. Mme. de Chevreuse did not resist his flame. Holland, and not M. de Chevreuse, was her first, and her real, love. Some years later M. de Châteauneuf was to declare that the young Englishman had been "the man whom Mme. de Chevreuse had loved the best, and whom she loved still." Holland was invited to the Hôtel de Chevreuse, and the house became the scene of an endless series of merrymakings, entertainments, and secret meetings. The husband saw nothing at all. Anne of Austria,

THE DUCHESSE DE CHEVREUSE

who was constantly in her friend's society, soon found out all about it. She thought the adventure very entertaining, and became the lovers' confidante. Holland, who had his *entrées* into the Louvre, had long conversations there with the Queen and Mme. de Chevreuse. In the course of these conversations, Buckingham came under discussion.

Holland was Buckingham's friend. He never tired of singing the praises of the King of England's favourite. He was the most attractive man in the kingdom, so he declared, "young, open-handed, dashing," successful in all his adventures, and, since he had gained the affections of the King of Great Britain, James I, and his son Charles I, strangely powerful. The influence he wielded was due to the qualities he possessed : brilliant, supple, with a fascinating glance, smiling sensual lips, gentle, coaxing, haughty, passionate, violent, all at once, Buckingham's personality might well have disturbed the most placid imagination. Anne of Austria's interest was roused, she listened eagerly, she began to ask questions. Then it was that Holland and Mme. de Chevreuse were inspired with the adventurous idea of fomenting an intrigue between the Queen of France and the English Duke. Princess and favourite alike were young, charming, and likely to attract the other; their minds should be worked up to the necessary pitch of emotion, then Buckingham, for some reason or other, should come to Paris, and nature would do the rest. Hardly had the plan been conceived before the pleasure its execution might afford became apparent. Holland and Mme. de Chevreuse threw themselves into the business with the fullest enjoyment. "To do honour to their own passion," writes La Rochefoucauld, "they planned an adventure of interest and gallantry between the Queen and the Duke of Buckingham, though neither had ever seen the other."

Mme. de Chevreuse set about her work cleverly. "Mme. de Chevreuse told me," writes Mme. de Motteville, "when

BUCKINGHAM

she was relating the follies of her youth, that she used to force the Queen's thoughts toward Buckingham by perpetually talking to her about him, and ridding her of the scruples she felt concerning such conversation." Portraits were exhibited. The business was not an easy one. "I have also heard Mme. de Chevreuse declare," adds Mme. de Motteville, "and with many exclamations on the subject, that the Queen's soul was noble and her heart pure, and that in spite of the climate in which she had been born—and in which, as I have already said, the name of lover is a fashionable one—she had found it the most difficult thing in the world to induce her to take some pleasure in the glory of being loved."

Holland and Carlisle, on their side, were at work in England. Certain persons talked to Buckingham, and he, being so pleased with himself as to believe no creature could resist him, was flattered at the thought of stirring the heart of a Queen of France. He had already seen Anne of Austria, whatever La Rochefoucald may say to the contrary. During a secret journey to Spain with the Prince of Wales, in 1623—there was a question at that moment of marrying the Prince to a Spanish Infanta—he had passed through Paris, and had been able, without revealing his identity, to be present at a ballet at the Louvre, where one of the King's under-tutors, M. de Préaux, quite unaware of his real quality, gave him a place from which he was able to indulge in a leisurely contemplation of Anne of Austria, whose charms found so brilliant a setting in the splendid festivities of her Court. He had never forgotten the fresh young beauty of the fair Princess.

And besides, moved, as it were, by some vague presentiment, he had long been seeking, by dint of humble attentions, to attract the sovereign's sympathetic interest. "I dare beseech you," he writes to the Duc de Chevreuse on April 26, 1620, "to take the trouble to cast your eyes on

THE DUCHESSE DE CHEVREUSE

eight coach horses which I am sending to the Queen, and to command that they shall be presented before her at some time when you yourself will be there, so that the wings of your authority may hide the blame which so much boldness will deserve; I rely on your favour for this protection." Now that he knew the way was being prepared before him, he entered eagerly into the plan. Whether sincerely or not, he fell in love. Anne of Austria was informed; she seemed touched, the adventure amused her. She had not realized, as yet, the import of the intrigue, nor the consequences it was likely to involve. "Thanks to the counsels of Mme. de Chevreuse," says Mme. de Motteville, "the Queen, in spite of the purity of her soul, had not been able to help finding pleasure in the charm of this passion (Buckingham's), which gave her a sense of complacency that flattered her pride more than it offended her virtue." Thus, on one side and the other, was a sentiment engendered which absence and the effect of a clever handling of the imagination were to cultivate, till a personal meeting should ripen it to a warmer feeling. This meeting had yet to be arranged.

Once the marriage of Henrietta-Maria had been decided, Holland and Carlisle suggested that Buckingham should travel to France to arrange the final details of the marriage contract. Louis XIII's Ambassador in England, M. Leveneur de Tillières, wrote, "The English Ambassadors in France ask that Buckingham should come to Paris, so that he may seem to have concluded the marriage, and keep the glory of it." The King of England accepted the proposal "joyfully."

The Cardinal de Richelieu was one of the French King's Ministers at this time. Contrary to general opinion, according to which the Cardinal ruled the whole government of the country from the very outset, Richelieu, at that date, was simply a Councillor, who gave his opinion, which was, indeed, treated with great respect, but who

BUCKINGHAM

by no means directed the affairs of the State. This matter of Buckingham's journey to Paris was debated in the Council. All its members were much perplexed. The French Ambassador in London was asked for his opinion. It was unfavourable to the plan. M. Leveneur de Tillières pointed out that Buckingham's character was "hot and haughty," that there were certain clauses in the contract over which he "would fly into a passion." M. de Tillières was quite aware of the intrigue in preparation as to the favourite of the King of England and Anne of Austria; he did not mention it, supposing, as he explained in his Memoirs at a later date, "that the understanding that was being formed between the Queen and the Duke was a known thing, and that, knowing it, all the drawbacks it entailed must have been foreseen." In reality the King's Council would seem to have known nothing at all about the matter. Richelieu wrote from his house at Limours, where he was then living in somewhat poor health, that Buckingham's journey was certainly not a desirable thing, but that it would have to be endured for fear of disobliging the King of England's Minister, and thus spoiling the whole situation. Marie de Médicis had set her heart on the English marriage for her daughter: she was begging that nothing might be done to retard it. Louis XIII, as though he had some obscure premonition of what was to come, stood out. These equivocations filled up the time a little: the arrangements for the marriage were actually concluded without Buckingham's presence. But Holland and Carlisle then put forward a proposal that the Duke should come to France to fetch the new Queen of England—he would seize the opportunity to settle various political questions. There was no possibility of getting out of it. The authorities in Paris agreed, and so it came about that a few days after the ceremony in the Cathedral of Notre-Dame, the English nobleman, so feared by some, so anxiously desired by others, entered Paris.

THE DUCHESSE DE CHEVREUSE

George Villiers, Duke of Buckingham, was at that time just three-and-thirty years of age. Of modest extraction, descended from a Norman family, and brought up in France, where he had learned the language, he had appeared when still a youth at the English Court, where he had been first noticed, and then doted upon, by James I, who soon raised him to high fortune. "Tall, good looking, of a pleasant wit, magnificent, liberal, fond of polite society," he seemed, so Fontenay-Mareuil tells us, "well suited to a Court." His fine presence was especially praised: he was a tall, strapping fellow, slight and vigorous, "the best built and the best looking man in the world," writes La Porte, "he appeared at Court with so much charm and so much splendour that he filled the populace with admiration, the ladies with delight and something more, the gallants with jealousy, and the husbands with something worse than that."

His character was disfigured by grave faults. His pride in his success among women made him exceedingly self-conceited. He was considered vain beyond all words. Fontenay-Mareuil considered him "so frivolous and so vain that he was quite unfitted for serious business, and still less for war." As a politician he proved himself capricious, violent, overbearing, carrying a spirit of muddle and imprudence into every negotiation he touched. Richelieu, whose Memoirs reveal the inextricable difficulties which the English Minister's behaviour caused him, describes him as a madman. "His enterprises," he says, "which were devoid of reason, were carried out in misfortune, but that did not prevent them from placing us in great peril and doing us a great deal of harm: for the wild folly of an enemy is more to be feared than his wisdom, seeing the madman does not act on principles which are common to all men." The favour with which Charles I regarded his Minister can only be explained by a lack of judgment on the sovereign's part, and a frivolity of mind,

THE DUKE OF BUCKINGHAM
(*From a picture by Rubens in the Pitti Palace, Florence*)

BUCKINGHAM

in the Prince's case, strongly resembling that of his favourite.

On the evening of May 24, 1625, Buckingham, who had travelled post, made his entry into Paris, accompanied by the Earl of Montgomery and a small following of English gentlemen. While he came, as the *Mercure* announced, "to pray his most Christian Majesty to permit the departure of the spouse of his King, and to place his confidence in the person of the said Duke to conduct her," he also proposed to define the exact meaning of certain clauses in the marriage settlement, and to discuss two questions of policy: that of preventing a peace between France and Spain, and that of laying the foundations of an alliance between France and England touching German affairs.

As was quite proper, considering the friendly relations subsisting between the family of Chevreuse and the Court of England, and more particularly Buckingham himself, the Minister took up his quarters in the family mansion in the Rue St. Thomas du Louvre. This had been decided by Louis XIII himself. Was the King still unaware of the plot Buckingham and Mme. de Chevreuse were hatching between them? We may well believe he was.

The Government, which was resolved not to annoy the Duke, had decided to make sure of various concessions it was anxious to obtain by treating him in the most friendly manner. Buckingham was received with great courtesy: he had audiences with Louis XIII, with Marie de Médicis, and with Richelieu. The moment for which those in the secret longed was that of the meeting between the Duke and Anne of Austria.

It took place in the Queen's apartments in the Louvre. Buckingham knew beforehand that he would think the Princess charming. Anne of Austria, moved by what had been told her of the fascinating nobleman, and aware of the feelings he nursed for her, felt herself drawn towards him by a lively and inexplicable sympathy. When they found

THE DUCHESSE DE CHEVREUSE

themselves together the result was that which might easily have been anticipated. "The Queen," writes La Rochefoucauld, "seemed even more charming to Buckingham than his imagination had painted her, and he seemed to the Queen the man in the whole world most worthy to be loved." By some spontaneous phenomenon, each recognized in the other a being whose heart overflowed with an infinite and mutual tenderness. "Buckingham," writes Leveneur de Tillières," was seen by the Queen Regnant with a great joy, which was not only written on her face, but went straight to her heart." From that moment there was a sort of intimacy between them, as if they had known each other for years. And this intimacy, thanks to Buckingham's assurance and the Queen's inexperience, soon became familiarity. "From the very first day," says Leveneur de Tillières, "the freedom between them was as great as if they had known each other for a long time. This was caused by Buckingham's boldness, and by the character of the Queen Regnant." There was some astonishment in Anne of Austria's circle. The Duchesse de Chevreuse calmed the Queen's mind, assuring her that when intentions were upright and behaviour irreproachable, mere talk should not stir scruples of conscience which were devoid of any justification. "Certainly," adds M. de Tillières, "this passion was perfectly harmless in its effects, but its appearances were anything but that, and in this matter the said Queen conducted herself as many other women have done, in the belief they have, and she herself thought she had, or assumed on the advice of others, that evil appearances are of little consequence, so long as the reality is good and innocent, and that if that was safeguarded, God and the world would both be content—which I do not believe." Thus, according to Mme. de Chevreuse and M. de Tillières, appearances only were wrong. After another, and a coarser fashion, the Princesse de Conti confirmed this impression when she declared that she would

BUCKINGHAM

answer to the King for the Queen's virtue, *depuis la ceinture jusqu'aux pieds*.

And indeed, the life led by Anne of Austria in the Louvre was so busy from morning till night, she was so constantly surrounded by her many servants and her household courtiers, she was so exposed to the general view, in that great apartment of hers on the first floor of the Louvre, next to the King's bed-chamber and his cabinet, that it would have been difficult for her to escape the watchful and curious eyes about her. Cardinal de Retz relates, in his Memoirs, a strange story, which he enlivens with somewhat objectionable details, and declares he heard from Mme. de Chevreuse, of an incident said to have taken place between Buckingham and Anne of Austria in the garden of the Louvre, now known as the Jardin de l'Infante. The Queen, so he avers, had appointed to meet Buckingham in this garden after nightfall. Mme. de Chevreuse accompanied her to the place of meeting, and then retired some distance, leaving the lovers together. After a time she heard an unusual and curious noise, "as of a struggle," she ran forward, found the Queen in great agitation, and Buckingham on his knees before her. In a state of feverish excitement, Anne of Austria took her way back to her own chamber, angrily exclaiming that "all men were brutal and insolent." And next morning she sent Mme. de Chevreuse to ask the English Duke whether he was sure she ran no risk of giving a Dauphin, who would be no Dauphin, to France.

This is not a likely story. Among all the spots in the Louvre which Buckingham and Anne of Austria might have chosen, had they desired to meet unseen, the very last would have been a corner overlooked by more than sixty of the palace windows—those of the King, the Queen, the Queen-Mother, the great officers of the Court, Anne of Austria's own Household, besides those of the much-frequented passage now known as the Galerie d'Apollon—

THE DUCHESSE DE CHEVREUSE

whence the whole Court might easily have detected the Sovereign's misconduct. Besides this, Retz is the only writer who makes any allusion to the episode, and historical critics are agreed in the opinion that the Cardinal's story arises out of some confusion with an incident of a similar nature which others have related, and which seems to have taken place shortly afterwards, at Amiens. His version is a mere transformation, with aggravations, of what then occurred.

During the very short time—not more than a week—Buckingham spent in Paris, the unceasing series of banquets, receptions and suppers offered to the English Minister certainly filled up all his leisure. Richelieu gave him a great dinner, about the splendour of which there was a world of talk. "All night long," says the *Mercure*, "the air was filled with the noise of cannon and mortar shots, and in the morning, with the story of the banquets given."

A great concert was organized at the Hôtel de Rambouillet in the Rue St. Thomas du Louvre, just next door to the Hôtel de Chevreuse, at which the famous singer of those days, Mlle. Paulet, sang before Buckingham. These gatherings must have been the only occasions on which the Duke can have contrived to meet Anne of Austria and approach her nearly. He did speak to her: we know he avowed his passion. The young Queen, in her agitation, did not know how to reply: Buckingham pressed her. She ended by giving him to understand that she did not regard him with indifference. In later days she was to confide to Mme. de Motteville that she had confessed to the Duke that "if it had been possible for a virtuous woman to love any man except her husband, he would have been the only one for whom she could have cared." She thought she had an inclination for him. The Duke, adds Mme. de Motteville, "was the person of whom I have heard the Queen speak in better terms than of any other. His suit had been received with a certain sense of satisfaction : the Queen made no secret of the fact."

But in the midst of this Court crammed with idlers, who had promptly guessed what was going on—many had remarked and grasped the significance of certain gestures and glances, of asides that were far too confidential and talk that was all too tender—Louis XIII, the Queen-Mother, the Ministers, could hardly fail to be aware of that which formed the subject of every courtier's conversation. The King was deeply grieved. Cold and reserved by nature, he contained himself. But he resolved, in agreement with his advisers, to hurry Buckingham's departure from Paris. His decision met with universal approval. "Nobody was able to conceal," writes Brienne, "the general satisfaction at the thought of being rid of the presumptuous foreigner, and sending him back to his own country." The Government at once evaded the settlement of the two questions which had formed the essential object of the English Minister's visit: the debate concerning the clauses of the marriage contract had caused some lively discussion, but however great the anxiety in Paris to oblige England, it was absolutely necessary that an end should be put to a state of things so painful for the King : the business was cut short. "The perpetual interviews and familiarities between the Duke and the Queen Regnant" were beginning to exceed the bounds. It was evident to every one, says Tillières, "that the Queen's affection was increasing day by day, and appearances were growing worse and worse, which enraged both the King her husband and the Queen her mother-in-law." Henrietta-Maria's departure was fixed for June 2, in the hope that "once the Duke of Buckingham had departed all these affections would die down." As a matter of fact, though Buckingham had been able to ascertain that the Queen nursed kindly feelings for him, he had not attained the full success for which he had hoped : there were too many obstacles in

THE DUCHESSE DE CHEVREUSE

that overpopulated Court to permit of so private a meeting as that for which he longed. In the course of the journey to conduct the new Queen of England to Boulogne, amidst the chances furnished by traveller's lodgings, a more favourable opportunity might perhaps occur.

According to the usual practice of the Court of France, the Royal Family was to accompany the young Queen as long as she travelled on French soil. Louis XIII himself was to go as far as Compiègne, the Queens—Marie de Médicis and Anne of Austria—and Monsieur, the King's brother, were to journey to Calais, and a bevy of French noblemen were to attend her to London. Precautions were forthwith taken to ensure that Anne of Austria and Buckingham should see as little of each other as possible, and that, when they did meet, the Queen should always be surrounded by a numerous court. On June 2, Henrietta-Maria, having bidden farewell to those she was to leave behind her, quitted the Louvre at five o'clock in the afternoon, carried in a litter covered with red velvet and gold embroideries, borne by two mules in red velvet trappings, and escorted by all the companies of the mounted archers of the city of Paris, by five hundred citizens, also mounted, and by all the officials of the city—the mayor, sheriffs, district police, for it was the privilege of the Paris burghers thus to escort any daughter of the Royal House who had espoused a foreigner and was about to quit the kingdom. Buckingham travelled with her. The Queens were neither of them present: they had already started by another route, attended by a numerous following of princesses, ladies, and court lords, mounted or in coaches. The two troops of travellers were not to meet till they reached Montdidier. Half-way to St. Denis the Parisians took their leave of the Queen of England; that night she slept at Stains, the next at Compiègne, and the third at Montdidier, where she was joined, on June 6, by Marie de Médicis and Anne of Austria: almost the whole

BUCKINGHAM

of the Court was present; the escort consisted of two companies of the Body-guard, strengthened by detachments from the Swiss Regiment of the King's Guard. Louis XIII had returned to Fontainebleau.

The solemn entry into Amiens took place on the 7th. The King had given orders that the same honours were to be rendered to his sister as to himself. The Duc de Chaulnes, governor of the province, was there to welcome the Princess, with all the nobility of the province, three hundred mounted gentlemen, about him. Five thousand armed burghers of the town of Amiens, divided up into companies, kept the road. The chief sheriff, garbed in a violet gown, harangued the Queen in the official terms habitual at that time. "Madam," he said, "when the sun rises, we see all things smiling upon us: a thousand gay colours adorn the sky, the birds pour out their little songs to greet his noble light, and the earth enamels her verdant bosom with a thousand flowers pearled with dew. So, too, when you do us the honour to come into this town, we open all its gates to you, and with them those of our eyes and of our hearts!" To the sound of trumpets and drums, of cannonades and arquebusades, the procession passed into the town, and after a Te Deum had been sung in the cathedral, the Queen took up her lodging in the episcopal palace.

Then there were merry-makings, balls, splendid banquets. Marie de Médicis fell ill—a cold, 'twas said—and the travellers stayed on. This delay filled Buckingham's heart with joy.

He was more splendid than ever. Bois d'Annemets, who saw him just then, relates in his Memoirs that the Duke did all he could to dazzle men's eyes. "It must be acknowledged," he writes, "that he wore the finest suit, and the best chosen, that ever will be seen." The English Minister was always covered with diamonds and pearls. At the receptions and collations and great banquets his magnificence astounded every one who saw him. But all he had been able to snatch for himself was a word, a glance here and there, exchanged with the Queen. Was he to leave France with nothing more? It was clear that stringent orders had been given to the people about Anne of Austria: Putange, her equerry, never left her; La Porte, her "cloak-bearer," was always on the watch; ladies and servants were perpetually on guard around her. Mme. de Chevreuse and Holland were to provide the much desired opportunity.

Anne of Austria was not lodged in the episcopal palace with her sister-in-law. She had been assigned a spacious dwelling with a good-sized garden which ran along the bank of the Somme. It was a very pleasant garden, and all the persons at Amiens connected with the Court knew it, and used to walk in it. One evening Mme. de Chevreuse came to pay a visit to the Queen, and with her, Buckingham and Holland. The sky was clear and the air was balmy. Somebody suggested a walk in the garden. The Queen agreed. Buckingham led the Queen, Mme. de Chevreuse took Holland's arm. A few paces behind them came Putange, La Porte, and a few ladies. Holland and Mme. de Chevreuse, as though by accident, contrived to let Buckingham and the Queen out-distance them, while they held back the attendants. The spot was a lonely one. Buckingham spoke. He was tender, pressing. Anne of Austria, frightened, stopped, and sat down. Her ladies joined her. After a moment, the Queen moved on again. Holland and Mme. de Chevreuse followed the same tactics. The moment was propitious: the half-solitude, the falling dusk, the emotion stirred in the young Queen's breast by a *tête-à-tête*, in the course of which Buckingham's declarations of adoration grew more and more fervent, threatened to end by moving her deeply. The Duke, bold as he was, fancied his hour had come. They were just at the corner of a wooded alley, hidden by

BUCKINGHAM

clustering shrubs, nobody could see them. He ventured. What happened?

There are two versions. According to Tallemant des Réaux and Retz—this last places the whole incident in Paris—there was a regular scene, and a violent one. But this story, a mere echo of the talk of courtiers, who embroidered on their theme to their hearts' content, will not bear investigation. The Queen did, as a matter of fact, call out loudly, and at once, hearing her cry, everybody hurried to her. If she had not called out, her attendants were so near her that they must have come up with her before Buckingham could have put his design into execution. Thus, if she did call out, it was because she was not a consenting party. In reality, La Porte, who was present, La Rochefoucauld, who had his information from witnesses of the incident, and Mme. de Motteville, to whom the Queen told the whole story, all agree in giving us an explanation which seems sufficiently satisfactory.

"Favoured by the darkness," writes La Porte, "the Duke of Buckingham permitted himself very insolent liberties, and even went so far as to attempt to caress the Queen, who at once gave a shriek, at the sound of which everybody ran to her." "One evening," says La Rochefoucald, "when the Queen was walking in her garden, they found themselves alone together; the Duke of Buckingham was bold and enterprising, the chance was a favourable one, and he tried to take advantage of it in so disrespectful a manner that the Queen was forced to call out for her women." Mme. de Motteville reduces the episode to still more modest proportions. "A great deal has been said," she writes, "(about this scene,) but it was very unjustly spoken, for I know from herself (the Queen), who did me the honour of confiding it to me in the simplest way, that finding herself at the corner of an alley where a palisade might hide them from the public glance, the Queen, startled at perceiving that she was alone, and apparently

THE DUCHESSE DE CHEVREUSE

worried by some over-passionate feelings on the part of the Duke of Buckingham, cried out, and calling her equerry to her, reprimanded him for having left her." Thus the nature of the scene is easily guessed; it was short, impudent, and commonplace. Its true commentary may be found in the rider added by the Princesse de Conti to her affirmation that she would answer to the King for his wife's virtue "de la ceinture aux pieds," to the effect that she would not undertake the same responsibility "de la ceinture en haut!"

Buckingham's behaviour proves that he knew very little about Anne of Austria. Out of youthful curiosity and childish giddiness, out of the vanity and caprice of a pretty woman, the young Queen, whose life had hitherto been dull enough, may have let herself be tempted for a moment to feelings that were new to her, and to a closer inspection of a forbidden delight to which she was a stranger; but her sentiment, whatever it may have been, was so weak, she was so cold by temperament, her regard for her own dignity was so great, that the brutal reality of an ill-judged and far too sudden gesture was more than enough to recall her to a sense of what she owed herself, and to stir all the scruples dormant in her conscience. Buckingham had bungled!

When everybody, hearing the Queen's cry, rushed to her side, the English Duke seemed quite put out of countenance: the best thing he could do was to disappear: he stepped backwards, and was lost in the darkness. The people about the Queen asked questions. Anne of Austria, in her embarrassment, stammered this thing and that. A few words were exchanged, and then, by common accord, it was resolved that nothing should come out. The King must be kept absolutely in the dark.

But in any case, Marie de Médicis was told. The very first consequence of the adventure was that the Queen-Mother, on the plea that her own health was still bad, and

BUCKINGHAM

gave no promise of immediate improvement, ordered Henrietta-Maria's immediate departure for Boulogne, under the escort of Monsieur only. On June 16, the Queen of England left Amiens. Anne of Austria was bound by etiquette to travel with her, in her own coach, two leagues out of the town. She accompanied her sister-in-law for the prescribed distance, and when she had reached the spot beyond which she was not to proceed, she bade her farewell. At that moment Buckingham approached her coach to take his leave. Anne of Austria, who had not seen him since the scene in the garden, treated him with great coldness. The Duke, deeply affected, bent forward between the curtains of the coach, as though he would have spoken a few words; he was weeping, and strove to hide his tears. The Queen continued quite unmoved. The Princesse de Conti, who sat beside her, was to reproach her, later, for what she called her "cruelty." Buckingham bowed low, and departed, more in love than ever, bitterly grieved by his failure, humiliated by the thought of his own folly, and in despair at the idea of the dislike which he believed the Queen had now conceived for him.

Henrietta-Maria and her train travelled by Abbeville and Montreux to Boulogne, where the Queen was to embark. There was a violent storm, and she had to wait, for the ships despatched by the King of England to carry over his bride had not yet come into harbour. A sloop conveying letters for the Court was anchored in the port. Mme. de Chevreuse and Holland suggested that Buckingham, under colour of treating some political matter with the Queen-Mother, might himself carry these despatches to Amiens. He would thus see Anne of Austria again, and his departure might perhaps have altered the feeling of that Princess towards him. The Duke took post-horses, and rode to Amiens without a stop.

He waited on Marie de Médicis. The Queen-Mother was still ailing, and in her bed. She received the English

THE DUCHESSE DE CHEVREUSE

Minister with some appearance of surprise. Buckingham explained the reason of his coming, and asked if he might pay his respects to Anne of Austria. The young Queen, who had been bled that morning and was likewise in bed, was extremely astonished. "Back again!" she cried. "I thought we were rid of him!" She sent word that she could not see anybody. Buckingham pressed his request. The Queen-Mother, he pointed out, had deigned to receive him while she was in bed. Mme. de Lannoy, the Lady of Honour, went herself to Buckingham to explain that "it would not be agreeable to the King that the Queen should allow any gentleman to come into her chamber, she being in bed at the time." Buckingham appealed to Marie de Médicis, and she, wearied by his persistence, replied to the objections put forward by Mme. de Lannoy, "Why not, after all? I do it myself!" There was nothing for it but to give in. Mme. de Lannoy took measures to ensure that the Queen's chamber should be full of people when the English Minister entered it. The Princesses de Condé and de Conti were both of them beside her bed. When Buckingham came into the room, he advanced to the bedside, fell on his knees, took the Queen's hand and burst into sobs. It was a painful scene. Mme. de Lannoy pointed out to the Duke that it was against the custom of the French Court for any man to speak to the Queen of France on his knees, and offered him a seat. Buckingham replied that he was no Frenchman, and was not bound by the laws of that kingdom. Anne of Austria remained as cold as ice. Everybody felt thoroughly uncomfortable. It was impossible that the interview should continue. The Duke retired, and took his way back to Boulogne, humiliated and sick at heart. He was resolved to find some pretext for returning to France at the earliest possible moment, even if he had to jeopardize and compromise his master's policy to do it.

Meanwhile, and in spite of the good resolutions as to the

BUCKINGHAM

complete silence to be observed, the story of the Queen's adventure, which every courtier was delightedly whispering to his neighbour, was handed on from one person to another till it reached Fontainebleau, and the King's ears. Mindful of his own dignity, Louis XIII held his peace. When Marie de Médicis became aware that her son knew all, she thought it her duty to undertake her daughter-in-law's defence. Nothing at all serious had taken place, she declared, and the King had no right to doubt the correctness of his wife's behaviour. "The Queen-Mother could not refrain from testifying to the truth, and asserting that there was nothing in the matter at all, and that even if the Queen had desired to do wrong, it would have been impossible, for there were so many people about her who watched her doings, and that it had not been in her power to prevent the Duke of Buckingham from feeling esteem and even love for her. She also quoted a number of incidents of a similar kind which had happened to herself in her own youth. These reasons, though they were unanswerable, did not extinguish the King's jealousy."

But at all events, though Louis XIII did not choose to say anything either to Buckingham or to his wife, he did not intend to leave the persons who should have watched over the Queen, and whose carelessness had been the cause of the incident, unpunished. He struck at the male members of her Household. The Queen had been attended in the Amiens garden by Putange, her equerry; La Porte, her "cloak-bearer; a gentleman in waiting, M. de Jars, and a servant of the name of Datel. On the morning of July 20—the two Queens had joined the King at Fontainebleau—the monarch's confessor, the Père Séguiran, waited on Anne of Austria, and informed her, in the King's name, that all the above-named persons were dismissed from the Court. The Queen was very much affected. She made no protest, she only sent the King a message to the effect that "she besought him to name all the persons he wished to remove from her Household, so that there might be no more of that kind to be done." She bestowed gifts of money on the dismissed persons, and before long she was to take them back into her service.

As far as Buckingham was concerned, the King's mind was made up: never again was the English Minister to set his foot in France. Every effort the Duke made to attain this end was doomed to failure. Buckingham did all he could to win over Richelieu, who still continued to treat him with consideration; but on this particular head Richelieu refused to attempt to alter the King's mind. "Neither did Buckingham's departure diminish the feelings he nursed for the Queen Regnant," writes Leveneur de Tillières, "nor did his extravagances prevent him from believing he might get back into France and there assuage his passion. As he knew his only hope of obtaining this was to gain the support of the Cardinal de Richelieu, he paid him frequent compliments by letter, and the Cardinal, who was bent on carrying out his designs for ruining the Huguenots, would accept them, on some occasions, with great civility, but on others with hearty scorn." In November, 1625, when Buckingham had made a fresh attempt, the Secretary of State de la Ville aux Clercs wrote as follows to Richelieu, in the King's name: "The King continues to be of the same mind, and cannot consent to allow the Duke of Buckingham to come here." In the earliest days of the married life of the young English sovereigns, when a bitter quarrel marred the understanding between Charles I and Henrietta-Maria, that Princess, in great distress, expressed a desire to go to France and seek some consolation in her mother's arms. Buckingham announced his readiness to consent to her taking the journey, provided he himself attended her. And Louis XIII, so great was his dislike of seeing the man he abhorred, preferred to refuse his sister leave to visit him, under such an escort. A thousand shifts and subterfuges

BUCKINGHAM

were planned by the Duke and Mme. de Chevreuse: on August 2, 1626, M. de Lamothe-Houdancourt, Grand Almoner to Henrietta-Maria in London, wrote to Richelieu as follows: "Pembrock tells me that it had been settled between Mme. de Chevreuse, the ladies (the Princesse de Conti and others), and the gallants (Buckingham and Lord Holland), that twice every year they would cross the water under pretext of settling the difficulties between the King and Queen of England, and that the Queen-Mother, in her fear that her daughter might be badly treated, would obtain this freedom for them. As they believe the Cardinal may cross their plans, they desire to bring about his ruin." Louis XIII was not to give in. Mme. de Chevreuse was to go on talking about Buckingham to Anne of Austria, and Holland was to continue expatiating on the subject of Anne of Austria to Buckingham; but the lovers were never to meet again. Many observers held Buckingham's hostile attitude with regard to France in 1627, his alliance with the Huguenot rebels, and his descent on the Île de Ré to be the outcome of his personal spite. Mme. de Motteville insinuates that "he set up a quarrel between the two crowns solely to create the necessity for his own return to France to negotiate a treaty of peace."

Meanwhile, at noon on Sunday, June 25, 1625, Queen Henrietta-Maria, who had been rejoined by Buckingham on his return from Amiens, embarked at Boulogne on board the great ship *The Prince*, which, attended by a splendid squadron numbering two hundred British sail, was to convey her to the English shores. In her marriage contract the number, rank and quality of her French attendants had been duly specified. Under the leadership of a Grand Almoner, M. de Lamothe-Houdancourt, Bishop of Mende, cousin to the Cardinal de Richelieu, a man still in the ardour of his youth, who was to correspond regularly with the Cardinal and keep the Court of France thoroughly well informed as to everything that happened

THE DUCHESSE DE CHEVREUSE

at Whitehall, some two score ecclesiastics, gentlemen, secretaries, equerries, serving-men, musicians, and physicians, with half-a-score of women—ladies-in-waiting, and waiting women—all of them of French nationality, were to travel to London with the young sovereign. They followed in her train. Besides these, there were three or four Ambassadors Extraordinary—Comte Leveneur de Tillières, the Comte d'Effiat, father of Cinq-Mars, the Duc de Chevreuse, and, at a later date, Brienne. M. de Chevreuse had been given his instructions. His mission was to secure the "satisfactory carrying out of the contract and of the marriage ceremony," which was to have nothing religious—that is to say, nothing Protestant—about it. A sprinkling of ladies accompanied the Ambassadors: the Comtesse de Tillières, the Comtesse de Sipierre, a charming young creature who was to die very young and deeply regretted, and finally, the Duchesse de Chevreuse. The Duke had at first refused to bring his wife over with him. He declared she was in an interesting condition, and ought not to undertake the journey. But she wept so much and begged so hard that he had been obliged to give in. Holland never left her side.

The ship on which Henrietta-Maria had embarked, a three-decker, "one of the greatest to be seen on the ocean," had been prepared for her reception with all the luxury known to that period: there were three saloons all on the same deck, hung with "high warp tapestries, adorned with golden threads." Henrietta-Maria dreaded the thought of being sick at sea, and an "orchestra of lutes, viols and other delicate instruments" had been provided on board, to entertain her, and "prevent the inconveniences of the voyage." The crossing lasted twenty-four hours. When the ship hove in sight of the English coast at Dover, it was saluted by salvos of cannon; the new Queen was greeted by the acclamations of the multitudes assembled on the shore, and the blaring of trumpets and bugles. She landed, and

BUCKINGHAM

was received in a wooden pavilion, "wherein sweet scents, perfume-burners and odours of the most pleasing kind caused the too strong air of the sea to change, for her, into a pleasant softness."

The next morning, at ten o'clock, Charles I arrived: "the flower of his nobility attending him." On the following day the young couple started for Canterbury, and thence they went to London. An epidemic was raging in the city, six hundred persons, it was said, dying there every day. The new Queen's solemn entry into her capital was hurried, and anything but brilliant. A special session of Parliament had been convoked to confirm the marriage arrangements, and on this occasion the King gave a great banquet, followed by a ball, at which M. and Mme. de Chevreuse were present. Then, on account of the sickness, Charles I retired to his palace at Hampton Court, outside London. He had assigned M. and Mme. de Chevreuse lodgings in Richmond Palace, about three miles away.

The beginnings of the married life of the English sovereigns were anything but peaceful. The King's first interview with his wife had not produced an agreeable impression on him. She was thin and puny in appearance, with but little beauty about her. The meeting with her husband had been a great disappointment to the young Queen. She had taken her way to London in sadness and melancholy. Charles had lost his temper. Hard words had passed between the two. Buckingham had made things worse by insisting on his own wife, sister, and niece being placed about the Queen, instead of three of her French ladies: the Ambassadors of Louis XIII had interfered. The Queen, speaking of her husband to M. de Tillières, told him that "with regard to his mind she had been deceived." She wept. And then Buckingham reproached her with being bad-tempered, and told her she must be merry with the King, or else she would be unhappy.

THE DUCHESSE DE CHEVREUSE

Everything suffered. The King of England, as though to atone to his people for having married a princess of a Catholic house, and permitted a Catholic bishop and bevy of priests to be about her, began to persecute the Catholics. This persecution was a contravention of the agreement entered into with the Court of France, and the Court of France protested against it. Louis XIII sent over M. de Blainville to express his displeasure, and Blainville was coldly received. Buckingham offered to go to France to arrange matters, and Louis XIII refused to receive him. The violence of the treatment meted out to Henrietta-Maria and to Catholics in England increased twofold. The Bishop of Mende writes to Richelieu in August 1625: "We have no more bitter enemy than Buckingham: he tries to damage the Queen in the King's mind; and the Queen, on the other hand, does not do all she might to win over the King: she sees him not at all, or no more than she is obliged. Buckingham's spirit is an evil one." Attacks were made on the French attendants of the young Queen: the English fomented complaints against them, and especially against the ecclesiastics. The situation was growing very difficult. Sorely puzzled, the French Government, in its inability to discover any efficacious means of obtaining satisfaction, tried one shift after another. Richelieu wrote to the Bishop of Mende that he "wept tears of blood over the sad position of the Queen of England."

Now, while Louis XIII did not know which way to turn, and while his Ambassadors in London, and notably M. de Chevreuse, were straining every nerve to discover some basis of settlement, Madame de Chevreuse was supplying the King of France, overwhelmed with annoyances already, with various other subjects of vexation and displeasure.

Both the Duke and his wife had been heartily welcomed in London. When the King assigned them lodgings at Richmond, he also provided them with a town residence,

BUCKINGHAM

Denmark House. The English were filled with admiration of the splendour of M. de Chevreuse. He sparkled with gems and diamonds, and never went abroad without "mules covered with the most splendid trappings that ever were seen." Great attentions were lavished on the Duchess. Her merriment and high spirits were immensely liked in a circle where the French of both sexes were otherwise but little appreciated. Lord Holland was constantly at her side. Thanks to the fashions then in vogue, when gowns were worn full and ample, draping the figure in their folds, the young Duchess was able to conceal her condition, which had indeed imparted a wonderful freshness and brilliancy to her skin. Buckingham was frequently in her company, and these three made up a little *coterie* of the most delightful kind, which grew more and more intimate as the days went on. At last, people began to gossip.

The Bishop of Mende, in his private correspondence, categorically accuses Holland of having permitted Buckingham to share the favours bestowed on him by Mme. de Chevreuse. "Mme. de Chevreuse," he writes, "is shut up for five or six hours every day with Buckingham : Holland has made over his prize to him." And indeed, Mme. de Chevreuse was to avow, in later years, that Buckingham had been very dear to her. Was the correspondence she kept up with Anne of Austria the cause of the English Minister's devotion to her? Or had her charm and her well-known easy sense of virtue inspired Buckingham with a fancy to number her among his many passing conquests? It was a strange sight! Then Holland suggested that Mme. de Chevreuse should go to his house to lie in : he himself, he declared, would only keep one small set of rooms for his own use. Mme. de Chevreuse was spending weeks on end, at this time, in Buckingham's mansion, and without her husband. M. de Chevreuse did not appear to know or understand anything of what was going on. On account of the strained relations between Buckingham and

THE DUCHESSE DE CHEVREUSE

Henrietta-Maria, Mme. de Chevreuse hardly ever appeared in the Queen's presence. She lived apart from all the French members of the Household. When she wrote to France, to Marie de Médicis, she gave her none but excellent news of the royal couple.

At last the Bishop of Mende, stung into anger, denounced the scandal caused by the misconduct of Mme. de Chevreuse and her husband's weakness, to Cardinal de Richelieu. "I am ashamed," he writes, "of the impudence of Mme. de Chevreuse, and of her husband's simplicity." He had endeavoured to prevent the Duchess from going to Lord Holland's house for her confinement. "Ashamed," he wrote, "of the fact that M. de Chevreuse was not (ashamed), I gave him to understand that it would give offence in Paris if she did not lodge in his own house. It is a public jest, and one which can only serve to dishonour the State. If it had been desired to ruin everything, nothing worse could have been devised." The French Government had flattered itself that the English marriage and the conditions imposed in favour of the Catholics, amongst others the despatch of a body of ecclesiastics to London, would have done some service to the Roman Catholic Faith in England: truly the result seemed likely to be of a quite contrary nature! "It seems," says the Bishop, somewhat coarsely, "as if these ladies had come over to establish brothels, rather than to serve religion!" As for the husband, he was simply ridiculous. "M. de Chevreuse is playing a shabby part over here: it is a vexation to me that he should be the laughing-stock of the foreigners as well as of the French."

These reports impressed Louis XIII and Richelieu in the most unfavourable way. The Cardinal's opinion was that Mme. de Chevreuse ought to be sent back to France at once. To this Charles I objected, on the pretext that the young Duchess was so far advanced in pregnancy as to be unfit to undertake so long a journey. The Bishop of Mende then reported that she was lodged in Lord Holland's house. "So great is the husband's weakness," he writes, "that one blushes for him." He adds that Mme. de Chevreuse was seeing a great deal of Mme. de Thémines, and that both these ladies were holding long conferences with Dumoulins, the Protestant pastor, and that they eat meat in public on fast days. Did they mean to turn Huguenot? What an example! It was unendurable! From Paris, Richelieu, in his rage, wrote in the most insulting manner regarding Mme. de Chevreuse. "When she does come back," he says, in one of his letters to the Bishop, "there will be no necessity for sending to fetch *des guilledines* from England!"—an allusion to the class of persons sought after by men who *couraient le guilledou*. To Schomberg he mentioned her in still more scathing terms: "These English, whom we call *bouquins* (in France Buckingham's name was pronounced *Bouquinquant*), say we may well call them so, seeing some of them have *bouquiné une de nos chèvres!* This billet will be seen, if you please, by no eye save your own!" Mme. de Chevreuse was to become aware of the language the Cardinal had applied to her: she never forgave him. From that moment there grew up between her and Richelieu a deep and bitter hatred, the effects of which were to make themselves felt till the mighty Minister was laid in his grave.

The Duchess was brought to bed at Hampton Court, the palace of the King of England, of a daughter, who received the names of Anne-Marie, and was ultimately to become a professed nun, and Abbess of Pont-aux-Dames. By M. de Chevreuse, Marie de Rohan had daughters only: this Anne-Marie, born in 1625; Henriette, born in 1631, who also became a nun, and Abbess of Jouarre; and Charlotte, who was born in 1627, was known as Mlle. de Chevreuse, and to whom I shall frequently refer in the course of this work. If there were other children their

THE DUCHESSE DE CHEVREUSE

birth was necessarily concealed, and she bore them in secret : we find no trace of them in history.

Once she was thoroughly recovered, Mme. de Chevreuse could find no excuse for remaining in England. A message from Paris warned her, and her husband too, that they must return forthwith. The Duke's mission was concluded : he asserted that the English Government had formally undertaken faithfully to adhere to every clause of the marriage contract. On the other hand, the violence of the epidemic which afflicted London had not abated : it was high time to get back to France.

The departure of Mme. de Chevreuse was viewed with the deepest regret by the English Court. "We do not know where to begin," wrote Charles I to the Duke, "whether by thanking you for your company and that of my dear cousin your spouse, or by complaining against Fortune, who, after long feeding us with the hope of a lengthy enjoyment of your presence, and the pleasure of your good company in our rustic sports, has deprived us of that happiness by the call and necessity of business, and the accident of this infection. Our dear cousin carries back with her the satisfaction we lose by her return, and with it the honour, the respect, the prayers and good wishes of all sorts, not of our own Court only, but of all other persons who have had the honour of seeing her, or hearing others speak of her."

Charles I also wrote to Louis XIII to thank him for having sent him Mme. de Chevreuse, and to sing the praises of the Duchess. "I would fain derive as happy an advantage from the return of our cousin the Duchesse de Chevreuse as you yourself have done by her coming here, the charms and perfections of which have so greatly increased and added lustre to the honour and favour you have been pleased to bestow on myself and my well-beloved spouse, that we feel ourselves in duty bound to express all the gratitude in our power for so singular an affection and

BUCKINGHAM

favour, and also for the wisdom with which you made your choice of a person in whom we have found so many causes of contentment and satisfaction: this it is which leads me to beg you to show me the kindness of assisting me to render her the honour and the thanks I owe her, for the great honour and felicity we have received through her, who now returns to you, well fitted to be the ornament of any place, and the very worthy pledge of our mutual affection."

As a proof of his regard, Charles desired to make M. de Chevreuse a Knight of his Order of the Garter. The Duke took the precaution of requesting his King's permission to accept the honour. "You did wisely not to accept the Garter without my permission," replied Louis XIII on July 9, 1625; "I have laid the matter before the Senior Knights of the Order (of the Holy Ghost): I give you leave to accept, on condition that the Garter is conferred upon you without any religious ceremony and independently of any Church." Neither the oath taken nor the service promised clashed in any way with the statutes of the Order of the Holy Ghost. The Garter was duly bestowed, and a handsome gift of jewels along with it.

On July 15, 1625, M. and Mme. de Chevreuse took their departure from London: two other French Ambassadors, d'Effiat and Brienne, travelled with them. The final interview of these two gentlemen with Buckingham took place at Richmond. "My lord," quoth Brienne, "I am not surprised that two of the greatest of our ladies should have fallen in love with you." The reference was to the Queen and to Mme. de Chevreuse. "It would have been difficult for me to gain the victory," replied Buckingham, "for I was nothing but a poor foreigner." "My lord," said Brienne, "it is the glory of our French ladies that they can stir love without accepting it, and if any of them cannot but accept it, their only care, when they bestow their good graces, is to be wooed by a gallant belonging to the Court, and not

83

THE DUCHESSE DE CHEVREUSE

by a foreigner, who, in our country, is held to be no more than a *passe-volant*."[1] It was a "setting down": Buckingham listened, and made no rejoinder.

M. and Mme. de Chevreuse were civilly received at Court —they were of use there. Richelieu, in spite of his just anger against the Duchess, remembered she was the friend of Anne of Austria, of Charles I, of Buckingham: he must treat her with consideration. He was very polite. "The news of your generosity to their cousin, Mme. de Chevreuse," writes Holland to Richelieu from London, "has been very agreeable to His Majesty and to the Queen: this is an action so noble that it adds to your own glory and serves those who serve you, for the whole of this Court, which has been honoured by the presence and the knowledge of this lady, holds her as good as she is beautiful, her perfections walking equally, hand in hand."

And still the discussions with the English authorities went on. The "solemn" promises given to the Duc de Chevreuse as to the articles of the marriage contract had not been kept. There was now some question of driving all the French members of Henrietta-Maria's household out of the country, and Charles had just signed a merciless proclamation against the Catholics. For many reasons, the French Government did not desire to break off relations and declare war. There was nothing for it but to nego-

[1] Under the old French Monarchy the great noblemen were colonels and owners of their regiments. They chose their own arms, uniforms, etc. Their obligation as regards the King only amounted, in time of peace, to keeping up the effective strength of the regiment to a certain minimum. This obligation, as a matter of fact, was not very strictly observed, and except in war time, the regiments were always far below their specified strength, and frequently mere skeletons. For this reason, whenever the King, through his military representatives or governors of provinces, or other deputies, ordered a review of any kind, the strength of the regiments affected was hurriedly made up by borrowing men from other corps, on the understanding that a like service should be rendered in return when the necessity arose, or by enlisting, for a few days only, any straggling trooper, or hired bravo, or good-for-nothing wandering fellow, on whom the colonel and his officers could lay their hands; and these stop-gap soldiers were known as *des passe-volants*.

BUCKINGHAM

tiate, and for that purpose "the best means of repairing the damage was to appeal to the private influence of M. and Mme. de Chevreuse." Cardinal de Richelieu kept M. de Chevreuse informed of the displeasure of Louis XIII as to the disregard of the promises given by the English Government: once, in a moment of irritation, the King had taxed the Duke and his wife with keeping up communications with England prejudicial to his own service and to the cause of religion. "As they had done the mischief," he went on to say, "he insisted on their applying the remedy." Richelieu had added, in conversation with M. de Chevreuse, "that he warned him, as a friend, that he had better see to the matter, otherwise the blame would be laid on him." Much abashed, M. de Chevreuse offered to send one of his friends, M. de Bautru, to London, to remind the English Government of the engagement into which it had entered. Bautru duly departed to London; to Charles I he pointed out that M. and Mme. de Chevreuse were being blamed for what was happening in England, and that if matters did not improve, the Duke and Duchess would both be obliged to retire from Court; to Buckingham he suggested, in the name of Mme. de Chevreuse, that he should himself come to France, to smooth over the various difficulties. In consequence of these representations, Holland and Carlton were despatched to Paris, to discuss the whole business: this was a result of a kind.

While he was thus using the Duke in his dealings with England, Richelieu was endeavouring to employ the Duchess as his tool to work on Anne of Austria and Gaston, the King's brother. La Rochefoucauld declares, in reference to these attempts, that the Cardinal, aware of the hostile frame of mind, as to himself, in which the Duchess had returned from England, trusted her but a very little way; Richelieu was right: the future was to prove it, and in cruel fashion!

CHAPTER IV

THE CHALAIS AFFAIR

Richelieu and Anne of Austria's Circle—The Ornano Plot—The activity of Mme. de Chevreuse—She appeals to Chalais—Chalais in love; his arrest; his death—Flight of Mme. de Chevreuse into Lorraine. 1626.

It was the peculiar lot of Cardinal de Richelieu to inspire not only the most unbounded devotion and the most ardent affection, but also the most implacable hatred. The merit —or the fault—that brought this about lay in his own character. His intelligence was transcendent, his feelings were most keen, and he inspired all who approached him with the liveliest admiration, to begin with, and fascinated them, in the next place, by his courteous manner, his eager politeness, and his great anxiety to please. But when he took action, the man was so positive and so resolute that, whether intentionally or not, he gave offence by the very harshness and severity of his will. His imperiousness made itself sharply felt. The tension of his mind alarmed those about him: he would stop at nothing to attain success, and thus inspired feelings of dismay. His one idea was to guide all the affairs of the country on continuous and rational lines, and his unswerving logic put the poor courtiers, with their futile and vacillating passions, quite out of countenance. Between him and Mme. de Chevreuse there was a radical divergence of temper. Even if the Cardinal had not offended her by his hard words, the Duchess would soon have become the great statesman's bitter enemy.

In Lorraine she found a field ready for her operations. As Louis XIII, who had the gift of sound judgment, learnt

THE CHALAIS AFFAIR

to value Richelieu's talents more and more highly, his attachment to the exceptionally remarkable man, who, so he would declare, had been sent him by Providence, had deepened. But as Richelieu's credit grew stronger the inevitable consequence had made itself felt, and an opposition had also grown up and was gaining strength. Louis XIII was known to be self-willed and harsh: people were well aware that he himself was generally responsible for the severe decrees issued by his Ministers; but as nothing could be done against His Majesty, a belief was simulated and disseminated that Richelieu alone was to blame: he became an object of general dislike.

Nowhere was this animosity stronger than in Anne of Austria's own circle. The young lords and ladies, giddy and superficial every one of them, who clustered about "the little Queen," were even less able than most people to reconcile themselves to the Cardinal's severe and unbending views. When Mme. de Chevreuse returned from London, she found the tone, when the Cardinal was mentioned in Anne of Austria's household, was one of ridicule. And there was more than that. Ever since the Buckingham incident there had lingered in the Queen's heart—with the indignation caused by the Duke's imprudent behaviour and that continued stir in her sentimental existence of which he was the author, and which had really been very agreeable to her—a secret grudge against the King, who had been aware of what had happened, and in his inability to strike herself, had punished those about her; and above all, against Richelieu, who, when informed of the incident, had no doubt advised the monarch to take the measures he had adopted. The Queen's own courtiers had guessed the sovereign's prejudices, and her friends of the female sex, while they poked daily scorn at the Minister, would occasionally venture on a veiled allusion to the King his master. Mme. de Chevreuse returned just in the nick of time to transform a mere inclination into a living force.

THE DUCHESSE DE CHEVREUSE

Chalais wrote of her to Richelieu, "She has a bitter animosity against your person." Mme. de Chevreuse stirred up the Queen against the Cardinal. "She never ceased," writes Mme. de Motteville, "talking about him to the Queen. The mistress and her favourite both hated Cardinal de Richelieu, and nothing delighted them so much as to annoy him, all the more so because the Queen was persuaded that he made mischief about her with the King." Finding herself listened to, the Duchess went a step further. She ventured on attacking the person of the King himself: she pointed out the possibility that Louis XIII, with his delicate and uncertain health, might very likely die, and his brother Gaston would succeed to the throne. Why should not Anne of Austria marry Gaston, then, and so continue Queen of France? The Queen lent an ear to these suggestions; but such fancies would have remained buried in the secrecy of confidential intercourse if an unexpected series of favourable circumstances had not given the audacious Duchess a chance of trying to realize them. Her love of intrigue and her constitutional impetuosity led her to engage in a wild conspiracy.

Gaston, then Duc d'Anjou, and later to become Duc d'Orléans, was then a lad of seventeen. He was an inferior sort of fellow. His great staring eyes, pendulous lower lip, and perpetually open mouth gave him a far from intelligent expression. His character was considered anything but sympathetic: he was timid, lazy, fidgety, nervous; he never could sit quiet, and was always making faces. Familiar, ill-mannered too, vain, insisting to the last tittle on the honours due to his rank, never allowing a woman to be seated in his presence, nor a man to speak to him save with uncovered head, he proved himself, as his confessor, the Père de Coudren, described it, "both violent-tempered and debauched." Chalais, when he lay in his prison, was to say: "Monseigneur is, of all men, the most

THE CHALAIS AFFAIR

frivolous. He is of small mind, and of no resolution: he has already lost the few servants he had by his own weakness." Later, when Anne of Austria's eyes had been opened, she was to reply scornfully to the King's reproachful accusation of having desired his death so as to marry his brother, that " she would have gained but little by the change." At the moment of which we write, Gaston was still young, there was some hope of improvement on his part; in any case, he was heir to the throne. The little Queen fell in with the plan suggested to her. From the confession made by Gaston to the King on August 2, 1626, it is clear that this plan had been mentioned to her by Mme. de Chevreuse even before 1624. And in 1625 came the announcement that Gaston was going to marry, and to marry Mlle. de Montpensier! This marriage would shatter all the cherished dreams!

It was Queen Marie de Médicis who desired the match. For years she had been working for it. Mlle. de Montpensier, the only child of a Bourbon of the Montpensier branch, and the last of his line, was one of the richest heiresses in France. Marie de Médicis had made much of the mother, a Joyeuse. She had showered proofs of a touching affection on the child from her earliest years, calling her "my daughter." After having destined her to be the bride of a son born before Gaston, and who died young, after having even gone so far as to get the marriage contract signed, in 1608—a wonderful contract it was, with a list of all the splendid domains of the ancient family of Bourbon, the duchies of Montpensier, Auvergne, St. Fargeau, Combraille, Dombes, and Beaujolais—she had lost no time, when her elder son was taken from her, about arranging the same alliance for the younger brother. Gaston was then three years old, his betrothed was six. Since that time the Queen had waited patiently. But now, the young man having reached his seventeenth year, and the young lady her twentieth, she felt it was time to

THE DUCHESSE DE CHEVREUSE

conclude the matter. Louis XIII, after some hesitation, had given his consent, and the news had been made public.

It came as a surprise. Everybody had known, of course, that such a project had been in existence, but it was believed to have fallen to the ground. In the absence of an heir, the families of Condé and Soissons had both conceived the hope of being some day called to the crown. They were sorely vexed: and the Comte de Soissons had made up his mind to marry Mlle. de Montpensier into the bargain! But of all the persons affected by the news, none was so severely hit as Anne of Austria.

If Gaston married and had children, while she herself had none, how humiliating would her position be, and how diminished her importance! What would become of her if the King were to die? "Ah, the poor Prince!" said Marsillac to Villelongue, "how badly is the King advised! That a childless King of five-and-twenty should marry a brother of eighteen or twenty, who may have children within a year! What harm may that not bring about! And that poor Princess (the Queen)! What is to become of her?"

Mme. de Chevreuse raised Anne of Austria's courage. Nothing was done yet, she pointed out: there was only one course open to her, the marriage must be opposed and stopped at any price. The best thing would be to persuade Gaston to refuse to marry Mlle. de Montpensier. "It is Mme. de Chevreuse," wrote Chalais to Richelieu, "who is the cause of the whole world's opposition to the consent (of Monsieur to the marriage), and she incited everybody to do harm to Mlle. de Montpensier." It was necessary to find somebody with influence over Gaston sufficiently strong to carry him away. Mme. de Chevreuse addressed herself to the Prince's Governor, Colonel d'Ornano.

Jean-Baptiste d'Ornano, a Corsican by birth, was the grandson of one Sampietro Bastelica, who had raised his fellow-countrymen in revolt against the Genoese, and the

THE CHALAIS AFFAIR

son of a certain Corsican called Alfonso and surnamed d'Ornano, who had come to France in the sixteenth century, had distinguished himself, been appointed Colonel of the Corsican bands, made a Marshal of France in 1596, and died in 1610. Jean-Baptiste, who was born in 1581, had succeeded his father in the colonelcy of the Corsicans; his intelligence, energy and power of command had won him rapid advancement, he had been made a Councillor of State in 1610, *Maréchal de Camp* in 1614, Lieutenant of Normandy in 1618, and in the following year, 1619, Governor to Gaston. Thanks to his prestige and his firmness of character, he had acquired great authority over the Prince, and was the only person able to lead him and make him do what he desired.

To tell the real truth, Ornano cared but little about the Montpensier marriage. The Colonel's chief consideration was connected with the fact that if Gaston succeeded to the throne, he himself, his favourite and confidential counsellor would become the most powerful person in the realm. Till that time arrived, the absence of a direct heir, which had a singularly weakening effect on Louis XIII, proportionately strengthened the hand of Gaston, whom the King was fain to treat with great consideration. It was quite possible that, as the result of a series of internal complications, the King might be driven to resign his crown. Complications, therefore, should be regarded with favour. Ornano might at all events, by dint of creating difficulties, make himself feared, and force the King into buying his temporary fidelity or submission by the bestowal of honours and dignities.

Mme. de Chevreuse offered him the alliance of the Queen Regnant. She proposed that he should foment a cabal between Anne of Austria and the heir to the throne, with a view to preventing the Montpensier marriage. The sovereign was sure to endeavour to procure peace by paying off the conspirators. The risks were slight and there

THE DUCHESSE DE CHEVREUSE

was profit to be made—past difficulties of the kind proved that fact. The offer was a tempting one, and Ornano closed with it.

The ladies about the Queen, Mme. de Chevreuse, the Princesse de Conti, Mme. de La Valette (formerly Mlle. de Verneuil), held long conferences with him. He was ill: they went to see him as he lay in bed, "which was of no consequence at all," says Fontenay-Mareuil, "because he was so ugly." Richelieu grew uneasy. His spies brought him warnings. To lay a finger on the Colonel was impossible. So powerful was his influence with the heir to the throne that his master would not endure it. Richelieu suggested that the King should draw Ornano over to his side, and bind his hands, by conferring favours upon him. He was made a Marshal of France, and appeared grateful for the honour. He took the necessary oaths early in 1626; and the Cardinal questioned him about Gaston's marriage, inquiring whether he had given the Prince any advice on the subject. The new Marshal replied that he never interfered in that matter, and left Monsieur to settle it as he chose. Some time afterwards Gaston asked to be admitted to share in the deliberations of the King's Council. Louis XIII took this to be a move of Ornano's, destined to lead to his own admission to the Council Chamber, where the heir-apparent's confidant might endeavour to exercise a preponderating action likely to end by creating a difficult situation. He refused. Gaston and the Marshal were both much annoyed, and Mme. de Chevreuse took advantage of their vexation to lay a complete plan of campaign before Ornano, which was to be carried out in opposition to the Montpensier marriage, and would result in serious changes in the State, likely to ensure a great advance in the Marshal's own fortunes. Deliberately, Ornano entered on the adventure.

Advised by him, Gaston made it known that he refused to accept the proposed marriage: the reason he put forward

THE CHALAIS AFFAIR

was not that he had "any aversion to the person of Mlle. de Montpensier, but that he was afraid to bind himself." Then the Prince, with his habitual inconsistency, told Richelieu, when the Cardinal came to see him, that he was ready to marry if a fine apanage was secured to him. Ornano was on the watch. Mme. de Chevreuse scarcely left his side, Anne of Austria, in the shadow, was close on her heels. Later on the Queen was to deny any active participation in the business. When Louis XIII lay at the point of death she sent M. de Chavigny to "beseech him not to believe that she had dabbled in the Ornano affair, or that she had ever had anything to do with the plan for her marriage with Monsieur." And the King replied sadly, "In my present state I am bound to forgive her, but I am not obliged to believe her!" It did not prove a difficult matter to induce Gaston to change his mind once more.

That done, the conspirators laid the foundations of an understanding with the grandees of the kingdom. At a later period Monsieur was to confess this, under cross-examination. "Monsieur," so runs the report, "acknowledged to his mother, in the presence of the Cardinal de Richelieu, that it was true that the Colonel had incited him to keep up habitual relations with as many as possible of the great nobility of the kingdom." Mme. de Chevreuse was busy too: she opened correspondence with the Prince de Condé, the Comte de Soissons, the Ducs de Montmorency and de Nevers, and even, to reach the Huguenots through her, with Mme. de Rohan. She found a ready and attentive hearing. Great lady as she was, the Queen's favourite, dealing with an affair in which Monsieur and Anne of Austria were both interested, and which was to involve a struggle with a too-powerful Minister, Mme. de Chevreuse was sure to find favourable ears. All these great lords knew, like Ornano, by their experience of the past fifteen years, how little danger there was about risings

THE DUCHESSE DE CHEVREUSE

of this sort, and how much profit was to be made out of them. They sent replies. M. de Nevers said that if war broke out he would raise troops in the province of Champagne; the Comte de Soissons promised 400,000 crowns on condition that Gaston made Mlle. de Montpensier over to him; Longueville undertook to bring 800 horsemen out of Normandy, and a group of smaller gentlemen, La Meilleraye, Mauny, Guitry, Bertechères; a force of from 500 to 600 men should be raised in that province as well. Let Monsieur give the signal for revolt by his own sudden departure from the Court, just as Marie de Médicis had done at the time of the last rising. Of all these accomplices, the members of the Vendôme family were the most eager.

Cæsar, Duc de Vendôme, and Alexandre de Vendôme, Grand Prior of France, the natural sons of Henri IV and Gabrielle d'Estrées, had never loved Louis XIII. As children their disagreeable and quarrelsome tempers had rendered them the objects of the young King's dislike, and this antipathy had grown and strengthened with age. In the course of the inquiry which followed on the Ornano plot, a letter from the Duc de Vendôme to the Marshal was produced, which explained his reasons for joining the conspiracy: he complained that "since the death of Henri IV, the King and Marie de Médicis had done him every sort of injustice," that they had tried to strip him and reduce him to a nonentity, and that he intended to defend himself; he added, and this flattered Ornano's secret hopes, "that the crown would look well on Monsieur's head." Four accusations were brought against the Grand Prior by his judges: that he had opposed Gaston's marriage, that he had openly professed his hatred for the King, that he had incited Monsieur to leave the kingdom, and proposed to play the Ministers an evil trick. The co-operation of the Duc de Vendôme was promised through his secretary, Dunault: he demanded that Gaston should leave the Court and proceed to Metz, Sedan, or the Havre, that if necessary

THE CHALAIS AFFAIR

he should "use threats and violence to Richelieu," and above all things, that he should take up arms.

The great families of the kingdom were not the only persons to whom application was made. An appeal was addressed to foreign countries. This was no new fashion. In the course of the three-quarters of a century during which civil wars had been raging in France, the habit of asking for extraneous help had grown up. The feeling of the country was against the practice. "I think it a shameful thing for me," writes Alexandre de Campion, later to become the faithful friend of Mme. de Chevreuse, "to serve the King of Spain against my native country." "I cannot honourably serve Spain against my country." Gaston, cross-questioned by Richelieu on July 23, 1626, himself admitted the gravity of the act: "Monsieur said that the greatest fault he had committed had been to treat with foreigners." When the Cardinal told him, thereupon, that this fault on the Colonel's part constituted a capital offence, he openly testified that he knew it very well. But the answers came in from abroad: efficacious help was promised; Mme. de Chevreuse and Ornano did not hesitate.

They entered into negotiations with England. Through Mme. de Chevreuse, Gaston was put into communication with the Earl of Carlisle. Monsieur's theory was that the King his brother treated him in a humiliating manner, that he did not give him his due, and tried to force him into a marriage he disliked. Guided by Buckingham, who sought to make every possible difficulty with France, Carlisle replied that he was to express the "annoyance with which it was realized that he was badly treated, and to assure him that if he would only make his views known, he would be served by England in whatever manner he might desire." Blainville, the French Ambassador in London, warned Louis XIII's Secretary of State for Foreign Affairs, on July 4, 1626, in these words: "The

THE DUCHESSE DE CHEVREUSE

Earl of Carlisle has reported Monsieur's discourse to him, which is so full of hatred and scorn for the King that, out of respect, I dare not write it." The Bishop of Mende wrote, for his part: "The King of England is expecting great results from the understanding between Monsieur and the Queen, and nearly the whole Court is conspiring in this design." The English Government, it must be said, was struggling at that moment with internal difficulties which made it far from easy for it to afford any really effectual help. It gave "fine hopes and promises."

Gaston wrote letters to Savoy. In his cross-examination he was to confess that "it was true he had written letters to Piedmont." The Duke of Savoy, who was watching the complications in French politics in the hope of snatching some addition to his own territories, replied that he would send ten thousand men.

Negotiations were opened with the Ambassador of the United Provinces, Aarsens, but he avoided replying—he had no faith in the business. The conspirators applied to the Nuncio, and tried to win him over: to the Spanish Ambassador as well. Gaston declared he had "tried in a general way to make himself as many friends on every side as he could get."

Thus the plot was being gradually organized. And the conspirators began to discuss the details of its execution. According to the confession made by Gaston to the King on July 12, 1626, it was arranged that advantage was to be taken of the King's absence in a distant province to raise the people of Paris, and take possession of the fortresses of Vincennes and the Bastille. If, as was most probable, the King hurried up with his troops, Monsieur was to fly to Dieppe or to the Havre. The Protestants of La Rochelle had offered to receive him in their town, but Gaston, advised by two of his confidants, Bois d'Annemets and Puylaurens, had refused the invitation. As the Duc de Longueville, Governor of Normandy, was his adherent, Dieppe or the

THE CHALAIS AFFAIR

Havre would be safe refuges for him. In case there should be any failure in that quarter, Gaston wrote, or was made to write, to the Duc d'Épernon, Governor of Metz, and deputed the Abbé d'Obazine to beg he would open the gates of the city to him. Everything was being set in order.

The Vendômes, on their side, were hoping to get something out of the adventure. The Duke, who was Governor of Bretagne, had long dreamt of setting up an independent government in that province. He had been paving the way, gaining over the local nobility, bestowing pensions and gifts of money, "seeking the favour of the people by every means which seemed to him likely to make him popular." The accusation against him, as it was eventually formulated, runs as follows: "M. de Vendôme's intention of making himself the sovereign of Brittany is apparent by various conjectures and various actions, for which he deserves to be called a madman." He, too, recognized the possibility of the disappearance of Louis XIII. The persons about him, his family, his brother, stood on no ceremony whatever: they all talked openly of the King's eventual deposition. And why should not a Vendôme, own son of Henri IV, ascend the throne? And if the King continued to hold out, what was there to prevent an end being put to his resistance by putting him out of the way? "The whole family," so the document concludes, "has been very free in its criminal talk against the person of the King. One said a Louis had been deposed once before, another, that bastards had reigned just as well as kings born in wedlock, another, that he would rather hang the King than let the King hang him."

Here we reach the most serious point of the whole plot. Was there really any idea of deposing Louis XIII, or of putting him to death? The King and Richelieu both believed it. "The vile attempt against the King's person," writes Richelieu, "has been confirmed, in the first place, by Chalais, who formally confessed that Mme. de Chevreuse nursed a special hatred against his Majesty." Dunault, secretary to the Grand Prior de Vendôme, told the Sieur du Fossé, in the presence of Mme. d'Elbeuf, that his master "begged for mercy, and acknowledged his two separate undertakings against the King's person and the State." Bullion reported to the King, on October 17, that "nothing was expected in Savoy save an absolute change in the State, to the prejudice of the person of the King, whom it was proposed to shut up." And the Cardinal repeats his assertion elsewhere: "Two persons of quality revealed to the King that there was a design to cast him down and lift Monsieur up. Confessors at the Jubilee reported that penitents had applied to them, accusing themselves of a great plan and party to elevate Monsieur at the King's expense." And Louis XIII, in his public declaration of August 5, 1626, which instituted a court of criminal justice to try the conspirators, affirms that he has "received notice of several conspiracies against our person and our authority." Richelieu thus concluded: "Here is the most fearful conspiracy ever mentioned in history: if this be so on account of the multitude of plotters, it is yet more so because of the horribleness of their design—for this design was not only to lift up their master (Gaston) above his proper condition, but to lower and destroy the sacred person of the King."

As a matter of fact, an examination of the evidence does not permit us to reach so decisive a conclusion. When Du Fossé and Dunault were confronted with the Vendôme brothers, and asked to repeat their asertions, the Grand Prior did not acknowledge the truth of what Dunault had said as to a design on the King's person. "My friend," said he to Dunault, "you have said a thing which will bring you into trouble, and me too." The judges followed up the track of certain compromising remarks in the hope of getting at their origin, but the results attained were exceedingly nebulous. When Chalais was cross-

THE CHALAIS AFFAIR

questioned, and even threatened with the torture, he denied having "ever heard anybody mention, or known of the existence of, any plan to touch the King's person, or of any evil talk against his said Majesty." He repeated that "he had never heard the King's person mentioned." And Gaston's favourite, Bois d'Annemets, enters an indignant protest in his Memoirs: "It is so great a wickedness to accuse Monsieur of having desired to have the King killed, that the mention of it fills me with horror." La Rochefoucauld comes to the conclusion that the "crime was not fully proven," and he is right. Mme. de Chevreuse, Ornano, and their confederates do not seem to have deliberately planned an attempt on the King's life. In their private conversations the eventuality of the King's disappearance by deposition or otherwise was no doubt discussed; but the idea never assumed any definite shape, and no steps were taken for its realization. The Vendôme family certainly indulged, in the presence of other persons, in imprudent language, which was reported to the King and stirred his fears. Further than this the matter does not seem to have gone.

It was towards the beginning of 1626 that the King and Richelieu became fully aware of the plot that was hatching. At first Louis XIII paid no attention to the warnings. Then things began to look threatening, and Ministers grew uneasy. No violent measure could be taken against Ornano. He ruled Gaston so completely, and was so well guarded, besides, that it was difficult to take any step regarding him without causing serious complications. He was privately warned that he must be careful, that the King had his suspicions, that he had better clear things up with His Majesty. He boldly replied that he would see about it in a month. And then, scorning the danger, or else desiring to aggravate matters so as to force on the wished-for rupture, he had Monsieur's request to be admitted to the Council Board renewed: with the addition that

THE DUCHESSE DE CHEVREUSE

Monsieur demanded an apanage of 500,000 *livres* a year as well. Mme. de Chevreuse, on her part, announced in the Queen's circle that a demand was to be made for the Marshal's own nomination to the Council—this, she declared, would make the Government's decision clear. The conspirators' course was taking definite shape.

Louis XIII summoned Richelieu and Schomberg to Fontainebleau, and the three sat in council. The proofs of the conspiracy were absolutely clear, so the two Ministers asserted. It was for the King, "by his own will, to see what it pleased him to do, and for his servants to carry it out." Two lines might be taken, so Richelieu explained. To exercise caution, to win over the conspirators by dignities and favours—which, it must be acknowledged, had not as yet succeeded very well, or to remove all the guilty persons from the vicinity of Monsieur—and this last course needed serious consideration, for Monsieur must not be allowed to flee from the Court. Louis XIII said he would think it over. Thereupon came a report—false or true, we know not—that the Vendôme brothers, taking advantage of the fact that Richelieu, who lived at the Château of Fleury, was in the habit of crossing the forest, with but scanty attendance, to sit at the King's Council Board at Fontainebleau, intended to waylay the Cardinal and kill him. Louis XIII ordered a troop of cavalry to escort his Minister's coach, and then he made up his mind.

On the plea of manœuvres to be performed in his presence, he summoned his regiment of French Guards to Fontainebleau. On the day of its arrival, May 4, 1626, and after it had occupied the Castle, he sent to his brother's Governor, desiring him to wait on him after supper that evening. At ten o'clock Ornano made his appearance at the door of the King's Cabinet: he was placed under arrest by a captain of the Guard, M. du Hallier. Resistance was out of the question. The Marshal was taken to the Castle of Vincennes and imprisoned there.

THE CHALAIS AFFAIR

There was a great to-do. Gaston hurried to the King's chamber. He wanted to see the King, he wanted to see the Queen-Mother. He was not admitted. The next morning he saw the Chancellor d'Aligre, and angrily demanded an explanation. D'Aligre replied that he knew nothing about the matter. Monsieur wandered to and fro, not knowing what to do next. Very soon, by his brother's command, he was to sign a declaration in which he cast off all his accomplices, and swore fidelity to the King.

In Anne of Austria's rooms there was general consternation. One witness, who saw Mme. de Chevreuse at that moment, said of her (with a thrust at her easy virtue): "I thought there could not be a man left in the kingdom, so deep was the dejection written on her features and her countenance!" For six whole days she stayed shut up in her rooms, terrified, expecting to be arrested every moment. Then, as time went on, and the danger seemed to pass away, she gathered courage again. Louis XIII had no proofs against her, he could not well put her in prison: such a measure would rouse the wrath of great and powerful families, whom it would be as well not to disoblige at such a moment. The instant she thought herself safe she began to plot again. Ornano must be delivered, at any cost, and the enterprise must be carried on. To secure her hold on Gaston, now his Governor was lying in prison, she turned her attention to M. de Chalais.

Henri de Talleyrand, Marquis de Chalais, third son of Daniel de Talleyrand and Jeanne de Monluc, was a youth of eighteen, well-built, pleasant-looking, "skilful in exercises of every kind," so Fontenay-Mareuil informs us; and the charm of whose manner had won him many successes among the ladies of the Court. He was well-received in every quarter. In his infancy he had been placed about the person of Louis XIII as a "child of honour," and he had grown up in close intimacy with the King and with Monsieur. His mother left no stone

THE DUCHESSE DE CHEVREUSE

unturned to secure his future. As soon as he reached man's estate she purchased him the post of Keeper of the King's Wardrobe. "It had cost her the greater part of her fortune, and left her with hardly anything to live on." But what would she not have done to advance the fortunes of the son she loved so tenderly? Thanks to the good offices of the Duc de Bellegarde, Grand Equerry to His Majesty, she had married him to a rich wife; Chalais had espoused the widow of the Comte de Charny, Charlotte de Castille, sister to the Treasurer Jeannin de Castille, an opulent financier. Thus he had everything, both dignities and riches. His post as Keeper of the Wardrobe gave him access to the Sovereign, he was "one of the King's servants," had his master's ear, was constantly in the company of Monsieur, and from every point of view, a prominent personage.

Unfortunately, so far as intelligence and character were concerned, he was a poor creature, vain, superficial, unconscientious, weak. We possess the letters he wrote from his prison: they are a medley of undignified self-abasement and tasteless pleasantries, supplications for mercy, offers to betray anybody and everybody so long as he himself may escape, denunciations, retractations, tears. There can be no excuse for him, save his youth, his lack of experience, and, no doubt, the distractingly difficult position in which he found himself.

If Mme. de Chevreuse cast her choice on him it was certainly because he was in love with her. His venal marriage had soon lost its hold on his heart. He threw himself with the greatest ardour into the passion with which the Duchess had inspired him. "He was passionately in love," writes Bois d'Annemets. "His attachment to Mme. de Chevreuse was something extraordinary," affirms La Rochefoucauld. He was observed following the fair lady whithersoever she went, "to the churches, to the public promenades, and more especially to the Chapel of the

THE CHALAIS AFFAIR

Louvre." He made a boast of his adoration. At his trial one witness deposed that "he had heard the said Chalais declare a hundred times over that he was in love with Mme. de Chevreuse and that he had the most beautiful mistress in the whole kingdom." Chalais was to reiterate the fact of his love for her to Richelieu: he was to speak of Mme. de Chevreuse as "that person whom I was known to have loved."

It would appear certain, in spite of Mme. de Motteville's assertions, that Mme. de Chevreuse did not respond to this passion: she did not love Chalais, and she did not yield to his prayers: the letters the unhappy man wrote from his prison prove this fact. But when Ornano was arrested, the Duchess perceived the advantage to which she might turn his adoration. Chalais, thanks to his post, was in a position to discover the intentions of the Government; being Gaston's friend, he might be able, just when Monsieur, all astray, knew not in whom to confide, to gain an ascendency over that Prince and lead him as the Marshal had led him. She resolved to make the attempt.

She pretended to accept the young man's adoration, she let him hope, and practised her arts upon him. As Chalais wrote to Richelieu, some time later: "I was in love with her: she did all she could to make me think she was well pleased it should be so." He was taken in, he allowed himself to be persuaded, they made him do whatever they wanted done. A bargain was struck: the Duchess was to accept the young man's homage, and he, in return, was to do his best to lead Monsieur according to the directions that were to be imparted to him. "This little bargain," wrote Chalais to Richelieu, "was very like those a man makes with the devil. She told me that if I gave myself over to her utterly she would scorn all the rest of the world. I replied that her good will would be very dearly bought. I failed in judgment. But I swear before God that, though I was well aware of the faction, I never

THE DUCHESSE DE CHEVREUSE

was its counsellor. It is very difficult not to be deceived by such devilish artifices; for who could escape a Princess so kindly looked upon at the Court of two of the greatest Queens in the world, whose commerce is so easy, and her rouge so well laid on?" Chalais pleaded extenuating circumstances, but in reality he gave way readily enough. Mme. de Chevreuse left no stone unturned. To excite his feelings against Richelieu, she went so far as to tell him the Cardinal was in love with herself, and consequently his rival. "When this Lady Lucretia spoke to me about this business," writes the young man to the Cardinal, "I had never failed in my service to you, and when she saw that I thought her proposal a dangerous one she tried to work round me from a different direction, telling me you were in love with her, and so to arouse my jealousy." What Chalais does not add is that he was all the more willing to be persuaded because he had a grievance of his own against the Ministers. He thought the two or three services he had rendered them had not received a sufficient reward. Certain astrologers and diviners who had cast his horoscope had told him he would be fortunate and powerful, or else, indeed, most unhappy: full of faith in the earlier part of this prediction, he fancied he now saw his chance of winning fortune, and made his venture.

If he was over-confident, Mme. de Chevreuse was hardly less so. It was an imprudent proceeding on her part to address herself to a young man of whom she knew scarcely anything, a youth so inconsistent and so devoid of strength of character. Chalais had given her a sample of his real nature when he came and acknowledged to her, as Bassompierre asserts, that it was he who had warned the Government of the Duc de Vendôme's plan to attack Richelieu on his way from Fleury: he explained to the Queen and the Duchess that when he had mentioned the secret to the Commandeur de Valençay, Achille d'Étampes, that officer had threatened to denounce him to

THE CHALAIS AFFAIR

the Ministers unless he went and reported the matter to them himself; but he begged the ladies to calm their minds, since his confession would be regarded as a proof of the straightforwardness of his character. And then, added Chalais, at his trial, "the ladies spent the whole afternoon, when dinner was over, laughing over the story of this affair."

Chalais opened his campaign. He spoke to Monsieur, he entered into an understanding with the Prince's immediate circle: Bois d'Annemets, who was a member of it, tells us that these overtures were at first somewhat coldly received. But Chalais was Keeper of the King's Wardrobe, he was in a position that ensured him the sovereign's ear: it was only wise to treat him with consideration; and then the new recruit did possess a certain value: he obtained a hearing. To Monsieur himself Calais addressed the most fervent protestations of devotion. Gaston told Louis XIII that the young courtier even offered to sell his post about the King, so as to be more free to serve his brother. The conspiracy, which had been paralysed for a moment by Ornano's arrest, began to lift its head once more. The Government was warned afresh.

Richelieu's first advice, as in the Marshal's case, was to try and win Chalais over. He might then be used to betray his accomplices. Advances were made to the young man. Much flattered, and thinking he would thus rise sooner and higher in the King's service, Chalais unhesitatingly accepted these proposals. The Commandeur de Valençay acted as intermediary. According to Fontenay-Mareuil, Chalais sent word that "if he was given something considerable he would get the marriage accepted, and anything else that was desired." His hand was trumped already. Richelieu offered him a post as *Maître de Camp* in the cavalry, to which he was to be appointed as soon as Monsieur was married. Chalais sent his acceptance of the bargain.

THE DUCHESSE DE CHEVREUSE

Meanwhile, and as a corollary to the imprisonment of Marshal d'Ornano, Louis XIII decided to arrest the Vendôme brothers. The thing would have to be carefully done; the Duc de Vendôme was fortifying his position in Brittany; he had openly declared he hoped he might never lay his eyes on the King again. Without a word of what he meant to do, Louis XIII left Paris, started for Brittany, and got as far as Blois. The Grand Prior took alarm, interfered, tried to induce his brother to come and wait on the King, and besought the sovereign to receive him. Louis refused. The Government began to collect troops, the situation became threatening for the Vendôme family. The two princes, thoroughly frightened, decided to proceed to Blois. They reached that town on June 11: on the 12th they were both in prison.

This arrest produced the same effect as that of Ornano; but it was less unexpected. Mme. de Chevreuse, who had received a warning of it, despatched a lackey to the Grand Prior, to advise him not to come to Court. As soon as the brothers arrived at Blois, Gaston sent them word that "they were very wrong to come to the King." But the event was calculated to cause Mme. de Chevreuse the most acute alarm. What was Chalais doing? What effect was he producing on Monsieur? It was given out that Gaston had now decided to agree to the marriage. The King, it was said, was resolved to have Mlle. de Montpensier brought to Blois forthwith, and have the betrothal formally celebrated: the Marquis de Fontenay had departed to Paris with orders to bring the Princess back, under the escort of fifty mounted men. And as a prologue to the marriage ceremony, the Duc de Vendôme and his brother were to be put in prison. Was Chalais playing a dishonest game? Or was he powerless?

The Duchess questioned the young gentleman: Richelieu had bought him over, there could be no doubt about it. She was not dismayed, she meant to win him back.

THE CHALAIS AFFAIR

Convinced, writes Fontenay-Mareuil, "since the imprisonment of Messieurs de Vendôme, that there was an understanding between Chalais and the Cardinal de Richelieu, she cast so many reproaches on him, and pressed him so hard, that he preferred failing the Cardinal and himself to failing her, and thus, having caused Monsieur to change once more, as well, he made him more rebellious than ever against the marriage." Once again Chalais had been turned round, and Louis XIII and the Cardinal, when they knew it, conceived a bitter animosity against the youth. The Cardinal cross-questioned him, and he, greatly embarrassed, answered in vague phrases, affirming his fidelity. The Minister ordered him to keep his promises, and he, so that he might boast later to Gaston of his devotion to him, evaded them. "The poor man," writes Bois d'Annemets, "tried to find his advantage with every party. He promised the Cardinal wonders and then came and told us the very opposite."

While this was going on, Mme. de Chevreuse decided that Gaston must fly at once. There had been some idea of sending the Prince to La Rochelle, but on reflection it was thought wiser for him to go eastward, so as to be near Lorraine, where the fugitive was sure to find a refuge. Chalais carried out the orders given him by the Duchess; he sent a gentleman who acted as his equerry, Gaston de la Louvière, to Sedan, with a letter to the Comte de Soissons. La Louvière came back without any answer: he had been shown the door! Then Chalais sent the same equerry to Metz, with another missive addressed to the Governor of that town, M. de la Valette, son of the Duc d'Épernon. "If you are disposed to entertain proposals from Monsieur," it ran, "I will undertake to have them made to you." M. de la Valette told M. de la Louvière that "he was surprised that Chalais, who belonged to the King's Household, should mix himself up with such matters. He had no power over the town of Metz—it was his father who

THE DUCHESSE DE CHEVREUSE

commanded there : let them apply to the Duc d'Épernon." Both attempts had failed!

The Government was on the watch. It was remarked at Blois that Chalais, who was lodged in the Castle close to Gaston, went to the Prince's chamber every night, and spent whole hours with him. Louis XIII decided to leave Blois. On June 27 he was at Tours, and thence he travelled to Nantes. Mlle. de Montpensier was expected. Richelieu kept telling Chalais that the King called on him to persuade Gaston to agree to the betrothal. Chalais shifted this way and that. He ended by declaring he was no longer in a position to keep his promises, and took back his word. But at the same time, feeling the ground crumbling under his feet, and convinced that his only hope of escaping from his difficulties was to take to flight himself, and make Gaston fly as well, he made his preparations.

His first idea was to make a sudden start, with the Prince and five or six gentlemen, "on swift horses"; but there could be no doubt, unluckily, that the party would soon be caught. He decided that a more prudent course would be to ride quietly out of Nantes on pretence of some excursion, as to Ingrandes, for instance. Once that far, they could have the King informed that Monsieur, not feeling himself safe at Nantes, was returning to Blois, and that done, they would gallop as fast as their horses could carry them to Chartres, and on to Paris. The day of departure was fixed, and then everything fell through, because, so Gaston asserted under cross-examination, "the *maîtres d'hôtel* had not had their dinner": the real reason was that the Government, duly warned, had sent companies of light horse along the roads to stop the fugitives. Chalais looked about him for some other plan : in any case, flight was an imminent necessity.

Thereupon Louis XIII told his Ministers that he was worn out by the behaviour of the Keeper of his Wardrobe,

THE DUCHESSE DE CHEVREUSE
(From a painting in the possession of the Duc de Vendôme, and now at Belmont Castle)

THE CHALAIS AFFAIR

and intended to have him arrested forthwith. This was on July 8. At daybreak on the 9th, M. de Tresmes, Captain of the Guard, proceeded to Chalais' room in the Castle of Nantes and took him into custody. He made no resistance. He was made over to an Exempt of the Body-guard,[1] and shut up in one of the Castle dungeons. A Commission of judges was appointed, and charged, so ran the royal decree which called it into existence, with the duty of inquiring into the accusation of high treason brought against Chalais. This trial was not to be mixed up with that of Ornano, who was still lying in prison at Vincennes, and whose condemnation had been delayed by various political considerations. The magistrates were to proceed diligently about their business.

That very day the Commissioners, d'Effiat and Valençay, proceeded to interview Chalais in his prison. He, quite crestfallen, only answered that he had never failed in his duty to the King, and that if it was desired to make use of him with regard to Monsieur's business he was ready to reveal anything and everything. The court began to hear witnesses, the prisoner was confronted with them: Richelieu took a hand in the cross-examination.

The accused man's behaviour was pitiful. He wrote to everybody, and his letters proved him foolish, terrified and worthless. He besought the Cardinal to get him pardoned, praised the King's virtues in the most exaggerated terms, loaded Richelieu with heavy and pompous flattery: he ran down all his friends of Gaston's set, vowing they were "great disturbers of heaven and earth," who were only fit to "*danser, baller, et coucher ensemble*"; he denounced their plots against Richelieu's life, telling the Cardinal about "all the great dagger-thrusts that were meant for

---

[1] The "Exempts" of the Guard, under the old French kings, performed certain police duties. They were half soldiers and half police officers. A prisoner condemned to the Bastille was conducted there by one or more exempts, who also had charge of prisoners when they were moved from place to place, and kept order at executions.

THE DUCHESSE DE CHEVREUSE

you"; he again offered to serve the King with Monsieur by giving that Prince good advice and playing him false. "I dare swear," he said to Richelieu, "that you will find yourself in great need of a very zealous, affectionate, and tolerably watchful man, such as your Lordship's humble servant." "I will bring everything into order," he wrote. But his letters lay unanswered.

As to Mme. de Chevreuse, Chalais' first act, after his arrest, had been to write to her, repeating the asseveration of his passion, and beseeching her to help him. "It is not at this hour," he wrote, "that I first recognized the divinity of your beauty, but I have now begun to learn that you must be served like a goddess, since I am not permitted to prove my love to you without running the risk of losing my life. Take care of it, then, since it is utterly dedicated to you, and if you judge it worthy to be preserved, tell this companion of my misfortune that you will sometimes remember that no man ever loved as I do." Mme. de Chevreuse, herself suspected, and sorely alarmed as to her own fate, could do nothing for him: she did not even answer his letter. Her silence stung Chalais: so the Duchess, having compromised him, was now going to leave him to his fate! During his next cross-examination he mentioned the part Mme. de Chevreuse had played in connection with himself, and then, growing angry, he made known her sentiments, her plans and her intrigues. Mme. de Chevreuse, counselled by Bautru, had just made up her mind to wait on Richelieu at Beauregard, and intercede with him in the prisoner's favour. Scoffingly, the Cardinal told her what her *protégé* ws saying about her. The Duchess, furious, lost her self-control. Her rage broke forth, and she brought counter-charges against her accomplice. Richelieu, of course, reported these assertions to the prisoner, who made still further revelations. He even wrote her vehement letters, which the Cardinal intercepted. Later he was to regret the intemperance of

THE CHALAIS AFFAIR

his language: he was to protest that "he had never said anything untrue in any of his answers except in those concerning Mme. de Chevreuse," but it was too late.

Then Chalais gave himself up to the darkest despair. He let his beard grow, "a wild beard"; the guards who watched over him related that he would rage up and down his cell foaming at the mouth, and crying out that he would rather be in hell, that he was "worse than damned," and when his keepers reminded him, "in God's name, that he belonged to a Christian communion," he exclaimed, "A fig for Christianity!" (the expression was far stronger,) "I am not in a state to have my duty shown me!" They strove to quiet him, he grew more and more excited. "He felt ready to do like the ancient Romans," he declared, "and was inclined to poison himself; he would crack his skull against the wall." Thoroughly scandalized, his guards remarked that "there was no paradise for those who destroyed themselves!" His answer was to the effect that "his misery was too great," and he swore he would "crack his head into four separate pieces." All these sayings were reported to his judges: the culprit, they were told, did nothing but utter impieties, would not say his prayers, blasphemed all the day long. The King's opinion of him was completely formed.

On August 5 Louis XIII signed letters-patent to institute a Court of Criminal Justice, charged with the duty of finally deciding the prisoner's fate. The court held its first sitting on the 11th, in one of the halls of the Franciscan Monastery at Nantes. After the usual formalities, the documents connected with the trial were read aloud. On the following day, the 12th, the Attorney-General asked for an adjournment, to summon several persons for the purpose of including them in the prosecution—among them Mme. de Chevreuse, M. de la Louvière, Bois d'Annemets, Puylaurens, and four other gentlemen. The court, in conformity with these conclusions, issued a warrant for the

THE DUCHESSE DE CHEVREUSE

arrest of the inculpated persons, with the proviso that the decree was not to be executed until the King had signed it. The King did not sign. Mme. de Chevreuse was interrogated, but privately, and she remained at liberty. On the 18th, the examination of the accused and the depositions of the witnesses were concluded and the court delivered sentence: Chalais was condemned to death!

When the condemned man learned his fate he was filled with bitter sorrow at the thought that he had denounced and compromised Mme. de Chevreuse. He declared to his keepers that his deposition concerning "that lady" had been false, and when one of his guards, Lamont, pointed out that it agreed with what he himself had told them in the course of conversation, and that it was confirmed by letters he had written and which had been intercepted, Chalais protested that "what he had written had been written out of the extreme fury into which he had been thrown by a false idea he had had, that she had deceived him." He was once more brought before his judges, and renewed his retractation.

The sentence, which dealt with the crime of high treason only, condemned Chalais to be beheaded in one of the public squares of Nantes; his head to be set up on a pike over one of the rampart gates, and his body quartered and hung on four gibbets erected in the four chief streets of the town. His mother wrote an imploring letter to the King: "Sire, I beseech you on my knees to grant me my son's life! Do not let the child whom I have bred up with so much tenderness cause the few years left to me to be desolate! I gave him to you when he was eight years old: he is the grandson of the Marshal de Monluc and of President Jeannin. . . ." The King consented to suppress the ignominious additions that aggravated the death sentence. The execution was carried out on Wednesday, August 19. Its details were of a horrible nature. The regular executioner was away, and the authorities had

THE CHALAIS AFFAIR

recourse to the assistance of a poor wretch who had been condemned to be hung, and who knew nothing of the grisly trade. Thirty-six blows were delivered with a "cooper's broad-axe" before the head was parted from the trunk, and the headsman had to "turn the head round the other way before he could cut it quite off." The victim groaned till the twentieth blow had been delivered, crying out "*Jésus, Maria!*"

On August 2, Chalais had written to the King, "May it please you to remember that I only belonged to the faction for thirteen days. Permit me, Sire, to appeal to your Majesty, with tears in my eyes, and as the most repentant of men, to grant me pardon, out of your extreme goodness." If Louis XIII showed him no mercy it was because, humiliated as he felt himself to be by this attempt to sow disturbance in his family and in the State, by this reckoning on his own death or deposition, and by the fact that one of the gentlemen of his own Household had dared to dip his hands into so vile a conspiracy, he allowed himself to be swayed by that instinctive and inflexible spirit of severity which was peculiar to him all his life.

But what fate had he reserved for the original authors of the plot, and more especially for Marshal d'Ornano and for Mme. de Chevreuse?

Ornano was still at Vincennes, awaiting the King's pleasure. There were great difficulties about his prosecution. Monsieur would have to be brought into it, cross-questioned, confronted with the prisoner. The judges would have to deal with the Queen, with the greatest nobles in the kingdom, with foreign States. And further, Gaston had declared that if his Governor was tried he himself would leave the Court. The Ministers, thoroughly puzzled, sought to gain time. Circumstances were to settle their difficulties for them.

For on September 2, after only a few days' illness, Ornano breathed his last. His death occurred too

THE DUCHESSE DE CHEVREUSE

conveniently for it to escape suspicious comment. The public vowed the Marshal had been poisoned. In vain did Ministers deny the report: the greatest publicity was given to the details of Ornano's illness: physicians made a post-mortem examination, and found no trace of poison; their report was printed; Louis XIII took the trouble of sending a letter to all the officials in the kingdom, which set forth that the prisoner had "been attacked by a sickness of dysentery and a retention of the urine, with constant fever, which had carried him out of the world after two or three weeks; that the person in charge of him had called in every assistance that could be desired, both as to remedies and advice, from the best and most experienced physicians in Paris." Still the world doubted. But these doubts were really unfounded. An examination of all the documents proves that the Marshal died a natural death. In any case, his departure simplified the King's business.

The King had settled it, to begin with, by insisting that Gaston should marry Mlle. de Montpensier at once. The young lady arrived on August 2: the King sent for his brother to the Council Chamber, and there, before the assembled Councillors, informed him of his "decision to give him a fine apanage and approve his marriage." It was a veiled order. In a fright, Gaston acquiesced. "Are you now speaking without the equivocations you have several times employed?" inquired the King. Monsieur vowed he was giving his honest word. That very evening there had been a scene in Anne of Austria's apartment. Mme. de Chevreuse had made it a case of conscience on Gaston's part not to give in and agree to the marriage. The Queen had added her own entreaties to her friend's. The two ladies had begged and prayed the Prince to such a degree, so Gaston afterwards acknowledged, "that they had both gone on their knees to me, to beseech me not to marry Mlle. de Montpensier." And he added that "the Queen Regnant had entreated him several times over, in

THE CHALAIS AFFAIR

the course of three days, not to carry out the marriage." But there was no possibility of retreat now.

On August 5, in the King's Cabinet at the Castle of Nantes, and in the presence of the parish priest, Cardinal de Richelieu himself performed the betrothal ceremony, and the marriage itself was celebrated, very quietly and in the most simple fashion, on the following day. Bois d'Annemets wrote that the business was a dull one, no music, no show, and the bride and bridegroom dressed in their ordinary clothes. "By the God who made me!" cried Chalais, when he heard the news in his prison. "Here's a high-handed stroke! They have caught Monseigneur on the hop! May the devil take me if ever there was a man as bold in his management of State affairs as the Lord Cardinal!"

And now, what was to be done with Mme. de Chevreuse? A council was held. Richelieu, with his usual precision and lucidity, summed up all the griefs against her. "She had done more harm," he asserted, "than any other person." She had personally acknowledged to him, on the occasion of her interview with him at Beauregard, the existence of the agreement between the great nobles to prevent Monsieur's marriage: Chalais had denounced her as the author of the whole cabal; through Mme. de Rohan, she had put the nobles into communication with the Huguenot rebels; she it was who had suggested the criminal plot against himself at Fleury; she it was who had constantly instigated Gaston to leave the Court, she, who had led Chalais astray, even as she had led the Vendôme brothers; and the Cardinal, piling proof on proof, recalled the prayer Mme. de Chevreuse had addressed to Gaston, on her knees, to refuse to make the marriage, "whatever it might cost him." She was the most guilty of all. But what was to be done? There was no possibility of arresting her and making her stand her trial: the difficulties in the Marshal's case would be repeated in hers, and in a

THE DUCHESSE DE CHEVREUSE

particularly aggravated form. Besides, it was against all custom to imprison a lady belonging to a great family, and hale her before Parliament or any Court of Justice, for criminal proceedings: such a measure would rouse several powerful houses to fury. The Ministers discussed the matter. The King broke in upon their debate by declaring that, to begin with, Mme. de Chevreuse should be sent into exile.

It was Bautru who brought the Duchess the news of the measure to be taken against her. Her blood boiled, her rage was ungovernable. "They little knew her!" she broke out; "they thought her mind was only equal to flirtations! She would show them, when the time came, that she was good for other work." She vented a string of imprecations. She poured forth a stream of threats: she swore she would have every Frenchman in England treated just as she was being treated in France; she fell on the King and the Cardinal and heaped abuse upon them. "The King was an incapable idiot!" she cried. "It was a disgrace that such a rogue as the Cardinal should hold the reins of Government!"

Anne of Austria, who had been informed of the King's decision by M. de Nogent, was in much the same condition of mind: she, too, flew into a fury. "Her anger burst forth. She said a great many spiteful things, to the effect that she would rather never bear a child than be parted from that creature (Mme. de Chevreuse), and she threatened that she would have her vengeance on the Cardinal, whatever it might cost her."

The Duc de Chevreuse was most painfully affected, he said some hard words of the Cardinal, declared he "had a deadly hatred of him." But just then the King wrote him a letter commanding him to hurry his wife's departure, and Chevreuse forthwith replied: "Sire, the bearer of this letter having joined me some four leagues from Dampierre, I have not been able sooner to satisfy your Majesty's will.

THE CHALAIS AFFAIR

I shall be at Dampierre to-morrow morning, to give orders, at the same time, for the departure of my wife, with all the obedience I owe your Majesty's commands."

There was nothing for it but to submit. Louis XIII had decided, so the Duc de Rohan writes, that Mme. de Chevreuse was to go to the Château du Verger, in Poitou, which belonged to her brother, the Prince de Guéméné, and there remain, without leaving its precincts, until further orders. Mme. de Chevreuse resolved to escape the performance of the King's behest by taking to flight. Secretly she took her way to Paris, and thence to the east of France, crossed the frontier, and took refuge in the Duchy of Lorraine. Thus, of her own free will, she began her first exile in a foreign country.

CHAPTER V

THE EXILE IN LORRAINE: THE PASSION OF CHÂTEAUNEUF

Montague's love for Mme. de Chevreuse—Their intrigues—Arrest of Montague—The Death of Buckingham—Mme. de Chevreuse returns to Paris—Châteauneuf's love for her—His disgrace—Mme. de Chevreuse is exiled to Touraine—1627-33.

"LET my reader imagine great villages full of inhabitants, set beside fine rivers, the banks of which are dotted with cattle of all kinds, hills covered with trees and vineyards, plains so rich that there is hardly any need to sow the wheat and other grain they bear: peasants who live in glass-windowed houses, and every one of whom has a great silver goblet in his oaken chest:—thus will he attain some faint idea of what this happy province is. Never did I behold so brilliant a picture of abundance, nor of labours that provide a better image of the felicity of human existence." Such is the description of Lorraine given by Nicolas Goulas in his Memoirs, just about the time when Mme. de Chevreuse sought a refuge in that Duchy. But it was not the charm of the country that had attracted her. Through her husband, the Duc de Chevreuse, she was the kinswoman of Charles IV, reigning Duke of Lorraine, and to him she had appealed for refuge, protection, and support.

The Duke was just one-and-twenty, five years younger than his visitor. Tall, thin, fair, with a bony face and highly arched eyebrows that gave him an astonished air, and an active body well-fitted for athletic exercises, and more especially for horsemanship, in which he excelled, Charles IV had an open and smiling countenance. He

THE EXILE IN LORRAINE

was brilliant and amusing. A contemporary biographer declared he had "a nose that smelt things a long way off." Though his studies had not been profound, he was no fool; he had a great power of assimilation, he was a good listener, a still better talker; but he was considered proud, heedless, and restless. Brought up in France, he had spent a great deal of time with the Guises, his own cousins, and had often been at Dampierre; he loved sport and pleasure; he was a frivolous prince. He had succeeded his uncle, Henri II, whose only daughter, Nicole, he had married. It was not a happy marriage. Henri II had not entertained any very high opinion of his son-in-law. "You will see that blundering fellow will ruin everything!" he had declared. The young Duke was certainly destined to bring his State into a very dangerous position.

Charles IV was overjoyed by the arrival of Mme. de Chevreuse. In her company he would have a whiff of the air of the French Court, of which he had so agreeable a recollection. "Not being able to forget the memories he had brought with him from France, he was to find great delight in the company of a person who would bring all the breeding of that country into his palace." Mme. de Chevreuse came to Lorraine heralded by her reputation as a fascinating woman, "beautiful and witty, very well informed as to Court intrigues, with a gallantry of appearance and a style of conversation quite different from those of this country, the proximity of which to Germany renders the methods of its people heavy and coarse." The Prince, who sighed for the "pleasantness of life in Paris," and had little taste for "German pride," would call on all the resources of his modest court to receive his cousin, the young and beauteous Duchess, in worthy fashion. The result was to exceed his wildest hopes.

What, indeed, was the most likely consequence of a meeting between a prince of one-and-twenty and a lady

THE DUCHESSE DE CHEVREUSE

five years his senior, a finished coquette, bent on using every fascination she possessed to charm the Duke whose protection she had come to claim? Charles IV fell in love with Mme. de Chevreuse. "Everything," says Richelieu, "began with love." "Though the relationship served as a pretext," writes Brienne, "it was her beauty which won Mme. de Chevreuse the power she obtained." Charles IV qute forgot Nicole!

There were entertainments of all sorts, hunts and joustings and horse-races, that delighted the Court of Lorraine, and of all these Mme. de Chevreuse was the queen. One of the most brilliant of these gatherings took place during Lent, at Shrovetide (February 14, 1627), in the great hall of the ducal castle at Nancy, at nine o'clock at night. The story of it is told us by Henri Humbert, and it was illustrated by Jacques Callot: "It is you, Madame," said Callot, in a dedicatory epistle to Mme. de Chevreuse, which reveals the depth of the impression produced at Nancy by the beauty of the Duchess and the passionate admiration with which it had inspired the Duke, "it is you who, France having recognized in you the light of all perfection, have come hither to receive the same approbation from our eyes, our voices, and our hearts. We confess, O fair Princess! that never before did Lorraine behold so many beauties, and all the more glorious because they are not of foreign growth. Madame, this is the sky wherein your sun must most naturally shine, there to be joined to that great Mars who draws from it his origin!" On a great platform, all the Duchesses, Princesses, and ladies of the Court had taken their places. Charles IV made his entry, sumptuously dressed. He was followed by a series of cars, magnificently adorned, surrounded by trumpeters, buglers, and torchbearers, and bearing the Princes of the House of Lorraine, garbed as classic gods, and ladies robed in carnation-coloured satin, who played on lutes. Then, the Duke of Lorraine having

THE EXILE IN LORRAINE

put on his armour, a barrier was set up across the arena, and the champions dashed upon each other, lance in hand. The victor of them all was to win the prize—a sword. It fell to the Duke, who instantly presented it to Mme. de Chevreuse.

But while the Duchess was thus apparently forgetting her distresses amidst the delights of this adoring little court, the Government of Louis XIII was preparing to act.

The King had not seen the Duchess pass over the frontier and into Lorraine without a feeling of extreme vexation. Once at Nancy, she was sure to cabal against France, and incite the Duke to raise all kinds of difficulties. Richelieu desired the King's Lieutenant at Metz, M. de Flavigny, to collect information for him. Precautions were taken. The garrisons of the three bishoprics of Metz, Toul, Verdun, were strengthened, and orders were given to rebuild the citadel of Verdun, all this to intimidate the Duke of Lorraine. When Charles IV begged the Bishop of Verdun to stop the building and excommunicate the workmen labouring on it, and the Bishop complied with his request, the French Government sent a judge, M. Charpentier, to Verdun, who declared the excommunication null and void, sentenced the Bishop to pay a fine of 10,000 *livres,* and had the works begun again.

Mme. de Chevreuse was not easy in her mind. Remorse was beginning to assail her. She had kept up her correspondence with Anne of Austria, and made an attempt, through her, to repair the mischief she had done, and get leave to return to France; if the King, she wrote, would only withdraw the order of banishment he had intended to send her, she would come back. Anne of Austria put forward this request as if it had been presented to her by some third person.

"I think," replied Richelieu to Bouthillier, on October 1, 1626, "that the Queen should content herself with telling the persons who speak for Mme. de Chevreuse that all she can do is to induce the King not to press for her return.

THE DUCHESSE DE CHEVREUSE

As for withdrawing the order he has given, that is quite impossible." Mme. de Chevreuse then applied to her own husband. M. de Chevreuse suggested that his wife should retire into the Bourbonnais or into Auvergne. He would conduct her there himself. Louis XIII expressed no objection. The Duchess made as though she would go a little way into France; then she changed her mind and went back over the frontier. A little later she made another appeal, this time through the Duke of Lorraine: "His Majesty has done me the honour of telling me," wrote Richelieu, "that I was to answer in his name that he cannot believe that this Princess, who finds so great a pleasure in living amongst foreigners that she has left his kingdom twice over, not only without his leave, but against his will, can really desire to return to his Court; that M. de Chevreuse, having asked as an act of grace that she might come back into the Bourbonnais, had set her on the road she should have taken to get back altogether, but that since that time, she had testified, by leaving it, that she had no desire for that which others were asking for her; and further, that the present time does not permit of His Majesty's doing what M. de Lorraine requests in this particular: in a word, her return is impossible, for the moment!"

Mme. de Chevreuse was exceedingly annoyed. It was clear, then, that she was despised; she was to be treated with severity. All that remained to her was to avenge herself. She would make use of the influence she had acquired over the Duke of Lorraine to stir him up against France. At that period, the King's Government, which found the Huguenot business very troublesome and difficult, was about to begin that siege of La Rochelle, which was to absorb all its energies for so long a time. Before long the effects of the Duchess's animosity began to make themselves felt. The Duke of Lorraine put forward unjustifiable pretensions, and made claims that

THE EXILE IN LORRAINE

were really nothing but spiteful attempts to stir up a quarrel. "In Paris," says Brienne, "everybody was persuaded the Duke was acting on the instigation of Mme. de Chevreuse." Just at this juncture there appeared at Nancy an Englishman, Lord Montague, who was to be singularly useful to the Duchess for the development of her gift of intrigue, and was to help her to spin one of those huge plots destined to prove the source of so much anxiety to the Cardinal.

Displeased by the King's periodical refusals to allow him to return to Paris, Buckingham was growing more and more bitter against Louis XIII. The perpetual violations of the treaty of marriage between Charles I and Henrietta-Maria gave rise to constant complaints on the part of the King of France, which were rudely received, and left without any answer. The relations between the two Courts were of the most precarious kind. Buckingham, resolved to do France a mischief if he could, was always on the look-out for favourable opportunities. The Huguenots were active, and he decided to support the rebels. As the plan worked itself out, the Duke began to dream of a grand coalition against Louis, in which Savoy, Piedmont, and Spain were all to be included; communications would be kept up with the interior of France, the King would find himself in a cleft stick, between the Huguenots and the great nobles, on one side, and the foreigners, on the other. It was in connection with the preparations for this understanding that Montague, Lord of King Charles's Bedchamber, arrived in Lorraine, to open negotiations with the Duke.

Montague was a young Englishman, reserved in manner, distinguished in appearance, elegant, very good-looking, who wrote and spoke French well; in later years he became a Catholic, took priest's orders, "an abbé, and a devout one," says La Porte, and he assisted Anne of Austria in her last moments. At the time of which we now speak, he was

THE DUCHESSE DE CHEVREUSE

a merry boon companion, not overburdened with prejudices. Having been mixed up in all the Duchess's affairs in London, he knew her well; he knew Anne of Austria also, and he was Buckingham's friend. Informed, too, of the conditions under which his mission must be performed, it was his intention, when he reached Lorraine, to enter into communications with Mme. de Chevreuse: the influence wielded by the Duchess over Charles IV was well-known in London: her continued correspondence with Anne of Austria was suspected there; thanks to her help, Montague would be able to treat both with the Duke of Lorraine and with the great families in France.

Mme. de Chevreuse was not at Nancy; she had settled at Bar-le-Duc, which at that time belonged to Lorraine, and was even the subject of a dispute with the French King, with regard to the investiture necessary if the Duke was to hold the place. "Mme. de Chevreuse," says Hugo in his *Vie de Charles IV*, "made this her usual place of residence, less for the sake of propriety than to avoid the offence her continued presence at Nancy would have given in France." The scruple was a very tardy one! Montague saw the Duchess, and unfolded Buckingham's plan to her. Buckingham, he said, proposed to equip three fleets, each to carry 10,000 men. One was to go to La Rochelle, one to the coasts of Guyenne, and one to Normandy. Each was to disembark the troops it carried, and then to blockade the mouths of the Seine, the Loire, and the Garonne. In return for this, England wanted the Duke of Lorraine and the Emperor to invade France, the Duke of Savoy to march on Dauphiné and Provence, and the Duc de Rohan to raise the Huguenots in the South. To attain all this, Montague begged Mme. de Chevreuse to help him.

Joyfully, Mme. de Chevreuse fell in with the plan. She received Montague in the most friendly fashion; and made herself so agreeable to him that the young man, fascinated

THE EXILE IN LORRAINE

by her beauty, was quite unable to resist the strength of the passion that soon fired him, and Hugo asserts that Mme. de Chevreuse offered no resistance. Thanks to her intervention, Montague was placed in communication with the Duke of Lorraine: thanks to her, once more, the Duke followed Montague's lead: "She pushed him over the precipice," says Richelieu. The French Government was kept informed, and Mme. de Chevreuse, on her side, was in correspondence with Anne of Austria, who was watching the progress of the business. The Duke of Lorraine sent word that he would declare himself as soon as the English had disembarked their troops.

Mme. de Chevreuse sent letters in all directions. By arrangement with Anne of Austria—so, at least, Richelieu clearly insinuates in his Memoirs—she entered into communication with the Comte de Soissons and the Rohan family. Women, adds the Cardinal, were intriguing for her, "feeding the Queen with perpetual discontents," stirring up the Comtesse de Soissons, urging Monsieur to take to flight. A message was sent to the Comte de Soissons that if the King died, he would be placed upon the throne. Wider and wider the net was being spread.

Meanwhile, Montague travelled to Savoy, and thence into Switzerland, to Holland, and to Venice, and entered into negotiations with the Duc de Rohan, on whom he waited. Buckingham, Rohan tells us in his Memoirs, was, so Montagu affirmed, to send over 500 horsemen; the Huguenot leader was to take up arms in Languedoc, to march to Montauban, to endeavour to make a junction with the English troops that were to land at Bordeaux. Rohan contented himself with sending a reply to the effect that he too would make up his mind once the English troops had succeeded in effecting their landing.

It became known at Court that the plot was to be put into execution forthwith. Mme. de Chevreuse had persuaded the Duke of Lorraine to give the signal to the

THE DUCHESSE DE CHEVREUSE

rebels by taking the field himself. Flavigny wrote from Metz that 10,000 men were being raised. Charles IV had asked his Germanic Majesty to send him a *corps d'armée*, and was only awaiting the arrival of these troops to cast off the mask. The English fleet, on its side, was preparing to disembark troops on the Isle of Ré.

The French Government took rapid measures. The Army of Champagne, under the command of Louis de Marillac, was reinforced, so as to be able to hold any invasion from the Lorraine side in check. Louis XIII himself started for the Isle of Ré, to meet the English in person. A captain of Chevau-légers, Blagny by name, volunteered to abduct Charles IV "close to a house whither he frequently went alone, to see the Duchesse de Chevreuse," but Richelieu advised against this step, because of the too great scandal such an attempt was likely to cause. Still, if the Duke's person was not to be touched, why not try to carry off Montague? The documents thus seized would provide useful information for the King's Government.

Montague, after his visits to Savoy and Lorraine, had gone back to London, to give an account of his mission to Buckingham, and had failed to find him, the Duke having departed with the English fleet to the Isle of Ré. Charles I gave him orders to return to the Continent. Richelieu had him watched, and two Basques, in convenient disguises, followed the English nobleman.

Having crossed the Channel, he travelled along the frontier, so as to keep out of France, and pushed towards Lorraine. French posts had been established all along that frontier. One evening, while the traveller was riding a stage in the Barrois, one of the Basque spies slipped away and warned the officer in command of the nearest post, M. de Bourbonne, that Montague was in his power, and quite close by. Bourbonne put a bold face on it, collected some half-score of his own friends, made a dash

THE EXILE IN LORRAINE

across the frontier, laid sudden hands on Montague and his serving-man (who carried a cloak-bag crammed with papers), conducted his prisoner to Bourbonne, in the first place, thence to Coiffy, a great fortress with mighty walls, and finally, to the Bastille.

This arrest, as might have been expected, made a great stir. The Duke of Lorraine vehemently protested against such a violation of his territory: he demanded the immediate release of Lord Montague, and the punishment of M. de Bourbonne. Louis XIII refused satisfaction. And meanwhile, Bullion and Fouquet proceeded to examine the English nobleman's papers.

They were exceedingly instructive: they revealed, as Richelieu put it, "that England, Savoy, Lorraine, the Emperor, and the Heretics in France, were all bound together in a pernicious design against the State: that they meant to make war both by sea and by land—by sea in Poitou and Normandy, by land in Champagne—attacking Verdun with the forces of the Duke of Lorraine and the Emperor, and Burgundy with those of the Duke of Savoy; that it seemed more than likely that Venice was mixed up in the business to some extent; that the Dutch had likewise proved by their actions, not only their connivance but their strong support: that the whole business had been set a-going by the Chevreuse, who had acted in the matter with the consent of the Queen Regnant."

The cloak-bag contained instructions from the King of England, memoranda in Montague's own hand, a quantity of correspondence, and a number of letters from Mme. de Chevreuse.

Everyone was very much alarmed. The Duke of Lorraine sent once more, this time by the Marquis of Lenoncourt, to demand Montague's release within the space of twenty-four hours, and added a threat that if he was not given satisfaction, he would not "fail to use any of the legitimate methods that justice permitted of his

THE DUCHESSE DE CHEVREUSE

employing, to obtain reparation for the insult offered to his person." No answer was vouchsafed him. The Duke of Savoy commissioned his confidential representative in Paris to "reply, if necessary, to anything found in Montague's papers which might be displeasing to his Majesty."

The most alarmed of all was Anne of Austria. La Porte has left us the story of her terrors. She fully expected her name would be found in Montague's correspondence. What would the King do? He would drive her out, no doubt—send her back to Spain! She "could neither eat nor sleep" for thinking of it. She sent for La Porte, bade him go to Coiffy, mingle with the armed men of the escort that was bringing Montague to Paris; get at the Englishman, and find out from him exactly what the perusal of the documents seized was likely to entail on her. La Porte departed, reached Coiffy just as the seven or eight hundred horsemen commanded by MM. de Bourbonne and de Boulogne were starting on their ride to Paris, with Montague in their midst, contrived to get near the prisoner, and was happy enough to learn from him that the Queen's name did not appear: if he was questioned, he would not say one word. When La Porte repeated his words to Anne of Austria, she "shook with joy."

Montague, in his prison in the Bastille, pleaded extenuating circumstances. In a letter to Louis XIII, he explained that "the King of England had only taken up arms against the King because he had thought His Majesty did not respond to the esteem and affection he felt for him; and that Savoy, Lorraine, and Soissons had joined him because they were hurt at the small regard the King bestowed upon them, and that if they could all be persuaded of the contrary, they might be led to make the hearty peace so needful in the interests of both kingdoms." Whether genuine or not, reasons put forward at so critical a moment were necessarily accepted. Louis XIII, whose hands were over-full with the business

THE EXILE IN LORRAINE

of the Isle of Ré, preferred an attempt to break up the confederation gently to an endeavour to reduce it by main force. He was willing, consequently, to negotiate. There was, indeed, the matter of the Duchesse de Chevreuse. Present events, as Goulas said, were "due to her instigation": Montague himself had insinuated that she had "induced Buckingham to do what he had done." Richelieu confirmed these assertions, and related that after the defeat of the English in the Isle of Ré, various papers had been discovered in Buckingham's lodging, and amongst them, a memorandum the Duke had drawn up to send to England, and which set forth that he had undertaken his enterprise "because Gerbier" (the English Resident in Flanders) "had reported to him from a person in whom he was bound to have confidence" (he meant Mme. de Chevreuse), "that this was what he must do." The Duchess was guilty indeed! But even with her, it would be wiser to use gentle means and recall her to her duty, than to put forward demands that would not prove obtainable.

Advised by the Ministers, Marie de Médicis, who was acting as Regent during the King's absence in Saintonge, explained to the Duke of Lorraine's Envoy, M. de Bréval, that His Majesty, who had been informed of his master's plans by the perusal of Lord Montague's correspondence, could hardly believe in their truth, and desiring to clear the matter up, requested the Duke would come to Paris; once there, he could "say his say." What was the matter with him? What was the cause of the attitude he had been assuming for the past six months? Bouthillier, the Secretary of State, undertook to speak to Bréval about Mme. de Chevreuse. To do this, he resorted to a subterfuge. He enlarged on the satisfaction the conduct of M. de Chevreuse had given the King, and declared His Majesty desired to show his appreciation of it by treating his wife with benevolence: that this lady need

THE DUCHESSE DE CHEVREUSE

only alter her line of conduct, and use her influence, in future, to settle the trouble, after having made it, and she would be allowed to return to France. Bouthillier even went so far as to hint at the possibility of Buckingham's travelling to Paris. The Duc de Chevreuse, duly warned, communicated with his wife: he was urgent with her: "I rejoice," replied Richelieu, when Bréval notified this fact to him, "that M. de Chevreuse should be undoing what others are said to have done," and he added, to save the King's dignity: "If M. de Lorraine does not lay down his arms, the King will take up his, and that as powerfully as he ought."

Meanwhile, and as a proof of his desire to conciliate, Louis XIII set Montague at liberty. Montague waited on the sovereign to express his thanks: he explained that the whole misunderstanding had arisen out of the refusal to receive Buckingham in Paris, and "the ill-treatment meted out to Mme. de Chevreuse," and added that when the agreement between the two crowns came under discussion, England would demand that the Duchess should be included in it. Louis XIII returned an evasive answer.

The Duke of Lorraine had agreed to come to Paris and discuss the situation with the French Government. He set forth his claims: they included one concerning Mme. de Chevreuse: he asked that the Duchess might, at all events, be allowed to go to Dampierre, or to settle at Jouarre; Mme. des Essarts—Charlotte des Essarts, Comtesse de Romorantin, a former mistress of Henri IV, who had become the wife of M. du Hallier—intervened, and assured the Ministers, in the name of Charles IV, that "in consideration of this change, the Duke of Lorraine would do anything he was asked to do": this proves the importance attached to the Duchess's pardon. "I think," wrote Richelieu to Marie de Médicis, on April 30, 1628, "that it is of no consequence whether Mme. de Chevreuse lives at Dampierre or at Jouarre, and that although the des Essarts

THE EXILE IN LORRAINE

is a bad woman, it will not be well to refuse her intervention to begin with, seeing that even as one thief can manage another of his own kidney better than any Capuchin, so the des Essarts is fitter to treat with Mme. de Chevreuse than the Marquise de Maignelay!" Thus his opinion, too, was that the King had better give in. So that the royal dignity might be safeguarded in the process, M. de Chevreuse was to be put forward. He had rendered many services, the authorities would give out that as a reward for these, his wife's situation was to be made less unpleasant, and Richelieu would write him gracious letters, preparing the way for the pardon, to the idea of which the public mind was to be accustomed. After all, so the Cardinal pointed out to his master, Mme. de Chevreuse was too dangerous in Lorraine; she spent her whole time hatching plots; it would be far better to have her in France, where they could keep an eye upon her. They would impose certain conditions for her return: she was not to come to Paris; she was to avoid any place where the King or Queen might be; if she desired it, she might live in the Abbey of Jouarre, of which one of her kinswomen was Prioress; she might even go and pay her respects to Marie de Médicis, whenever the Queen-Mother went to Monceaux; she might reside at Dampierre whenever the French Court was not in Paris. M. de Chevreuse agreed to all these conditions, offered to append his own signature to them, and undertook to make his wife accept them too. The King gave his consent.

Mme. de Chevreuse, duly informed of her husband's undertaking on her behalf, made no sign. A person who had been in her service, and whom she had turned away, came and reported that she was talking more scornfully than ever about both the King and Richelieu. The same informant added that the intercourse between the Duchess and Anne of Austria had never been so close; that Mme. de Chevreuse kept on telling the Queen she had nothing to

THE DUCHESSE DE CHEVREUSE

fear, because Buckingham, England, the Emperor, Spain, Lorraine, and other forces were all on her side. A tragic event was to shatter all this splendid confidence.

On August 23, 1628, Buckingham was at Portsmouth, whither he had gone to hurry on the preparations for sending important reinforcements to La Rochelle. He had just accompanied a visitor to the door of his cabinet, when a man of the name of Fulton, a Puritan, and the son of a sergeant, came close up to him, and suddenly plunged a knife into his heart! Death was instantaneous. This sudden departure was singularly favourable to the arrangement of French affairs.

Mme. de Chevreuse was unspeakably affected. She fainted away, and had to be bled several times over before her consciousness returned; she was distracted with despair. Her love for Buckingham, who was her strongest supporter, still endured. His death broke up all her dreams, and destroyed all her plans. She was thoroughly overwhelmed.

All this time, Louis XIII and Richelieu were actively prosecuting the siege of La Rochelle. Now that Buckingham was no more, and that all hope of help from England had failed them, the besieged rebels, already exhausted by a struggle that had lasted over a year, felt the end of their resistance was at hand. Two months later, the capitulation was signed, and on November 1, 1628, Louis rode into the vanquished town at the head of his victorious troops.

His triumph was a brilliant one, and produced a deep effect on the mind of his contemporaries. The Huguenots were believed to be finally undone, and the King's Government free, consequently, to turn all its forces against the foreigner. The King's prestige was strengthened, and his adversaries were proportionately weakened.

By degrees they gave in. England sued for peace, and

THE EXILE IN LORRAINE

discussion ensued. Mme. de Chevreuse, who clearly perceived that, as far as she was concerned, the game was up, did not propose to be left out of all the arrangements. She appealed to Charles I to secure her interests in the course of the negotiations. The English King consented to tell Louis XIII "that he felt a particular affection for Mme. de Chevreuse, and would certainly demand that she should be included in the Peace, if he were not ashamed to mention any woman in connection with it." Louis XIII and his advisors feigned to attach no importance to this communication. "His Majesty," wrote Richelieu, "finds great difficulties concerning the return of Mme. de Chevreuse, who has done a great deal of mischief, and may do more in future, and may, for the same reasons, do good, and bring advantage to the King's service."

But one by one, discouraged by the victory at La Rochelle, all the prominent persons compromised in the late intrigues were obtaining the King's pardon; His Majesty would certainly have to end by granting the Duchess hers. But in any case, Louis XIII did not intend to allow her name to figure in his Treaty of Peace with England. Nevertheless, before that document was actually signed—this was to take place on April 24, 1629,—he consented to her return to Dampierre; she was to go back unobserved, to live there quietly—there were to be no more cabals. The Duchess acquiesced.

Thus, towards the end of 1628, less than two months after the fall of La Rochelle, Mme. de Chevreuse was back in France. She returned as untamed as ever, as full of bitterness against Cardinal Richelieu. At Court, the King's pardon produced divers impressions. Gaston d'Orléans made a mock of it, remarking to Marcheville with his usual levity (and a thrust at the part Mme. de Chevreuse had played as go-between in the business of Anne of Austria and Buckingham), that the lady had "been brought back so that the Queen might have more

THE DUCHESSE DE CHEVREUSE

opportunities of bearing a child!" "A devilish idea!" adds Richelieu, who reports the observation.

The Duchess had hardly reached Dampierre when, having no intention of living shut up in her country-house, she caused a request to be addressed to the King of England to intercede in her favour, and get her leave to go back to Court. The Duke of Lorraine and Anne of Austria added their prayers to the English King's request. Charles I spoke to the French Ambassador, M. de Châteauneuf: he wrote to Louis XIII "in order that it might please his Majesty to reinstate the Duchesse de Chevreuse within his Court": he added that "she was his kinswoman, that she had suffered for her love for him, that he felt himself obliged to assist her and address this prayer to His Majesty, that he would confide the business to his Ambassador, and would request him to write the King the instances he had remitted to him." Châteauneuf replied that there were difficulties; Mme. de Chevreuse, he declared, "was a woman whose spite surpassed that of her sex, however spiteful that might be, and it was a proved thing that several persons of power and condition had been turned away from their duty to the King by their adherence to her passions." Then Charles I sent a special messenger to Louis XIII to press his request.

This fresh interference made the King angry. Just at that moment, a sharp discussion was going on with the English authorities about a French Lady of the Bedchamber, whom the King of France desired to place about the person of his sister Henrietta-Maria, according to the terms of the marriage contract, which Charles refused to carry out. "He makes difficulties," wrote the King of his brother-in-law, "about a Lady of the Bedchamber whom he does not know, and whom I would choose gentle and good-tempered, because he says she would disturb the peace of his Household and the understanding between himself and the Queen, and he wants me to take one whom

THE EXILE IN LORRAINE

I know only too well, and who has always brought trouble into my house!" On April 30, 1629, Richelieu wrote to M. de Rancé, private secretary to Marie de Médicis: "England asks for Mme. de Chevreuse: we do not care to agree, for reasons well known to the Queen-Mother."

These reasons grew more and more numerous. That very year, 1629, when Louis XIII and the Cardinal had departed to the Italian frontier, whither they had been summoned by external complications, Gaston d'Orléans, then a widower—for Mlle. de Montpensier had died in childbirth, not very long after her marriage—had betrayed his intention of marrying the Princess Marie, daughter of the Duc de Nevers, as his second wife. Louis XIII was determined this marriage should not take place. As early as in March 1629, he had been cognizant of the fresh intrigues to which the plan was giving rise. The foreign foe was finding its account in them. Both Charles I of England, who still clung to a policy hostile to France and Spain, and the Duke of Lorraine, regarded these external dissensions as a means of causing difficulties for Louis XIII on his Alpine frontier. Bérulle reported to Richelieu, in the name of Marie de Médicis, then acting as Regent in Paris, that Anne of Austria had arranged with Mirabel, the Spanish Ambassador, that Gaston should slip over into Flanders, so as to be married at once. This idea had come from Mme. de Chevreuse. She had wanted to go into Flanders herself, nobody knew why, or rather people easily guessed: Marie de Médicis had forbidden her to move.

On the other hand, the business with the Duke of Lorraine was in a bad way. Mme. de Chevreuse kept Charles IV informed of everything that could affect him; and Anne of Austria, instigated by the Duchess, gave the Duke information too, sent La Porte to him, and opened communications of her own with Spain, through Mirabel.

THE DUCHESSE DE CHEVREUSE

A gentleman who had been sent to Paris by the Duke of Lorraine travelled to Dampierre to see Mme. de Chevreuse. On July 7, 1629, Richelieu writes to M. de Rancé: "The cabals in Lorraine and Spain, due to the Duchesse de Chevreuse, are unendurable. The King very much wishes Mme. de Chevreuse could be seized and taken to the Forest of Vincennes, in that case it would be necessary that nobody should see her." But once more unexpected events were to alter the views of the Government, and lead it to show favour to the dangerous Duchess it would fain have seen in prison!

To prevent her son Gaston from marrying the Princess Marie, the Regent had induced the young girl to come to Paris, and had then shut her up—or something very like it—in the Castle of Vincennes. Louis XIII and Richelieu both disapproved of this step; they considered it quite incorrect. Marie de Médicis took offence. Monsieur was so furious that he left France, and took refuge in Lorraine; whence he was only got back with the greatest difficulty. This business hurried on the quarrel that had long been brewing between the Queen-Mother and Richelieu.

From the day on which the King's mother succeeded, in spite of her son's wishes, in procuring the entrance of Richelieu into the Council—a thing she had done out of her conviction that she was thus introducing a creature of her own, and that she herself would now be sovereign mistress of everything—the Cardinal, deeply conscious of what he owed the King and the State, and impelled by the highest sense of his duty, had been far more zealous in his defence of the interests of the kingdom, than in his obedience to the suggestions of his former benefactress. Marie de Médicis, harsh-tempered, shrewish, and anything but intelligent, had not been able to stomach what she called the Cardinal's "ingratitude": the relations between her and Richelieu had become embittered. But, and this was

THE EXILE IN LORRAINE

only just, Louis XIII, who had stood out so long against his mother's wishes, before he would admit the prelate, whom he so heartily disliked, to his council board, having learnt, as he had, day by day, to appreciate more and more highly the merits of a Minister whose incomparable value made itself increasingly apparent, now defended the Cardinal against his mother's attacks. When she, in her rage, suggested that Richelieu should be driven out of the post of high confidence in which she herself had laboured to place him, the King refused to listen to her; the disagreement between the Queen-Mother and the Cardinal was to transform itself into a struggle between mother and son, and to end in steps of the most extreme nature.

Anne of Austria, who had never liked Marie de Médicis, to whom she ascribed her own domestic unhappiness, took up the cudgels against her. Mme. de Chevreuse, faithful to her sovereign, did the same. Richelieu fancied the two fair ladies were pronouncing in his favour; he was gratified: "Mme. de Bouillon has told me," wrote the Cardinal, "that Mme. de Chevreuse is going on well, and giving good advice to the Queen." From one episode to another, the Queen-Mother's aggressive hostility reached such a pitch, at last, that Louis XIII, thoroughly wearied out, resolved to bring matters to a crisis. In the month of July, 1631, he was at Compiègne, and his mother with him. Suddenly, one morning, he quitted the palace, leaving the castle—an ancient edifice dating from the Middle Ages, and built against the walls of the town, on the site of the present one—surrounded by troops, and caused it to be signified to Marie de Médicis that she must retire to Moulins and remain confined to that place for the future; he was sending her into exile, in fact. The Queen refused to obey, and in her anger, took to flight, crossed the frontier, and shortly afterwards sought refuge on foreign territory, in Flanders. She never was to enter the kingdom again.

THE DUCHESSE DE CHEVREUSE

In the course of all these events, Richelieu had drawn nearer to Anne of Austria. The price of their reconciliation was the return of Mme. de Chevreuse. "The Cardinal de Richelieu," says Mme. de Motteville, "to win her (the Queen) over, brought back Mme. de Chevreuse. No doubt she promised everything he asked of her. After his quarrel with the Queen-Mother, his benefactress, he tried to make it up with the Queen (Anne of Austria), and bind her to him through her favourite, and so put her back about her."

Highly delighted, Mme. de Chevreuse paid a visit to the Cardinal. "She made him a thousand protestations of friendship and sincerity in the King's service and his own." A conversation ensued. Agreement was likely to serve both parties' ends. They came to an arrangement. Mme. de Chevreuse vowed she would be frank and loyal, that she would henceforward avoid all commerce with the Duke of Lorraine and other foreigners, and reveal everything that might come to her knowledge to the Cardinal; Richelieu promised to stand by her.

Then she and the Cardinal began to vie with each other in attentions, civilities, and mutual respect. Mme. de Chevreuse having fancied, for a moment, that the Cardinal had betrayed the existence of their understanding, Richelieu lost no time about writing to reassure her: "I should esteem myself very unworthy to be honoured by your kindness if I were capable of abusing it as I have heard you had some idea I might have done. If I had been guilty of such a meanness as to reveal that which it pleased you to confide to me, I should have been a traitor to myself. I confess to you that I could not have believed you would have suspected me of committing such a fault. But instead of being scandalized at that, I only beseech you to have greater confidence in me for the future, and to believe I would rather fail to my own self than fail to prove to you, on every occasion, that I am, and always shall be, ready

THE EXILE IN LORRAINE

to give you testimonies far more difficult than those in question here."

Was the Cardinal sincere? He was making use of Mme. de Chevreuse for the time being, at any rate. The French Government was desirous of detaching the Duke of Lorraine from the cause of the House of Austria, and the Duchess served its purpose in this matter. The Duke pledged his faith. Urged by Mme. de Chevreuse, he came to Paris. A treaty between Lorraine and France was signed at Vic on January 6, 1632. Mme. de Chevreuse was the author of the agreement; she had kept her word.

Her fortunes had risen high indeed! After having inspired Richelieu and Louis XIII with the feelings of which I have made my readers aware, after having herself given vent to opinions which should naturally have proved an eternal barrier to her return to the Court, she found herself back in that same Court, considered, respected, spoilt, powerful, hedged in with homage and deference. A short time after her return to France, M. de Chevreuse had a quarrel with M. de Montmorency, whom he had called a knave, because he had written some insulting rhymes about him. He drew his sword, in the lower court of the Louvre, between the guardroom of the Swiss Guard, and that of the French Guard; several thrusts were exchanged, and before the soldiers were able to part them, both combatants were lying on the ground. It was a serious business! M. de Chevreuse jumped upon his horse and fled. Any other man would have lost his head for his pains. Richelieu went to Mme. de Chevreuse, and told her the Duke might come back. He returned, and was made over, as a matter of form, to an officer of the Guard, who was ordered to keep his eye upon him; and he was desired to go and spend a fortnight at Dampierre; the punishment was light, and he owed it to the favour his wife enjoyed.

And Mme. de Chevreuse responded to Richelieu's asseverations by expressing the deepest feelings of devotion.

THE DUCHESSE DE CHEVREUSE

"Sir," she wrote, in the course of the earlier months of the year 1632, "I should not have thought myself so fortunate as to be remembered by you amidst the occupations you now have: I find myself agreeably mistaken in this opinion; this leads me to hope that I may be so to my still greater advantage, touching the sentiments you entertain for me; I desire it with equal passion and sincerity. I am resolved to prove to you by every action of my life that I am, Sir, your very humble and obedient servant." So close was the understanding between the Duchess and the Cardinal, that Richelieu would dictate the letters he desired she should write to Lorraine, for instance, with the object of preventing the Duke from listening to the suggestions of Gaston d'Orléans; we still possess rough drafts of these missives in Richelieu's own hand; on the back of the documents we find, written by the Cardinal's secretary, de Cherré, the words, "To M. de la Ville, the Duke of Lorraine's Gentleman-in-waiting, by the hand of Mme. de Chevreuse." Was she sincere either? Had not Richelieu his own reasons for doubting her faithfulness? Among these, one, surely, ought to have stirred his suspicions, and kept them on the alert—the intimacy between the Duchess and Anne of Austria!

It was a very close intimacy. The Duchess and the Queen were never apart: they were seen together everywhere. Now Anne of Austria had never forgiven the Cardinal. Richelieu was perfectly well aware of this; he suspected that any conversation concerning him, in which the sovereign bore her part, handled him in a manner the reverse of kind. Just about this time, he received intelligence that the then Keeper of the Privy Seal, Charles de l'Aubespine, Marquis de Châteauneuf, was holding long interviews and frequent conferences with the Queen and Mme. de Chevreuse. What was the meaning of all these secret meetings? What was the Keeper hatching with the two Princesses? Richelieu began to wonder.

THE EXILE IN LORRAINE

M. de Châteauneuf, the scion of an ancient race, many members of which had been Privy Councillors and Secretaries of State, had, as was customary amongst such families, spent a regular career in the King's Household. He had subsequently been appointed to the Treasury, with Jeannin and de Thou, in 1611; had been selected for special missions, such as that of Ambassador to the English Court, and had shown much intelligence in his performance of these functions. After one of the crises in the struggle between Marie de Médicis and Richelieu, he had been appointed Keeper of the Seals, in the place of Marillac, who had fallen into disgrace. He was an active, hard-working, and what was exceedingly precious, a very compliant man; he had been selected to preside over the judicial commission charged with the prosecution of his predecessor's brother, Marshal Louis de Marillac, who had been compromised with him in the same intrigues, and had sentenced him to the scaffold—the punishment had been considered severe. Appointed, at a later date, head of the commission that was to decide the fate of the Duc de Montmorency, he had sent that nobleman to his death: he gained the reputation of being an over-obsequious courtier. He was full of ardour, energy, and fire; he thirsted for glory: he was well versed in business affairs, and his friends were many. His enemies, who reproached him with his sentences on Marillac and Montmorency, declared his ambition had led him basely to betray his conscience and his honour, but they nevertheless treated him with extreme consideration; of this Mme. de Motteville assures us.

One grave weakness disfigured his character: he was too fond of women, and this brought about his ruin. He delighted in female society, in paying compliments, and being flattered by fair ladies. When he rose to be a Minister, in whose hands the power of showing grace and favour lay, he was immensely courted; he could hardly have stood out against his flatterers. In spite of his two

THE DUCHESSE DE CHEVREUSE

and fifty years, his feelings were still easily fired; his love affairs had been numberless. "His weakness," writes Mme. de Motteville, "was the cause of that the ladies had for him; their intrigues contributed greatly to his grandeur and good fortune, and also to his wretchedness."

He was fascinated by the Duchesse de Chevreuse. Where was the man who was not? She was thirty-one, in all the splendour of her fresh and brilliant beauty. The man of fifty could not resist her. This autumnal passion was fierce, devoid of reserve, devoid of dignity. We have his love-letters. "I await your commands with impatience," he writes, with reference to some service she had asked him to do two of her friends, "if you would give them to me by word of mouth, I should be happier than I deserve, or dare expect to be. The King will be here to-morrow, and will only stay two days. Good God! Must I spend one day of my life without serving you? How mean I think myself to spend my care on any other thing, and how good you are to permit me to swear my eternal fidelity and obedience to you, without being able to prove them by my service! As to the two persons concerning whom you have spoken to me, it is enough that you should say 'I desire,' for it is for you to command, and for me to obey."

And with reference to another recommendation he writes:

"It is enough that I should know the person of whom you speak is your servant, to oblige me to do what he wishes. Good God! How unhappy am I to find so few means of serving you, with all my desire to do it! But your bodily resemblance to the divinities is too great for you to fail in possessing all the qualities of their souls. That is the cause which makes you accept, even as they do, the adoration which is rendered you, though that can in nowise add to your glory, when it is paid you from a heart filled with obedience, fidelity and respect!"

THE EXILE IN LORRAINE

After Châteauneuf's arrest, at a later date, his papers were searched, and some threescore letters from Mme. de Chevreuse discovered among them. Charpentier, secretary to Cardinal Richelieu, made a copy of them for his master's use. That copy is now in our hands. In its pages we follow the Duchess day by day, amidst the refined subtleties of an extraordinarily finished coquette, applied to the service of the boldest possible spirit of intrigue. Few of the documents left us so thoroughly portray her real character. She did not care for Châteauneuf, of that there can be no doubt whatever; but she made it her business to feed his passion, keep it alive, and continually excite it; she made advances to him; she kindled his jealousy; she drove him distracted: her aim (and she attained it) was to have him at her beck and call, so as to use him to carry out her plans: the strangest thing of all was the part played by Richelieu in the course of this correspondence.

Alarmed, in fact, by the lengthy conversations that were going on, as he discovered, between Mme. de Chevreuse and the Keeper of the Seals, the Cardinal commanded his people to be on the watch. The execution at Toulouse of the Duc de Montmorency, betrayed by Gaston d'Orléans, might quite conceivably drive that Prince to seek safety in flight. Could it be that Anne of Austria, Mme. de Chevreuse, Châteauneuf, and his friend the Chevalier de Jars were in connivance with Monsieur, and endeavouring to induce him to take this step? Some certainty must be obtained. The Cardinal grew restless and anxious. The complications of his political existence—Heaven knows they had been numberless enough!—had thoroughly upset his over-sensitive nerves. He ended by watching the sayings and doings of Mme. de Chevreuse and Châteauneuf with an attention so anxious that his irritation, at times, assumed all the appearances of downright jealousy. Was he in love with the lady himself? The Duchess gives

THE DUCHESSE DE CHEVREUSE

us to understand he was; Richelieu was Châteauneuf's junior, he was only forty-seven. Then the Keeper of the Seals took fright. Mme. de Chevreuse vowed she cared for no one but him, but at the same time laid artful stress on the Cardinal's attentions to her.

"I think," she wrote, "the Cardinal is resolved to have no patience with me, night or day; he sends at nine o'clock in the morning to know how I am. I sent him word I have necessary business to transact with you. Since that he has written to me twice; the first time to know what the business was, about which I had to speak to you, the second, to beg me not to proceed until he had first seen you, or sent me word: you perceive his foolishness, and how much trouble he gives me! You shall soon have news of me, and hear when I can see you." And again: "It is not because I have promised you, but because I believe you deserve it, that I hold you in such high esteem; do not grieve at not having let me see all the pain it cost you to leave me, if only it be as great as that you showed me: I am well-pleased with that, and glad to have seen your true feelings for once, shorn of all pretence, and to have reason to be content with them."

When Châteauneuf reproaches her with having neglected him, because, as he believes, she has promised Richelieu to do so, she protests: "You are wrong to have nursed such a thought," she writes, "and my soul is too noble to admit a feeling so vile; for that reason I regard the Cardinal's favour no more than I dread his power, and never will I do anything that is unworthy of myself; I shall take great delight in pleasing you, and it will be a great trouble to me to cause you pain." Notwithstanding all this, she proceeds to reveal the advances Richelieu is making to win her over. A person had come to see her from the Cardinal, she says, who offered her the Minister's support, and told her in his name, "that it is his great desire to oblige me in the most important matters, and that

THE EXILE IN LORRAINE

he alone is in a position to do it; that nobody can be equal to him: all his protestations," she adds, "are mere fine words, followed by very paltry doings, and I put but little faith in any of them." And she continues: "I believe you so heartily mine that the best news I can give you is news of my health, which is better than it has been: for as to my resolve to value you above anything else in France, it is so firm that nothing can ever alter it."

And, thereupon, she holds forth to Châteauneuf concerning a young nobleman who is likewise in love with her, and passionately too, and whose presence about her is a source of much annoyance to the Keeper of the Seals, M. de Brion, to wit: François de Lévis Ventadour, the future Duc d'Amville, Chief Equerry to Monsieur.

This behaviour only makes the lover's heart more sore. The Duchess tells him a long story of a scene she has had with Richelieu, in the Queen's apartments. Richelieu had come to see Anne of Austria; he stayed two hours: "He paid her (the Queen)," writes Mme. de Chevreuse, "many compliments, and loaded her with praises in my presence, whereas to me he spoke most coldly, and with a great affectation of carelessness and indifference, while I, according to my custom, behaved as if I did not notice his bad temper. When he tried to tease me about some small matter, I jested at him to the point of crying scorn upon his power: he was more astonished than angry, for he changed his tune then, and plunged into civilities and humilities of the lowliest kind. I know not whether it was because he would not betray his bad humour in the Queen's presence, or because he did not want to quarrel with me. To-morrow I am to see him at two o'clock: I will let you know what happens. Rest assured that when I cease to be yours, it will be because I have left this world altogether."

And then she goes on to M. de Brion. That gentleman is growing urgent, and passionately eager; he might be taken to be a lover who had rights over her : he talks like her master; Mme. de Chevreuse declares herself very much vexed : but that is on Richelieu's account. "M. de Brion has sent to me, and, without any regard for my entreaties, or for the reasons I have represented to him, insists on going whithersoever I go, and says that nothing can prevent him from so doing, even if, in my fear of the Cardinal's anger if he should find it out, I should desire the contrary. I assure you this talk on de Brion's part has both vexed and afflicted me, for I really could not endure it, and am very much grieved that he should have given me so great cause for quarrel, after having given me so much reason for praising him : I am resolved I will not see him, if he comes against my will, and I will not even accept messages from him, if he does not repent him of the fashion in which he has spoken to me."

Then, at last, Châteauneuf lost patience. Was the Duchess his property or not? He insisted on being told! Rather alarmed, Mme. de Chevreuse protested her devotion in still stronger terms. She found herself impelled to make advances on her own account : "It will never grieve me to see marks of your affection," she writes to the Keeper of the Seals, "so do not fear to weary me with your letters, but continue rather to delight me by giving me proofs of your recollection of me as often as you can : I promise you a larger share of mine than that you have asked of me."

But, unfortunately, the position taken up by Richelieu was meanwhile growing more and more alarming. Mme. de Chevreuse is not playing with Châteauneuf, this time, when she communicates the fears with which the Cardinal's sentiments inspire her. "Never," writes the Duchess to her friend, "have I had so much trouble about holding converse with you as at this moment. You shall know all the details of my conversation with the Cardinal at our first meeting, for I can say no more in writing, except that

THE EXILE IN LORRAINE

it was not without good reason that I begged you to speak ill of me to the Cardinal. I shall not see you till to-morrow: M. de Chevreuse will speak to you at six o'clock in the evening: he is going to see the Cardinal, who is beside himself."

Richelieu seems, indeed, to have grown more and more angry about the dangerous understanding he had discovered between the Queen, Mme. de Chevreuse, and the Keeper of the Seals. His rage betrayed itself: he grew impatient, domineering, tormenting. The Duchess attributed his jangling nerves to his passion for herself! "The Cardinal's tyranny," she writes, "increases every moment, and his extravagances are worse than those of M. de Brion. He rages and swears because I do not go to see him, and because I do see various people here, and amongst them M. de Brion, whom I am resolved not to have in my own house again, because I know the King vows he is a spy. Judge of the point the Cardinal's spite reaches when he makes an affair of State out of that! The thing that vexes me is that the reason I have, on account of the love I bear my own self, for not seeing him, will be taken by the Cardinal to be my fear of making him angry again, which has led him to act in this fashion. I wrote to him twice, paying him compliments of which he is quite unworthy, and which I would never have made him but for the persecution of M. de Chevreuse, who told me I should thus purchase peace. I think the King's favour has swelled his arrogance beyond all measure. He thinks he will terrify me with his fury, and persuades himself, in my opinion, that there is nothing I would not do to appease it: but I would rather make up my mind to perish than make my submission to the Cardinal! His glory is not only unendurable to me, but odious! He told M. de Chevreuse that my temper was insufferable to a man of feeling like himself (it is his meanness that has led him to this opinion of it), and that he was resolved not to pay

THE DUCHESSE DE CHEVREUSE

me any particular duty, since I was not capable of bestowing my friendship and confidence on him alone! M. de Chevreuse has had a little quarrel with me, because the Cardinal's insolence has so intimidated him that he would fain have persecuted me into basely submitting to it."

The Cardinal appears to have done everything he could to bring Mme. de Chevreuse back to the performance of her former promises. Did he feign to be in love with her? The Duchess herself wondered. "I hardly know how to represent my interview with the Cardinal to you," she writes, "except by telling you that he betrays as deep a passion for me as I perceived, in old days, in the heart of Lord Holland. But even as I have always held that one to be real, I believe it (the passion) to be false in the case of the Cardinal, who vows he keeps nothing back from me, and desires to do absolutely everything I command him, on condition that I live with him after such a fashion that he may feel certain he stands higher in my esteem and confidence than any other person on the earth."

Richelieu persevered, raining supplications on her; his persistence became alarming. He tormented Mme. de Chevreuse. "I am in despair," writes that lady, "over what the Cardinal has communicated to me this evening. He has sent me an express messenger, to beseech two things of me. One for my own interest, and the other for his satisfaction; which were: the first—not to speak to M. de Brion, the second—not to see you: this last, alone, is any trial to me. Nevertheless, my determination to prove my affection for you is stronger than all the Cardinal's importance. Send me word how I may see you without the Cardinal's knowledge, for I will do whatever you think best for that purpose, since I passionately long to talk with you."

And in another letter: "I have seen him this evening

THE EXILE IN LORRAINE

[the Cardinal], and find him more resolved than ever to persecute me: never have I found him so troubled in mind as to-day, nor heard him so uneven in his talk, so that often he was in a desperation of anger, and in another moment he would calm down, and fall into the most extreme humility. He cannot endure that I should esteem you, and can do nothing to prevent it. Farewell! I must see you at all costs! Send me an answer, and beware of the Cardinal, for he is spying on us, both you and me!"

And in yet another: "Although I am not well, I will not omit to tell you how my visit to the Cardinal passed off. He spoke to me of his love, which he declares to be so great as to have caused his illness, by the distress of my behaviour to him! He enlarged on my conduct in long speeches of complaint, especially as regards your person, and concluded that he cannot live on, in his present feeling for me, if I do not assure him I have changed my feeling for him: to which I replied that I had always endeavoured to give him reason to be pleased with me, and desired to do so more than ever. He pressed me hard to know how things were between you and me, saying that all the world believed us to be in the closest possible understanding, which I absolutely denied. I will say no more at this moment, but believe me that I esteem you as much as I despise him, and that I shall never have a secret for you, nor any confidence in him!"

A curious situation, indeed! Châteauneuf, bitterly annoyed, poured forth his rage against Richelieu, and Mme. de Chevreuse responded: "I have a hatred of the Cardinal's tyranny, which is even greater than yours; but I am resolved to overcome it, and not to complain about it. Never have I so longed to talk with you as in this hour. The Cardinal vows that I shall soon be on bad terms with you, that you do not care for me, and jeers about it: as far as I am concerned, I laugh at all that: I believe in your

THE DUCHESSE DE CHEVREUSE

fidelity and your affection, and will give you the same all my life, provided that, even as you have deserved that I should form this good opinion of you, you do not make yourself worthy that I should lose it. I counsel you, not being able as yet to say that I command you, and not choosing to say, that I beg you, to wear the diamond I now send you, so that when you look at the stone, which has two qualities—one, that of hardness, and the other, of a brilliance so great that it can be seen afar off, and reveals its smallest blemish—you may remember that you must hold firmly to your promises, if they are to be pleasing to me, and that you must never make a blunder."

And as Châteauneuf's bitterness against Richelieu rose higher, Mme. de Chevreuse increased the fervour of the expression of her attachment to the Keeper of the Seals: "I believe you to be mine utterly," she writes, "and I promise that I will treat you eternally as mine; though the whole world should neglect you, I shall esteem you so faithfully, all my life long, that if you love me truly, as you say you do, you will have reason to rejoice at your good fortune, for all the powers of the earth will never drive me to change my mind: this I swear to you, and charge you to believe it, and to love me faithfully." And then comes her final word, to which she has been leading up. "I assure you I will command you always, and I order you to obey me, not only so as to follow your own inclination, if it so leads you, but to satisfy my desire, which is to dispose absolutely of your will: this is the secret which I did not tell you yesterday, and which I promised you should know to-day."

From that time forward she ceased coquetting with Châteauneuf, she swore that Richelieu might do what he chose, she would never yield to his advances: "Not all his prosperity," she writes, "will have the power of bringing me into subjection to the point of making me dependent on his whims; if he has an extravagant fancy

THE EXILE IN LORRAINE

for me, do not let that matter disturb you. Never was there anything to compare with his folly! he has sent, and written me, the strangest complaints: he says I am perpetually making game of him, that he knows of a surety that I have an understanding with you, and that your people never budge out of my house: that I see Brion because he is his enemy, and on purpose to vex him: that the whole world says he is in love with me, that the King believes it, that he cannot endure my behaviour any longer: this is the Cardinal's condition!"

Was the Cardinal really in love with Mme. de Chevreuse? She thought so, and desired to produce that impression on others. But could Richelieu himself have discerned, in his own eager and passionate heart, how much of his feeling was pure political anxiety, and how much a disturbance of his sentimental being? His Memoirs confine themselves to the political aspect of the business. They set forth his anxiety in connection with the understanding between Châteauneuf and Mme. de Chevreuse: and assert that the Keeper of the Seals, swept off his feet by his passion for the Duchess, had thrown himself into the cabals of the "factious ladies": that these ladies were plotting with foreign powers against the safety of the State: and events were destined to justify the correctness of this version of the story.

Affected by a multiplicity of causes, the incidents of Gaston's revolt, the growing hostility of Anne of Austria to the Cardinal, and Mme. de Chevreuse's own hatred of him, the Queen and her adherents had again begun to intrigue with foreign courts. Châteauneuf had allowed himself to be carried in their train. He was in a position to supply information as to the councils of the Government. Richelieu was soon advised of the "sincere and faithful admiration" for Spain professed by the Queen's circle: he knew the praises of the Spanish alliance were being constantly sung in that quarter; that through Mme. de

THE DUCHESSE DE CHEVREUSE

Chevreuse, the Keeper of the Seals was in communication with divers persons in the service of England; that he was well acquainted with all Monsieur's projects. Louis XIII, in his anger, desired to take severe steps at once. But Richelieu thought it wiser to wait: "I have just received notice," writes the King to his Minister, on February 4, 1633, "that a craftsman, newly come from England, has gone to wait on Mme. de Chevreuse at Jouarre. If she reports this to you herself, it will be some proof of her amendment; if she says nothing of it, confess at least, for the last time, that she is deceiving you and laughing at both you and me. I will confess to you that two things vex me beyond measure, and sometimes rob me of my sleep!—the insolence of Parliament, and the mock the persons you wot of make of me, not forgetting you. You know how I trust you in every business of mine; believe me in these two matters, and we shall set them right."

It was useless to fly in the face of facts. Before long, they demonstrated that Châteauneuf, at the prayer of Mme. de Chevreuse, was betraying State secrets to her; he had given the Duchess notice of an attack to be made on a fortress in Lorraine; she had warned the Duke, who had taken his measures accordingly, and the attempt had failed. Plans of campaign had leaked out, the Duke of Lorraine was kept informed of the undertakings against him discussed at the King's Council Board. Certain letters written by Châteauneuf were intercepted, they contained proofs of his treason. From the English Court, Louis XIII received warning that the Keeper of the Seals intended to get the Cardinal driven out, and to step himself into his shoes. The adherents of Gaston d'Orléans, it was asserted, reckoned on Châteauneuf's help, and were in correspondence with him. Mme. de Chevreuse went about openly retailing information which could not have reached her through any channel save that of the Keeper of the Seals.

THE EXILE IN LORRAINE

In a Memorandum dated the end of February, 1633, Richelieu set forth the piled up grievances of the Government against Châteauneuf; it was impossible for the King to retain a Minister who had behaved himself in such a fashion; he announced his intention of dismissing the Duchess's friend; he had come to the end of his patience.

On the morning of February 25, 1633, the King, then at his palace of St. Germain en Laye, sent an order to Châteauneuf to deliver up the Seals; very shortly afterwards, a Captain of the Guard, M. de Gordes, arrested the Minister. Châteauneuf made no complaint. He was conducted to Angoulême, and placed in confinement there. His nephew was arrested likewise, and the Chevalier de Jars as well; the family and friends of the disgraced Minister took to flight. By the King's order, Bouthillier and Buffon searched Châteauneuf's lodging, and there found a quantity of correspondence, amongst which were three-and-thirty letters from Montague, two-and-thirty from Henrietta-Maria, and all those of Mme. de Chevreuse. The prisoner, under cross-examination, "accused himself, as much as anybody chose, of having loved the ladies too dearly," but declared all the rest to be "women's nonsense and silly talk." He was left in his prison, and was to lie there till the death of Louis XIII.

As to Mme. de Chevreuse, the Government's perplexity, as always, was extreme. Any rigorous treatment of her seemed fraught with the most serious difficulties. And further, her services were really needed at that particular moment. Monsieur had left the kingdom, and was stirring up the Duke of Lorraine against the King. The Duke had raised an army, and there was a fear that he would call on the Emperor to come and help him; in Richelieu's opinion, Mme. de Chevreuse was the only person likely to be able to induce him to lay down his arms. The Duchess was invited to proceed to Lorraine and enter into negotiations for this purpose. She, who had been living in great anxiety ever since the arrest of Châteauneuf, and was, indeed, thoroughly frightened, did not dare to refuse. "Although this negotiation was not to her taste," writes La Porte, "Mme. de Chevreuse, to prove her zeal, acted in the matter against her own feelings, in the belief that the Duke of Lorraine would not be so easily moved: but she was deceived, for the Abbé du Dorat (who had been sent to act with her), so exerted himself that he induced his Highness to disband his army."

But this service once obtained, Louis XIII found it impossible to endure the idea of having Mme. de Chevreuse, whom he so detested, against whom he had so many just reasons of complaint, under his eyes, at his own Court. He waited awhile; but in the month of June, he made up his mind, and requested M. de Chevreuse to be so good as to conduct his wife to Couzières, near Tours. There was nothing for it but to obey.

Anne of Austria begged the King's leave to see the Duchess before she departed: unwillingly, His Majesty consented. Richelieu sought the same permission, on the plea that Mme. de Chevreuse desired to speak to him. "You ask me," wrote the King, "if you may see Mme. de Chevreuse, who wishes to bid you farewell; you know very well what pleasure the Queen has given me by asking my leave to see her; I know that her visit cannot serve your interests: you know very well that it will not be agreeable to me: that said, do what you will, and be assured that I will always be the best master to you that the world has ever seen."

Mme. de Chevreuse departed; she made no protest. The punishment meted out to her was, on the whole, a gentle one: it was better for her to betake herself to Touraine, than to go and vegetate in some foreign country, which would have been the only other resource open to her.

THE EXILE IN LORRAINE

Before she quitted Paris, she had a long interview with Anne of Austria; and they agreed to exchange constant letters. Did Louis XIII gain much by driving the fair intriguer out of his Court? Far or near, at home or abroad, the Duchesse de Chevreuse was destined to remain a thorn in his side!

CHAPTER VI

THE FLIGHT INTO SPAIN

Couzières—Mme. de Chevreuse intrigues with Anne of Austria—The affair of the Val de Grâce—Mme. de Chevreuse in danger—She takes to flight—Her journey across France in disguise—Marsillac, Malbâti, Spain—1634-37.

COUZIÈRES is a charming little country house on the slopes of the valley of the Indre, near Tours. Woods lie all round it. A great pleasure-ground, the outline of which may even yet be traced, though its area is now covered by a thick growth of trees, stretched its wide space, bright with sunlight and gay with flowers, in front of the cheerful dwelling. The house, though of small dimensions, is tolerably convenient. The partitions of the rooms as they were in the old days may still be traced. In one wing there remains a room, with a heavy stone chimney-piece and open rafters, which has preserved its ancient title, "the chamber of M. le Prince"—the Prince de Guéméné. The park, with its ancient walls, is just as it was in the seventeenth century. The surrounding country is pretty, one of those smiling landscapes characteristic of Touraine, with undulating lines full of dignity and charm. Couzières had known its hour of fame when, after a quarrel followed by a brief armed struggle, Marie de Médicis and Louis XIII met within its park walls, for the purposes of a temporary reconciliation. This was in 1619. Mme. de Chevreuse took up her quarters in her new residence attended by a numerous following—comptroller, equerries, lackeys, waiting-women, grooms, and so forth.

She had not been condemned to live in seclusion; she

THE CHATEAU DE COUZIÈRES, NEAR MONTBAZON IN TOURAINE

THE FLIGHT INTO SPAIN

was free to go to Tours. She was even obliged to be there frequently, to see her men of business and discuss her affairs, which had fallen into great confusion, with them. And having no taste for living alone, she desired to frequent the society of the province, which included several of her personal friends. Further, she was sure to find better facilities, inside the town, for carrying on her secret correspondence without attracting attention, or being caught by Richelieu's agents. So she hired a house at Tours, belonging to the Archbishop, and called the Hôtel de la Massetière, and in it she often stayed.

The life she led in this new residence was active and brilliant. She entertained, she went out hunting. Local gossip credited her with love affairs; so at least Tallement des Réaux assures us. Of one of these, the Archbishop of Tours was the harmless hero.

He was an aged prelate—eighty years old—and had already been Bishop of Bayonne. M. Bertrand d'Eschaux —this was the Archbishop's name—by birth a Basque, far from good-looking, blind of one eye, very learned and very kind-hearted, had performed the marriage ceremony between Marie de Rohan and the Duc de Luynes. He was a constant visitor in the house of Mme. de Chevreuse, who had the greatest confidence in him. Once, when she found herself in a difficulty, he lent her money, 25,000 *livres*, and looked after her correspondence. In spite of his great age and the dignity of his high rank in the Church, the charms of the young Duchess had produced their effect upon him, so at least she believed and declared: her boast was that she could make him do anything she chose. At certain critical junctures in her life he was to give her proofs of a really touching fidelity and devotion.

As a member of their social circle, the ladies of the city of Tours found Mme. de Chevreuse less satisfactory. They thought her decidedly in the way. The Duc d'Orléans, passing through the town at a slightly later date, wrote

THE DUCHESSE DE CHEVREUSE

to M. de Chavigny, in the somewhat cavalier style he usually affected: "The players are at Tours. Everybody there is in good health. Mme. de Chevreuse came to see the performance of *Le Cid*, and stayed one day, on which I paid her as short a visit as I could contrive. Neither I nor the ladies of the town were the least grieved at her departure; rather the contrary, for she played us a thousand dirty tricks." Two other persons were even less pleased with the goings on of Mme. de Chevreuse: these were Louis XIII and the Cardinal de Richelieu.

They knew a regular correspondence was being carried on between the Duchess and Anne of Austria. What did those letters convey? The King would fain have found out. "On my arrival here," he writes to the Cardinal, "I found, in the Queen's apartments, a certain Plainville, who goes to and fro for Mme. de Chevreuse, and who was welcomed into the Queen's presence like the Messiah. I write you this, to find out whether you think that when I know he has been dismissed I had better have him arrested and his letters taken from him." But Richelieu did not think it wise to act too hurriedly. And, indeed, apart from Plainville, Mme. de Chevreuse possessed many other means of corresponding with her friends in Paris: modest and obscure folk, some of them, others who were important personages; amongst these last, some Englishmen.

First and foremost there was Lord Montague. He had been sent into France on a diplomatic mission by the King his master, and had betaken himself to Tours, to pay his duty to Mme. de Chevreuse. As much in love with her as ever, he had placed himself at her disposal, to ensure the safety of her communications with Paris. His attentions to Anne of Austria and to the Duchess were the subject of many a merry jest and gibe between the two young ladies. "The excess of your kindness," writes Mme. de Chevreuse to the Queen, "which leads you to

THE FLIGHT INTO SPAIN

wish you could spend an hour in this place, so as to make the happiness of those who live in it, gives me freedom to answer the joke you make at M. de Montague's expense, as to his stay here. I acknowledge that you have good cause to think it an advantage to him to spend some time at Tours, but for a reason very different from that you give, for it is certain that he needs to be a great deal away from you, to make him see that he is still a mortal man, since he is no longer dwelling with the angels. If I have any credit with you, he will soon be enjoying that felicity."

Montague had not come over alone. He had brought a young English gentleman with him. His name was Craft. He had been presented to the Duchess, and the usual fate had overtaken him—he had fallen madly in love with her: Mme. de Chevreuse accepted his adoration. This young man's letters, which were intercepted, are still in existence. They afford proofs of one of the liveliest passions the Duchess ever inspired. "I cannot rest two days in the same place," he writes her from Calais, where he was waiting for weather calm enough to permit of his crossing to England, "without rendering an account of them to you: I hope to embark when I have finished this letter, and the thought of you will console me in all my misfortunes. I often see your portrait, and often kiss it. I pray you to think upon your poor servant, and upon the love he bears and always will bear you, having nothing in the world that is worth a thought, save yourself! My heart and my soul are both yours utterly!" "My passion for you is greater than I can express, and the resolve I have taken to be true to it will never suffer change! I dread my own country, for I can never hope to see anything there that will bring me contentment. . . . I will never love any but you, and that with all my heart and soul, and all my life long." Then, after he has reached London: "You owe me less thanks than ever for the passion I feel for you, for everybody here is so mean and contemptible that I know neither contentment nor comfort till the night falls, and I can be alone, and think of you."

Apart from these Englishmen, there were other persons on whom the Duchess could rely to forward her correspondence: Marsillac, son of the Duc de la Rochefoucauld, the future author of the *Maximes*, who had been presented to her by Anne of Austria, and whose regard for her was tinged with a deeper feeling; he was only twenty-four; M. de la Thibaudière, a gentleman from the province of Poitou; M. Chennetier, a burgher of Tours, who lived in the Hôtel de la Massetière; a certain M. Julien, who gave writing lessons; and above all, La Porte, Anne of Austria's own confidential servitor, the Queen's "cloakbearer," a young man from Anjou, three-and-thirty years of age, intelligent, devoted, discreet, and, in a certain sense, the soul of honour. La Porte acted as secretary to Anne of Austria, kept the cyphers and seals, copied and sent or carried the letters.

What was the object of all this correspondence?

On November 8, 1636, Richelieu wrote as follows to Chavigny: "As for the Queen, I will not tell you anything more, save that the old-established generosity of Mme. de Chevreuse has ever been the cause of the fact that in that country" (the Queen's circle) "the reverse of the King's will is always what is desired." To avenge herself on King and Cardinal, the Duchess had resolved to oppose his Majesty's policy in every foreign Court to which she herself had access. She would negotiate, and the Queen should back her up: Anne of Austria simply sailed in her wake. In England, the two Princesses made use of Craft and Montague; in Lorraine they had a sister-in-law of Mme. de Chevreuse, the Abbess of Jouarre, who had the letters brought her by La Porte delivered in Nancy; in Flanders, the secretary of the English Ambassador, Auger, took in the letters, and passed them on to the Spanish Ambassador in Brussels, the Marquis de Mirabel, who

THE FLIGHT INTO SPAIN

undertook to see they reached their various destinations. "Thus," says La Porte in his Memoirs, "the Queen had news from every quarter without anybody being aware of it; and this went on for some considerable time." It went on for nearly four years.

The letters which the Government of Louis XIII succeeded in stopping give us the general outline of the plot in which Mme. de Chevreuse was the chief mover.

The first idea was to stir up Spain against France, and induce that country to join forces with those of Lorraine, Savoy, and the Empire. Instead of corresponding directly with Madrid, which was too far off, Mme. de Chevreuse addressed herself to the great personages of Spanish nationality then ruling the Low Countries. At Brussels she had lighted upon an intriguing woman, worthy of the part assigned her, in the person of Madeleine de Silly, wife of Charles d'Angennes du Fargis, a former Lady of the Bedchamber to Anne of Austria, who, after having disgraced herself by her numerous love affairs, had been driven from Court because her foolish imprudence during her husband's embassy to the Court of Spain had deeply irritated the French Government. She had taken refuge in Brussels, and spent her time there fomenting cabals against her own country. Since open war had been declared between France and Spain, she had been keeping the Cardinal-Infante, brother of Anne of Austria, who commanded the Spanish troops in the Low Countries, fully informed of the movements of the French army, and suggesting to the Spanish authorities the measures they should take, the diversions they should create, and the attacks most likely to be attended with success, so as to embarrass the Cardinal's government.

We have her letters to Anne of Austria, the Queen's replies, and the letters addressed by Anne of Austria and by the Duchess to Mirabel and to the Cardinal-Infante. Word was sent from Brussels to the Sovereign and to

THE DUCHESSE DE CHEVREUSE

Mme. de Chevreuse of every happening in the camp of those of Richelieu's enemies who had sought refuge in Flanders, among whom Marie de Médicis was the chief figure. It was the scene common to all emigrations—illusions, jealousies, discord, suspicion and penury. Mme. du Fargis, a most needy woman, was perpetually begging. "I beg to point out," she writes, "as I did in my last letter, how extremely necessitous my condition is, without a serving-man, without a coach, without any attendants, and without even the wherewithal to make me a gown! What the Infante has given me hitherto has just sufficed to pay the debts my husband contracted! Good God! will these times never change? I am dying of hunger!" She entreats the Queen to recommend her to the Cardinal-Infante, so that he may increase the pension he gives her. She promises to write every week. Anne of Austria watches eagerly for her letters. Everybody in the Low Countries seems to be involved in this correspondence. Craft carries letters from Anne of Austria to Mme. du Fargis which tell her what she is to say to Mirabel, to the Cardinal-Infante; the Queen writes to them direct, and Mme. du Fargis reports to her. And, more serious still, the Queen, under the guidance of Mme. de Chevreuse, writes other letters to the King of Spain's Prime Minister, the Duque d'Olivares.

The results attained are not, indeed, commensurate with the efforts made. The Spaniards do not attach much importance to these feminine tricks. The frivolity of the French refugees in the Low Countries has prejudiced their hosts against them: these "Frenchmen," according to Mirabel, "have not a grain of prudence in their heads!" Mirabel sends no reply to the letters from the Queen and the Duchess. Mme. de Fargis makes a complaint about it. Anne of Austria has to write three times over to the Infante before he condescends to give her any sign of life. "I beg you will tell Mirabel," she writes to Mme. du Fargis, "that

THE FLIGHT INTO SPAIN

I do not write to him until I see letters from him, because I think mine weary him, and if you have a convenient opportunity, say the same thing to the Infante on my behalf." The humiliation of it! But why should the Spaniards have taken the plottings of two foolish young women, who had no real influence in France, to be anything serious? The Queen herself acknowledges this. "I would gladly shed my blood to serve the Queen-Mother," she writes to Mme. du Fargis, "but that is not in my power, for I have very little influence over the Cardinal, though we appear to be on very good terms: but this is not the case, in fact, whatever anybody may think: here, in a few words, is the absolute truth." And in another letter: "Do not rely on my intervention in the matter of the Queen-Mother, and seek out some other means, for that you count on is not good. From my side you must expect nothing, for it is impossible for me to do anything." Marie de Médicis herself is so well aware of it that in her poverty and dejection she begins to think of being reconciled to her son, if he will only consent, and of abandoning her advocacy of the Spanish cause. But how, indeed, was any confidence to be placed in her, in the Frenchmen about her, in the people in Paris who were keeping up intercourse with her?

Mme. de Chevreuse, alone among them all, held on her way. The more hopeless her undertakings began to look, the more fiercely she laboured on them. In a document Anne of Austria was forced, at a later period, to draw up for the satisfaction of the King her husband, she supplies proof of the untiring activity of the Duchess. She admits that Mme. de Chevreuse received at Tours not only the intermediaries who habitually transmitted her correspondence, but persons who came to her direct from Lorraine; she confesses that her friend was in the habit of sending this correspondence on to her, to the convent at the Val de Grâce, in Paris, whither she herself repaired

THE DUCHESSE DE CHEVREUSE

under pretence of performing her devotions, but with the real object of being alone, away from the Court, and free to deal at her convenience with the business of these intrigues; and that when she was absent from Paris, the letters were forwarded to her by the Superior of the nuns, Mother Saint-Etienne, who, when she saw the superscription, "Give this letter to your kinswoman, who is in the county of Burgundy," knew what that meant and for whom the letter was intended.

Did Anne of Austria realize the gravity of her own acts, and the danger to which she was exposing herself? La Porte, in his endeavour to save his mistress, was to protest that the letters written by the Sovereign contained "nothing but gibes against the Cardinal de Richelieu, and that assuredly she never spoke of anything that was against the King or the State." But he was mistaken. Anne of Austria was a traitor. When one of the Cardinal's agents, the Abbé du Dorat, said to him on August 28, 1637, "You must be prepared for every kind of frivolity and impertinence in that sex," he accurately defined the qualities of levity and thoughtlessness inherent in ladies who dabbled in such intrigues as this one. The most conclusive proof of this thoughtlessness lies in the fact that it never for one moment occurred to either of them that the day might come when Louis XIII would find out all about it!

From the very outset, in fact, Louis XIII and Richelieu, fully advised of the comings and goings between Couzières and Paris, had been on the watch. "According to the orders of your Eminence," wrote Bullion to the Cardinal, "I have kept my eyes open. It is true, and I have always recognized the fact, that the Queen has no kindly feeling for you, and if she has not sinned with her tongue, her ears, it may be, have played you false—and this I do not doubt. I am working to find out all particulars without betraying myself. There can be no doubt that the

THE FLIGHT INTO SPAIN

cabals at Tours are still being carried on." Information came in from divers quarters. It was reported that two gentlemen had travelled out of Lorraine to Couzières to see Mme. de Chevreuse, "one, named Mortale, a cavalry officer, dark, curly-haired, tall and stout, with full lips and wide nostrils; the other, Rochevalon, fair and blue-eyed, riding a white horse, and wearing a scarlet coat, a hat trimmed with a silver braid, and two white feathers and a yellow one." La Porte's movements were watched. The King was informed, one day, that he had gone to Tours, to request Mme. de Chevreuse to proceed in disguise to Orleans, there to meet Anne of Austria, who would be passing through the town. In a fury, Louis XIII vowed that if the story turned out true he would have La Porte thrown out of the palace windows. Thereupon La Porte, who had come to join his mistress at Orleans, entered the Queen's chamber, where the King was standing in front of the fire.

"Whence come you?" said the King sharply.

"From Fontainebleau."

"I did not see you there!"

"I arrived very late at night, and your Majesty left very early the next morning."

"But I met the Queen close to Artenay, and I did not see you in her suite!"

La Porte explained that his horse had lost a shoe, which had delayed him, and that he had galloped after his mistress to Artenay, where he had actually seen the King "hawking magpies in the vineyards."

"Indeed!" quoth the King.

But how find out the truth? How acquire the initial proof that would place the authorities in a position to open an inquiry, and force the culprits to confess their guilt? The King and the Cardinal waited—they waited for months. It was not till early in the summer of 1637 that they were to discover the document they longed to

THE DUCHESSE DE CHEVREUSE

find: it was La Porte who, all unwittingly, was to deliver it into their hands.

La Porte had a room in the Hôtel de Chevreuse, in the Rue St. Thomas du Louvre, which he had furnished himself, and in which he lived. He went for his meals to a tavern in the Rue Fromenteau, but it was in the Duchess's house that he made the necessary preparations for his missions and kept all his papers.

Now one fine day, a letter from Anne of Austria, addressed to Mirabel, and which he was to hand to Auger, the secretary of the English Embassy, was intercepted—how, we know not—and carried to Louis XIII. This time there could be no doubt about the matter. The proofs were in the King's possession. Richelieu, alarmed, would have temporized even then; but Louis XIII had made up his mind. The letter was known to have passed through La Porte's hands. "Of his own accord," writes the Cardinal in his Memoirs, "the King decided to arrest La Porte." This was in August. On the 10th of that month, Louis XIII, who was at St. Germain, sent a message to Anne of Austria, desiring her to repair at once to Chantilly, where he desired to speak with her. La Porte suspected nothing. He had to send another letter of the Queen's for Mme. de Chevreuse, of which M. de la Thibaudière, who was going to Tours, was to take charge. Meeting La Thibaudière in the courtyard of the Louvre, he tried to give him the packet, but the other, on the plea that he was not to start quite yet, begged the Queen's servant to keep it till the next day. After supper La Porte went into the St. Eustache quarter of the town to inquire, in the Queen's name, after the health of M. de Guitaut, a captain of the Guard, who had received a bullet wound in the thigh. About ten o'clock at night he left M. de Guitaut's lodging, and was just about to pass between a two-horsed coach and the wall close to which it was standing, at the corner of the Rue des Vieux-Augustins and the Rue Coquillière,

THE FLIGHT INTO SPAIN

when he was suddenly seized from behind, one person put his hands over his eyes, others laid hold of his arms and legs, and in the twinkling of an eye he was picked up, thrown, before he could utter a cry, into the coach, and held down, while the vehicle was driven rapidly away. When it stopped, and La Porte was allowed to get out, he saw he was in the gloomy courtyard of the Bastille; his assailants had been five of the King's Musketeers, commanded by their lieutenant, M. Goulard, and fifteen or sixteen other Musketeers had formed the escort.

He was searched. The letter to Mme. de Chevreuse was found. Who was the writer of that letter? demanded Goulard. They only had to look at it, replied La Porte; it bore the Queen's seal. He was thrown into a dungeon, protected by three locked doors; a truckle-bed and an earthen pot were the only pieces of furniture it contained. A soldier was left to guard the prisoner. Food was brought; then La Porte was left under lock and key.

An official, M. le Roy de la Poterie, was deputed to make a search at the Hôtel de Chevreuse. This search revealed nothing but some unimportant letters and cyphers. La Porte had hidden all the compromising papers in a hole in the wall at the corner of one of the windows. The hiding-place was concealed under a lump of plaster, and nobody knew anything about it. A servant-boy was seized, but he could only cry and vow he had nothing to tell. When La Porte was questioned about the letters and the cyphers, he gave the most hazy answers.

The only real proof, in fact, was Anne of Austria's letter, but that was sufficient testimony of her relations with Flanders and with Spain. The letter to Mme. de Chevreuse established that lady's complicity in the business. Richelieu decided to question La Porte himself.

At eight o'clock the next evening, a coach escorted by the Provost's Lieutenant and four archers carried the prisoner from the Bastille to the Cardinal's palace. By

THE DUCHESSE DE CHEVREUSE

way of the kitchen yard, the gardens and the ante-chamber, La Porte was led into Richelieu's chamber, where the Minister awaited him, attended by Séguier, the Chancellor, and Des Noyers, a Secretary of State. Richelieu began his examination. It was proved, he said, that the Queen had been keeping up a correspondence with Flanders and Spain, and that La Porte had been her intermediary. If he would acknowledge the facts, his fortune was made; he would not even have to go back to the Bastille. La Porte, who was quite unaware that the Queen's letter to Mirabel had been found, denied everything; he was absolutely in the dark. Then, said Richelieu, some other person had been carrying the letters: who was it? La Porte declared he did not know. Thereupon Richelieu grew angry. If La Porte would not tell him anything, he should be tried, and the business would be a short one; a subject's first duty, when his King ordered him to speak, was to obey. La Porte protested: his conscience could not command him to accuse the Queen of sending letters into Spain if he did not know she had been doing it! "But she has given us proofs of it!" cried Richelieu, in a rage, "and we know she makes use of you to carry her correspondence!" "If the Queen says that, it is because she wants to save the persons who serve her to keep up these communications, by saying it is I who did it!" Richelieu mentioned the letter addressed to Mme. de Chevreuse which had been found on the prisoner's person, and which was to have been handed to M. de la Thibaudière. La Thibaudière, as a matter of fact, having heard what was happening, and fearing he might be compromised, had spontaneously reported what had passed between La Porte and himself. La Porte, who knew nothing of this, told a story. "You are a liar!" cried Richelieu. "You tried to give the letter to La Thibaudière in the courtyard of the Louvre; he asked you to keep it till the next day; and after that you expect me to believe

THE FLIGHT INTO SPAIN

you! You must write to the Queen, and tell her she does not know what she says when she declares she has no communications with foreigners and enemies of the State, and that it is of yourself she makes use for her intrigues!" La Porte refused; he could not, he said, take such liberties with the Queen. "Very well," was the Cardinal's reply; "you shall go back to the Bastille!" At one o'clock in the morning La Porte was taken back to his prison!

Meanwhile, Louis XIII had commanded that a search should be made at the Val de Grâce. The convent was not then the magnificent building of the present day. It was at a later date that Anne of Austria commissioned Mansard to erect the great pile as it now stands. The convent of those days, a far more modest edifice, was that the Queen had built when she founded the house in 1624. Its Abbess, Mother St. Étienne—Louise de Milly, the daughter of a family belonging to the Franche-Comté, but in the service of the King of Spain, and whose brother was governor of the town of Besançon—was an intelligent and strong-minded woman of fifty-six. Respect for canonical rights rendered caution indispensable. Louis XIII wrote to the Archbishop of Paris that, having ordered the Chancellor to proceed to a search in the Val de Grâce, on account "of certain despatches which were there, and which might cause great prejudice to his affairs," he begged the prelate to accompany his Minister, induce the Superior to furnish all the information she might be requested to give him, and that done, send the said Superior into exile in some provincial convent.

The Archbishop and the Chancellor proceeded together to the Val de Grâce. They found nothing except some unimportant letters. The Superior had begun by declaring she could not receive the gentlemen, because she was ill. A doctor was consulted, and gave it as his opinion that she was well enough to answer questions. The Archbishop and the Chancellor were conducted to the nun's cell, and

THE DUCHESSE DE CHEVREUSE

cross-examined her. After he had made her take an oath "on the damnation of her own soul and the truth of the Holy Eucharist, which is the most religious thing on earth, and the most potent for the human conscience," so runs the official report, the Archbishop commanded her to reveal everything, "in virtue of her holy obedience, and on pain of excommunication." The Superior denied everything. The Queen, she said, certainly received visitors in the parlour, but she was never present, and so could not know who came there; she did not know La Porte; and the Queen had never confided any papers to her care. Thereupon the Archbishop called together the chapter of the community, gave it notice that he was deposing the Superior from her office, sent her to the Convent of La Charité-sur-Loire, and ordered the nuns to proceed forthwith to the election of another abbess; all of which was done on the spot.

Mother St. Étienne protested that the treatment meted out to her was unjust, "and that it would not last long!"

The inquiry at the Val de Grâce had borne no fruit at all. The only thing left to be done was to question Anne of Austria.

The news of all these discoveries had overwhelmed the Queen. The impression produced at Court had been disastrous for her. At Chantilly, whither she had gone by the King's order, everybody avoided her. The King and the Cardinal did not see her at all; the courtiers passed beneath her windows and never looked up. The people about her hardly waited on her as they should. She felt herself an object of universal scorn. She fell into a state of terror; twice the physicians had to bleed her; she could not eat and could not sleep.

The Chancellor, sent by the King, waited upon her; he questioned her. Had she really been in communication with the Spaniards? She denied it. Then he laid the intercepted letter to Mirabel before her. With a sudden

THE FLIGHT INTO SPAIN

gesture she snatched the paper up and tried to hide it in the bosom of her gown. La Porte and Monglat both assert that the Chancellor did his best to take it back by force! This closed the conversation!

On the following morning the Queen sent her secretary, Le Gras, to assure the Cardinal she had never employed La Porte to carry any letters but those to Mme. de Chevreuse. On August 15 she received Holy Communion, and again requested Le Gras to go and tell the Cardinal that she swore by the Blessed Sacrament she had not had any dealings with foreign Courts. She was beside herself! Two days later her secretary came and told her the authorities knew more than she thought. Then she sent Le Gras to ask Richelieu to come and speak to her.

He came; and she acknowledged, in substance, that she had written to the Cardinal-Infante in Flanders; but, she declared, "it was only on subjects of no importance." "There was more than that, Madame!" was the Cardinal's grave reply; but if her Majesty would make a clean breast of everything, the King would certainly forgive and forget. Desperately agitated, Anne commanded the persons present in the room to retire. Yes! she then confessed, she had written to her brother the Infante, and to the Marquis de Mirabel; she had complained, in the letters transmitted to Auger by La Porte, of the situation in which she was kept in France; she had warned Mirabel to be careful to counteract the understanding in preparation between the King and Lorraine, or the King and England; yes! M. de la Thibaudière was to have carried one of her letters to Mme. de Chevreuse; yes! she had forced Mme. de Chevreuse to come and see her in disguise! And she wept, and talked of her remorse, and confessed she had been false to her oaths, and acknowledged the sins of which she had been guilty. Richelieu was touched; the King, he told her once more, would certainly grant her his pardon. As for himself, he would do his best to serve her. "Ah, Monseig-

THE DUCHESSE DE CHEVREUSE

neur," cried the Queen, "how full of kindness you must be!" And she would have taken him by the hand, but Richelieu, embarrassed, respectfully eluded the honour, and took his leave.

He made his report to the King. But what action could they possibly take against the Queen of France, whose bestowal of a Dauphin on the nation was so eagerly and impatiently awaited? They must e'en bow their heads and forgive her!

The King was determined that the Queen should at all events renew her confession and sign it. Anne of Austria obeyed. This was on August 17. She wrote the document from dictation. After acknowledging that she had sent letters into Flanders and received answers to them, she added: "Among other things, I have sometimes expressed my discontent with the situation I myself occupied, and I have written letters to the Marquis de Mirabel, and received letters from him, which were couched in terms that must have been displeasing to the King. I warned the Marquis de Mirabel that there was talk of an understanding with Lorraine, and that he must take his measures. I have manifested my anxiety and distress about the news that the English were making peace with France, instead of remaining at one with Spain. The letter that was found on La Porte was to have been given to the Duchesse de Chevreuse, and the said letter referred to a journey which the said Dame de Chevreuse intended to take, and nominally without our knowledge." She closed her confession by a promise never to offend again. Below this statement Louis XIII added, with his own hand, one of his own, to the effect that, in consideration of this confession and of the oath the Queen had taken never again to place herself in a similar position, he pardoned her. The husband and wife exchanged kisses. As far as they were concerned, there was an end of it all.

But the King meant to take his compensation out of the

THE FLIGHT INTO SPAIN

Queen's accomplices. He gave orders for the cross-examinations to begin afresh, and be actively carried on. La Porte continued to deny everything, so he was handed a letter which Anne of Austria had been forced to write, and in which she told him: "I desire you will acknowledge the truth about everything concerning which you may be questioned." Still La Porte refused to confess. He would not, he declared, be guilty of such a piece of "meanness"; the Queen's letter had been dictated to her! Under fresh pressure from the Chancellor, he wrote to Anne of Austria, to ask what she really wished him to reveal. Through Mlle. de Hautefort, the Queen contrived to give him an idea, to some extent, of what had happened. La Porte behaved in a most chivalrous way. That formidable agent of the Cardinal's justice, Laffemas, entered his cell, and, finding all his attempts to break down his opposition useless, held out a paper, saying, "Here is an order to put you to the question, ordinary and extraordinary!" La Porte did not flinch. He was led into the torture-chamber; the instruments of torture were laid out before him—planks, wedges, cords, and so forth. The prisoner's sole reply was that he would only speak if the Queen ordered him to do it. "But she has written ordering you to speak!" "That letter was dictated to her!" If the Comptroller-General of the Queen's Household, M. de la Rivière, came and repeated her order by word of mouth, said La Porte, perhaps he might obey him. M. de la Rivière came. In his presence the Chancellor asked his questions. Then La Porte consented to confess the business of the intercepted letter to Mirabel. All the rest he denied. They threatened him; but it was all in vain. Tired out, his judges left him in the Bastille; he was to lie there for nine months, and at last, in 1638, the Queen was to be granted her faithful servant's freedom, on condition that he went into exile at Saumur.

But what was to be done with Mme. de Chevreuse?

THE DUCHESSE DE CHEVREUSE

Once more the question arose, and, as always, full of inextricable difficulties. There was no doubt as to her guilt. There were proofs by the score of what she had done. Louis XIII began by notifying the Queen that he forbade her to have anything to do with the Duchess in future. He put his order into writing: "I do not wish the Queen to write to Mme. de Chevreuse in future, and principally because this pretext has covered all the letters she has written elsewhere." Anne of Austria pledged her word.

Apart from the Queen, this business of the Duchess was full of complications. Since the month of April the Government had been aware that she was planning to get out of France, and take refuge in England. In a memorandum laid before the King, Richelieu detailed the dangers to the Government this course involved. "Mme. de Chevreuse," he said, "is in friendly relations with the Duc de Lorraine, with the English, with the Queen, with the Fargis, and, generally speaking, with all the mischief-makers. If she is outside the kingdom, she will prevent the Duc de Lorraine from coming to any arrangement, as much on her own account as because the Queen, who favours the Spanish party, will desire it; she will give a great impulse to the English to do what she wants them to do; she will be open to all the impressions conveyed by the mischief-makers. Hence my conclusion is that she must not be allowed to leave the kingdom."

But how was it to be prevented? There were two methods: the first was to use force; to this course, which must end in failure, Richelieu saw serious objections; the other was "the ways of civility"; in other words, to write to the Duchess, and make her understand that if her desire to go abroad was caused by reasons connected with her own necessities—she was known to be heavily in debt—the Government was ready to come to her assistance: that, if it was only "for the satisfaction of her own mind, the

THE FLIGHT INTO SPAIN

Government had nothing against it, but that she ought to consider that she would leave her whole family in perdition." The Cardinal's final conclusion was that it would be better to send her money. "So dangerous is her spirit," he said, as he closed his statement, "that, once outside the kingdom, it may cause one knows not what unforeseen disturbances." Louis XIII approved this view. A large sum of money was despatched to Tours. Mme. de Chevreuse expressed her thanks, but refused to accept the gift; she declared she was in no need of money. Finally, after thinking it over, she did accept it, but merely as a loan.

What was to be done next? The King decided that anyhow he would send somebody to Tours to question the Duchess. After that he would see. He confided the mission to an old servant of the House of Lorraine, an ecclesiastic, treasurer of the Sainte-Chapelle in Paris, the Abbé du Dorat, a man of faithful and reliable character. "Madame," wrote the Cardinal to the Duchess, on August 15, "I have requested M. du Dorat to wait on you for an affair that you will consider of some importance. As I desire to give you fresh proofs of my affection and my good offices, I beseech you will give me proofs of your sincerity, and assure yourself that by this conduct you will extricate yourself from the business in question without any annoyance whatsoever, even as you have been extricated, in the past, from others which were of not less importance." On second thoughts, a certain Abbé de Cinq-Mars was appointed to act with du Dorat. The duty imposed on the envoys was to induce Mme. de Chevreuse to give them all the information they could extract from her as to her dealings with foreign Powers. Despatches from the Duc de Lorraine and from the Spanish Ministers, containing certain circumstantial details, had been seized in Burgundy. If the Duchess would make a frank confession, she would be given a full pardon.

THE DUCHESSE DE CHEVREUSE

Du Dorat and Cinq-Mars found Mme. de Chevreuse in an extraordinary state of agitation. When the news of what had been happening in Paris reached her, the Duchess, like the Queen, had been quite overwhelmed. She was too conscious of the gravity of her own faults, and too well informed, by the fate of Chalais, Boutteville and Montmorency, of the fashion in which the King knew how to punish, not to dread chastisement of the most terrible description. The arrival of the two inquisitors put the finishing-touch to her terror. She denied everything wholesale. When they pressed her with questions, she ended by acknowledging that several times over she had intended to go and see the Queen in secret, but that the Queen had dissuaded her from carrying out the plan, because of the insuperable difficulties attending its execution. As regarded the Duc de Lorraine, she had no understanding with him, and it had never entered her head to prevent him from treating with France. As to the despatches intercepted in Burgundy and which were now being held over her head, she knew nothing at all about them. When du Dorat made his report to Richelieu, he declared himself convinced that Mme. de Chevreuse had induced the Queen to prevent the alliance between France and England, and concluded thus: "Your Eminence will permit me, if it so please you, to assure you that this lady is the greatest enemy you have, and the one who has done you the most displeasure." On August 24 he made Mme. de Chevreuse set down in writing, and sign, the few items to which she had confessed, and carried the document with him to Paris, after having assured the Duchess he would keep her informed of the progress of events.

The effect produced in Paris was exceedingly bad. Mme. de Chevreuse was made acquainted of this by her friends. The King and the Cardinal were both of them deeply irritated. La Rochefoucauld sent Craft to warn the

THE FLIGHT INTO SPAIN

Duchess. She lost her head. Du Dorat wrote her not to fret herself, reiterating his assurance that all the cross-questioning had only been a test of her frankness; that everything would come right; that his Majesty was resolved to pardon her, whatever she had done. The Duchess, beside herself with terror, watched anxiously for his letters. She besought the Queen and her friends in Paris to give her timely warning of any decision to take strong measures against her. It was arranged with Mlle. de Hautefort that within the next week she was to send Mme. de Chevreuse a Book of Hours. If the binding was green, it would mean that all was going well, but if it was red, the Duchess was lost; she must think of nothing but her own safety. Mme. de Chevreuse watched on.

Then what happened? Du Dorat's letters ceased. Later on she was to know that he had fallen ill. Next, at Tours, on Saturday, September 5, at eleven o'clock in the day, the Duchess received two packets: the Book of Hours—in a red binding! The fatal colour!—and a letter from Anne of Austria: "Her Majesty sent her word that as soon as she received it" (this letter) "she must escape, somehow or other; if she did not, she was lost, and would certainly be arrested on the Sunday morning!"

Mme. de Chevreuse was distracted. For two hours she lay prostrate. Towards one o'clock she called for her coach, and went to the King's Lieutenant-General at Tours, M. Georges Catinat. She told him she was exceedingly anxious, that she had no news of du Dorat, and that it was a very serious matter. The Lieutenant-General, standing leaning against the window, told her several times over that she need not be so much alarmed; that something must have happened to prevent du Dorat from writing; that he was sure to send her a letter by the next post. The Duchess, who had been walking up and down in a fever, suddenly moved towards the door, saying she was going back to Couzières, and would first go and bid

THE DUCHESSE DE CHEVREUSE

the Archbishop farewell. Her state of agitation surprised Catinat.

At the archiepiscopal palace, Monseigneur d'Eschaux had been ill in bed for five or six days. Mme. de Chevreuse was admitted to his chamber, and sat down on the edge of his bed. To him she told all she had in her heart. There was no letter from du Dorat: his silence had filled her with deadly fear, and this fear had been transformed into certainty that very morning by the Queen's missive. She held out the letter—a very long one—and only read him one passage, that concerning her present danger. Now she must fly; she must get out of France! The Archbishop, greatly surprised, asked her if she had ever thought of flight before? No! she replied. And whither did she intend to go? To Spain! The Archbishop was at a loss to know what he should say. The Duchess reminded him that he had a nephew, the Vicomte d'Eschaux, who lived on his property at Eschaux, near the Spanish frontier, in the Basque country, some six or seven leagues from Bayonne. Let the prelate give her a letter of recommendation to his kinsman! After some hesitation, the Archbishop complied. He even went so far as to make out the itinerary of the journey to the Pyrenees. The Duchess asked for a pen; she wrote three or four letters, and then tore them up. The Archbishop began to make more inquiries: And who was she taking with her? Only one manservant, Hilaire. Indeed, she meant to put on male attire herself. The Archbishop pointed out that one manservant was really not enough; the Duchess replied that she would take Renault as well. Towards four o'clock in the afternoon, M. Catinat put in an appearance. Alarmed by the state of agitation in which the Duchess had been when she left him, he had gone to inquire for her at the Hôtel de la Massetière, and, not finding her there, had come on to the palace. Mme. de Chevreuse bade farewell to the Archbishop and to the Lieutenant-General, returned

THE FLIGHT INTO SPAIN

to her town house, took several packages and a sum of money, and started for Couzières, attended by her equerry and a couple of waiting-women. She was deadly pale, absorbed in her own thoughts, sorely troubled; now in a sort of dream, now shedding tears.

By seven o'clock she had reached Couzières. Supper was served—meat of some kind. She scarcely touched it. Then she went to her own chamber, and, calling her women together, told them she had received reliable warning that she was to be arrested, and that she was about to depart. She did not tell them where she meant to go, because she was sure to be sought for at Couzières; and the King's emissaries, finding her gone, would persecute them to find out whither she had betaken herself. If she could only get two and a half days' start she would be out of danger. She desired her waiting-woman, Anne, to order the comptroller of her household, whom she had left at Tours, to keep her house there going as if she was still in it, and to tell everybody that she was ill and not receiving any visitors. She wrote a letter to M. Catinat, and confided it also to her waiting-woman: in it she confessed to the Lieutenant-General that she was leaving France, and begged him to look after her affairs for her. Secrecy was enjoined on all; nothing was to be said even to the other members of the household, except that their mistress was ill; then everybody was dismissed, except Anne. The two menservants, Hilaire and Renault, had received their orders to be in the road close to a certain gate into the park, at nine o'clock, with three horses, one of which was the Duchess's own ambling hackney, "a mare, all white, splashed with black, like a magpie."

She dressed herself in man's attire: a black coat, jerkin and breeches, and high boots. To conceal her features, she dyed her face with a mixture of soot and brickdust, which made her look like a gipsy; on her head she put a fair wig, which she fastened on with a strip of black silk bound

THE DUCHESSE DE CHEVREUSE

round her forehead—meaning to say she had been wounded in the head in a duel; she was quite unrecognizable. When she was ready, she betook herself to the park gate, where Hilaire and Renault were waiting for her: "She had neither linen, nor clothes, nor packages, nor bags"; nothing but a little enamel watch, and some *rouleaux* of gold in her pocket. She gave her final orders to her waiting-woman, mounted her horse, and passed out of sight.

All that night she travelled, all the next day (Sunday, the 6th). That evening, worn out with fatigue, she reached the little market town of Couhé, some eight leagues beyond Poitiers: she had ridden thirty leagues! At dawn next morning she was off again, and by eight o'clock she was at Ruffec. She could not go another step! At the hostelry of the Chêne Vert she asked for a room, three napkins, and a fire; she took off her jerkin, threw herself on the bed, and slept for two hours. At ten o'clock Hilaire and Renault came to tell her she must dine. When the meal was over, she remounted her horse. The inn servants stood around, watching the handsome young gentleman; one of the maids remarked that he seemed hardly able to sit in his saddle, into which, helped by a stableman, he had climbed with considerable difficulty. Mme. de Chevreuse answered that she was "extremely weary and ill"; she was going to seek repose in a friend's house; she gave the servants a crown, and they judged her to be a "person of condition." The little party departed once more on its travels.

But the Duchess had come to the end of her strength; there could be no doubt about it! Thereupon she recollected that she was not very far from Verteuil, the home of M. de la Rochefoucauld and his son, M. de Marsillac. Why not send and ask M. de Marsillac to lend her a coach? She would write that young gentleman an anonymous note, which Hilaire should carry to him, and in which she would tell him a tale. Her servant had his inkhorn on him. So

THE FLIGHT INTO SPAIN

she wrote: "Sir, I am a French gentleman, who asks you to do him a service to save his liberty and perhaps his life. I have had the misfortune to fight a duel, and I have killed a well-known nobleman. This drives me to leave France, and that quickly, because I am being searched for. I believe you to be sufficiently generous to serve me without knowing me; I want a coach, and a few lackeys to attend me." Then it struck her that M. de Marsillac was not likely to act on so vague a request. She told Hilaire what he had better say, and gave him another letter. He rode off, on the Duchess's own hackney.

He reached Verteuil, and was ushered into M. de Marsillac's chamber, where he was still in bed. He tendered him the note the Duchess had given him; he explained the position: the Duchess was close by; she was on her way to Saintes, in a great hurry about some urgent business; she had not the time to stop now, but on her way back she would visit Mme. de la Rochefoucauld; she begged M. de Marsillac would be good enough to lend her a coach and four saddle-horses.

Marsillac was living alone at the château with his mother and his wife. He hastened to do as he was asked. What! he cried, Mme. de Chevreuse was in the woods close by? But he would go to her himself, and at once! He would be pleased to do nothing of the sort, protested Hilaire. The Duchess would not see him on any account. Marsillac did not press it. He called his own bodyservant, Thuillin, had four horses harnessed to a coach driven by a coachman of the name of Ardouin, ordered four more to be saddled, and desired the two servants to follow Hilaire and carry out whatever orders they were given. Hilaire helped them to harness the horses; and when he departed he left the Duchess's hackney, which was broken down with fatigue, in the stables at Verteuil.

Some five hundred paces from Ruffec they found Mme. de Chevreuse. She asked Thuillin "if there was not any

THE DUCHESSE DE CHEVREUSE

place in the neighbourhood where she might go and rest for a few hours?" Yes, replied the man, only two leagues off there was another house belonging to M. de la Rochefoucauld, called La Terne. Mme. de Chevreuse got into the coach and lay down. Very soon they reached La Terne. The man who took care of the house—Potet was his name—made ready a room and a bed, on which Mme. de Chevreuse stretched herself out, without taking off her clothes. He inquired whether she would not have something to eat. She asked for some fresh eggs. Then she desired Renault to give her the itinerary the Archbishop had made out for her; it was not to be found. She questioned Potet and Thuillin as to the best road to take so as to get to Eschaux, on the Spanish frontier. Thuillin said that Potet knew the way, and would be too happy to conduct her. Potet, who had been in the service of the Duc de Luynes, had recognized the Duchess. Mme. de Chevreuse, too, kept telling him she had certainly seen him somewhere; Potet was only too glad to put himself at her disposal. He pointed out that they must go either by Cahuzac or by Tonneins; for the first stage, they might go as far as Condour, near Marthon, and sleep there in the house of a certain Dulorier, who was an acquaintance of M. de la Rochefoucauld's; at Cahuzac they would find a lodging in the house of one of M. de la Rochefoucauld's men of business, Malbâti by name.

When night fell, Mme. de Chevreuse got into the coach once more. Potet, Hilaire, Thuillin and Renault rode after it. Towards three o'clock in the morning they were at Condour, and the following evening they reached Saint-Vincent de Connezac. Mme. de Chevreuse was a little rested; and she could not keep M. de Marsillac's coach for ever. At Saint-Vincent she bought a tolerable mare for eight *pistoles*, and the next morning, when she had reached a spot about two leagues from Mussidan, she told Ardouin he might drive the coach back to Verteuil.

THE FLIGHT INTO SPAIN

As a precaution, she kept Thuillin with her. In the course of the night between Wednesday the 9th and Thursday the 10th of September she reached Cahuzac.

Potet and Thuillin went and knocked at the door of the attorney, M. Jean-Paul, otherwise called Malbâti. It was opened by his wife; her husband was out. Potet and Thuillin made themselves known; they had with them, they told the good lady, a gentleman of quality, and friend of M. de Marsillac's, who had been fighting a duel, and whom M. de Marsillac commended to her husband as though he had been his own self. They were admitted. As they were all sitting down to table, Malbâti himself appeared. He was a good-looking man of about sixty, with a straightforward and friendly countenance. He gave his five visitors a most cordial reception. He made a very favourable impression on Mme. de Chevreuse. During the repast, she told him she wanted to go and take the waters, "to cure a wound received in a recent duel, which still caused a great deal of pain." Malbâti replied that the only waters he knew of for that kind of trouble were those of Ax. No, said the Duchess, those were not the waters she desired to take; she wanted to go to Bagnères: did he not know the way there? Ah! quoth the attorney, if the traveller had only come five or six days later, when the vintage would have been over, he would gladly have ridden with him as far as Notre-Dame de Garaison, close to Bagnères, whither he himself was bound to go, to accomplish a vow. The Duchess asked him if he could not come at once. No! he said, that was quite impossible. But she pressed him so hard that he ended by giving in. Everybody went to bed, Malbâti giving up his own room to the young gentleman, as he believed him to be.

The next morning, when the whole household was up and about, Mme. de Chevreuse asked her host if he had not a suit of clothes he could sell her. Yes, he replied, he had a suit that M. de Marsillac had given him two years previously,

THE DUCHESSE DE CHEVREUSE

and which he had never put on. Though it would be rather large, it might do. Reassured at finding herself with Malbâti, a sensible man of experience and respectability, the Duchess requested Thuillin to go back to M. de Marsillac, taking two of the saddle-horses with him, and to assure him that she would "everlastingly feel the obligations under which she was to him." She directed Renault and Hilaire to stay on at Cahuzac until they had fresh orders from her, and then she started forth once more, accompanied by Potet and Malbâti.

The grace and charm and delicate features of the young traveller had not passed unnoticed by Malbâti. He drew Potet aside: Who was this young gentleman? he inquired. Potet made a gesture indicating his own uncertainty. He would hear that later. Mme. de Chevreuse, guessing the purport of the conversation, broke in upon it by inquiring about the noble families living in the part of the country through which they were travelling.

That evening they slept at an inn about five leagues from Douzains. Malbâti was thoroughly puzzled. The evident exhaustion of the young man, when he had dismounted at the end of this last stage, "and the beauty of the said young gentleman," so the good man was to assert at a later date, "made me somewhat suspect that this was a lady in disguise; which led me to resolve I would discover the truth the next day, by frequent questions, and by the entreaties I would make that I might be told it."

That next day, Friday, the 11th, the three horsemen crossed the Garonne at Agen, and slept at Gondrin. Malbâti cross-questioned the Duchess. At last he said, in the most determined fashion, "Who are you?" The Duchess gave evasive replies, but he pressed her so hard that she finally confessed she was the Duc d'Enghien, son of the Prince de Condé; and then, to change the conversation, she began to talk about the *Cid*, poured forth praises of Corneille, and recited whole passages out of the play.

THE FLIGHT INTO SPAIN

On the morrow, Saturday, the 12th, the halt for the night was at Montastruc. Malbâti returned to the charge. "How is it," he inquired, "that a great Prince like you travels as you are travelling, alone, in such distant parts as these?" Mme. de Chevreuse said something about the duel she had been fighting, and began to spout poetry again.

On the Sunday, September 13, they stopped at Bernadets. It was a wretched lodging, and Mme. de Chevreuse preferred sleeping on some straw in a barn. The next morning she was offered, for her breakfast, a quarter of a goose, boiled in a very dirty earthenware pot. She refused to eat anything at all. A peasant woman, who had seen her as she slept, and been struck by her appearance, brought her four fresh eggs on a pewter dish, covered with a clean napkin. "That's the prettiest boy I ever saw in my life!" quoth she. Mme. de Chevreuse smiled at her, and accepted her eggs.

They had five leagues more to ride before reaching Bagnères. Touched by Malbâti's devotion, the Duchess told him she was not the Duc d'Enghien, but another person, whose name she would reveal to him when they reached the end of their journey the next day. Potet confided to the attorney that though he might admire their comrade's face now, "it was nothing to what it was when the gentleman had not rubbed tile-dust and soot all over it."

At two o'clock in the morning the three horsemen rode into Bagnères, and dismounted at a hostelry close to the baths. Mme. de Chevreuse asked the innkeeper which waters were the best, those of Bagnères or those of Barèges. He replied that it would depend on the sort of illness the patient had. The Duchess said she thought she had better consult a physician. She knew one at Tarbes, a man of high reputation; she would go and see him the very next day. The innkeeper pointed out that the road to Tarbes was long and difficult to travel.

THE DUCHESSE DE CHEVREUSE

On the morning of Monday the 14th, Mme. de Chevreuse went over to the baths. There were a great many people there, and one of them, a gentleman, recognized her, and, with an air of great surprise, respectfully approached her. The Duchess at once begged him to conceal his former acquaintance with her, and asked him to do her the kindness of procuring her a guide to take her into Spain. The arrangements were made: it was settled that the guide was to meet her in the mountains at an appointed spot. Then she returned to her inn.

Malbâti had promised to accompany the young gentleman as far as Bagnères; he had never said he would go on from there to Tarbes. He was very ill-pleased at this fresh development of the Duchess's plans, and tried to dissuade her from attempting the journey, saying the country was full of thieves, and the roads most unsafe. Mme. de Chevreuse persuaded him to come with her.

Once more they got into their saddles, led by a single guide. The attorney of Cahuzac wore a gloomy look; the Duchess told him she saw clearly how vexed he was; that he was very possibly thinking of forsaking her; but he had served her so faithfully thus far that she could not doubt he would render her the final service of accompanying her this once more. They travelled across the mountains all that day and the next night. Towards three o'clock in the morning they reached one of the little huts that serve as shelter for the shepherds of that country. Mme. de Chevreuse had deceived Malbâti. She was not taking him to Tarbes, but to the frontier. While the horses were being fed, the travellers stretched themselves out upon the hay and slept.

At dawn Mme. de Chevreuse rose to her feet and led Malbâti aside. She had promised, she said, to tell him who she really was, and now the hour had come: she was not the Duc d'Enghien; she was a woman, and the Duchesse de Chevreuse. She was deeply grateful to him for the

THE FLIGHT INTO SPAIN

service he had just done her. She was going to Spain. She was leaving France against her will, because if she did not, ruin would overtake her. And she added, so that Malbâti might repeat her assertion, that she was on her way to England, and had not been able to discover any other means than this of getting there. She had escaped from Tours because she knew she was to be arrested. Her conscience was clear: she had never done, and would never do, anything against the King or the Cardinal; she would write to them to that effect; she would rather "throw herself into the fire than be shut up in a prison." She trusted Malbâti would report all she had said: let him say she was only going to stay a few days in Spain; that she did not intend to see either the King or the Queen; that she meant to go straight to a seaport, whence the King of England was to have her fetched on one of his ships of war. She was expecting a guide from Bagnères to meet her at the spot they had now reached. Now they must part; she would be able to spare Malbâti and Potet, and they might return to their own homes.

Malbâti was amazed. He listened in the deepest astonishment. His heart was filled with mingled feelings of emotion, regret and pity combined. What could she be thinking of, he asked at last, gently, to dream of crossing the mountains alone, and in such troublous times, with a man of whom she knew nothing at all? She would come to destruction, she would fall among "a thousand thieves!" Mme. de Chevreuse replied that she was quite confident about her journey, which would not cost her more than two or three hundred *pistoles*: she would halt at the hospice, four leagues away, where there were Spanish priests who would take care of her; she would then write to the Viceroy of Saragossa to send her a coach to Barbastro. There was no danger at all. She would send back news by the guide.

Malbâti was sorely troubled. He had not spent so many

THE DUCHESSE DE CHEVREUSE

long hours in the company of the beautiful woman whose life he had been sharing for some days without experiencing a dim sense of her charm, and an inner feeling that was alike mysterious and tender. But just at this moment a Spanish peasant—the promised guide—made his appearance, climbing up the path. Mme. de Chevreuse asked Malbâti to take charge of a letter for the Archbishop of Tours, and after a certain amount of hesitation the attorney consented. If you have any fears, said the Duchess, burn it, but "if he would take her word, she swore to him, on the faith of an honourable woman, that it contained nothing against the King's service." She also asked him to return M. de Marsillac's horse to him, and to thank him for the service he had done her: "She would never forget the obligations and the courtesies she had received from him." To indemnify Malbâti for his outlay, she offered him a *rouleau* of *pistoles*. He would not accept it. But she succeeded in making him take a sum to cover the expenses of his return journey—seven *pistoles*.

The moment of parting had come. Malbâti was shaking with agitation. With an impulsive gesture, the Duchess threw her arms round his neck and kissed him. The guide was in a hurry to start. Mme. de Chevreuse made Potet give her the map and the inkhorn, reminded him as to the road he would have to follow on his return, and then, having bestowed a final embrace upon Malbâti, took hold of her horse's bridle, and walked briskly up the mountain path. . . .

Malbâti, lost in thought, took his way down the mountain-side. The next day he made his Communion at Notre-Dame de Garaison; then he went home to Cahuzac, and despatched Hilaire and Renault to perform the commissions with which the Duchess had entrusted him, amongst them the letter to the Archbishop, which he sent to M. de Marsillac; this gentleman had it carried to Tours by a lackey in the service of M. d'Estissac. Meanwhile,

THE FLIGHT INTO SPAIN

Mme. de Chevreuse had succeeded without any difficulty whatever in crossing the frontier and reaching Spanish territory.

She had fled from Couzières on the evening of Saturday, September 6. On Monday, the 8th, at Tours, M. Catinat received the letter the Duchess had desired her waiting-woman to send him. The Lieutenant-General asked the lackey who brought it "where his mistress was?" "At Couzières," he replied, knowing no better. Catinat at once sent a messenger to Couzières, who returned with the news, which he had already suspected, that the Duchess had fled. He instantly wrote three despatches, one to the Duc de Chevreuse, one to du Dorat, and the third to his own brother, a Councillor of the Parliament of Paris, telling all three of his correspondents what had just happened, and requesting them to inform the Government.

On the receipt of this letter, M. de Chevreuse, greatly alarmed, fetched the Abbé du Dorat and the steward of his own household, M. de Boispillé, and waited on Louis XIII, who was at Conflans. There had been no intention on his part of placing Mme. de Chevreuse under arrest. Anne of Austria and Mlle. de Hautefort, deceived by flying rumours, had acted too precipitately.

Both the King and Richelieu were exceedingly annoyed. They requested Boispillé to proceed at once to Tours, to find out exactly what had happened, and to report to them. Finally, on Saturday, the 12th, Richelieu, after thinking the matter over, ordered Boispillé, in the King's name, to hurry after the Duchess, catch her up, and assure her that if she would come back at once, her flight would be overlooked; she might even return to Dampierre.

On the Sunday, Boispillé started on his journey. At Tours he saw the Archbishop and the Lieutenant-General. From the Archbishop he learnt the road the Duchess was to take, as he believed, to get to Eschaux. Boispillé went on his way. On Sunday, the 6th, the prelate had received

THE DUCHESSE DE CHEVREUSE

letters from Paris which assured him Mme. de Chevreuse had no reason to be so alarmed. He had at once despatched two men, Dolce and Mazuel, to join her, reassure her, and induce her to turn back. These two men had not returned. Boispillé found them at Bordeaux. It was then arranged that Dolce should go to Eschaux, that Mazuel should search the banks of the Garonne, and that Boispillé should endeavour to collect information on the spot. When, after a few days, the three men met again, none of them had found out anything. There was no news of Mme. de Chevreuse at Eschaux. Mazuel turned back towards Tours, going by Blaye, Saintes and Saint-Maixent, looking about in case the Duchess should be lying ill anywhere along the road. Boispillé remained at Bordeaux till the 22nd. It was then over a fortnight since Mme. de Chevreuse had started. He went back to Tours, and there heard that the Duchess had ridden by Ruffec and Verteuil, where she had borrowed M. de Marsillac's coach. He hurried to Verteuil, and when he put his horse into the stable there, he recognized the Duchess's hackney. Marsillac assured him he did not know what had become of the lady; he told him all that had happened as far as he himself was concerned; beyond that he knew nothing. Boispillé brought the hackney back to Tours.

Then he went to see the Archbishop again. That prelate, meanwhile, had received the letter Mme. de Chevreuse had written him from the Spanish frontier, and confided to Malbâti. "Ah," said he, "you have been working hard to try and get news, and I, who have never set my foot outside this place, have news to give you!" He read the letter aloud. Boispillé thought the Duchess was at Eschaux. He took post-horses, and went there as fast as he could. He arrived on Sunday, October 11; but Mme. de Chevreuse had not been there as yet. He returned to Tours, and thence to Paris. His undertaking had failed.

THE FLIGHT INTO SPAIN

Meanwhile, Louis XIII and Richelieu had received information from other quarters.

When Marsillac's servants and his coach returned to Verteuil, he learnt, to his great astonishment, that instead of going to Saintes, as she had declared she intended doing, Mme. de Chevreuse had gone in a quite different direction. And the strange disguise she wore, and which his servants described to him, caused him still greater perplexity. Suspecting some unpleasant business at the bottom of it all, he at once wrote and desired his secretary, who happened to be in Paris, to report the whole matter to his father. And at the same time Mme. de la Rochefoucauld, whose mind was as uneasy as her son's, wrote to her husband, giving him every detail. "If it is all of no consequence," wrote Marsillac, "I should be very glad if no fuss were made about it." M. de la Rochefoucauld, as soon as he received the two letters, went to see the Chancellor, and then hurried down to Rueil to speak to Richelieu. He was very much alarmed, and accused his son of carelessness. Five or six days after that, Potet returned to Verteuil with the horses, and told Marsillac that Mme. de Chevreuse had crossed over into Spain. Marsillac instantly sent the news to his father, who carried it to Richelieu. He was received in the most frigid fashion. "This business places me in such a difficulty," he wrote angrily to his brother, M. de Liancourt, "that I cannot write to you about anything else. It is not that my son can be excused, either as regards myself or other persons, for he has shown me very little consideration; I pray God he may be wiser in future."

But Mme. de Chevreuse was safe in Spain. There was no use in trying to stop her. At all events, Louis XIII and Richelieu would now find out exactly what had happened, and if there had been accomplices, they should be chastised. An inquiry was opened, and placed in the hands of a magistrate of the Parliament of Metz, President

THE DUCHESSE DE CHEVREUSE

Vignier. He departed to Tours, cross-examined the Arch bishop, the Lieutenant-General, the servants at Couzières; he went on to Verteuil, saw Marsillac and the servants there; he questioned the owners of the taverns and inns where Mme. de Chevreuse had rested, and finally he questioned Malbâti himself. Then he sent in his report. Thanks to this inquiry and report, we know all the details of the flight. It seemed far from easy, all things considered, to lay the blame anywhere, since the King, at the very beginning of the business, had declared himself ready to forgive the chief offender.

Public rumour accused Marsillac: he, so it was said, had carried off Mme. de Chevreuse, had helped her out of the kingdom, had even brought her to La Terne, and there "held revels" with her. He was ordered to Paris to give an explanation of his conduct. His friends, M. de la Meilleraie and M. de Chavigny, were defending and excusing him, on the score of his having been the lover of Mme. de Chevreuse, which was quite untrue. Richelieu commanded him to tell him the whole truth. Marsillac took a high tone, and gave sharp replies. Richelieu grew angry. When the young man answered somewhat haughtily, the Cardinal said: "Very good. Then you must go to the Bastille." The next day Marsillac was in prison. His friends pleaded his cause, and after a week had gone by, Meilleraie managed to obtain his release. He was to be the only victim of the flight of the Duchess, and his punishment was of the lightest kind.

CHAPTER VII

IN ENGLAND: MADAME DE CHEVREUSE AND RICHELIEU

Mme. de Chevreuse in Madrid—In London—Her negotiations with Richelieu: she slips through his fingers—M. de Chevreuse is sent to London: Mme. de Chevreuse flees into Flanders—Death of Richelieu—1638-42.

FROM the Hospice, where the monks had received her with great kindness, Mme. de Chevreuse had pursued her journey into Spain. From Sant Esteban, the first fortified town she reached, she wrote a letter to Cardinal de Richelieu. In it she set forth the reasons of her conduct: since the Châteauneuf business, she asserted, she had striven to live in peace, and to avoid anything likely to cause displeasure: she had been suddenly warned that she was about to be arrested, to answer for things "of which she had never even thought, and to be told that the truth of them was in her accusers' hands. This had made her imagine her destruction was a settled thing." So she had departed! She also wrote to the Archbishop of Tours, telling him she had reached Spanish territory, requesting him to do certain things for various people, and adding that she had not yet decided what her next step should be.

From Sant Esteban, she went to Saragossa. Thence she sent more letters into France. Forgetful of her promise to Malbâti, she resolved to go to Madrid. From that city she sent news of herself to Boispillé. But a courier from France brought her a curt message. "We send no answers into Spain." The Government had issued its orders.

Mme. de Chevreuse solicited an audience with the King

THE DUCHESSE DE CHEVREUSE

of Spain. She was kindly received: the fact that she was the friend of Anne of Austria was not forgotten. Philip IV, the sovereign of the Spanish kingdom, was then a man of thirty-five. "Splendid presents were given to Mme. de Chevreuse," writes Mme. de Motteville, and she adds: "The King of Spain appeared to have some little tenderness for her, and although she told me, in the days of the Regency, that the prince had never said a soft word to her except once, and then only as he passed by, report tells quite another story." There was a persistent belief, indeed, that the King of Spain had been on the most intimate terms with Mme. de Chevreuse. Louis XIII was pleased to affirm the fact to Anne of Austria, before her assembled Court, after a decidedly coarse fashion. "The Queen," writes the English Ambassador, Digby, to Montague, on May 19, 1638, "told me, with great emotion, that the King had given her a very pleasant piece of news, to wit, that the King of Spain had certainly '*couché avec Mme. de Chevreuse!*'" He used these very words in a loud voice."

But for many reasons it was not possible for Mme. de Chevreuse to remain at Madrid. Her position there was of the most precarious kind. She had made an attempt to obtain a certain rank at Court by getting herself appointed what was called *posada en palacio:* her application had been refused. This had deeply offended her. Lost in that stiff serious society, in which her lively French ways were very ill received, she soon felt it would be wiser to leave the country and make up her mind to go to London. The King of Spain courteously provided her with all the necessary facilities. He even charged one of his gentlemen, Don Domingo di Gonsalvo, to conduct her to Fontarabia, and attend her to England. So after a stay of a few months on Spanish soil, the Duchess took ship, and on Sunday, April 25, 1638, she disembarked at Portsmouth. Her fate was to undergo a change, indeed!

IN ENGLAND

She was joyfully received. Lord Goring and Lord Montague, who had been sent to meet her by Charles I, welcomed her when she landed: she settled for a time at Greenwich. Friends crowded about her. The English Court had not forgotten the merry days of 1625, and hailed with delight the return of the fair lady who, in spite of her eight-and-thirty years, was still the fascinating Duchess it had then admired.

Mme. de Chevreuse recovered her confidence. Now that she was no longer in an enemy's country, the powers in Paris would perhaps agree to enter into relations with her. And besides, she was short of money, she must really look into her affairs, which had been sorely neglected.

The pregnancy of Anne of Austria had been formally announced in February 1638, and she lost no time about writing to the Queen to offer her congratulations, and thus reopen intercourse with her. It was the first time she had communicated with her since she had left Couzières. "The remembrance," she wrote, "which I cannot doubt your Majesty has of what I owe you, and that I have of what I should pay you, will persuade your Majesty, without a word from me, of the pain it has been to me to remove myself so far away from you, so as to escape penalties which I feared the unjust suspicions stirred up against me might cause me to suffer." Necessity alone had forced her over the Spanish border, where the respect felt for her Majesty had caused her to be received and treated far better than she deserved. "That I bear you led me to hold my peace till I was in this kingdom (England), which, being in a good understanding with France, gives me no reason to apprehend that it will cause you displeasure to receive letters coming thence."

And she congratulates the Queen on her condition, and beseeches her to help her: "May your Majesty's protection

THE DUCHESSE DE CHEVREUSE

preserve me from the misfortune that the anger of the King and the bad graces of Monseigneur the Cardinal would bring on me!"

Anne of Austria, who had learnt prudence, showed the letter to Louis XIII. As it happened, Mme. de Chevreuse had done just what the King most desired when she wrote it. Now that she was out of Spain, so Richelieu opined, it was as well to reopen relations with her, and bring her to reason. The Queen should make a beginning, and initiate a corespondence which might ultimately assume wider proportions. The sovereign's interesting condition supplied the necessary opening. Anne of Austria had better announce it to her friend herself: a rough draft of her letter was supplied her, and that rough draft we now possess. Anne of Austria was to make no reference to the terrors with which she herself had inspired the Duchess, and which had really been at the bottom of her sudden flight: she was to reassure her, saying, "There is no intention here of doing you any harm"; she was to make a joking reference to the hurried journey across France, the details of which, revealed by the inquiry conducted by President Vignier, had so entertained the Court that certain facetious persons had embellished the tale, which did indeed lend itself to the process, with all sorts of merry adventures, the echoes of which have been transmitted to us by Tallemant des Réaux. "I have not been able to help laughing over certain adventures with which I know you have met." She was to advise the Duchess to repair the mischief done in the past by adopting, during her stay in England, an attitude the very opposite of that she had hitherto assumed with regard to France: "I entreat you, for the love of your own self, and of me, to do nothing in the country in which you are, likely to rouse any just displeasure against you outside it, and I confess to you that while I have a passionate desire for peace, I should be in despair if England, either during the

IN ENGLAND

time you are there, or after you have left it, should do anything against France." The request was as definite as possible. But on consideration, some doubt was felt, and the letter was not sent.

Thus Madame de Chevreuse's letter to the Queen arrived in the nick of time. In response to it, Richelieu caused the Duchess to be informed by a third person, but on his own authority, that her attempt to correspond with Anne of Austria had not been ill received, and that she might write again. Mme. de Chevreuse at once wrote to the Cardinal himself. "Having learnt," she said, on June 1, "that which I easily believe, seeing how great is my desire to do so, that it will be agreeable to you to receive this letter, I write it to you with much contentment. I hope the misfortune which has constrained me to leave France has grown weary of having pursued me for so long, and that the suspicions which have filled me with dread may have partly justified that fear, of which I should be well pleased to be cured, by the knowledge that my enemies are not more powerful than my own innocence. I thought myself obliged to remove myself far away, so as to gain the only thing needful for my justification, that is to say, time. The assurances I have received of your kindness towards me, since my arrival here, make me hope for the success on which I have set my desires." She begged Charles I and Henrietta-Maria to write and urgently plead her cause both with Louis XIII and with Richelieu. And at her request the King of England went so far as to desire his Ambassador in Paris to intercede in her favour, and beg an immediate permission for her return to France.

But this time Richelieu thought things were going too fast. In a carefully prepared memorandum, the Cardinal set forth, for the King's information, the reasons which made it necessary to take indispensable precautions before Mme. de Chevreuse was given leave to come back: "If

THE DUCHESSE DE CHEVREUSE

the English Ambassador mentions Mme. de Chevreuse," he wrote, "the King will say that when she acknowledges her faults, he will be ready to grant her his pardon." There were to be conditions, and these were still more clearly set forth by Chavigny, the Secretary of State, to M. de Bellièvre, the French King's Ambassador in London : "We impatiently await news of what may have passed between you and Mme. de Chevreuse, and whether, in your judgment, she intends to render some useful service in the place where she is, so as to reconcile herself with France." The Government meant Mme. de Chevreuse to pay for her pardon, and to give pledges beforehand. These conditions were exceedingly distasteful to her. Counselled by Montague, she was to fool the Cardinal, and enter on a perfidious struggle with him, in the course of which she was to give proofs of extraordinary subtlety and consummate duplicity.

From Greenwich she had removed to London. She had no money, and was living "at the King of England's table"—in other words, at his expense. Her first care was to have a lodging of her own and her own furniture. She applied to her husband : she made Montague write to the English Ambassador in Paris, Digby, requesting him to see M. de Chevreuse on the subject. M. de Chevreuse replied that the matter was one that required looking into, and that he was sending the Abbé du Dorat to London for that purpose, subject to the Cardinal's consent to his taking the journey.

But it was not du Dorat who arrived, it was a mere serving man. Digby wrote to Montague : "The Sieur de Boispillé brought M. de Chevreuse leave from Court yesterday to send a servant to ask after the health of Mme. de Chevreuse." It was a mockery. Mme. de Chevreuse sent the lackey back with a civil letter to her husband. "I promise myself that you will take care to send me what I ask. I beseech you to do it, for I cannot

IN ENGLAND

remain much longer in the state in which I now am, and I trust it will not become so bad as to drive me to use any other help than that I expect from you, for my subsistence." Thus pressed by his wife, M. de Chevreuse made up his mind to send over Boispillé. Boispillé was a faithful servant, devoted, but somewhat credulous. Richelieu sent for him, and told him he would consent to his going to England, but on one condition only, that he should take the Duchess in hand and induce her to make her submission to the King. He gave him a letter for the Duchess: he was to address all his correspondence to du Dorat, who would transmit it to the Cardinal.

The letter carried by Boispillé from the Cardinal was somewhat haughty in tone. "Madame," wrote Richelieu, "M. de Chevreuse having desired the King's permission to send the Sieur de Boispillé to you, I have not chosen to let him go without testifying to you by these few words that even as I have an interest in all that affects you, I shall never feel content when I think that you have not reason to be so. If you are innocent, your safety depends on yourself, and if the frivolity of the human mind, not to say that of your sex, has led you to stumble in a manner that has given His Majesty reason to complain, you will find in his goodness that which you may expect, and should desire."

Mme. de Chevreuse made as though she would accept the Cardinal's overtures. Boispillé wrote that he had been very well received, that Mme. de Chevreuse was in an excellent frame of mind, that there was nothing in the world for which she longed so much as to get back to France. Only whenever he tried to have a clear explanation with her, she put him off. He begged and prayed her to tell him what her wishes were, at all events. "We are in treaty for Mme. de Chevreuse," writes Montague; "we are much pressed to formulate her demands, but we have not made any at all." In the meantime Montague

THE DUCHESSE DE CHEVREUSE

contrived to have a snub administered to the French Ambassador, M. de Bellièvre. Mme. de Bellièvre was informed that she must not expect a seat in the Queen's coach: only a few days previously a "tabouret" had been granted to the Duchess, and the same honour had been withdrawn from the French Ambassadress. Mme. de Chevreuse and her friends were to continue to set Richelieu at naught by dint of a cunning mixture of apparent goodwill and real hostility.

Boispillé urged matters on. He was full of confidence. The Duchess, he wrote, "charges me to say anything that is desired on her part, to hurry on the moment of her return, promising to give every kind of satisfaction in the future, and never to fail: she protests that she will do so well, and so faithfully serve and attach herself to the interests and the orders she may receive from his Eminence, that she will repair all her past faults, and that every one will find the greatest satisfaction in her." By dint of entreaties, he had induced her to confess that she must, at the least, have a formal declaration from the King, which would constitute a general abolition of her whole past, including her departure from France. And she insisted that this promise should also be made to the King of England, who would be answerable for its being kept.

Louis XIII and Richelieu were well inclined to grant this abolition; Boispillé had sent over a memorandum setting forth various affirmations made by Mme. de Chevreuse, which were of a nature to satisfy the Government. The Duchess declared, he said, that she had never entered into any undertaking either with England or with Spain. She had never received any pension from either country; she had no dealings with Lorraine: she certainly did see the Spanish Ambassador and the other foreign envoys, but that was simply because they came to pay their respects to her. Her present conduct

IN ENGLAND

appeared quite correct, and she had promised that she would behave well in future. Under these circumstances, thought Boispillé, the Government might safely send the document for which she asked. Louis XIII and Richelieu came to a decision. "Madame," wrote Richelieu to the Duchess on July 24, "the King has given his willing consent to your request. Since you feel you are free from all guilt, save for having left the kingdom, he has commanded me to inform you that he gladly grants you the abolition, as he would have granted it for any other thing you had declared to be on your conscience. The sureties you have asked for are being sent to you. If you need others still greater, I will gladly serve you in that particular."

The abolition was couched in solemn terms: "Louis, by the grace of God, King of France and of Navarre. . . ." The King "remitted, forgave, pardoned, and abolished" all the faults committed by Mme. de Chevreuse, assured her she should never be pursued or punished on their account, forbade all officers of his justice to prosecute her because of them; but twice over in the document did he enumerate the sins of which the Duchess had been guilty, to wit: that she had fled from Tours without the King's consent; that she had left the confines of his kingdom without his permission; that she had retired into a country belonging to the open enemies of the State; and that she had "negotiated with le Duc de Lorraine against the service" of his Majesty.

When Mme. de Chevreuse read this document she started, and flew into a rage. What! she cried. She was accused of having been in treaty with the Duke of Lorraine? But it was a lie! She could not possibly accept a document enshrining such a calumny as that! She would have nothing to do with their abolition! She would not go back to France! "After the certainty expressed to me," she wrote to du Dorat, "that I used my

THE DUCHESSE DE CHEVREUSE

entreaties to prevent Monsieur le Duc de Lorraine from coming to an arrangement with the King, and to keep him on the side of Spain, a thing of which I never thought, I cannot believe myself to be safe in France; for I could not, while he holds such an opinion, hope for the protection of Monseigneur the Cardinal, unless it shall please him to rid himself of this suspicion by giving me the means of justifying myself, and himself that of thinking me worthy that my fault in leaving France should be forgotten, for which I will wait till his goodness affords me the necessary surety." Nothing had been gained, after all!

From that moment all Bellièvre's letters were full of warnings that in all her dealings with him Mme. de Chevreuse was affecting an air of open hostility. She openly consorted with the enemies of France. She held frequent conversations with the agent of the Spanish Court, she spoke publicly in favour of Spain. Richelieu was very much vexed. He made an attempt to reopen negotiations. He had it conveyed to Mme. de Chevreuse that his personal feelings for her were unchanged, that she might reckon on his friendly offices, that the great thing was to find some common ground on which they might come to an arrangement. "Consider, sir," wrote Mme. de Chevreuse, "the position in which I am, quite content, on one hand, with the assurance you send me of your continued friendship for me, and much distressed, on the other, by the suspicions, or I should rather say the certainty, you declare you possess as to a fault which I have never committed, and which I confess would be doubled by another if, once committed, I were to deny it. I confess, sir, that all this places me in so great a difficulty that I can see no repose for myself in such a meeting. If indeed you had not so certainly persuaded yourself that you know it (the fault), or that I could acknowledge it, it would be a means to an understanding: but since you let yourself be carried away to such a firm conviction

IN ENGLAND

against me that it will not admit of any justification, and since I cannot make myself guilty without becoming so, I have recourse to yourself, sir, and entreat you, by that quality of friendship which your generosity promises me, to find some expedient whereby his Majesty may have satisfaction, and I may be able to return to France in safety." The only possible course was to wait.

Thereupon Richelieu was informed that the Duchess was trying to get Marie de Médicis brought over to London, so as to set up a more efficacious opposition to the French Government in England. "Ah," exclaimed the poor Cardinal, quite disheartened, "men think sometimes that animals can do no great harm because they can do no good at all, but there is nothing more capable of bringing a State to ruin than evil minds protected by the weakness of their sex!" The King of England did not care, indeed, to have his mother-in-law at his Court, for her bad temper was well known to him, and he refused to allow her to come. Then Mme. de Chevreuse made Henrietta-Maria write and advise her mother to take ship without the King's leave. Marie de Médicis acted on the hint. Unwelcome wherever she went, first driven out of Flanders, and now forced to leave Holland, where everybody was sick of her presence, the only refuge left her was her son-in-law's kingdom. She reached England in the course of the month of November.

Immediately a great friendship was struck up between the old Queen and the Duchesse de Chevreuse. They saw each other every day: Mme. de Chevreuse, well knowing that nothing could be more disagreeable to Louis XIII, kept entreating the King of England to press the Queen Mother's recall to Paris on his brother-in-law. She kept up the closest relations, too, with the Spanish Ambassador. Richelieu asserts in his Memoirs that she was even in correspondence with the Spanish Prime Minister, Olivares. She welcomed all the Cardinal's per-

THE DUCHESSE DE CHEVREUSE

sonal enemies, as, for instance, the Duc de la Valette,—who had fallen into disgrace with Louis XIII on account of his humiliating defeat before Fontarabia, and had crossed the Channel rather than face his judges—Le Coigneux, Monsigot, and others. Bellièvre wrote that Mme. de Chevreuse was making arrangements to go over to Flanders, so as to be in more direct communication with the Spaniards. Never had the Duchess been so dangerous! How reopen negotiations with her, bring her back to her duty? Richelieu appealed to her husband.

Distressed beyond measure by his wife's behaviour, living in perpetual terror of being compromised by her proceedings, M. de Chevreuse was doing everything he could invent to prove his personal zeal for the King's service. He was more than attentive to Richelieu: he sent big game, snared in his park at Dampierre, to stock the Cardinal's lands in Poitou: he never lost any opportunity of affirming the fact that he was too good a servant of his Majesty to dream of undertaking any business without his master's consent. Somebody suggested that he should beseech the King to permit his wife to return to France. He did it. Richelieu pretended to take his petition seriously. "Madame," he wrote to the Duchess on January 5, 1639, when he sent du Dorat and Boispillé over to her, "the perpetual entreaties of M. de Chevreuse to save you from your ruin, joined with the affection I have always felt for whatever concerns you, have led me to obtain from a King a passport for the Abbé du Dorat and the Sieur de Boispillé, who go to you with the intention of doing you service, and leading you to think of yourself more than you have ever done." As always, Mme. de Chevreuse received this suggestion with the most perfect courtesy. "I could hardly receive," she says in her answer to the Cardinal, dated January 28, "greater proofs of my husband's regard for me than his prayers that I may be able to return to France; nor

IN ENGLAND

can I hope for their success, save by your assistance, to which I acknowledge I owe the good beginnings I see, and I trust I may owe their happy ending to your good offices." But she warned him beforehand that if there was any more talk of the abolition, she would never give in on the subject of her negotiations with the Duke of Lorraine—such negotiations never having had any existence in fact. "If the suspicions of me which my misfortune has engendered," she wrote, "touching the business of M. le Duc de Lorraine, were true, I would confess them to you, not doubting that your generosity would obtain me pardon for that, as well as for my departure from France."

When du Dorat and Boispillé reached London, they found the Duchess on her guard. She paid them compliments. "What I have been able to discover as to her intentions," writes du Dorat to Richelieu on January 31, "is an extreme passion to return, a feeling of gratitude for the kindness shewn her by your Eminence, and a longing to tell you many things, if she had the good fortune to be able to see you." But when the two envoys tried to arrive at some definite conclusion, the conviction that Mme. de Chevreuse was evading the question forced itself upon them.

Their mission was a difficult one: Richelieu had given them the very same abolition that Mme. de Chevreuse had refused to accept; and had even forbidden them to hand it over to the Duchess till she had furnished them with a written acknowledgment, signed with her own hand, of the truth of the facts it set forth. Mme. de Chevreuse had been furious. "I will confess to you," she wrote to Richelieu, "that I was doubly astounded to see it (the reference to Lorraine) in the abolition shown me by du Dorat, and to hear on what conditions he had undertaken to hand it to me!" On the other hand, du Dorat and Boispillé had informed the Duchess that the

THE DUCHESSE DE CHEVREUSE

King would allow her to return to France, but not to Court—only to Dampierre;—and even then they did not know how long she would be permitted to stay, nor whether she would enjoy her liberty there. She had thereupon demanded an abolition, pure and simple, without any mention of the Lorraine business, and with full liberty to go and come as she chose, all over the kingdom.

Du Dorat and Boispillé tried to reason with her. She would have leave to go to Dampierre to begin with, and after that she would certainly be allowed to come back to the Court. The Duchess replied that she refused everything. "If your Eminence," wrote du Dorat, in his despair, to Richelieu, on February 25, "will give me leave to say what I think of this person, I will assure you that there never was so unquiet a spirit: necessity and the loss of her liberty are two furies that tear her in pieces."

In Paris, now, all was silence. Boispillé and du Dorat did not know what to do next. "Time is getting on," wrote Boispillé on March 10; "I had better get back. As for the poor Abbé du Dorat, he is bored to death." And on the 17th: "We are in a state of misery and impatience here which cannot be described. We are quite at a loss, the poor Abbé and I. M. du Dorat has fallen into such a state of melancholy that truly I think he will fall ill of it!" On that very day, the 17th, Richelieu despatched his answer to du Dorat. If the Government, he said, insisted that Mme. de Chevreuse should acknowledge her negotiations with Lorraine, it was because this "was necessary to its safety." The Cardinal declared he would keep her confession a dead secret. Nevertheless, he announced, in his desire to reach some solution, he had induced the King to grant the abolition pure and simple, without any reference to the Lorraine business, which the Duchess had insisted on obtaining. Mme. de Chevreuse, he added, expressed her astonishment at not being

IN ENGLAND

allowed to go and come as she chose within the frontiers of France. Only a year previously, just before her flight from Couzières, she had been ordered to keep within the boundaries of Touraine. There was no evidence that she had done anything since then to deserve any amelioration of her condition. From this Richelieu drew the conclusion that the lady's fate lay in her own hands. With his letter he enclosed the new abolition: the passage touching the Lorraine business had really been suppressed.

When the Cardinal's courier arrived, at nine o'clock at night, Boispillé and du Dorat at once hastened to wait on Mme. de Chevreuse, and informed her of the contents of the packet sent them from Paris. Then permission to move about within the borders of France was refused her? She would not go back, the Duchess answered curtly. In vain did the two envoys, in sore distress, return to the charge on the following day. "Never was there unreasonableness nor ingratitude to compare with hers!" wrote the indignant du Dorat to Chavigny on the 24th. They discussed, they entreated. "She bade us retire," wrote Boispillé, "telling us the thing was settled, and that no amount of rhetoric would now persuade her. We saw her again, at three o'clock in the afternoon, a short time before the despatch of this letter—just the same thing! So we have resolved to depart on our way back on Saturday or Sunday, God helping us. I can say naught, save that this is a very poor, unfortunate lady, with a temper that is very contrary to her own good, and an enemy of her own self."

On the 28th, Mme. de Chevreuse sent her own answer direct to Richelieu: her letter was full of ironic deference. "Sir," said she to the Cardinal, "I have seen the answer you were pleased to make me by your letter to M. du Dorat. How deeply you have obliged me! And how unhappy am I to find you so good to me, and yet to remain in so much evil fortune! I pray God that some

THE DUCHESSE DE CHEVREUSE

day my services may prove to you that I am not altogether unworthy of the kindnesses I have received from you!"

Before du Dorat and Boispillé left London, they made one final effort. At all events, they said to the Duchess, would she acknowledge that she had behaved ill in the past, and that she was sorry for it now? If she was given leave to return to France in perfect freedom, would she promise to have no more intercourse, inside the frontiers or beyond them, with persons whom the King regarded with suspicion? If she was convicted of guilt, would she consent to be considered guilty? After some little reflection, Mme. de Chevreuse agreed to reply in the affirmative. Du Dorat and Boispillé then added that they themselves would vouch for the truth of her assertions to the Cardinal. Mme. de Chevreuse assented.

When the travellers reached Rueil, they explained the concession they had succeeded in obtaining. The Cardinal accepted the indirect method thus suggested to him. "We, the undersigned," the two envoys now wrote, "declare to Monseigneur the Cardinal that the Duchesse de Chevreuse sincerely acknowledges the evil conduct of which she has been guilty in the past, and repents of it with her whole heart," etc. . . . No more explicit attestation was forthcoming, and the Cardinal must e'en be content with this declaration. Louis XIII thought it would be better to give in. He would allow Mme. de Chevreuse to go to Dampierre, provided she would undertake to live there quietly, and enter into no more cabals. Richelieu himself informed the Duchess of the King's decision.

From London, whither they had returned, du Dorat and Boispillé wrote that Mme. de Chevreuse was behaving in a quite satisfactory manner. Everything was going on well: the business was apparently quite settled, all that remained to be done was the winding-up, when letters from the Duchess were delivered to du Dorat and to Richelieu. In her letter to du Dorat, she said: "I will only write you

IN ENGLAND

three lines, to bid you express to Monseigneur the Cardinal the sense I have of the kindness he has induced His Majesty to show me. I leave the rest to Boispillé, who will write you, within the next two days, in the most particular way, concerning the reasons which delay me here." To Richelieu she wrote: "Sir, I have no words wherewith to thank you in a sufficiently worthy manner for the kindness you have won for me from the King, but I have the determination it is my duty to feel, to deserve it by my very humble services. You will hear, sir, through M. du Dorat, the reasons which prevent me from going to enjoy it as soon as I should have desired, and I pray you to believe that I continue to preserve the deepest sense of the kindness you show me, and in which I have the fullest confidence."

What was the matter now? Boispillé made inquiries: the Duchess, it appeared, was hampered by difficulties about money. She was heavily in debt, and her creditors would not let her depart: it was a question, so Boispillé wrote, of paying up or letting the whole thing go. Mme. de Chevreuse wanted the Government to help her to find 12,000 *livres*. Was that all? Richelieu was not so pinched that he could not find money: he sent over 18,000 *livres*. This time every difficulty seemed cleared away.

Boispillé made his preparations for the journey: the route had been chosen—the travellers were to go by Dieppe; the governors of Dieppe and Rouen had received orders to welcome the Duchess with every sign of respect. The Queen of England had undertaken to get a ship supplied by the Government, and as this ship could not sail for another fortnight, the date of the departure from Dover had been fixed for the 13th of June. The Duchess had bidden all her farewells: she had waited on Queen Henrietta-Maria; she had written to the King of England; she had asked her husband to send her coaches and horses to meet her at Dieppe, and had requested the Abbé du

THE DUCHESSE DE CHEVREUSE

Dorat to await her there; Boispillé was counting the hours, when all of a sudden, on the 4th of June, Mme. de Chevreuse sent for him.

He found her in a state of extreme agitation. She told him she had just received two letters from Lorraine which had caused her the greatest perplexity; she held them out to him : the first, which was anonymous, informed her that if she went to France her ruin was a certain thing; she was only being coaxed back to Dampierre so that her enemies might more easily lay hands upon her. The Cardinal had said too much about her conduct with respect to Spain and Lorraine for him to allow her to go unpunished now. The second letter, which was dated from Sierck, on the 26th of May, bore the signature of the Duc de Lorraine. "I am certain," he wrote, "of the designs of the Cardinal de Richelieu, which are to offer you every imaginable thing, so as to oblige you to return to France, and then at once to cause you to perish miserably. The Marquis de Ville, who has talked both with him and with M. de Chavigny, can make you more learned on this subject, since he heard it with his own ears. I expect him every minute, and if I believed I had enough power over your mind to divert you from taking this resolution, I would go and cast myself at your feet, to make you realize your absolute destruction, and beseech you, by everything that may be most dear to you in this world, to avoid this misfortune, too cruel for the whole of this earth, and more unbearable to me than to all the rest of the world."

Boispillé exclaimed loudly : What did these letters mean ? He tried hard to nullify the effect they had produced. But the impression on the Duchess's mind had been too deep. After all, she said, the Cardinal had not given her any assurance ! As the Marquis de Ville was coming over to explain matters to her, she desired at any rate to wait and see him. "A wretched business," wrote Boispillé to Paris; and he advised Richelieu to send Mme. de Chevreuse the

IN ENGLAND

assurances for which she seemed to wish. "Remember, sir," he wrote, "if it so please you, that in the letters you have done her the honour to write to her, and which are truly full to the brim of affection and kindness, you say nothing to her as to her safety, for which she looks to you alone. I think that if it pleased your Eminence to write a word as to this, to her, or to me, it would overthrow all these counsels, past or to come."

Richelieu was irritated beyond expression. He contented himself with writing three lines, as follows, and desiring Boispillé to lay them before the Duchess: "Those who alarm Mme. de Chevreuse are in the wrong: she has nothing to fear in France; anybody who tries to make her believe to the contrary is wickedly deceiving her." Mme. de Chevreuse merely replied that she intended to wait for M. de Ville. "I have told her, and represented to her," wrote Boispillé on the 9th of June, "all the reasons which I believe led the Duke Charles to write as he did to her, which was simply to prevent her from going back on account of their own private interests. I still hope, Monseigneur, that the goodness and generosity of your Eminence will overlook all this, and pardon all these formalities, or, if I dare call them so, these tendernesses, of a mind which, I believe, only needs a little time to learn patience and gentleness." Madame de Chevreuse, for her part, wrote to du Dorat, who was then in France, on the 13th of June: "I am in the same state as Boispillé has told you, impatiently awaiting the arrival of the person he has mentioned to you (M. de Ville), to obtain a complete explanation, without which I cannot, and must not, leave this country."

So they had to wait; and they waited till the 3rd of August: then, at last, M. de Ville arrived. Mme. de Chevreuse insisted that his explanation should be given in Boispillé's own presence. M. de Ville related that in the course of the preceding winter he had travelled, on his

THE DUCHESSE DE CHEVREUSE

way from Paris, with a certain Lange, who had told him that, knowing the affection with which Mme. de Chevreuse was regarded in Lorraine, he felt it his duty to warn him that if the Duchess returned to France she was lost. Two days previously, it appeared, the Cardinal, in the course of a conversation with M. de Chavigny as to the Duchess, had declared himself exceedingly angry because that lady denied having advised the Duc de Lorraine not to treat with France, and added that he had letters of hers which formally attested the fact, "that this affair was perfectly clear, and that when Mme. de Chevreuse came back to France, they would force her to talk good French, and that if she fancied she could deceive them, she was deceiving herself!" Boispillé protested. Who had told Lange this tale? That he had not divulged. The discussion was carried on apart from Mme. de Chevreuse: no definite result was possible. M. de Ville, having consented to draw up a copy of his communication and sign it, departed on the 7th: he had formally advised the Duchess not to go back to France!

On the 9th she wrote to Richelieu, formulating her definite request for his categorical assurance as to her safety. "I very humbly entreat you, sir," she wrote, "to do me the kindness of telling me frankly whether you are so satisfied as to the past that I need not preserve the smallest reason for suspicion as regards either the business of M. de Lorraine before I left France, or other things which have happened since."

Richelieu was sick of it all. He replied on August 30 —a curt letter, in which he consented to give the fresh assurance demanded from him. "Madame," he said, "the King has thought it very extraordinary that after having received your abolition more than three months ago, just as it had been desired for you at that time, you should have made difficulties about using it as you had said you intended to do." She was being deceived, he added, by

IN ENGLAND

imaginary fears. "You are too judicious not to be aware that for nothing on earth would his Majesty grant you an abolition of a thing for which he intended to prosecute you in France, later. However, since the Sieur de Ville has tried to persuade you that there was an intention of prosecuting you for that business of M. de Lorraine, I do not fear to declare to you that the King's intention has never been, and is not, such; and that you will enjoy the benefit of your abolition in its full and complete effects, without any further mention of the negotiations with M. de Lorraine." That was clear enough: what more could she want?

Mme. de Chevreuse responded, in dilatory fashion, in a letter dated September 16. She thanked the Cardinal, "but," she added, "the apprehensions with which I have been filled have been so great that my mind has not been able to cast them off, all at once, so as to permit of my returning to France at present. You must, if you please, forgive my weakness." To du Dorat and Boispillé she wrote that she had received fresh details, which prevented her from setting off.

"I despair of inducing Mme. de Chevreuse to return," wrote the disgusted du Dorat to Richelieu on September 23, "after so many evasions and puttings off." The reasons the Duchess put forward were "ridiculous," she was asking for "leisure to rest her mind, after all the terrors which, she declares, have been inflicted upon her! She thinks minds ought to be dieted as well as bodies! That is a treatment to which hers should not be subjected, for it might very easily escape for good!" "I have neglected nothing," added Boispillé on September 24, when he had returned to France, "that might make Mme. la Duchesse de Chevreuse realize the deep obligations she owes your Eminence." Nothing moved her! "So being convinced, Monseigneur, that my presence with her was no longer necessary, I have thought your Eminence would not take

THE DUCHESSE DE CHEVREUSE

it ill that I should travel to this place." Mme. de Chevreuse was to hold her peace, and let six months roll by, before she gave the Cardinal another sign of life.

But her existence during that period was anything but inactive. Day after day despatches reached the Cardinal from London, crammed with details of the annoyances caused by her sayings and her doings. It was the Secretary of the Embassy, M. de Montreuil, in the absence of M. de Bellièvre, the Ambassador, who kept Richelieu informed. Mme. de Chevreuse was making her house the meeting-place of all those of the Cardinal's enemies who had emigrated to England—La Valette, Soubise (the Protestant leader, who had fled from France after the defeat of his co-religionists), La Vieuville (a former Minister who had fallen into disgrace, and had been tried and sentenced), Monsigot, Le Coigneux, etc. She was on the most intimate terms with the representatives of the foreign powers at war with France. M. de Ville had come back to England to recruit a thousand men who were to fight on the Continent against the troops of France. "Mme. de Chevreuse had used her credit" to aid the success of his undertaking. M. de Ville lodged in her house, sat at her table, used her coaches. Another time it was the Spanish Ambassador, the Marquis de Velada, who had gone to see Mme. de Chevreuse the moment he arrived in London: the Duchess lent him her finest coach; she went to considerable expense to do him honour. An anonymous informant, signing himself "Titus" supplied details of the splendour of this gathering. On another occasion M. de Montreuil reported the intercourse between Mme. de Chevreuse and Prince Thomas of Savoy, commanding the armies acting in Flanders against the troops of Louis XIII. The Savoyard Envoy in London, Hallot, was constantly in the Duchess's house. Even Rossetti, the Nuncio, was inveigled by her into opposing the French Government. In years to come, when Rossetti (who has

IN ENGLAND

been made a Cardinal meanwhile) is sent by the Pope to represent him at the Congress of Münster, Mazarin will put his pen through his name, with a reminder that Rossetti, when in London, "held very secret and frequent communications with the Duchesse de Chevreuse," and that the Pope's Ministers know how Mme. de Chevreuse "strove to harm the State" at that period.

Richelieu knew not what to do. His exasperation against Mme. de Chevreuse had reached the boiling-point. Boispillé relates in one of his letters that it had become impossible to mention the name of the Duchess in the Cardinal's presence, so furious did the subject make him. Was there no possible means at all of putting an end to this noxious creature's caballing, and making sure of her? Thereupon—this was in May, 1640—the Duc de Chevreuse once more offered his services: he proposed to go to England himself, and to bring his wife back with him to France by fair means or foul.

The Duke had been groaning more and more under his wife's conduct. He had stood by the Government to the utmost of his power. He had always prevented the sending over of anything the Duchess had asked for. In vain had she begged him to let her have the most humble or the most useful of her possessions: "the small wearing apparel in my cabinet, the perfume-box mounted in silver with the papers in it, at Couzières; above all, the coffer with the silver nails, and, if possible, La Porte, my tailor, with my clothes." The Duke had sent no answer. He openly complained of his wife. One day, at St. Germain, the Queen met him and asked him for news of the Duchess. He replied, with much bitterness, that he was sorry indeed that Her Majesty was preventing her from coming back. He had written over and over again to the exile, setting forth the dangers in which she was involving himself and all their house, and the difficulties in which she was placing him, even reducing him "to starvation." He had gone so

THE DUCHESSE DE CHEVREUSE

far as to send Renault, the serving-man, to her, to beg her to return. "I have learnt by Renault," wrote the Duchess in reply, "the feelings you have as to my return, and your desire to be informed as to mine. To which I will answer you very truly that I dare to say they are even greater than yours, in my longing to find myself in France, and in a position to remedy the state of our affairs, and live in peace with you and my children." Unhappily, that was not possible! Some means had yet to be discovered. "That, I swear to you, is what I daily pray God to grant me, and I do all I can to find it." M. de Chevreuse had replied stiffly that she was telling him untruths, and that she was not making any effort to get back. "I have laboured for my return as much as you, and more," answered the Duchess; "I have been so overwhelmed with various terrors that I know you would have pitied me for the anxieties in which I have lived." It was after the endless evasions and equivocations of the year 1639 and the early part of 1640, that the Duke made up his mind to join his wife in England, and bring her back on his own authority as her lord and master.

He asked Richelieu's leave. "Sir," he wrote to the Cardinal, "permit me, if it so please you, to speak to you of the despair into which the slowness of my wife's return has cast me. Having considered all the care and importunity she has caused your Eminence, her promises and her delays as to her return, none of which she has carried out, notwithstanding the entreaties I myself have addressed to her; considering your Eminence has always done me the honour of treating me with kindness, I have resolved humbly to beseech and entreat you to get me leave from the King to go to England and fetch her back, with the assurance of being honoured by the kindness of His Majesty, and your own, sir." Richelieu gave his consent. But he had not much confidence in this particular method.

IN ENGLAND

And, in fact, when, thanks to an indiscretion on the part of Auger, the Secretary to the English Embassy, the news of the Duke's intended journey reached London, a most indescribable scene took place in the Duchess's house. "Never was such agitation seen," wrote M. de Montreuil. Mme. de Chevreuse vowed she would not wait for her husband; that if he persisted in coming over, she would go away to Flanders. She waited on the King of England, to entreat him to stand by her. To calm her mind, Charles assured her that "since she had placed herself under his protection he would not allow her to be forced to go back to France." Mme. de Chevreuse sent a courier to her husband, beseeching him not to undertake the journey. The Duke replied that his only intention in going to London was to see her, and talk over their business matters with her. Why was she in such a state of alarm?

He had begun his preparations. Louis XIII had given him a letter to the King of England, passports for himself and the Duchess, a note containing the names of the persons he had better avoid while he was in London—La Valette, La Vieuville, Le Coigneux, Monsigot. Chevreuse had not a halfpenny left: he was in debt in all directions; he had asked for an advance of 12,000 crowns, and it had been granted. He was just about to depart.

When the Duchess heard of all these arrangements, she wrote her husband another letter, dated April 23. She besought him to "change his intention, which was capable," she declared, "of absolutely preventing her return to France instead of hastening it," she being firmly resolved, she added, "if you override all the reasons I have given you, and come here, to start the instant you arrive, and pass over into the countries of the King of Spain." An ultimatum and a threat!

When that letter reached M. de Chevreuse, he took up his pen, and the poor man poured out all his distress and indignation and alarm, in his answer to his wife. "I cannot

THE DUCHESSE DE CHEVREUSE

understand," he said, "on what pretext you can desire to fly when I want to go and see you, after having written you the reason for my journey, and made you so clearly understand that I have no definite object save that of seeing you and finding out the state of your affairs. I speak to you now as your husband, and one who loves you as he should, but who is beginning, too, to open his eyes and his ears. The times, our private affairs, and your behaviour, force me to this: for as for trying to make me believe you really fear my using violence to force you to return, I am quite certain you do not dream of that! Why, then, this pretence? It must be to my person alone that you have so much aversion: that is passing strange! After having assured me, this long time, that you desired to return, and when, amidst all these uncertainties, I desire to go and see you, and fetch you back, you are pleased to tell me that as soon as I arrive you will take to flight and retire into an enemy's country. How can I, in my own person, cause so great an extremity and change in your intentions as not only to make you delay them, but absolutely alter them, and so bring us both to ruin and destruction? Think well of this! Avoid your own shame and mine, rather than my person! To conclude: I cannot change my plan, and if I could, I would not; I have gone too far in this matter of my journey. I must depart: and with the promise that I shall not only be at Calais on the fourth day of next month, but I will there await news from you until the eighth, and then, if you are still in the same wise mind as that you have so often written me, and which you would have all the world believe is yours, I will not travel farther, and will wait for you in France, wherever you choose. But remember, I pray you, that you must not deceive me again! I am not a fool; I know very well what I am writing to you: I have thought about it only too much! It is a very sore thing to me to see you treat me as you do, and to see myself and our children brought

THE DUC DE CHEVREUSE
(From a contemporary painting in the Blois Museum)

IN ENGLAND

down to starvation and to the extremities to which your behaviour has reduced us, with the impending ruin of our house. I will confess to you that I am in great distress, and that I do not know to what cause I am to ascribe your behaviour, which is that of a very worthless person. Recollect, once more, that I well know what I am saying!"

M. de Chevreuse was resolved to start. He was to leave Paris on May 3, a Thursday; Friday, the 4th, would see him at Calais, as he had explained to his wife. He would cross afterwards. Just as he was departing, he received the news that his Duchess had put her threat into execution, had left England, and landed in Flanders, on Spanish territory!

She had taken her departure on Tuesday, May 1, at eleven o'clock in the morning, accompanied by the Spanish Ambassador, the Marquis de Velada; the Duc de la Valette, La Vieuville, Montague, Craft, and De Ville. By the King's order, Lord Newport had attended her as far as the Downs, in case she should meet M. de Chevreuse. Charles had presented her, as a parting gift, with a diamond worth 10,000 crowns. She had embarked at Rochester on the 5th, and on the 8th, after an alarm, had landed, with Craft, at Dunkirk, then a foreign port.

M. de Chevreuse was quite overwhelmed. He sent word at once to Chavigny, the Secretary of State: he waited on Richelieu; he handed over all the letters he had received from his wife, so terrified was he lest he should be suspected of being in the plot with her. Richelieu desired him to write to Charles I and beg the King to have the goodness not to receive the Duchess into his kingdom in future. M. de Chevreuse obeyed: he presented his request, so he declared, on bended knees and with clasped hands." Charles I replied: "Your wife being of the quality she is, and never having given me, during her stay at my Court, the smallest cause for displeasure, I do not see how I can refuse to allow her to return if she so decides. That

THE DUCHESSE DE CHEVREUSE

is a favour that all private persons may claim; how much more, then, may it be hoped for by a lady of eminent quality!" He was in the right.

Meanwhile, Mme. de Chevreuse, at Dunkirk, was suffering, from the very moment of her landing, from the miserable consequences of the false position in which she had placed herself. She had no money, and hardly a friend. She hesitated about proceeding to Brussels. But where else was she to go? In her dismay, she made up her mind to try her chance in Paris. She wrote a letter to Louis XIII, accusing her "misfortune" as the cause of what had just happened: she had gone to Dunkirk, she said, with as much regret as "I felt when I went into Spain, and with the same determination to leave it as soon as the necessity which has brought me here permits it." She made a great declaration of her respect for the King, and "the affection she owed his person and his service." It was too late. Louis XIII did not reply.

Then she wrote to Anne of Austria, appealing to her kindness, begging her to pity her in her suffering, beseeching her to influence the King in her favour. The letter was intercepted. By the King's orders, it was handed unopened to the Queen. Her Majesty refused to take it, and said, "she did not care to open any letter from a person who conducted herself as Mme. de Chevreuse did, and who was in the place where she was. She did not know what fancy or what artifice had induced that woman to write to her!"

Mme. de Chevreuse addressed herself to Richelieu. "I acknowledge," she wailed, "that at this hour I do not know what to think of my misfortunes!" She implored the Cardinal to show her mercy; she mentioned the dangers to which her husband's journey to London had exposed her, without specifying what those dangers were: she avowed "the pain it cost her to make up her mind to go further into this country": she wanted to return to France;

IN ENGLAND

she besought the "good graces of the King," the "goodwill" of the Cardinal. Richelieu, too, sent no answer.

She wrote to her husband. M. de Chevreuse ordered the servant who brought him the letter to carry it instantly, with the seal unbroken, to the Secretary of State, M. de Chavigny.

The Duchess was in despair. Nobody at Brussels seemed to desire her presence; she was advised to go to Bruges. The King of Spain and Olivares were disposed to think she had better come to Madrid. At the bottom of her heart she would rather have gone back to France. She was forsaken, without resource of any kind. "I am ruined, and as it were in a desert," she wrote; "nobody gives me any consolation, I cannot see any one without rendering them an object of suspicion, and my solitude is stuffed with a thousand mortifications."

But she was not the sort of woman to let herself be disheartened for long at a time. She would pull herself together; she would defy misfortune. What did it matter, after all? "I shall always have the satisfaction," she said proudly, "of having tried to sacrifice myself a second time for my own blood, and despised all the dangers I risked in the doing of it! Nothing makes one so bold as a good conscience! Nobody shall ever have cause to cast the smallest reproach on me, but rather the reverse: I will always behave to every one like a Christian, and a very generous one!" M. de Chevreuse, she said, was the cause of everything that had happened to her. "If the husband had not ruined everything, things might have been ordered just as people desired!" She invoked the help of Providence: "I have so recommended my intentions to God that I shall accept all that may come of them as being sent by His hand. . . . I hope, God putting His hand to this business, that all things will shortly fade away!"

It was impossible for her to stay on at Dunkirk. She went to Brussels. She busied herself there, began her old tricks. She saw the governor of the Low Countries, Don Antonio Sarmiento, circumvented him, made love to him. Though she was near her fortieth year, her charm must still have been irresistible, for—so Mazarin tells us—Antonio Sarmiento fell into her clutches. Through him she recovered her power. On November 6, 1640, M. de Montreuil reported to Bellièvre that she was offering to act as go-between for the King of Spain on one hand, and La Valette and Soubise on the other—these gentlemen having promised to raise a rebellion against Louis XIII in Guyenne, in consideration of their being allowed a thousand crowns a month. A few weeks later, she was throwing herself heart and soul into the revolt of the Comte de Soissons.

The Comte de Soissons, who had taken up arms against Louis XIII on the frontier, near Sedan, had sent one of his gentlemen, Alexandre de Campion, a young and brilliant cavalier about thirty years of age, as his envoy to win over the Duchess. Campion had not found it difficult to obtain the adhesion of Mme. de Chevreuse. She wrote to Olivares, she swept Don Antonio Sarmiento into the business; she helped Campion to raise troops and to find officers for them. The sudden close of the undertaking is a matter of history. Soissons was killed on the battlefield of Marfée, in the moment of victory. "I was so persuaded," wrote Campion to the Duchess on July 21, 1641, "of the sorrow the death of M. le Comte would cause you, that even if you had not testified it in your letter, I should have believed in it none the less. The interests of all those to whom Monseigneur the Cardinal bears ill will were so bound up with his, that as many illustrious and unhappy persons lose all their hope in losing him, and as of these you are the chief, you lose in proportion to the advantage you would have gained by his victory."

"You are the chief of all those to whom the Cardinal bears ill-will." Campion was right! Till Richelieu

IN ENGLAND

breathed his last, the Duchess was to continue his inveterate enemy, and obstinately to adhere to her refusal to return to France: she was never to see his face again.

In a Memorandum, tinged with melancholy, drawn up by the Cardinal on June 15, 1640, he demonstrates to the King that there is no hope of peace with external enemies, the Spaniards being determined not to conclude any treaty, and Mme. de Chevreuse having set forth to them all the reasons likely to make them adhere to this resolve. He sums these reasons up: A sick monarch, weary of the war; an invalid prime minister, who has but a short time to live; and, when both Sovereign and Cardinal shall have passed away, the return of all the exiles, and France a prey to disorders in which the Spaniards will surely find their account. Richelieu was a true prophet!

Mme. de Chevreuse was resolved to await the realization of his prediction. She was not to await it long. On December 2, 1642, after a few weeks' illness, the Cardinal, worn out in body, exhausted by prolonged bad health, drew his last breath.

CHAPTER VIII

THE DEATH OF LOUIS XIII: THE RETURN OF MADAME DE CHEVREUSE

Animosity of Louis XIII against Mme. de Chevreuse—The King's Death—Return of Mme. de Chevreuse—Her Intrigues: The "Importants"—The plot against Mazarin—Mme. de Chevreuse in exile —Her underhand dealings—Her flight into Flanders—1643-47.

As long as Richelieu lived, and Louis XIII, worn by suffering, grew weaker and weaker, the contemporary conviction that the monarch was the Cardinal's prisoner, a mere toy in his Minister's hands, grew continually stronger. The King's attitude, on the very morrow of the Cardinal's death, may well have undeceived it.

To the great surprise of Louis XIII, St. Germain was invaded, the moment the breath was out of the Cardinal's body, by a host of suitors, all convinced that everything in the kingdom would now be changed, that Richelieu's friends were to be driven out, fresh Ministers summoned to power, the exiles recalled, the prisoners set free, and all the victims of the late régime reinstated in their dignities and honours. The King grew angry. He was well aware of the theory which represented him to be a "sluggard king," ruled with absolute power by a "mayor of the palace." All that had been seen in print, often enough, in the libels published during the fifteen years of his reign: his own brother had written it to him, in disrespectful letters which their disputes had made public property. A score of times Louis had endeavoured, directly or indirectly, to assert the contrary: no attention had ever been paid to his denials.

He now began by making it known all over the king-

THE DEATH OF LOUIS XIII

dom, in letters addressed to the Governor of every province, that the Cardinal's death did not in any sense modify the policy of the Government: the Minister's former collaborators retained their offices, the exiles remained in banishment; as for the suitors, His Majesty announced that "he would send those who had the boldness to speak to him of banished persons, prisoners, and other wretches, to the Bastille." One of his former favourites, Barradas, fancying he had only been sacrificed to a personal antipathy on Richelieu's part, caused his entreaty for leave to return to the Louvre to be submitted to the King, and Louis XIII "curtly replied that he (Barradas) had better stay quietly at home, and if he should need his services he would let him know it." Wearied at last by the influx of people, Louis XIII left Saint-Germain and betook himself to Versailles, where etiquette permitted of his living alone, far from the Court and Court intriguers. Goulas thus sums it up: "All the persons who presented themselves in the hope of serving their friends or relations who had been persecuted under the late Government, or of finding their advantage in the death of his Eminence, were extremely disappointed, and as the same Ministers remained in office, and followed the same maxims, there was no sign that the Cardinal de Richelieu was dead, and that fortune was likely to disturb and confuse the affairs of France."

Less than any other person was Mme. de Chevreuse warranted in the hope the King's displeasure might be softened. She knew how deeply he disliked her, she knew too well how many and various were the elements that went to make up his personal animosity against her. She thought it wiser to put no request forward. In the course of the few months he had to live, Louis XIII was to give public proof of his inveterate rage and hostility against her.

Even while his vital powers slowly failed, consumed as he was by a slow decline, his mind, clear and resolute as ever,

THE DUCHESSE DE CHEVREUSE

was haunted as by a fixed idea—the thought of Mme. de Chevreuse. In his talks with Mazarin, with Anne of Austria, with Chavigny, he constantly referred to her, and spoke of her "hotly, saying that confusion, disorder and misfortune would never be absent from the place where the said lady might be, and that wherever she had gone she had done fatal harm!" Not only did he refuse to admit he could possibly be asked to allow Mme. de Chevreuse to return to France, but he was careful to say, over and over again, that she must not be allowed, at any price, to come back after his own death. He laid the greatest stress on this, asserting that no one knew better than himself what complications that woman was capable of causing: they must protect themselves against her "like the plague." In one of his letters Mazarin, recalling this advice, sadly writes: "The late King was inspired by God for the good of this kingdom!"

And it was this particular anxiety, in part, which caused Louis XIII so much perplexity as to the arrangements he should make for his son's Regency. One of his reasons for refusing to leave Anne of Austria full authority as Regent was that he feared the Duchess might recover her former influence over the Queen's mind, and foresaw the lamentable results, from the political point of view, of the power of a creature concerning whose intrigues with the Spaniards he was only too well informed. "He could not make up his mind," writes La Rochefoucald, "to proclaim the Queen Regent, having always suspected her of a secret understanding with Spain, and not doubting that it (the understanding) would be still further fomented by Mme. de Chevreuse." Mme. de Chevreuse, to carry her own ideas through in the Council Chamber, would certainly demand the recall of Châteauneuf to the Ministry: so the necessity for keeping Châteauneuf at a distance was bound up, in the mind of Louis XIII, with that of leaving the Duchess in her exile.

THE DEATH OF LOUIS XIII

Thus when, on April 21, 1643, just three weeks before he actually passed away, the King, feeling death close upon him, at last drew up the Declaration whereby he refused Anne of Austria sovereign authority as Regent, and nominated the Council which was to rule the State in the name of his infant son, Louis XIV, he took care that the exclusion of Mme. de Chevreuse from the kingdom and the continued absence of Châteauneuf should be specifically mentioned in it. "Seeing it is our intention," he wrote, "to provide for all the subjects which might in any manner disturb the good settlement we here make, to preserve the peace and quietness of our realm, our knowledge of the evil conduct of the Lady Duchess of Chevreuse and the artifices she has hitherto used to make quarrels within our kingdom, the factions and intelligences she keeps up outside it, and with our enemies, leads us to judge it wise to forbid her—as we do now forbid her—to come into our kingdom during the war; and our will is that, even when peace has been made and carried out, she shall not return into this kingdom save by the order of the said Lady Regent, with the consent of the said Council, and nevertheless on condition that she shall never make her dwelling, nor be, in any place near the Court, or the said Lady Queen."

And as to Châteauneuf: "Seeing that for great and important reasons, affecting the welfare of our service, we have been constrained to deprive the Sieur de Châteauneuf of the office of Keeper of the Seals of France, and to have him taken to the Castle of Angoulême, where he has remained until this present time, according to our orders, our will and pleasure are that the said Sieur de Châteauneuf shall remain in the same state, and in the same said Castle of Angoulême, until after peace shall have been concluded and carried out, on condition, nevertheless, that he shall only then be set at liberty by the order of the said Lady Regent and with the consent of the said Council,

THE DUCHESSE DE CHEVREUSE

which will give orders concerning the place to which he shall retire, either within the kingdom, or beyond the borders of the kingdom, as may be thought most expedient."

Mme. de Motteville, in her Memoirs, and Mazarin, in one of his letters, tell us how, while the rough draft of this Declaration was being read aloud to the dying King, he lay listening, in silence and with closed eyes. When the reader reached the passage dealing with Mme. de Chevreuse, Louis roused himself, and lifted himself up in the bed, with a feverish light in his eyes; then, when the last words had been spoken, he cried, with anger in his voice, "That is the devil! There! That is the devil!" Goulas adds that M. de Chevreuse, who was in the adjoining room, was much distressed by the King's words, and Louis sent him a message to the effect that he had the greatest personal esteem for him, and "testified that he had always served him well."

On May 14, 1643, Louis XIII died.

Anne of Austria, advised by Mazarin, caused the King's will to be set aside by Parliament, laid hands on the sovereign power as Regent which her husband had refused to give her, and set out to rule the kingdom. At the solemn session held to proclaim the Parliament's decision, the little King, "a baby in a bib, was carried in by the Duc de Chevreuse, his Great Chamberlain." Was this a portent? M. de Chevreuse was full of hope. If the new Government, thought he, had paid so little heed to the late King's wishes on the point which had lain nearest his heart, surely it was still less likely to insist on less important injunctions, such as that connected with the exile of his Duchess! M. de Chevreuse was mistaken!

When Anne of Austria took up the Regency she assumed the reins of power with a heart that was far from brave. She knew nothing at all about State affairs, and besides, "her lack of confidence in herself and her humility

THE DEATH OF LOUIS XIII

were so great," writes Mme. de Motteville, "that she could not be otherwise than convinced of her own incapacity for government." Convinced himself as to this incapacity, Louis XIII, on his death-bed, had earnestly charged her not to part with the Minister he was leaving with her—Mazarin. An Italian by birth, noted by Richelieu and by the King himself on account of his remarkable qualities as a politician, his immense experience of business, and his exceedingly sound sense, Mazarin had devoted himself to the service of France. Louis XIII, anxious to leave a statesman behind him who—amidst frivolous and carping courtiers, and a public opinion that varied from day to day, and was apt to call out for peace at any price—would realize the object of the policy of the country and carry that policy through, had made Mazarin a Cardinal and his Minister, had initiated him into his own views, had insisted on his standing Godfather to the future Louis XIV, so as to force on him certain duties as the boy's helper and protector which would bind him closer to the child, and had extracted a promise from him that he would never abandon Anne of Austria or the young King. Mazarin had given his word. Anne of Austria, in her ignorance and her alarm, could not do otherwise than accept the statesman thus recommended to her; she continued him in his office, and learning as she did, day by day, to value his powers, she kept him about her, faithfully, till he died. History and her own contemporaries have been surprised by this fidelity. They have sought to explain it by asserting that the two were bound together by an affair of the heart, and that in the end they were married. The correspondence of Anne of Austria and Mazarin, which proves the exceedingly lively friendship and close understanding that existed between them, has seemed to confirm this explanation, put forward originally by various pamphleteers. But, mysterious though some passages in these letters are, as a matter of fact they supply

THE DUCHESSE DE CHEVREUSE

no decisive proof. The silence on this subject of all those who approached the Queen and her Minister most nearly, whether as enemies or friends, strengthens our doubt. As yet we have no clear reason for believing there was any feeling between Anne of Austria and Mazarin beyond that affectionate friendship and perfect mutual understanding which naturally grows up out of the necessity of sharing daily duties.

Now Mazarin, who had spent many months in close intercourse with Louis XIII and Richelieu, knew how the King had hated Mme. de Chevreuse. In his own hand we shall find, in later days—and how much more richly deserved—the very same complaints against the Duchess! Mme. de Chevreuse could not reckon on any goodwill on the part of the new Minister. Luckily for her, Mazarin's nature was neither adamant, like that of the dead Cardinal, nor inexorable, like that of the late King. A foreigner, with few friends, and little prestige, his cue was to wear his adversaries out instead of breaking them down, like his mighty predecessor; he must be supple, conciliating. He has been accused of cowardice: Ritz wrote of him: "On the steps of the throne, whence Richelieu, the harsh and terrible, had crushed, rather than ruled, the human race, we saw a successor who was gentle, mild, who asked for nothing, who was grieved to the heart because his dignity forbade him to humble himself in the sight of all men, as he would fain have done!" The Minister's foes were to turn his weakness and lack of energy to the best advantage. The first to benefit by them was Mme. de Chevreuse.

The dawn of the Regency was full of promise. This time the reaction which had failed to appear when Richelieu died was really taking place. Anne of Austria was said to be very kind-hearted. The Queen and Mazarin, not feeling strong enough to stand against the reaction, began to give way. "All those who had been beyond

THE DEATH OF LOUIS XIII

the frontiers of the kingdom," writes Lenet, "came back, one after the other, and at that poor Prince's funeral (Louis XIII), we beheld all the people who had been banished, hung, broken on the wheel, beheaded, or thrown into prison!" In the eyes of the public the Government of the Regency seemed a Government of reparation. The victims of the previous reign were all hurrying back. Mme. de Chevreuse was quite sure she might come back too!

But her dignity demanded that she should not do it too quickly. Now that her old friend Anne of Austria, whose sorrows she had shared for so many years, either as confidant or accomplice, for whom she had suffered so much, and endured all the severities of her long exile, was sovereign mistress of the realm, she owed her a brilliant reception, at least! Who, as Mme. de Motteville puts it, "had reigned" like her "in the Queen's heart, and through all her disgrace had kept up her intercourse with her, and had appeared to possess her friendship more completely?" But Mme. de Chevreuse was deceiving herself.

Towards the end of the life of Louis XIII the Queen's feelings for Mme. de Chevreuse had undergone a change. Was it as a matter of prudence that she began, in Richelieu's presence, to express hostility to the Duchess? Once already she had refused, and in somewhat scornful language, to accept a letter from her friend. On July 28, 1642, Chavigny wrote to Richelieu: "The Queen has carefully inquired from me whether it is true that Mme. de Chevreuse is coming back, and has intimated to me that she would be grieved to see her shortly in France again, that she knew her for what she really was, and commanded me to beg your Eminence from her, if you desire to do something for Mme. de Chevreuse, to do it without allowing her to return to France. I assured Her Majesty she should have satisfaction on this head." And again on August 12: "The Queen protests that not only will she

THE DUCHESSE DE CHEVREUSE

not permit Mme. de Chevreuse to come near her, but that she is resolved, as on her own salvation, never again to allow any person to say one word to her against her duty." Was the Cinq-Mars business, in which Mme. de Chevreuse was suspected of having had a hand, and thus, possibly, the Queen as well, the cause of these prudent assertions? That may have been, but far more probably Anne of Austria, as she grew older, as her experience widened and her intelligence matured, was beginning to realize the frivolity and inconsistency of character of the woman who had led her to play parts so unworthy of herself. She came to the conclusion that the influence exercised over her had been disastrous, and made up her mind to free herself from it.

When, after the death of Louis XIII, she took up the reins of power, her anxiety as to her responsibilities, the gravity of mind resulting from the habit of exercising power, a clearer appreciation of real political necessities, strengthened feelings which had already taken firm root in her heart. Mme. de Chevreuse found her former crony had become a Princess to whom her return to France was no more welcome than to Richelieu or Louis XIII: and in this feeling she was approved and encouraged by Mazarin.

Amongst the friends of the Duchess, Marsillac—la Rochefoucauld—was the first to realize the change in the Queen's views. He had remarked the coldness of the Regent's manner whenever Mme. de Chevreuse was mentioned to her. He tried to obtain an explanation, and Anne of Austria made no difficulty about declaring to him that she still regarded the Duchess with affection, but that after the late King's express orders that she should not be allowed to return to France, she found it very difficult to grant her permission to do so. And, she added, with some hesitation, that "as she (the Queen) had no taste now for the amusements that had bound them together in their youth, she feared she might appear changed to her."

THE DEATH OF LOUIS XIII

Much astonished, La Rochefoucauld argued the question. In the course of the conversation, Anne of Austria went so far as to say "that she knew by her own experience how well able Mme. de Chevreuse was to disturb the repose of her Regency"; that she was sure to plot against Mazarin just as she had plotted against Richelieu, that she would make endless difficulties for the Government. La Rochefoucauld tried to defend his friend: he pleaded her cause eagerly. "I pointed out to her," he writes, "what confusion and surprise so unexpected a change would cause in the public mind and among her own old servants, when they saw her first marks of severity fall on Mme. de Chevreuse. I set forth the fidelity of her attachment to her, and the long duration of the misfortunes it had entailed on her; I besought her to consider the levity of which she herself would be thought capable, and the interpretation that would be put on that levity. The conversation was long and stormy." There was something in the arguments put before her, and Anne of Austria was sorely perplexed. If everybody else was to come back, how could she, indeed, keep out Mme. de Chevreuse, whose former friendship with the Regent was a matter of common knowledge? "Ah!" cried the poor Queen to one of her ladies, Mme. de Fruges, "I was much happier at Saint-Germain, where I had nothing to do with State affairs, for I understand nothing about governing, and yet govern I must! Still, I trust to God to help me, since He has given me good intentions, and a very well-disposed Minister, full of wisdom and impartiality."

Just at that moment the position of that same Minister was beginning to cause her serious alarm. A most threatening opposition was rising up against him. The Duc de Vendôme's son, François, Duc de Beaufort, a young fellow of eight-and-twenty, presumptuous, thoughtless, passionate, was attacking him fiercely. Thanks to the name he bore, and the power and splendour of his family,

THE DUCHESSE DE CHEVREUSE

he had succeeded in gathering a dangerous group of partisans about him. Anne of Austria grew anxious. The friends of Mme. de Chevreuse took advantage of the situation to point out to the Queen, and to Mazarin, that there was a method of counterbalancing the too great influence wielded by the Vendôme Princes—this was to use the Guise-Lorraine Princes against them. Now, through Mme. de Chevreuse, the Regent might lay her hand on these! Let her bring back the Duchess, and she would stand by the Government. Thus, the return of the exile was becoming a political necessity. Anne of Austria wavered, she knew not what to do.

At all events she would write to Mme. de Chevreuse. She advised her, vaguely, to live, when she did come back to Paris, "in good understanding" with the Cardinal. Mazarin, on his part, sent Lord Montague with a somewhat clumsy offer to the Duchess of any sum of money she might need to pay off her debts. "He hoped there would be a close friendship between her and him." Here was a change, indeed, and more—these were advances! Mme. de Chevreuse felt some surprise. She had been informed that neither the Regent nor the Cardinal had at first been favourably disposed towards her. This sudden right-about filled her with satisfaction, but it puzzled her, too. So they wanted to make use of her! On the other hand, she had been warned not to trust the Cardinal: her friends, she had been told, had already declared themselves against the Minister: she must not leave them in the lurch. And besides, Mazarin was certainly playing some deceitful game: he was on the best terms with Richelieu's family, and the Duchess loathed them all. Alexandre de Campion, who was still her close friend, advised her to decide nothing, to wait, to see for herself: "The advice I take the liberty of giving you on this subject," he wrote, "is that you should make no final decision till you have seen the Queen, according to whose feelings you will have the

THE DEATH OF LOUIS XIII

joy of guiding your conduct." On this advice Mme. de Chevreuse resolved to act.

She now had virtual leave to return to Paris. She begged Alexandre de Campion to come as far as Péronne to meet her, desired La Rochefoucauld to join her at Roye, and then, Boispillé, the faithful steward, having brought her all she wanted for her journey, she set out.

She left Brussels on June 6, 1643. Her coach was followed by twenty more, filled with ladies and gentlemen, Spaniards and Flemings, who desired to do her honour by attending her a few leagues on her way. She reached Mons, where she traversed the lines of the Spanish army. Passing through Condé, on the 9th, she arrived at Cambrai. By Mazarin's orders she was received at every halt with the greatest respect. Governors of castles and governors of towns went to meet her a league outside each fortress, and attended her for another league beyond it. Monsieur d'Hocquincourt, who had gone to receive her on the frontier, conducted her to Péronne; here the Duc de Chaulnes and his Duchess entertained her splendidly. Thence Mme. de Chevreuse travelled to Roye, where she found La Rochefoucauld waiting for her, and likewise Montague, sent once again by Mazarin to make her "all the advances which might draw her into his friendship and his interests." She and La Rochefoucauld held a long conference. He warned her that she would find great changes at Court: he advised her to follow the Queen's lead, to get herself into the Cardinal's good books, to accept any offers he might make her, if she wished them to be continued. Mazarin, he declared, was not guilty of any crime: he had had nothing to do with the violent measures taken by Richelieu: he was almost the only man who knew anything about foreign politics. As for thinking she would lead the Queen as she had done in old times, she must put that idea out of her head. "Mme. de Chevreuse," writes La Rochefoucauld, "assured me she was

THE DUCHESSE DE CHEVREUSE

resolved to follow my advice in every particular." Her counsellor had perhaps made her realize that what he said to her was said in the Queen's name.

From Roye, on the 13th, Mme. de Chevreuse went to Versine. On the 14th, ten years after she had left the city, she was in Paris! Her return took the proportions of an event! Everybody talked about it. Crowds of people went to the house in the Rue St. Thomas du Louvre to greet the Duchess. In the *Gazette* we read: "The great procession of continual visitors from the Court, which makes the great spaces of her hotel seem all too small, does not fill any of us with so deep an admiration as the remark made that the fatigues of her long journeys, and the effects of the severity of her fortunes have not brought about the smallest change in her natural magnanimity, nor, which is still more extraordinary, in her beauty!" Mazarin's permission for the insertion of this notice in the "official" newspaper of that period proves the importance he attached to the co-operation of the Duchess. He stood in need of it!

The struggle between the Cardinal and the Beaufort-Vendôme party had, in fact, taken evident shape. On each side the adversaries were reckoning on help from Mme. de Chevreuse. "The Court was so divided," says La Rochefoucauld, "that the return of Mme. de Chevreuse was being waited for to decide everything: she was not looked on as a person who would be satisfied with supporting one side, but as one who would certainly destroy whichever side was the least connected with her." The Duchess estimated her own power very highly. In spite of the counsels given her by La Rochefoucauld, she was persuaded that once she was back with the Queen she would recover her former influence, be told all about public affairs, and called on to give her advice. These pretensions disturbed Anne of Austria's mind. And further, "not knowing," as d'Estrées tells us, "what engagements the Duchess might still be under to the Spaniards, from whose

THE DEATH OF LOUIS XIII

company she was so lately come," the Regent was quite determined to maintain the greatest reserve in her dealings with her former friend.

Wherefore, when Mme. de Chevreuse went to the Louvre to pay her duty to her sovereign, she had a most chilly reception. La Châtre tells us that after a few civil words, Anne of Austria, looking somewhat uncomfortable, explained to the Duchess that "the allies of France might become suspicious if they knew her to be with her so soon after her return from Flanders, and that for this reason she must take a little journey into the country"—to Dampierre! The Duchess was amazed. After a certain amount of hesitation she replied that she was ready to obey, "but that she besought the Queen to recollect that the whole of Europe knew she had been persecuted for her love of Her Majesty, and that she would perhaps be doing herself an injury if she sent her away so quickly"; she entreated the Queen to ask the opinion of the Cardinal, who was present. Mazarin, thus tackled, did not dare to advise the Queen to persist.

This first meeting had been unsatisfactory. As a matter of fact, the two ladies hardly recognized each other. Mme. de Chevreuse "no longer found the Queen as she had left her; and as a consequence of this change the Queen, on her side, no longer found in her the charms which had delighted her in former days." After a period of dissimulation, Mme. de Chevreuse declared herself openly against Mazarin. The plot was thickening!

She put herself into communication with the Beaufort party, and was soon informed of all that party's interests and ambitions. Greatly distressed, Mazarin went to her, questioned her: what did she really want? He was ready to do anything to be agreeable to her! Would she like 20,000 francs? Or 200,000? Mme. de Chevreuse refused; she held forth about the complaints and claims of her friends: the Duc de Vendôme wanted the Admiralty and

THE DUCHESSE DE CHEVREUSE

the Governorship of Brittany, which Richelieu had taken from him; the Duc d'Épernon wanted to be reinstated in his offices; M. de Marsillac wanted to be Governor of the Havre. But all these demands were dangerous, expostulated Mazarin : to give away the governship of the Havre he must take it from Richelieu's heirs; to please Vendôme he would have to make the Duc de Brézé, another of the late Cardinal's relations, resign the Admiralty. Well, he would do his best! And Brienne, who carried out the negotiations, did attain a measure of success. Then Mme. de Chevreuse demanded the release of Châteauneuf, and his appointment to the Ministry. This time Mazarin gave her a flat refusal : nothing would induce him to consent to Châteauneuf's return. "He plainly showed the Queen," says Goulas, "the inconveniences to which she would expose herself if she summoned Châteauneuf to the Council Board."

Then Mme. de Chevreuse, emboldened by Mazarin's apparent humility, and by the concessions she had already obtained, took a high tone. She grew impatient : she ventured to speak to the Queen, "complaining of the Cardinal, and expressing herself in terms which led the Regent to suspect she had come back persuaded she still had full power over her mind." Anne of Austria was much displeased. She, too, was resolved Châteauneuf should not come back. There was thunder in the air! Mazarin, like his predecessor, was sick and tired of the the Duchess. "You are most happy!" he said, later, to the Spanish Minister, Don Luis de Haro. "In your country, as in all others, you have two sorts of women, an abundance of coquettes, and very few good women : the first think of nothing but pleasing their lovers, the second of nothing but pleasing their husbands; in both cases their only ambition is for luxury and vanity. But our women, on the contrary, whether they be prudes or light women, old or young, clever or fools, all want to interfere

THE DEATH OF LOUIS XIII

in everything! An honest woman would not sleep with her husband, nor a loose one with her lover, unless he had first told her something about the affairs of the State. They must know everything, see everything, be told everything, and what is worse, they must do everything and muddle everything. We have some here who daily throw us into a greater confusion than ever there was in Babylon!"

The reason for which Mme. de Chevreuse insisted so much on Châteauneuf's return was not only on account of the personal interests of her accomplices: she had certain theories as to general politics which she proposed to realize, thanks tó the return to power of the former Keeper of the Seals. Now these theories were neither more nor less than peace at any price with Spain, and a reconciliation with the House of Austria—in other words, a complete reversal of the policy of Richelieu.

Châteauneuf, after his ten years of vegetation in his prison at Angoulême—whence, on March 23, 1643, he had written to Chavigny concerning his great longing to "leave the rough and miserable condition in which he was kept there, at an advanced age, and full of sicknesses which left him no peace," had been set at liberty early in the Regency, and allowed to live in his own house at Montrouge, near Paris: he kept very quiet indeed.

Mme. de Chevreuse opened her campaign. She began by praising the former Minister's qualities to the Queen: she talked about his "lengthened business experience; he was firm and decided," she declared; "he cared for the State, and was more fitted than any other man to re-establish the old form of government, the destruction of which Cardinal de Richelieu had begun." Anne of Austria gave her evasive answers. By this time she was deliberately putting aside whatever Mme. de Chevreuse asked her to do, while Mazarin amused the lady "with submissive and flattering words." Mme. de Chevreuse lost her patience.

THE DUCHESSE DE CHEVREUSE

"Nothing," she said over and over again, "was being done for her nor for her friends, and the Cardinal's power was growing greater every day." The civilities Mazarin heaped on her were nothing but "artifices." She made noisy complaints. "She expressed her dissatisfaction to the Queen," writes La Rochefoucauld, "and with her complaints she always mingled something sharp and scornful about the Cardinal's personal weaknesses." She certainly had immense confidence in her own strength.

This strength had its root in the power her friends of the Beaufort-Vendôme party claimed to possess. The members of this party were derisively nicknamed "The Importants." They thought themselves masters of the position. But a very strong opposition was rising up against them. When Mme. de Chevreuse had demanded the recall of Châteauneuf, the Princesse de Condé, by birth a Montmorency, who had never forgiven the former Keeper of the Seals his death-sentence on her brother, the Duc Henri de Montmorency, at whose trial he had presided, had made a fierce attack on the Duchess and her partisans. Her daughter, the brilliant Duchesse de Longueville, who was to play so active a part in the intrigues of the Fronde, shared her mother's indignation. Mazarin was overjoyed: here were allies! The Condé family poured out the vials of its wrath on Mme. de Chevreuse: its members complained of her to the Queen; she was an intriguing woman, they cried, as dangerous to the Regent as she had been to the late King, a criminal! Willingly enough, Anne of Austria listened. She was realizing the extent of the justification for the late King's hatred of Mme. de Chevreuse, and the necessity for the measures he had taken respecting her.

Informed as to the Government's arrangements, or ignorant of them, we know not which, Mme. de Chevreuse, either as a deliberate move in her tactics, or out of sheer imprudence, made herself twice as troublesome as before.

THE DEATH OF LOUIS XIII

In June and July, Mazarin set down in his notebooks that, thanks to her, the Vendôme party was gaining adherents: she had brought over the Duc de Guise, who had consented to act as mediator in the hope of attracting the Duc d'Elbeuf. The Cardinal had also been warned that the Duchess was preparing the way for the realization of her projects, and to that end was thinking of buying an island on the Breton coast, where she might find a refuge in case of danger: she was actually negotiating with Mme. d'Assérac for the purchase of Belle-Île; Campion was to be governor of the island; she was to proceed there with her lover, Don Antonio Sarmiento; with the Vendôme Princes masters of the Admiralty and of Brittany, Belle-Île would be a safe resort. Mazarin was resolved to put a stop at all costs to these arrangements. His notebooks prove him to have been very much taken up, at this moment, by the Duchess's behaviour: he mentions her constantly, notes her smallest actions, grows angry, breaks out into expressions of rage and impatience: "We must get rid of this Chevreuse, who sets up a thousand plots!" he says. "This woman will be the ruin of France! All this will grow worse and worse as time goes on, till at last there will be no possibility of curing it!" But what was to be done? At one moment the Cardinal, thoroughly disheartened, thought of giving up the struggle, and leaving France himself. But circumstances were leading up to a crisis that was to give him a chance of using strong measures, and the difficulty was thus to be solved.

Court life had begun again, more brilliant than ever: banquets and festive gatherings followed one upon the other in quick succession, all of them crowded with numerous and busy guests, frivolous enough as far as their outward appearance went, but whose passions, well alight, were none the less smouldering only just below the surface. The hatred between the Duchess and the Condé family grew deeper every day. The most trivial incident

THE DUCHESSE DE CHEVREUSE

might cause a scene at any moment. The incident did crop up, thanks to Mme. de Montbazon, step-mother of Mme. de Chevreuse.

Madame de Montbazon was then a woman of thirty-three. Tall, well-proportioned, flexible in figure, with a bosom, so Mme. de Motteville used to say, "modelled like that the most gifted sculptors shew us as having been possessed by the ancient Greek and Roman beauties"; "fine-looking, of a noble stature and an exquisite carriage," adds Goulas—Mme. de Montbazon was one of the most admired beauties of the Court. She was not reckoned intelligent, it is true—she was vain, haughty, full of disdain; but she had "a free and bold manner which was natural to her," and which was considered most attractive. Very much sought after, a great coquette, many men had fallen in love with her, and she had been kind to them all. "Never," says Retz, "was there a woman of so easy-going a composition. . . . I never saw anybody who, in the midst of vice, had preserved so little respect for virtue." She had lived with Gaston d'Orléans, she had lived with her own husband's son-in-law, the Duc de Chevreuse: at that moment she was living with Beaufort.

Exceedingly intimate with Mme. de Chevreuse, her senior by ten years, the Duchesse de Montbazon, for Beaufort's sake, was one of her step-daughter's most eager partisans. No other was so aggressive, nor so quarrelsome. It was in her house that the incident took place.

One day in August, 1643, not being very well, she was receiving her friends in her bedroom. A number of people had come to see her, and amongst them Comte Maurice de Coligny. Some anonymous letters of a passionate nature, written in a feminine hand, and filled with reproaches, threats of rupture, and expressions of a tender and melancholy affection, fell out of this gentleman's pocket, and were picked up in the room. M. de Coligny was believed to be the lover of Mme. de Longueville, and

THE DEATH OF LOUIS XIII

Mme. de Montbazon concluded these love-letters had come from the Duc de Condé's fascinating sister: this was perfectly untrue. They were proved, at a later period, to have been written by Mme. de Fouquerolles, and addressed to M. de Maulévrier. Beaufort published the incident abroad: he carried the story from house to house, there was a world of talk about it. The Condé family rose up in wrath, protested fiercely against the calumny, accused Mme. de Montbazon and Mme. de Chevreuse of having slandered a member of their house. Anne of Austria, thoroughly annoyed, sent for the letters, showed them to Mme. de Longueville's friends, convinced herself they had not been written by the Duchess, and caused them to be burnt. She forced Mme. de Montbazon to apologize, and formal communications of the most curt and chilly kind were exchanged between the ladies—somewhat stiff on Mme. de Montbazon's side, and haughty on that of the Condé Princess.

Now very shortly after this episode, Mme. de Chevreuse was to entertain the Queen at a "collation"—an afternoon lunch—in an exceedingly fashionable garden, which a man of the name of Renard had planted at one end of the Tuileries, and made, as Guy Joly tells us, "a delightful retreat, where people of the highest quality went to divert themselves." Mme. de Montbazon was of the party, and helped her step-daughter to do the honours. Anne of Austria arrived, accompanied by the Princesse de Condé, who had only consented to go with the Queen because she had been assured Mme. de Montbazon was ill and would not be present at the gathering. When she saw the Duchess she would herself have retired, but Anne of Austria begged her to remain. Pressed by the Princess, the Queen sent a message requesting Mme. de Montbazon would be good enough to help her out of the difficulty by taking her departure. This Mme. de Montbazon refused to do. In great displeasure, the Queen took her leave, and

THE DUCHESSE DE CHEVREUSE

a large proportion of the lady guests followed her example: there was a regular scandal.

Great was the perturbation that ensued! The affront had been a public one! All the "Importants" took sides with Mme. de Montbazon and Mme. de Chevreuse. Anne of Austria commanded Mme. de Montbazon to go into exile at the Castle of Rochefort-en-Yveline, which belonged to her husband. This piece of severity made matters worse. Excitement reached the boiling-point, and the most excited person of all was Beaufort. Bold, "clumsy-minded and false, with an intelligence much below the average" (thus does Retz describe him), Beaufort was "an uncivil man," with "coarse manners, an envious creature, spiteful and unreliable." The members of the cabal poured forth threats innumerable. The sole responsibility for everything that had happened was cast on Mazarin, and the whole attack was levelled at him. Secret meetings took place at the Hôtel de Guise: Beaufort, the Guise Princes, a certain M. de Beaupuis, son of the Comte de Maillé, the two Campion brothers, Henri and Alexandre, attended them. A spy named Carré, a Dominican monk, who had bombarded Richelieu with his reports, in the Cardinal's lifetime, kept Mazarin informed.

The outcome of all these secret councils was a deliberate plan to carry Mazarin off and put him to death. From what Henri de Campion says in his Memoirs, the idea of this attempt appears to have originated with Mme. de Chevreuse: she mentioned it to Beaufort, he agreed to her proposal, and then secured the assistance of Beaupuis and Alexandre de Campion. The theory the Duchess put forward was that Mazarin was re-establishing Richelieu's old tyranny in a more autocratic and merciless form, and that the only way to get the better of the Minister was to take his life. When Alexandre de Campion had promised his adhesion, an attempt was made to secure that of his brother Henri. He refused: he simply was being asked, he

THE DEATH OF LOUIS XIII

pointed out, to commit a murder : it was a vengeance taken on Mazarin for Richelieu's violent measures : they were jealous of Mazarin. Seeing how Henri held out, Beaufort and Alexandre began to hesitate. Mme. de Chevreuse raised their drooping spirits. Henri ended by giving in, on condition the Cardinal's life was not attempted, and he himself should not be expected to do anything except defend Beaufort in case of necessity. The other conspirators pretended to accept his terms. Beaufort also enlisted the services of the captain of his guard, De Lie, his equerry, Brillet, and a few resolute fellows—Ganseville, Héricourt, and Avancourt.

All the details were planned out. Some evening, when the Cardinal, as was his wont, drove out of the Hôtel de Clèves, attended by a mere handful of lackeys—five or six at most—and some churchman or other, the coach was to be attacked. Servants posted in all the neighbouring taverns were to watch and give the signal. The conspirators would crowd round the coach in one of the small, narrow, ill-lighted, deserted streets that lay round the King's palace; Brillet and Ganseville were to stop the horses, Héricourt and Avancourt were to open the coach-doors and strike, Beaufort and the rest, who would stay behind it on their horses, were to prevent any interference from outsiders. Once the work was done, everybody was to make himself scarce. Mme. de Chevreuse was to remain at Court, to appease the Queen's rage, and try to bring about a reconciliation between her and Beaufort—a strange fancy, for "this Duchess," as Campion writes, "was but little able, at that moment, to do anything for her friends' advantage!" Retz scoffs at the whole plot, which, he asserts, was invented "by four or five melancholy wights who looked as if their brains were of the shallowest! A cabal," he adds, "got up by people who all died mad!" Some contemporary authorities deny its existence; but Campion's Memoirs leave us in no doubt as to that.

THE DUCHESSE DE CHEVREUSE

Mazarin's notebooks, too, prove him to have had vague information about it, though all its details did not reach him.

For a moment the conspirators thought they would be able to execute their plan outside Paris. It was announced that the Cardinal intended to make an excursion to La Barre, a property belonging to Mme. de Vigean, at the mouth of the Montmorency valley: in this case it would have been easy to attack him in the open fields. Unfortunately, Mazarin took the Comte d'Harcourt with him on a journey into Lorraine: the assassins would have been obliged to kill him too, and he was related to Mme. de Chevreuse; the idea was relinquished. Another time the Cardinal was to go to Maisons, but the Duc d'Orléans went with him: again the plotters had to defer their attempt. The least eager among them, such as Henri de Campion, began to waver again. If no opportunity for doing the deed offered itself, they said, it surely was because the hand of God was against them! Beaufort, too, vain and changeable as ever, grew unsettled in his mind. Mme. de Chevreuse resolved to put an end to all these hesitations.

She settled that Mazarin was to be attacked at night, on his way to the Louvre. She took all her precautions. The Colonel's company of the Guard was on duty at the palace, and she arranged that the commanding officer, the Duc d'Épernon, should order his men not to budge, whatever noise they might hear, and simply to see the palace doors were kept shut. The date fixed was August 30. On that evening the accomplices were to meet at the tavern of "The Two Angels" on the Quai du Louvre, after sunset. They all assembled at the appointed hour. But the sight of eight or ten horses, saddled and bridled, at the door of an inn close to the King's palace was remarked, and with surprise. The matter was mentioned to Anne of Austria, who warned the Cardinal. That night he never left his house.

THE DEATH OF LOUIS XIII

At dawn next morning the incident was noised about the Court. What was the meaning of those horses and riders all clustered together so close to the Louvre? There was only one possible explanation: Mazarin was to have been attacked. With one consent Beaufort and his friends were accused of having plotted to kill the Cardinal. Feeling ran high: the Government was forced into taking strong measures. A Council was called, at which the Duc d'Orléans, the Prince de Condé, the Ministers, were all present. The proofs were in Mazarin's hands, and it was settled that Beaufort must be arrested.

That very day, September 1, Beaufort attended an entertainment given by the Comte de Chavigny, Governor of Vincennes, in the Queen's honour. Mazarin was not present. Anne of Austria treated the Duke with the most distant coldness. His friends warned him to be careful. He only shrugged his shoulders. The next day, heedless as ever, he presented himself at the Louvre: M. de Guitaut, Captain of the Guard, arrested him, took him to Vincennes, and left him in confinement there: the whole thing was done in the quietest manner.

The measure, as may be imagined, produced a deep impression. "This severe blow," writes Retz, "delivered at a time when authority had been so gently wielded as to be well-nigh imperceptible, made a great stir." Terrified, the conspirators fled, and took refuge with Beaufort's father, the Duc de Vendôme, at Anet; he welcomed them, concealed them, and said he would protect them.

Meanwhile, Mme. de Chevreuse, in her house in the Rue St. Thomas du Louvre, was more than anxious, and asked herself what her own fate was to be?

Anne of Austria thought it better to proceed with caution. She would wait a little, some five or six weeks, and then she would send the Duchess into exile, and do it in a somewhat ceremonious way, telling her it was necessary

THE DUCHESSE DE CHEVREUSE

she should retire from Court for a time. "She would advise her to live contentedly in France, not to mix herself up in any intrigue, to enjoy, under her Regency, the repose she had not been able to obtain in the late King's time; she would point out that it was time for her to find pleasure in a life of retirement, and to order her existence according to thoughts of the next world, and she would assure her of her own friendship for her, under these conditions." When, in the month of October, the Queen made up her mind to speak to Mme. de Chevreuse after this fashion, that lady received what she called "these remonstrances and counsels," in a very rebellious spirit. She forced Anne of Austria to lay her formal commands on her. The Duchess received orders to retire to Dampierre, and thence to Couzières. She was granted a sum of 200,000 *livres*, and she had to do as she was told.

She departed: she went to Dampierre. Her exile seemed to give universal satisfaction. "The Sieur de l'Estrade," wrote Gaudin to Servien, a Secretary of State, on October 31, "has complimented Her Majesty in the name of the Prince of Orange, on the departure of Mme. de Chevreuse, saying that by this action the Queen has demonstrated her good intentions with regard to her consideration for her allies: for immediately on her arrival, the said lady had proposed peace to her on very easy terms, and that the Spaniards would very willingly give up everything France had taken from them, if they were granted only one thing—which was, to abandon the Swedes and the Dutch."

Under the Regency, as in the days of Louis XIII, Mme. de Chevreuse was never to give the Government a moment's peace.

When she reached Dampierre she begged Alexandre de Campion to come and join her there secretly, travelling at night. "I could not desire any greater consolation in my misfortunes," writes Campion to her, in reply, "than

THE DEATH OF LOUIS XIII

the permission you give me to go to Dampierre. The fear you express lest I should be surprised on the highroads is most kind, but I will be so careful that this mischance will not overtake me. I do not travel in the daytime, and the nights are so dark that nobody will see me." He arrived. Through him Mme. de Chevreuse reckoned on reopening communications with all her accomplices. She organized the whole business; she would write to the Vendôme Princes, to Bouillon, to Spain, to England. She put herself into direct correspondence with Charles I's Ambassador, Lord Goring. According to Mazarin's notebooks, Goring was quite convinced that if the French Ministry underwent a change, and the Cardinal was dismissed, the friends of Mme. de Chevreuse—Spain, in other words—would come into power; and a peace would ensue, which could not be otherwise than favourable to the interests of English internal politics, then in a most difficult situation. Advised by the Duchess, those of her accomplices who had taken refuge at Anet crossed the frontier. Brillet and Henri de Campion, disguised and "wearing great beards," contrived to reach Holland; Mazarin, learning this, desired the French Envoy to the Prince of Orange, Beringhen, to keep his eye upon them. Beaufort took refuge on Papal territory.

From Dampierre, whether she would or not, Mme. de Chevreuse had been fain to take her way to Couzières. There she was to remain for many a month. She had leave to go to Tours; but the Government had taken measures to ensure her isolation. The Queen, it had been given out, would not look kindly on courtiers who frequented the Duchess. Anne of Austria personally expressed her vexation to La Rochefoucauld, telling him how great had been the ingratitude displayed by Beaufort, by the "Importants," above all by Mme. de Chevreuse; she particularly begged him "to have no more dealings with the Duchess, and to cease to be the instrument of her friends." La

THE DUCHESSE DE CHEVREUSE

Rochefoucauld, with some emotion, replied that he would certainly obey, but that he could not, "with justice, cease to be the friend of Mme. de Chevreuse, so long as she committed no other crime save that of being disliked by the Cardinal." His boldness was to involve him in disgrace.

Mazarin issued orders that Couzières was to be watched. He was quite sure everything would begin again, just as in Richelieu's time. Things had altered strangely! No longer was the Duchess plotting with Anne of Austria against a mighty Minister! This time it was the Queen herself who was suffering from the actions of her quondam friend. The Regent knew right well how dangerous she could be, and the measures taken by her Government grew more and more severe.

One of the Duchess's comptrollers, suspected of carrying her letters abroad, was seized and thrown into prison. An Italian physician, who had come to see her in his professional capacity, and on whom suspicion of having undertaken to carry letters for her had fallen, was arrested likewise, and his arrest was carried out after a most brutal fashion: he was dragged out of the coach in which Mlle. de Chevreuse and her waiting-women were seated with him. Police officers put their pistols to his throat, with shouts of "Kill! Kill!" and forced everybody out of the coach. Mme. de Chevreuse was furious. "Madame," she wrote the Queen from Tours, on November 20, 1644, "although the only good I had hoped from the withdrawal of the honour of your presence was to deserve that of your remembrance, by a continuation of the duty I paid you, I deprived myself of both, as soon as I became aware that this deprivation would be a more welcome sign of my obedience. But I confess that fresh one which has occurred within the last four or five days, by the imprisonment of an Italian physician who has been with me for some time, has touched me so nearly that I cannot believe your

THE DEATH OF LOUIS XIII

Majesty will refuse access to my just indignation : this has been done with a violence such as has never been seen before in such a matter, the occasion having been seized when he was in my daughter's coach, who was forced to get out of it, while two police officers held a pistol to her throat, constantly crying out 'Kill! Kill!' to her, and likewise to the women who were with her. This proceeding is so extraordinary that even as I reckon on your justice to give me satisfaction as to what I feel so keenly on account of my daughter's person, I dare promise myself your kindness will ensure my own future safety against such encounters!" Anne of Austria sent no reply.

Thanks to his spies, Mazarin knew every little thing the Duchess said and did. Through a certain nobleman, M. Cangé de la Brétonnière, he had the names of all the persons who frequented her society: a Mlle. Galland, a M. de Vaumorin, who was in the service of the Duc de Vendôme, M. du Tillac, who was about the Comte de Montrésor. To M. de Cangé's thinking, Mme. de Chevreuse made use of all these people for her communications with foreign parts, especially with England. Craft had been seen at Tours: he had lodged in the house of the Abbé de St. Julien, and had held divers conferences with the trusty friends of the Duchess, especially with Mlle. Galland, with whom he had sat up talking one night, in the Abbé's lodging, from eleven o'clock till two in the morning. M. de Cangé asserted the subject of this long interview to have been the escape of Beaufort.

In Paris, continued Cangé, Mme. de Chevreuse had a correspondent of the name of Mandat, who was in the habit of holding frequent conversations with the Magistrates of the Parliament, then carrying on a struggle with Mazarin—the prelude to the Fronde. A gentleman named M. de Molière had been sent to see Mme. de Chevreuse by the Duc d'Enghien: M. de Cangé had made his acquaintance, had made him talk, and had found out that Campion had

THE DUCHESSE DE CHEVREUSE

been in Paris for some days, disguised as an Englishman, and lodged in the Hôtel de Nemours. Another person who served Mme. de Chevreuse in connection with her private correspondence was a young Carmelite monk, five- or six-and-twenty years of age, the son of an official connected with the Parliament of Rennes, and a M. de Lussan, of Amboise, whom she was in the habit of sending to Paris, and who was always lodged, on these occasions, in the house of the Duc de Chevreuse, in that of M. de Montbazon, or in that of M. de la Rochefoucauld. M. de Cangé would shortly "send news of their intentions in these quarters."

From this and other information—though the details were not absolutely clear—Anne of Austria and the Cardinal arrived at the conclusion that Mme. de Chevreuse was certainly plotting with foreign powers. If peace with Spain was so difficult of attainment, if the dilatory methods of the Spanish Court rendered the discussion of its conditions so endlessly slow, that was surely because Mme. de Chevreuse was always stirring up hopes at Madrid! "Letters from Spain have been intercepted," writes Nani, the Venetian Ambassador, "which prove that the delays about making peace are attributable to the hopes entertained in Spain that there will soon be changes and disturbances in France." These changes and disturbances, he adds, were foretold by Mme. de Chevreuse and her friends: the Spanish Government reckoned on them, and was waiting for them.

Thus the Duchess's love of intrigue was an incorrigible vice, and a never-ceasing danger to the good management of public affairs. Anne of Austria became extremely angry. She gave orders that nobody was to consort with Mme. de Chevreuse on any pretext whatever, on pain of incurring her displeasure. Her commands were obeyed. Little by little the Duchess found herself forsaken, everybody left her alone. Montrésor tells us in his Memoirs that

THE DEATH OF LOUIS XIII

living as he did close to Tours, he watched the steady growth of this state of isolation. "The fact that Mme. de Chevreuse lived near Tours," he says, "resulted in my seeing her from time to time. The way in which she had been forsaken by all those on whom she had conferred obligations, and who had been bound to her by ties of friendship and interest, led me to judge how little reliance can be placed on the men of the present century, by the state in which I saw a person of her quality so universally forsaken in her disgrace, which increased my own desire to render her my services with all the more care and affection, on any occasion that might present itself. The esteem and interest I felt for her person led me willingly to run the risks involved, only taking care to regulate them in such a manner that no one could remark them as being too frequent, nor any affectation about them on her side or my own." Thus, and in spite of his good will, Montrésor himself was careful. He knew how angry the Government was. When the Queen of England came to France, the Regent requested her not to have anything to do with Mme. de Chevreuse; Henrietta-Maria, wrote Mazarin in his notebooks, was not to have any meetings with "a person who, by her bad conduct, had lost the good graces of Her Majesty."

It would have been difficult, under such conditions, for the Government to abstain from further action, and Anne of Austria, seeing the plotting was still going on in Touraine, could hardly have failed to come to the conclusion, that it was impossible for her to tolerate that Couzières should continue indefinitely to be used as a permanent centre of cabals against the State, carried on by Mme. de Chevreuse in perfect freedom.

And, indeed, the Duchess manifested no particular surprise when, one April morning in 1645, an exempt of the King's Bodyguard—his name was Riquetti—appeared upon the scene. He came to inform her, by the Queen's

THE DUCHESSE DE CHEVREUSE

order, that she must leave Touraine and betake herself to Angoulême, there to stay in the castle, and not move beyond its walls, till further orders: he himself was to conduct her thither. Instantly Mme. de Chevreuse perceived the extent of her misfortune. This time she would not have the semi-freedom she had enjoyed at Couzières, she was to be shut up in the citadel at Angoulême, and kept under lock and key. This prospect, so Montrésor tells us, "made such an impression on her mind that she resolved she would expose herself to every other peril that might threaten her so long as she escaped from that of being imprisoned, and which she thought inevitable." Her terrors of the year 1637 were on her again, and this time they were not imaginary, but most real and pressing.

Instantly she made up her mind: she would take to flight once more. She asked the officer to give her a few hours for her preparations, and he, unsuspectingly, it may have been, or perhaps because he had private orders, granted her request. That night, with her daughter Charlotte and two attendants, Mme. de Chevreuse got into her coach, and had herself driven, by La Flèche and Laval, straight to St. Malo. According to the custom of that time, she took jewels with her, to be turned into money. When she reached St. Malo she went boldly to the governor of the fortress, a gentleman of her acquaintance, the Marquis de Coatquin, and asked him to help her to get over to England. If Richelieu had been in power, M. de Coatquin would have lost no time about stopping the fugitive, only too certain, as he would have been, that any other course would have brought down the thunder of the sovereign upon his own head. But times were changed. He sent down to the port, and found an English barque just sailing for Dartmouth; the skipper agreed to take the passengers; Mme. de Chevreuse confided her jewels to the governor's care, and the boat hoisted sail and steered for the Cornish coast. The hull had hardly disappeared before M. de

THE DEATH OF LOUIS XIII

Coatquin, like a faithful servant of the King, began a letter to Mazarin, informing him of the departure of the Duchess, and setting forth the excellent reasons that had prevented him from arresting her. He deputed one of his gentlemen to carry the missive to the Cardinal, and give him further explanations by word of mouth. Mazarin's reply—it may have been ironically intended—ran: "I have seen, by that (the letter) you have been so good as to write me, the notice you give me that Mme. de Chevreuse has passed through. I have received, as I should, the proofs you give me of your affection for the King's service in this matter: I have not failed to represent everything I ought to the Queen, excusing what has happened by the reasons you send me, and those which the said gentleman has deduced." In Louis XIII's time, M. de Coatquin would not have got out of it so easily.

Mme. de Chevreuse intended, as soon as she landed at Dartmouth, to ask for a passport, get to Dover, and so across to Dunkirk, and thence to Liège. Once there, she would plead her innocence to Anne of Austria and crave her mercy. She did not care to make a long stay in England. The moment was one of the most critical of the Revolution in that country. In the course of his struggle with Parliament, Charles I had taken up arms. Cromwell's Roundheads had beaten the King's men at Newbury and Marston Moor, and within a few weeks Charles was to undergo a crushing defeat at Naseby, and to be forced to take refuge with the Scots, who were ultimately to hand him over to his own subjects. Mme. de Chevreuse, who was the King's kinswoman and friend, was anxiously wondering what reception she herself was likely to be given by the Parliamentarians: she had no desire to have any dealings with them. Her fears were not without reasonable foundation.

Hardly, in fact, had her boat come within sight of the English coast when two ships of war, flying the Parlia-

THE DUCHESSE DE CHEVREUSE

ment's flag, bore down upon her. The vessel was searched. Mme. de Chevreuse was recognized, and the English captains informed her they could not allow her to land; they would convey her to the Isle of Wight, where she must await the decision of Parliament regarding her: she had to submit. When she reached the Isle of Wight she found that the Governor of the island was the Earl of Pembroke, with whom she had been intimately acquainted in old days, at the English Court. He was absent in London. She wrote him a letter: "Sir," she said—this was on April 29, 1645, "my continued misfortunes having forced me to leave France hurriedly, so as to preserve, in a neutral country, the liberty of which the power of my enemies would have deprived me in my own, the only favourable means I could find to escape this ill-fortune has been to embark at St. Malo and cross into England, and thence over into Flanders, and so go to the country of Liège, whence I shall assuredly be able to justify my innocence. I trust to your virtue and courtesy not to refuse the supplication I make you to entreat the gentlemen of the Parliament to grant me a passport to get me hence to Dover, and so pass over to Dunkirk, whither the wretched state of my affairs forces me to betake myself as soon as possible. This is a grace for which I hope from the justice of the gentlemen of the Parliament, and which they will be free to confer on me without delay."

But Parliament refused. The order given was that Mme. de Chevreuse was not to be set at liberty. On May 20, 1645, Gaudin writes to Servien: "Letters from England inform us that Mme. de Chevreuse is still in the Isle of Wight, that the gentlemen of the Parliament have refused to give her either a ship or a passport to get to Dunkirk." Better still, the English offered to hand the Duchess over to Mazarin! The Cardinal, delighted to know her safely detained in the Isle of Wight, declined this offer. What could he have done with her? Like Riche-

THE DEATH OF LOUIS XIII

lieu, he had no wish either to shut her up or to bring her to trial: if he sent her to the most retired spot in the kingdom of France she would contrive to flee out of it! Far the best thing was that she should be kept a prisoner by the English! "It may be imagined," he wrote in a letter dated June 22, 1645, "how much Mme. de Chevreuse is hated, since when she was in the power of the English Parliamentarians they offered to hand her over to us, and we did not care to accept her."

June came, and still the Duchess was in prison. She was in despair. She fell ill; digestion and heart, she declared, were both seriously affected, and she was in a high fever. To provide herself with means of subsistence she had requested M. de Coatquin to send over her jewels, which were to be despatched to the care of Montrésor, in Paris, whence a reliable man would bring them over to her. A Breton gentleman, M. de Châteaubriant-Beaufort, did convey them from St. Malo and handed them over to Montrésor, from whose hands the person sent by the Duchess received them. But Mazarin, hearing of the incident, had Montrésor arrested and shut up in the Bastille. His house was searched, but nothing incriminating was found: a judicial cross-examination bore no more conclusive fruit; after a fortnight's detention in the Bastille Montrésor was transferred to Vincennes, where he spent fourteen months; at last, thanks to the intervention of the Guises and of the Prince of Orange, he was set at liberty.

Not knowing which way to turn, Mme. de Chevreuse finally addressed herself to the Spanish Ambassador. He expressed his willingness to come to her aid, and thanks to his intervention she at last obtained leave from the Parliament to depart from England; the Ambassador advanced her a sum of money—400 *jacobuses*.

She started, went to Brussels, and thence to Liège. Mazarin had her followed, every day he noted down the reports he had received about her. He could not flatter himself the Duchess would not continue her intrigues. He had entered into correspondence with the Duke of Lorraine's sister, the Princesse de Phalsbourg, in the hope of using her to detach Lorraine from the Austrian cause. This Princess kept him informed as to the movements of Mme. de Chevreuse; from her he knew she was writing to the Duke of Lorraine to counteract the Cardinal's own efforts; to Piccolomini, the Emperor's general, to enlighten him as to the movements of the French troops; to the Duc de Bouillon, to stir him up against France. His notebooks reveal the fact that she was abusing him in every letter she wrote, and working more ardently than ever in the cause of Spain. He even adds that it really would be very difficult to desire greatness for France and please Mme. de Chevreuse at one and the same time! How merrily had she gone to her ruin! he exclaimed, she who might, if she had chosen, have been one of the most fortunate women upon earth! On September 30 he wrote that the Duchess served her friends in Madrid very ill when she made them believe there was any hope for them, and begged the Princesse de Phalsbourg to find out what proposals she really was making to the Spaniards. "We have some light here already," he writes, "from Liège, on the subject of certain proposals she has made to the Spanish Ministers over there."

Thanks to a memorandum drawn up for the Archduke Leopold, Governor-General of the Low Countries, by a certain Abbé Ernest de Mercy, with the object of acquainting the Spanish Government with the nature of the assistance to be expected from Mme. de Chevreuse, we know what these proposals were.

At that moment Mme. de Chevreuse had a friend and confidant in the person of a French gentleman named M. de Saint-Ibal. Henry d'Escars de Saint-Bonnet, Lord of Saint-Ibal, was a thoughtless man, stoically brave, wanting in judgment, exceedingly broad-minded, independent, of

THE DEATH OF LOUIS XIII

uncertain temper, low-spirited and melancholy—thus at least he is described by Lenet: Saint-Evremond considered him simply a madman. Mme. de Chevreuse proposed to make a league between Spain and the Condés, the secret of which was to be confided to Saint-Ibal, and for the purposes of which he was to act as go-between. Condé hesitated to cast in his lot with the plotters, but only—so at least the French party at Brussels asserted—because he did not think the Spanish Ministers in the Low Countries set a sufficiently high value on Saint-Ibal: all they had to do was to come to an understanding with him. This Saint-Ibal was the mainspring of the whole business. Mme. de Chevreuse guaranteed the adhesion of d'Épernon, la Rochelle, the Huguenots; they would carry off Tancred de Rohan, a posthumous son of Henri de Rohan, the former chief of the Huguenot party, and place him at the head of the Protestant rebellion; let Spain have troops ready to disembark at the mouth of the Gironde: Saint-Ibal would go to Münster to the Duc de Longueville, and beg him to join the plot; Spain must give him a sum of 12,000 francs, and a monthly pension of 1000 francs. Thus Mazarin would be overthrown, and peace would be imposed on France! These plans proved Mme. de Chevreuse to be a prey to strange illusions.

And yet the Condé family, at that moment, seemed to be making a great effort to induce Anne of Austria to bring the war with Spain to an end. Henrietta-Maria, who had sought refuge in Paris, was adding her entreaties to those of the Princess Dowager. Had she a hope that if peace was restored on the Continent, France would intervene in English affairs, and come to the help of her unhappy husband in his defeat? That may well be! No stone that might influence Anne of Austria was left unturned. The nuns of the Val de Grâce were entreated to speak to the Queen: M. Vincent (de Paul) of the Mission, the Oratorian priests, were all canvassed.

THE DUCHESSE DE CHEVREUSE

But Mazarin, faithful to his task, was resolved to carry the policy bequeathed to him by Louis XIII and Richelieu to its logical conclusion : he was determined not to give in until the Spaniards accepted the consequences of the struggle as he foresaw them. The Venetian Ambassador, Nani, tells us that to protect Anne of Austria from the pressure put upon her he suddenly removed her out of Paris.

And we have a proof that Mme. de Chevreuse had no very great personal confidence in the complicated and foolish plan she had communicated to the Abbé de Mercy, in the fact that, at that very moment, and quite privately, she was making M. de Chevreuse entreat Mazarin to grant her his forgiveness and give her leave to return to Paris.

True to his old-standing habit of keeping on good terms with the man in power, M. de Chevreuse had openly sided with Mazarin against the Duchess his wife. "Chevreuse has been to see me," writes Mazarin in his notebooks; "he blames his wife." The Duke had written to the fugitive, had endeavoured to read her a lecture, had addressed her in his usual good-natured strain. "I can have no greater consolation in the retirement to which necessity has reduced me, replied the Duchess on August 23, 1647, "than that of learning that you are in good health, and seeing the recollection you have of me and the kindness you express to me : continue them, I beseech of you, so as to secure me my return to France, with a safety I have not hitherto been able to obtain there; assuring you that I desire nothing so much as to be with you in peace, and see the affairs of our house in good condition. But I fear my usual evil fortune will prevent me from enjoying this great good." On September 24, at Namur, she returns to the charge : "I am well pleased when I see that you remember me, and should be yet more so if you could obtain a safe return for me to you, but I fear that happiness will not come to me yet awhile. I impatiently await the

THE DEATH OF LOUIS XIII

news you tell me you will send me on that head, for I am now in a place where there is not much comfort, seeing it is a frontier town; I am much troubled, for it is only necessity which causes me to stop in Flanders—but to that I am forced to submit. It is not that I do not receive much politeness from the Governors of the Flemish fortresses, but as my aim is not to do anything for which I shall reasonably have cause to reproach myself, nothing but the necessity of which I tell you could ever keep me here."

Neither Mazarin nor Anne of Austria were to capitulate. Mme. de Chevreuse could not hope to return to France. And indeed, how uncertain would her position there have been! "The steps of the Palais Royal," wrote Guy Patin, "are as slippery as those of the Louvre ever were: this is a strange country, where there is little to be done by honest folk. M. de Mazarin is the chief ruler: all the rest tremble or bow down before the grandeur of his Cardinalship!"

But, happily for Mme. de Chevreuse, in France, that country of fickleness and change, political circumstances were soon to alter the face of all things, and thanks to a popular tumult of the most unusual kind, which was to shake the Cardinal's power to its foundations, and even, for a moment, to overthrow it altogether, she was once more to find a way of escape from her exile.

CHAPTER IX

AMIDST THE INTRIGUES OF THE FRONDE

The Intricacies of the Fronde—The return of Mme. de Chevreuse—An understanding with Mazarin—Flight of Mazarin—The majority of Louis XIV—The Cardinal's return—Mme. de Chevreuse goes into retirement—1648-53.

IT is a singular historical fact that the duty of carrying forward the essentially French policy of Richelieu should have devolved, after the death of Louis XIII, on a moderately intelligent Spanish Queen, and an Italian Minister whose energy was not his strongest point. Anne of Austria and Mazarin felt their position to be a difficult one, and their authority suffered. Haunted by thoughts of the revolution in England, in which Charles I had been punished for his opposition to the will of his people by the loss of his throne, they strove to avoid a similar catastrophe by coming to an arrangement with their enemies. The confusion grew proportionately greater, and the outcome of it all was the Fronde. In the face of the weakness of the sovereign's authority, the Parliament of Paris, which was no more than a mere judicial assembly, sought to play the part of States-General, tried to lord it over the Government, cut down taxes, dismiss treasury officials. The only answer Anne of Austria and Mazarin dared make to these usurping measures took the shape of concessions and delays. The King's power began to fall into abeyance, and the autocratic reaction of the reign of Louis XIV gives the measure of the depths the evil had reached.

Financial difficulties were at the bottom of the begin-

THE INTRIGUES OF THE FRONDE

nings of the struggle, but a great many other causes had led up to it. Parliament opposed the registering of fiscal edicts. The sovereign courts—Parliament, the Court of Accounts, the Board of Excise, the Grand Council—all joined together to oppose the creation of new posts: that was a revolutionary proceeding. They deputed a certain number of their members to form a common chamber, known as the "Chambre de St. Louis," which undertook to reform the kingdom: here was another revolutionary act—it took place in May 1648. Parliament would not have been so bold, but that public opinion, which loathed Mazarin, supported it. When the Government, after the Prince de Condé had won his brilliant victory at Lens, thought itself strong enough to try energetic measures, and arrested certain of the magistrates who had compromised themselves the most, such as Roussel, the populace, on August 27, 1648, rose up, and barricaded the streets. It became necessary to release the prisoners. Among the most fervent partisans of the popular cause was the coadjutor of the Archbishop of Paris, Paul de Gondi, afterwards Cardinal de Retz. After a whole succession of incidents, attempts at resistance, and conferences, Anne of Austria and Mazarin, convinced that the intrigues of the coadjutor and the flood of abuse poured out upon their heads in the innumerable pamphlets known as "*Mazarinades*" had rendered their position utterly untenable, suddenly left Paris, with the whole Court, in the course of the night between the 5th and 6th of January, 1649: that spelt open rupture. The Government was about to take up arms and lay siege to the city.

From Flanders, where she was living, Mme. de Chevreuse attentively watched the course of events. She was overwhelmed with delight. With Saint-Ibal, and through the Abbé de Mercy, she was inciting the Spaniards to increase the Regent's difficulties by moving their troops

THE DUCHESSE DE CHEVREUSE

forward. She laid stress on the success the Spanish arms might expect, thanks to her own intelligences within the kingdom. "It is her habit (Mme. de Chevreuse)," writes Mazarin, who had been duly warned, to M. de Coatquin, on September 16, 1648, "to talk very big about the understandings she has in France, so as to make the Spaniards think more of her; and I know that in the last conference, held at Spa a few days since, between her, Saint-Ibal, the Abbé de Mercy and the secretary Galareta, she spoke very freely of the absolute power which, she declared, she had over you and other persons of quality within the kingdom, who know no more about it than you do." In the course of that summer of 1648, the Archduke Leopold did, in fact, set out for Flanders with some 25,000 or 30,000 men, to attack Condé. "Mme. de Chevreuse," notes the Cardinal, "and the other French persons who supply information outside this country" (Saint-Ibal and others), "assert that when that is done, everything will be in disorder"—Paris in an uproar and the whole kingdom in a state of revolution; but the bloody defeat at Lens was soon to prove the futility of the suggestions put forward by the Duchess.

She did not lose courage. And, indeed, the subsequent complications caused by the Fronde were of a nature well calculated to raise her hopes. The news, in January 1649, that the Court had fled from Paris, that the city was in a state of insurrection, and that the King was about to be constrained to lay siege to his own capital, increased her confidence. It was the story of the League over again. Like Henri III, Louis XIV had been driven out of Paris. In the absence of States-General, the Parliament had assumed the responsibilities of the power reft from the sovereign's hand. Why should not the Spaniards offer their help, as they had done in the days of the League, to the Parisian insurgents? Thereupon there arrived in Brussels a gentleman who was destined to play an important part in the rest of the life of Mme. de Chevreuse,

THE INTRIGUES OF THE FRONDE

and who, for the moment, was to give form to the ideas that bubbled in her brain. This was M. Geoffroy de Laigue, Baron du Plessis-Patay, and Seigneur de Bondoufle.

Laigue, whose family was settled in Dauphiné, a brave man and a fine horseman, but, so Retz affirms, "exceedingly coarse, and of the most changeable character ever seen, with little sense and a great deal of presumption," was then thirty-five years of age, the fifth son of a family of ten children. He had been intended for the Church, but this idea had been relinquished on account of his turbulent nature, and he had found his way to Paris, had obtained a company in the Gardes Françaises, had been at the siege of Gravelines in 1644, during which he had been one of the leaders of the assault, and at the battle of Lens, where he had behaved with great valour. His close intimacy with the head of the younger branch of the la Trémoïlle family, first Marquis and then Duc de Noirmoutier, had attracted attention to his person. During the Lens campaign, the two friends, as a consequence of some difficulty with the Prince de Condé, and a scene with him which had resulted from it, had left the army in a fit of temper : Laigue had sold his company, and they had both gone back to Paris, where they had thrown themselves into the agitation of the Fronde.

After the rupture between the Court and the members of the Fronde, Gondi, like Mme. de Chevreuse, thought it necessary to appeal to Spain. "A grain of Spanish catholicon," he said, was indispensable. Laigue offered the Coadjutor his services. He would go to Brussels, he said, he would see Mme. de Chevreuse, and through her he would get into communication with the Spanish authorities. Gondi accepted his proposal unsuspectingly. "I had some repugnance," he wrote in his *Memoirs*, "to sending a man of my own cloth to Brussels." Laigue had had himself recommended to the Coadjutor by Montrésor.

THE DUCHESSE DE CHEVREUSE

A strange idea now occurred to them both: this was, to propose to Gondi that Laigue, to win over the Duchess to the cause, should go to Flanders and become her lover. The situation was vacant. Mme. de Chevreuse was forty-eight, of course, but age had not destroyed the coquette in her; she would be flattered. The Coadjutor laughed, and agreed. "We told Laigue," he writes, "that he was to live near the Archduke."

Laigue started. Arrived at Brussels, he began to pay his court to Mme. de Chevreuse. His first experiences were not encouraging. The Duchess acknowledged, at a later date, that her suitor had struck her as being an insipid sort of fellow, and that his dull face had reminded her unpleasantly of an actor at the Hôtel de Bourgogne, Bellerose by name. But by degrees her prejudices wore off. She allowed herself to be conquered; and Laigue was her final and her most enduring passion.

They took their steps in unison. It was high time. Mazarin's blockade of Paris was drawing closer and closer; Saint-Cloud, Saint-Denis, Meudon had been occupied by the King's troops. With feverish haste the Parliament had raised an army, which, during an attempt to seize Corbeil, on January 23, 1649, took to precipitate flight. On February 8, Condé, who had remained faithful to the Regent, attacked Charenton and took possession of the town, and 40,000 Parisians, who had sallied forth to repulse him, retired ingloriously. Haste was becoming urgent. Mme. de Chevreuse and Laigue asked the Archduke to write a letter to the Parliament offering peace: this step would prove that the Court of Spain was disposed to put an end to the war, and all the odium of its continuation would thus fall on Mazarin; the Archduke complied. The Duchess herself chose the herald-at-arms who was to carry the letter—a certain Don Joseph Illesca Arnolphini. When this herald reached Paris, he had to wait: there was a difficulty about his credentials; as a matter of fact, a great

THE INTRIGUES OF THE FRONDE

many of the magistrates objected to treating with foreigners; finally, the Parliament referred him to Anne of Austria; the business was a failure.

Laigue and Mme. de Chevreuse looked about for something else. The Archduke must be persuaded to make some decided move into French territory. Laigue, in his letters, declared he was already sure of the Archduke and the commander of his troops, the Conde di Fuensaldagna. "I never met such a fool!" said Gondi; "he thinks he can manage Fuensaldagna already!" Noirmoutier, who likewise thought his friend's assertions were "impertinent," suggested going to Brussels himself to make sure of things. Retz let him go. At the bottom of his heart, the Coadjutor was in a difficulty. In view of the successive defeats suffered by the troops of the Fronde, the murmurs of the populace, which was greatly divided in opinion, and the famine which was beginning to make itself felt, the Parliament had resolved, on February 28, to attempt to reach some agreement with the Court. Conferences had already begun at Rueil. This was a bad moment for trying to get the Spaniards to interfere! Gondi had written to Brussels and declined the proffered intervention, and Noirmoutier and Laigue had replied by setting forth the reasons which made the help of Spain so necessary. The Coadjutor had answered that these reasons did not meet with his approval. Early in March, just when the representatives of the Parliament and the Court were beginning to come to an understanding, Laigue was writing Gondi a series of despatches in cypher, in which he announced that the promised intervention was about to take effect. "The bulk of the Spanish army," he said, "would be at Vadencourt" (near Guise, in the Aisne) "on such a day; the advance-guard at Pontavert, on such another; it would stay there a few days, and then the Archduke intended to come and take up his quarters at Dammartin" (near Meaux). These letters threw the Coadjutor into "cruel agitations": "there was not a syllable in them," he moaned, "that did not cause him mortal pain."

Mme. de Chevreuse shared Laigue's illusions. The Prince de Conti, who had kept on the side of the Fronde, sent his equerry, de Bréquigny, to Flanders, to talk with the Archduke and see Mme. de Chevreuse; this lady told him she was just about to start for France with the Spanish army, 25,000 men strong. The Archduke, so Mathieu Molé tells us in his Memoirs, confided to Bréquigny that he had hesitated a great deal before entering on this campaign, and had only made up his mind to it at last under pressure from Mme. de Chevreuse.

But Mazarin had no intention of waiting for the Spaniards: he was hurrying on the Rueil conferences, and things were very nearly settled.

Then Mme. de Chevreuse, finding this out, turned round again. If peace was to be concluded, thought she to herself, she had better give up the struggle and secure her own inclusion in it. Instantly she wrote to her friends, begging them to do their best for her.

She applied to everybody. Through Bréquigny she obtained the intercession of the Prince de Conti; she addressed herself to her own son, the Duc de Luynes, to her husband, who had sided with the Fronde because he had fancied it the strongest. They all did what they could. M. de Luynes, who had also adhered to the Parliament, and had suffered from the war—the Comte de Grancey, at the head of a body of the King's troops, had seized, and sacked, and burnt his house at Lésigny—was formulating a whole list of claims, and inserted one with regard to his mother. "To bring back the Duchesse de Chevreuse, his mother," it ran, "with all the necessary provisions for her safety, so that she may go here and there, and live in any part of the kingdom, as it may please her, without being sought for on any account what-

THE INTRIGUES OF THE FRONDE

ever, or on any pretext of any kind." The Prince de Conti, who was also sending in his claims, likewise added a clause touching the Duchess: "That Mme. de Chevreuse may return to France, and live there in complete safety and liberty, either at Court, or wherever else she may prefer." As for M. de Chevreuse, he went to Saint-Cloud, with the intention of making a direct appeal to the Regent.

The scene has been related by Mme. de Motteville and by Monglat. M. de Chevreuse had reached his seventy-second year; he was deaf. When Anne of Austria saw him, she began to reproach him, at the top of her voice, for having kept to the rebel side, and been present on horseback with the insurgents, during the engagement at Charenton. "He replied to the Queen," writes Monglat, "that he was her very humble servant, but that he would never forsake Paris, his very good friend; that he would always be on that side as long as he was comfortable there; and that if she desired to have him on hers, she must not go out of it" (the city). When the Duke had laid the object of his suit before her, Anne of Austria, schooled by Mazarin, refused his prayer: she could not, she said, allow the Duchesse de Chevreuse to come back into "a town that was still full of rebellion; she had made a thousand plots against her service; she" (the Queen) "could not be pleased with her, nor content with the submission she offered, if she did not show her a real repentance of her last behaviour." M. de Chevreuse protested that he would answer for his wife's fidelity, but the Queen burst out laughing: what power had he over her? M. de Chevreuse said something about his daughter Charlotte, who, he declared, had immensely improved in looks: "she had eyes that were capable of setting the whole world on fire." "You are too fond of beauty," said the Queen, with a smile; "you must begin to turn your affections on virtue and on Heaven!"

THE DUCHESSE DE CHEVREUSE

Anne of Austria's refusal was only a feint. In reality, Mazarin had no intention of making any difficulties as to the Duchess, and she was to be included in the treaty arrangements. There was stiffer discussion about Laigue and Noirmoutier, to whom the Minister was not disposed to grant more than an abolition, considering them more guilty than the others, on account of their having served in the ranks of the Spanish army.

Peace was concluded at Rueil on April 1. Mme. de Chevreuse was pardoned.

In accordance with custom, she could not return to France without a special permission from the Queen. She waited a week, ten days; no sign! What did this silence portend? Laigue, a much humbler personage, had taken on himself to go back at once; the Duchess decided to follow his example. Quite suddenly, she left Brussels with her daughter Charlotte, and travelling all at a stretch—she drove the thirty-four leagues from Cambrai to Paris without any rest at all—she reached the capital towards eleven o'clock on the morning of April 12.

Her unexpected arrival astonished Anne of Austria extremely. The Queen, so Goulas tells us, considered this behaviour on the part of Mme. de Chevreuse as "a low and most shabby proceeding." The Duchess had contented herself with writing a short letter of excuse; the Queen refused to take it from the messenger. She insisted that Mme. de Chevreuse should leave Paris instantly, and at all events go as far away as Dampierre. The Duchess was very much mortified. She addressed herself to Molé, the First President of the Parliament, as though to seek shelter with that body, once so formidable to its opponents. But Molé had been won over by the Court. On April 16 he wrote to Le Tellier, the Secretary of State, that he had seen Mme. de Chevreuse, and had tried to "keep her to her duty." Le Tellier, in reply, reiterated the order for her immediate departure to Dampierre, and added, threateningly: "I do not doubt that what you said to Mme. de Chevreuse, in the conversation you had with her yesterday, invites her, more than anything else could do, to return to her duty, and if she fails in that respect, I can assure you there are means of forcing her to do it: we have that in hand which will bring her to reason, without the smallest contradiction!"

When the First President failed her, the Duchess appealed to the Coadjutor. The matter was pressing: the Court had given her twenty-four hours' law. Laigue went and fetched Gondi. "I went with Laigue to the Hôtel de Chevreuse," writes Gondi, "and there I found the fair lady at her toilette, and in tears; my heart grew tender, and I begged Mme. de Chevreuse not to obey until I had had the honour of seeing her again." After various unsuccessful attempts, he went to the First President, and he says: "When I began to point out how necessary it was for the King's service that people's minds should not be embittered by any infraction of declarations of so solemn a nature, he stopped me short, saying, 'Enough, my good sir. You do not wish her to go; she shall not go!' And he added in my ear, 'Her eyes are far too fine!'" This story does not appear to coincide with Molé's previous attitude, as depicted in his own letters. It is true, nevertheless, that on the very evening before his interview with Gondi, the First President had written to the Court, deprecating any hasty action as regarded Mme. de Chevreuse. Radiant, the Coadjutor took his way back to the Hôtel de Chevreuse; he was most warmly welcomed. Mlle. de Chevreuse—Charlotte—made herself extremely charming to him. Gondi was only six-and-thirty, and, in spite of his cloth, made no pretence of being severely virtuous. The young girl's fascinating grace produced its effect upon him: he began by coming back often, he ended by coming every night; the incident, in fact, was to be the starting-point of a love affair with the beautiful

THE DUCHESSE DE CHEVREUSE

Mlle. de Chevreuse which was not destined to be altogether unsuccessful.

If the First President really did intervene, and request Mazarin to delay taking any severe measure as to Mme. de Chevreuse, he may well have relied for support on the argument supplied by the favour with which public opinion had received the Duchess. The public, in fact, had learnt with satisfaction that the Duchess had sought to bring aid to the Parisians. A few days before her return, a "*Mazarinade*" had appeared which extolled her heroic virtues: *The French Amazon, or the Help of the Parisians, or the Approach of the Troops of Madame la Duchesse de Chevreuse, reprinted under the title of The Illustrious Conqueror, or the Generous Constancy of Madame de Chevreuse.* In this work, the author vaunts the qualities of Marie de Rohan in poetic terms. She is called "the incomparable Amazon," "a flower, the hope of our peace, which came to our help against the oppression of monsters"; "a sun that seemed to rise to drive away the fogs which our misfortunes piled above our heads"; "a delightful sunrise, appearing at the dawn of our highest hopes, all red with the fire of a righteous anger." The Queen was advised that it would be very imprudent to raise fresh difficulties. "It was not possible for the Regent," writes Jean Vallier, "whatever orders she might issue, to force Mme. de Chevreuse to leave Paris, nor even to go and await her Majesty's pleasure in her house at Dampierre, which is only six short leagues distant, so greatly was her authority diminished since she had taken the King away."

The twenty-four hours Mme. de Chevreuse had been given were prolonged. But after a few days Anne of Austria, unable to endure the thought that the Duchess was defying her, caused her to be requested to go to Dampierre for a few hours, at all events, so as to save her own dignity. Molé undertook to suggest this. The

THE INTRIGUES OF THE FRONDE

Duchess consented; but she insisted on having assurances as to the duration of her exile. Negotiations ensued: Mazarin gave his word; Molé pledged his own that it should be kept. Towards the middle of July, Mme. de Chevreuse complied.

But she had hardly settled at Dampierre before she began to ask leave to come back. The Court made no difficulties. "Mme. de Chevreuse," writes Le Tellier to Molé on July 19, "having sent to entreat the Queen to permit her to go wheresoever her business may call her, with every kind of freedom, and even to come and make her obeisance to Her Majesty, and having caused her to be assured that she will behave herself so that Her Majesty shall receive complete satisfaction, both these things have been granted unto her, and you are released from the word that you gave to the said lady."

Now that Mme. de Chevreuse had been received back into favour, propriety demanded that she should go and make her obeisance to the sovereign. She fell ill, and this delayed the ceremony until August 8. On that day the Duchess and her daughter Charlotte appeared at Compiègne, where Anne of Austria was then residing. The Duchess was pale and worn after her recent illness. It was the hour at which the Council sat, and the Regent's antechamber was crowded with courtiers. In spite of the promises given her, the Duchess had not come without a certain feeling of alarm. Le Tellier and Molé had been obliged to calm her by the assurance, on the Queen's word of honour, that there was no reason for her to have any fear. When she reached the Queen's presence, so Mme. de Motteville tells us, Anne of Austria, who had been in the habit of embracing her friend, failed to honour her with this mark of her favour. The Duchess bent low before the sovereign, beseeching her "to pardon all her past behaviour, and promising her the greatest fidelity in future." The Regent received these asseverations kindly,

THE DUCHESSE DE CHEVREUSE

and addressed no reproaches to the suppliant; but the friendliness of former days had utterly disappeared. Mme. de Chevreuse paid her duty to the young King, Louis XIV, then just eleven years old, spoke a few words to Mazarin, and retired. She had hardly passed out of the room before Anne of Austria remarked, quite audibly, on the change in her former friend's appearance: "There was hardly a trace of her past beauty." But everybody had admired Mlle. de Chevreuse, "whose beauty was celebrated," adds Mme. de Motteville slyly, "although it was not perfect; so true is it that what is novel is almost always pleasing, and even what is not pleasing is admired in spite of that!"

Still, Mme de Chevreuse had recovered her place at Court. A few days later the *Gazette* reported: "On St. Augustine's day, August 28, the Queen, accompanied by Mademoiselle, and attended by the Duchesse de Chevreuse and other great ladies of the Court, went barefoot to the Church of St. Augustine, where Her Majesty heard evening prayers." On September 5 there was a great ball at the Hôtel de Ville in honour of the King's eleventh birthday: the young monarch "led out Mademoiselle to dance," and Mlle. de Chevreuse danced with the Prince de Condé. The past seemed forgotten, and all the old hatreds wiped out; but this was a mere pretence.

Mazarin was too well acquainted with the character of the Duchess to believe her capable of casting off her life-long habit of intrigue. That being so, and considering the perpetually recurring political difficulties stirred by the half-subdued Frondeurs, he felt it better to have her with him than against him. On the very morrow of the Peace of Rueil, he had sent Charles de Mouchy, Marquis d'Hocquincourt, Governor of Peronne, to propose an understanding between himself and the Duchess. Mme. de Chevreuse, delighted, had raised no objection. When

THE INTRIGUES OF THE FRONDE

she came back to Paris, d'Hocquincourt had waited upon her again. There had been fresh parleying, not very definite, and it was the existence of these negotiations, more than the intervention of Molé and Gondi, which had ensured the comparative gentleness with which Mme. de Chevreuse had been treated by the Court. Through the Duchess, Mazarin hoped to reach the leaders of what was known as the Old Fronde, the great men of the opposition —Beaufort, Gondi and the rest. This we know by a letter from De Laulne, secretary to the Duc de Chevreuse. At the time of the Duchess's journey to Compiègne, so Goulas tells us, this agreement had taken definite shape. Mazarin's notebooks prove that all through September and October he had frequent interviews with Mme. de Chevreuse. She was interesting herself in the Cardinal's plans, and becoming his ally: she agreed to be responsible for the behaviour of her party. She was on excellent terms with the Duc d'Orléans, who was lukewarm in his attachment to the Regent, and boasted her ability to win him over completely. Through Mme. de Montbazon, she would also secure the adhesion of Beaufort, who had been released. Thanks to Laigue and Gondi, she would be able to keep the Frondeurs in hand. A strange accomplice, truly, for the Cardinal! A strange house in which to seek support for his policy!

Ever since her return to Paris, in fact, Mme. de Chevreuse had been living with Laigue, just as she had lived with him in Flanders; she had lodged him in her own house, under the nose of her husband, who had made no objection whatever. Everybody was perfectly well aware of the relations between this gentleman and the Duchess. He was invited everywhere. The Duc d'Orléans was more than civil to him. At Court he was surrounded by friends; he was present at the Queen's "petit coucher," and cracked jokes with Her Majesty! Above all things, he strove to push his own private advantage: he had begun life without

THE DUCHESSE DE CHEVREUSE

a penny, and was now busied, thanks to expedients of his own, in piling up a very fair fortune, which was to allow of his giving his niece, Marguerite de Laigue, a dowry of 350,000 *livres*, in the year 1650. He himself had never married, and the Duchess, in spite of her eight-and-forty years, and the disappearance of charms which no longer sufficed to explain the passions she might stir, permitted this gallant of five-and-thirty openly to play a part which did not seem to raise the faintest blush upon her cheek.

But Gondi's behaviour was more suspicious still.

A curious figure! Born of a family of Italian bankers who had rendered precious financial services to the French Kings during the sixteenth century—lending them many sums of money—and who had been rewarded with a shower of honours, Gondi had been destined for the Church from his earliest youth, and in 1644, at the age of thirty, had been chosen by his own uncle, the Archbishop of Paris, as his Coadjutor. No man could have been less fitted to be a Churchman. Of elegant appearance, carefully dressed as any cavalier, crowned with waving feathers, always on the look-out for a love-affair, in which he had considerable success, he was quite without virtue, and paraded a long array of vices. Richelieu, who knew him well and liked him ill, declared he had a "hang-dog look": he thought him a restless and rebellious man, whose "bad qualities surpassed those of which the house of Retz was generally accused." In the eyes of Mazarin, who had so much cause to complain of him, and may not be quite impartial in his judgment, Retz was "a monster," a man without religion, addicted to "godlessness, debauchery and wickedness"; "the most haughty, ambitious and evil-intentioned of men, and the enemy of all peace and order, utterly faithless." The worst of it was that Gondi knew his own worthlessness, and boasted of it. "My poor friend," said he to somebody who had been remonstrating with him, "you waste your time when you preach to me!

THE INTRIGUES OF THE FRONDE

I know very well I am a rogue, but in spite of you and everybody else I mean to go on being one, because that is what I like best!" He had set his heart on playing a great part in the disturbances of the Fronde. Mazarin declares that he said to him one day: "If M. de Beaufort is Fairfax, I am Cromwell!" That was a great delusion! Meanwhile, he was giving himself out to be a strong republican: he would have had the same thing done in France as had been done in England. He lacked the strength of character which had given Cromwell his power, and tried to make up for his want of talent by his intrigues.

And this it was that attracted him to Mme. de Chevreuse! Through her, he thought, he would get into touch with the Old Fronde, with such men as Montbazon and Beaufort, and with the Spaniards, that supreme resource in case of danger! And the Duchess, on her side, believing in his popularity, fancied that through him she would be able to influence the Paris mob, and so made overtures to him. Her chief means of attracting him, and keeping him about her, was her own daughter!

Mlle. de Chevreuse—Charlotte-Marie de Lorraine—had then reached her twenty-fourth year. Of middle height and distinguished appearance, with a pretty mouth and "a fine contour of face," she was considered a handsome woman. It has been said, indeed, that she was too thin, and that her complexion was not clear enough; but it was a woman, Mme. de Motteville, who brought this accusation against her. In any case, so Gondi declares, she had "the most beautiful eyes in the world, and a way of using them that was admirable, and peculiar to herself." Elsewhere Retz, who certainly penned his Memoirs after his passion had died down, speaks rather severely of her. "All she possessed," he says, "was beauty, of which one quickly tires when it has no other accompaniment. Her wit was always confined to the person she loved; but then she never loved the same person long; therefore nobody

THE DUCHESSE DE CHEVREUSE

thought her witty for long. . . . She had more beauty than charm, and was by nature silly to the point of being ridiculous!" The truth is that Mlle. de Chevreuse was exceedingly capricious: she was a spoilt child; when she lost her temper she would throw "her petticoats, her hoods, her gloves into the fire," and even Venetian laces, which her "girls—her waiting-women—only saved with the greatest difficulty in the world." Retz adds: "If she could have thrown her gallants on the fire too, when she was tired of them, she would have done it with the best will in the world!"

Her mother had not as yet been able to find a husband for her. There had been some question of marrying her to M. de Beaufort, who had believed her to be very rich. It would have been a splendid alliance; but Beaufort had not persisted in the matter. Then the Duchesse d'Aiguillon, niece of Cardinal Richelieu, thought of her for her nephew, the Duc de Richelieu, but the Duke was in love with Mlle. de Pons, and ended by marrying that lady. There was soon to be some idea of the Prince de Conti. While awaiting her entrance into the bonds of matrimony, Mlle. de Chevreuse found entertainment in the homage of the gentlemen who surrounded her: the Coadjutor became her prime favourite.

Before long, Gondi's constant attendance at the Hôtel de Chevreuse was common property. "The Coadjutor," writes Lenet, "was in close intimacy with the Duchesse de Chevreuse, and it was said in the world that he was endeavouring to enter into still more cordial relations with Mademoiselle, her daughter." "The Coadjutor," says la Rochefoucauld, "had a great friendship with Mme. de Chevreuse, and the beauty of her daughter was said to have still greater power over him." "Mlle. de Chevreuse," writes the Great Mademoiselle in still more straightforward fashion, "was the Coadjutor's mistress." Retz, in his Memoirs, details his own successes in the most vain-

THE INTRIGUES OF THE FRONDE

glorious manner. He declares that Mazarin, in his desire to separate him from Mlle. de Chevreuse, did all he could to get him ousted by rivals in the fair Charlotte's affections —M. de Candale and M. d'Aumale—and that their attentions gave rise to scenes of jealousy and heated explanations, as a consequence of which both gentlemen were dismissed.

What is more certain is that the picture presented by a household in which mother and daughter lived under such conditions, under the complaisant eyes of the deaf old Duke, was anything but edifying. Besides seeing Charlotte at the Hôtel de Chevreuse, the Coadjutor met her in the house of her cousin, Louise de Lorraine, the wife of the Marquis de Rhodes. On April 16, 1651, Mazarin wrote as follows: "Mme. de Chevreuse, to whom I had said that I did not see how the Queen was to make sure of the Coadjutor's mind, and that I was greatly afraid he would soon fail her, confided to me that she would keep him in hand through her daughter, who behaved to the Coadjutor in such a fashion that she made him in love with her, and this she has confirmed to me several times since. And the said lady did in fact rule him in this way, having laid the bridle on her daughter's neck, so that she appointed meetings in the house of Mme. de Rhodes with the Coadjutor, who constantly saw her at the Hôtel de Chevreuse at unseasonable hours, so that the scandalmongers said her marriage with the Prince de Conti could not but be a very good one, seeing the priest had been there already!" Retz tells us in his Memoirs that he used to go to the Hôtel de Chevreuse every evening, and went home again between midnight and one o'clock in the morning. "Nothing could have been more completely the opposite of everything that happened at the Hôtel de Chevreuse," he modestly remarks, "than the confirmations (I was holding every morning in the churches), the lectures I was giving (to pious seminarists)

THE DUCHESSE DE CHEVREUSE

at St. Magloire, and other occupations of that kind. I possessed the art of reconciling them all, and in the eyes of the world this art justifies all that it reconciles."

And all this immoderate existence was attended by the procession of distresses, disputes and low quarrels which are its usual concomitants. Mme. de Montbazon, whose moral conduct was no better than her stepdaughter's, and who, according to Mazarin, allowed her own daughter to follow Charlotte's example, was to be seen, in her jealousy of that young lady's success, handing about a letter from Mlle. de Chevreuse to Noirmoutier, in which she complained of his faithlessness, as if he, too, had been her lover, and reproached him with having cast her off for the sake of Mme. de Rhodes, "and a great deal more abuse of that kind." This affair made a great stir. Mme. de Chevreuse called her stepmother to account, but she replied, with a laugh, that one ought to scorn all scandal, and that they themselves were both of them accused of having a lover of seventy-five! On another occasion, when Mlle. de Chevreuse had angrily complained to Gondi of the disagreeable stepfatherly fashion in which Laigue seemed disposed to treat her, lecturing her perpetually about her behaviour, and boring her with his remonstrances, Retz held a council with Charlotte and Mme. de Rhodes, and all three came to the conclusion that to rid themselves of the tiresome mentor, they must supply Mme. de Chevreuse with a new lover! As a matter of fact, M. de Haqueville, on whom their choice had fallen, took himself out of the way.

Easy-going though contemporary opinion was as to the necessity for observing certain principles of morality in daily life, such scenes as these could not fail to cause painful astonishment in many quarters. Mazarin was fully aware of the depths to which the frequenters of the Hôtel de Chevreuse had fallen. He would speak of it in the bluntest manner. "In the presence of a numerous

THE INTRIGUES OF THE FRONDE

company," he ventured to write in one letter, "Mme. de Chevreuse and Mme. de Montbazon separately asserted that it was quite permissible . . . for one's own pleasure, for the persons one loved, to satisfy feelings of ambition or of vengeance. This is the doctrine these ladies practise and preach. And when age prevents the said ladies from turning their own beauty to profit, they have recourse to their daughters'. . . ."

And thus it came about that these three—Mme. de Chevreuse, Laigue and Gondi—held together by so strange a bond, laboured in unison to support the policy of Mazarin!

Now there was one party which could not regard this understanding between the Cardinal and the Chevreuse-Gondi faction with any feeling but one of the deepest displeasure—the Condés. The Prince de Condé, who had been faithful to the Regent through all the late troubles, after having gained victories over the Spaniards which had greatly strengthened the Government's position, felt the favour bestowed by the Queen and Mazarin on persons who had once caused him to be thrown into prison to be an insult to himself. He lost his temper. Looking about for a pretext, he protested that he and his family had not been given what they had been promised—the County of Montbéliard for himself, and Pont-de-l'Arche for his sister, the Duchesse de Longueville. A whole troop of young noblemen gathered about him, spurring him on: a new Fronde began to rise up—the Fronde of the princes and the dandies. On September 14, 1649, after a somewhat lively altercation between Mazarin and Condé, there had been a scene, and some fear of a rupture; with much difficulty, a reconciliation had been arranged. Condé, haughty and impatient by nature, now became absolutely aggressive in his dealings with the Cardinal: challenged him, declared he would call on Parliament to

THE DUCHESSE DE CHEVREUSE

put an edict of the year 1617, which forbade any foreigner to serve a French sovereign as Minister, into force; talked of demanding that the Regent's powers should be made over to himself. His outrageous pretensions, his arrogance and threats, made him a standing danger to Mazarin.

The enmity with which the Dowager Princesse de Condé and her daughter, the Duchesse de Longueville, had inspired Mme. de Chevreuse seven years previously, now flamed up in her heart against her former foes. Her plan was swiftly made: she would induce the members of the Old Fronde, so the Duchesse de Nemours explains to us, to join forces with those of the Parliamentary Fronde, and all of them together would call on Anne of Austria to arrest Condé. She laid her proposal before the Queen. Prudently, as Monglat tells us, laying stress on the difficulties against which the Regent was struggling, she dwelt on the harm the Prince was doing, and proffered the friendship and devotion of her own friends. "The Queen," so Mme. de Motteville acknowledges, "was so sick of the Prince de Condé's pride that she was more and more inclined towards the Frondeurs, who were being led to serve her by the Duchesse de Chevreuse." And in his notebooks the Cardinal wrote, on October 16, 1649: "Mme. de Chevreuse, twice over, has talked to me, forgetting nothing, to make known to me, in the first place, that it" (the arrest of Condé) "was a certain blow, and further, to persuade me it was an infallible means of re-establishing the King's authority in Paris and in all the provinces. Peace, so the Duchess explained, would most certainly follow: (she said) that I should be able to avenge myself on M. le Prince, who had offended me in sheer wantonness, and who, if a prompt remedy was not used to put some obstacle in the way of his elevation, would soon be master over everything; that Monsieur le Prince was not what he is thought to be; that he is strong among the weak, but very weak among the strong; that the nobility and the

THE INTRIGUES OF THE FRONDE

Princes are all furious against him. Finally, the said lady would answer to me for the whole party—M. de Beaufort, De Bellièvre, the Coadjutor, Noirmoutier—and that entirely." All the Duchess asked in return was to be well treated by the Queen. Mazarin confined his answer to a few vague sentences.

But the idea was making headway. Anne of Austria was realizing that she would have to arrest Condé. Mme. de Chevreuse was full of exultation. At last her influence in State affairs was assuming the importance which had been her dream! "She saw herself," writes Mme. de Motteville, "in a position to call back to life those old longings to rule the Queen which she had conceived in the early days of the Regency." For the Government, the question was one of keeping the mob on its side, and preventing disturbances in the streets. Could Gondi reassure the Regent on this point? Anne of Austria resolved to see the Coadjutor herself, at the Palais-Royal. Mazarin made the first advances, in a conversation with Mme. de Chevreuse, on January 1, 1650; the Queen confirmed his action; she had even drawn up a note, in which she said: "I cannot believe, in spite of the past and the present, that Monsieur le Coadjuteur is not on my side; I beg I may see him without the knowledge of any persons save Mme. and Mlle. de Chevreuse: that name will guarantee his safety." Gondi agreed, and the interview took place at midnight in the Queen's oratory, whither the Coadjutor had been conducted by one of her Majesty's cloakbearers. Anne of Austria poured out her complaints against Condé; Mazarin added his own entreaties; the Coadjutor professed his devotion to the sovereign.

But this time there must be rewards! Mme. de Chevreuse asked for a cardinal's hat for Gondi; a captaincy in the Guard of the King's brother, the Duc d'Anjou, for Laigue; a duchy, and the governorship of Charleville, for Noirmoutier; and certain indemnities for Vendôme and

THE DUCHESSE DE CHEVREUSE

their friends. There was probably some mention, also, of the return of Châteauneuf to the Ministry; the Queen's answer was not unfavourable. Further conferences ensued, and at these Mme. de Chevreuse, bringing Laigue and Noirmoutier in her train, was present. Her proposals were accepted, and the Government spoke, in return, of the simultaneous arrest of Condé, Conti and Longueville. The agreement was concluded. For another five or six days Mazarin hesitated, and finally, on January 18, 1650, when the three Princes came to the Council, Condé was placed under arrest by Guitaut, a captain in the Guard, Conti by Comminges, a lieutenant, and Longueville by Cressi, an ensign in the same regiment; the three prisoners were conducted to Vincennes under an escort composed of *gendarmes* and *chevau-légers*. There was no resistance at all.

That was a day of triumph at the Hôtel de Chevreuse! While the arrests were being made, writes Guy Joly, "the Coadjutor was at the Hôtel de Chevreuse with the Duc de Beaufort, who had dined there; the door of the house was kept closed, and the servants forbidden to allow any visitor to enter." Beaufort's equerry, Brillet, brought the news; and letters announcing it were forthwith written and dispatched in all directions.

Thus the alliance with Mazarin had resulted in success, and a perpetual interchange of attentions, civilities, offers of service, between the Cardinal and the Duchess, ensued. Mme. de Chevreuse expressed her opinion on business matters: it was listened to; she made suggestions, and her advice was received with respect. On certain occasions the Secretaries of State even went to her house to hear what she had to say. "Yesterday afternoon," wrote Le Tellier to Mazarin on June 14, "Mme. de Chevreuse sent to ask me to go to her; I went, and she told me the Deputy for Provence had paid her a visit, that things were going very ill in that province, and that it was much to be feared

THE INTRIGUES OF THE FRONDE

it would take up arms again. I pointed out to Mme. de Chevreuse that this was not a thing that need necessarily lead to bad consequences. When I was leaving her, she requested me to send your Eminence the memorandum here enclosed, in order that it might please you to use your influence with the Queen to induce her to order the confiscation of the persons therein mentioned." In all his letters Mazarin reiterated his expressions of respect, fidelity and devotion.

And Mme. de Chevreuse made the most of her favour. She begged incessantly: for herself she asked the ransom money paid for the liberation of the Prince de Ligne, who had been made prisoner in a battle, 150,000 florins—300,000 francs. Mazarin laid her request before Anne of Austria, who granted her 80,000 francs. For Laigue she demanded, besides certain honours from the Duc d'Orléans, a pension of 10,000 *livres*, and a sum paid down of 5000 more. Above all, she insisted that Châteauneuf should be recalled to power. After more or less evasion, Mazarin and the Queen gave in; the Seals were taken from Séguier, and handed over to the Duchess's friend. Châteauneuf was then seventy; but, says Retz, "his strong and vigorous health, his royal way of spending money, his absolute unconcern as to everything which did not rise above the average, his rough and savage temper, which was taken for frankness, made up for his age, and caused him to be regarded as a man not yet past his work." Never had the authority of Mme. de Chevreuse seemed more efficient, nor her understanding with Mazarin more close!

Were they sincere, either of them? Did not the Cardinal, at the bottom of his heart, dread his new ally's duplicity? And knowing what Gondi's ambition was, did he not expect him to play the traitor? As early as on June 26, Le Tellier was writing to the Cardinal: "This evening I have seen a man of quality who certainly must know what is happening, and who told me he had learnt

THE DUCHESSE DE CHEVREUSE

for certain that M. le Coadjuteur and Mme. de Chevreuse were resolved to use strong measures to drive your Eminence out of your office; that Mme. de Chevreuse has proposed this to Monsieur, and strongly pressed him to exert himself for this purpose; but that his Royal Highness has not undertaken to do so; that M. de Châteauneuf is aware of this cabal, but nevertheless acts as if he did not approve of it." Mazarin was so convinced, and rightly, that he was to be betrayed, that from this time forward he was to do all that lay in his power to separate the Coadjutor from Mme. de Chevreuse. Gondi, at all events, had one motive for turning against the Minister—he knew he was resolved to oppose his advancement to the rank of Cardinal with all his might.

At a very early stage in the proceedings, the Coadjutor had had his doubts on this subject. He had mentioned them to Mme. de Chevreuse, who had conveyed his fears to Le Tellier. "As to that point in your memorandum connected with the Coadjutor's desire of being made a Cardinal," writes Colbert, Mazarin's secretary and steward, to Le Tellier, "his Eminence was much astonished, and afterwards desired me to tell you that no reason on earth would induce him to grant the Coadjutor his request." Colbert went on to say that steps must at once be taken to separate the Duchess from the Coadjutor: that Le Tellier had better see her, "and sound her mind as far as he could, find out whether there was any sincerity in her perpetual protestations of friendship, and in connection with these, should unbosom himself, and speak to her confidentially; his Eminence could not grant what he (the Coadjutor) asked: apart from that, he had authority (from the Queen) to offer him anything he might desire. It would be more correct and more advantageous for Mme. de Chevreuse to work with the Queen, and to throw herself entirely into the plans of the Cardinal, or turn the Coadjutor's mind away from this design." Mme. de

THE INTRIGUES OF THE FRONDE

Chevreuse returned an ambiguous reply to these overtures. Colbert persisted. It was necessary, he declared, that the Duchess should be forced into choosing between the Minister and the Coadjutor. "If the said lady," he explained, "would not accept the proposal, his Eminence (the Cardinal) would conclude she was working to obtain his place for the Coadjutor." The proceeding was rather a hasty one. Mazarin was mistaken in thinking his hold on Mme. de Chevreuse to be so great. Some time afterwards, in September, 1650, M. de Boislève informed the Minister that the Duchess was certainly trying to compass his overthrow, and this time her object was to get Châteauneuf appointed to the head of the Ministry. She had mentioned her idea to Retz, who, in some astonishment, it must be said, had protested against it, asserting that "he did not intend to play second fiddle." At that very moment, she was multiplying her expressions of fidelity and attachment to the Cardinal's person; there could be no doubt about her bad faith!

Then the Minister responded by dealings as double as her own; he sent word through Colbert that on the one hand discredit must be cast on the Coadjutor and his friends, and on the other the efforts to detach Mme. de Chevreuse from the Coadjutor's cause, by parting her from him, must be persisted in. "You might," writes Colbert, "agree with her about everything, assuring her she will be left perfectly quiet, that the Queen will show her extraordinary favour, and bestow more solid advantages on her, if the plan is carried out; you might even speak of some marriage for her daughter, the success of which should be ensured by favours the Queen might grant." In reply, Mme. de Chevreuse poured out more and more expressions of gratitude. To prove how completely she shared the Cardinal's views, she went so far as to abuse Retz, and bring accusations against him. But all the same, she pertinaciously demanded the Cardinal's hat for him.

THE DUCHESSE DE CHEVREUSE

She defended his cause, pointing out to Le Tellier that he had suffered from the injustice done him, which he had bitterly resented. And, she went on, Gondi was powerful; the princes and their party were making advances to him, which he might very likely end by accepting. When the Court came back, in November, from a long journey through France, and Mme. de Chevreuse began to plead the Coadjutor's cause again with Anne of Austria, declaring Gondi's conduct to have been "a tissue of important services," and repeating her assertion that he had been unjustly served, that he was treated with scorn, the Regent had lost her patience and her temper too, and Mazarin had avoided giving any direct answer at all. Gondi told Le Tellier that "he was being reduced, against his own will, to such a condition that he would have to be one of two things, either the head of a party, or a cardinal." This was a threat!

Thus Mazarin's plans were now a failure. He had not obtained that support from the Duchess on which he had reckoned: and he had not separated her from the Coadjutor. Morosini, the Ambassador, wrote his home government that the Minister had no confidence in the Duchess. Already, in the month of April, Anne of Austria had "betrayed much bitterness of feeling against Mme. de Chevreuse, whom she accused of playing everybody false in too open a fashion," wrote Colbert to Le Tellier. Mazarin, completely undeceived, now regarded all the persons who frequented her company with suspicion: he found fault with Lionne, the Queen's secretary, because he saw her too often. He was alarmed by the regard shown her by the Duc d'Orléans. Then the Duchess made a thrust at the Cardinal in the Queen's own presence. Talking to Her Majesty one day, so Montglat relates, she ventured to tell her what the outside world was saying about Mazarin: she herself, she acknowledged, was astonished at the way he was hated: everything he did

THE INTRIGUES OF THE FRONDE

was criticized: as the Cardinal's friend, she was deeply grieved by this attitude of public opinion: so great was the aversion of the nation to Mazarin, that whatever happened, he would never be liked, and no doubt, she added, the Queen, finding her difficulties growing constantly greater, would be obliged, one of these days, to dismiss him. There could be no doubt as to the meaning of this insinuation. Anne of Austria was exceedingly displeased by it. She reported the whole story to Mazarin, who, Monglat goes on to say, was "so surprised that he threw his skull-cap on the floor in a rage, being clearly convinced that the Duchess was deceiving him!" All things were ripe for an open rupture.

It was of a rupture that Mme. de Chevreuse was thinking. Her assertions as to the increasing power of the party led by the princes imprisoned at Vincennes were no idle boast. It was quite true that Condé's trusted agents had sounded the Coadjutor. As a matter of precaution, Mazarin had removed the prisoners from Vincennes to Marcoussis, towards the end of August, and in November, from Marcoussis to the Havre. These removals had not been carried out without lively opposition, and difficulties with the making of which the Coadjutor had been connected. Thanks to the Cardinal's unpopularity, the princes' party was gaining strength; and it was to its interest to acquire as many adherents as possible. It was at this moment that the project for reconciling Mme. de Chevreuse and Condé, and attaching that lady to the princes' cause by proposing a marriage between her daughter and the Prince de Conti—the whole arrangement to end in a united campaign against the Cardinal—was conceived by two feminine brains.

The two ladies thus inspired were the Princess Palatine—Anne, daughter of Charles I, de Gonzague, Duc de Nevers, who had married the Prince Palatine, and resided in Paris—and Mme. de Rhodes, niece of Mme. de

THE DUCHESSE DE CHEVREUSE

Chevreuse. Guy Joly tells us that when the idea had been talked over between them, they betook themselves to the Rue St. Thomas du Louvre, to discuss it there. Mlle. de Chevreuse, charmed by the idea of marrying Conti, gladly fell in with the plan. Laigue and Noirmoutier were against it: they were afraid of Condé's imperious temper, and dreaded his vengeance. Mme. de Chevreuse was rather uncertain at first; she was torn between her longing for so brilliant a marriage and her old spite against the princes. The negotiations were pushed forward: Gondi's adhesion was secured. Mlle. de Chevreuse, Mme. de Rhodes, and the Coadjutor joined together in working on the Duchess: "Mlle. de Chevreuse cried shame on her mother for the hesitation she showed about procuring her establishment," says Retz. They ended by carrying their point. It was settled that a treaty was to be signed; Conti was to marry Mlle. de Chevreuse: and as a consequence of the marriage there would be a fusion of the two parties. Not that this Conti, who was suggested as a husband for Mlle. de Chevreuse, was a very attractive individual. "He was of poor composition," writes Mme. de Motteville, "but owing to the great plans that were built on this marriage, the best aspect that could be given to it was shown, and it became a thing of great importance to Mme. de Chevreuse." The Duchess followed her friends' lead. Mazarin knew nothing of the plot. Events were to hurry all these complications to a dramatic conclusion.

Mme. de Chevreuse, discussing the clauses of the treaty to be drawn up, in the presence of the persons deputed by the princes, had boldly set forth her conditions: Mazarin must be driven out, she said, and Châteauneuf must replace him as chief Minister: the Prince de Conti, who was to marry her daughter, must be made Governor of Provence: Condé must be Governor of Guyenne: and Gondi must have the Cardinal's hat. All these matters she settled as by her sovereign authority. To what might

THE INTRIGUES OF THE FRONDE

she not aspire? This business meant the welding together of all the Frondes: the Duc d'Orléans was in the plot: the Court would soon find itself at the conspirators' mercy, and Mazarin would be forced to capitulate!

When the Cardinal found out what was going on, as he did at last, he was quite confounded. This time the matter was serious indeed! He tried to come to terms with the Duc d'Orléans, in the first place, but the Prince, led by Mme. de Chevreuse and the Coadjutor, exacted as a first condition that the Queen should consent to the Chevreuse-Conti marriage and release the three princes. At the same time, so extraordinary were the falseness and love of intrigue of the whole band of conspirators, the Princess Palatine sent an underhand proposal to Mazarin to enable him to enter into direct negotiations with the princes! The Cardinal's notebooks show that crippled as he found himself to be by all these various complications, he paused, not knowing which way to turn, waiting on events, looking this way and that: his irresolution worked his ruin.

His enemies, noting it, completed their own pact. The draft treaty was drawn up and signed on January 30, 1651, in the house of the Princess Palatine. The conditions put forward by Mme. de Chevreuse were accepted: the princes were to be set at liberty, the Cardinal was to be dismissed: the Duc d'Orléans was to have a preponderating voice in the Government as to the choice of the members of the Council. Special agreements guaranteed the various interests of the signatories: the Duc d'Enghien, Condé's son, was to marry one of Gaston's daughters: Conti was to marry Mlle. de Chevreuse: the Duchesse de Montbazon and her family were to have sums of money: Châteauneuf was to be appointed Minister in chief: Paul de Gondi was to be made a Cardinal. The Princess Palatine made the following stipulation in the name of the absent princes: "We, Princess Palatine, do

THE DUCHESSE DE CHEVREUSE

promise in the name of and in virtue of the power we have received from Messieurs the Princes and the Duchesse de Longueville, and pledge the faith and honour of M. le Prince de Conti, that as soon as he is set at liberty he will accept the conditions that shall appear reasonable as between himself and Mlle. de Chevreuse, and will marry her in the face of our Holy Mother the Church."

And thereupon the conspirators began to take decisive action. The Coadjutor caused Gaston to demand the immediate release of the princes from Parliament. This was a bold step. There was a lively quarrel between the Duke and the Cardinal at the Palais Royal, the outcome of which was Gaston's refusal to reappear at Court. On February 4, at Monsieur's request again, Parliament demanded the dismissal of Mazarin, and then the Paris burghers, under the command of Gaston, who was Lieutenant-General of the kingdom, took up arms, barricaded the streets, occupied the city gates: the situation was growing critical.

Mazarin, defenceless, and threatened with imprisonment, was constrained to give way and take to flight: in the course of the night of February 6, 1651, after a long conversation with Anne of Austria, during which all the arrangements for her future conduct were made, he departed in haste. On the 8th, the Parliament passed an edict according to the terms of which the Cardinal was expelled the kingdom, and the enlargement of the princes demanded from the Queen. Anne of Austria was outflanked. She would have fled too, taking the King with her: but Châteauneuf gave Mme. de Chevreuse timely warning, and she sent word to the Duc d'Orléans and the Coadjutor; instantly, the Palais Royal was surrounded by armed burghers; the Queen was a prisoner, the Government was vanquished; on the 10th, the Court made its submission, and the Queen signed an order for the princes' release.

THE INTRIGUES OF THE FRONDE

Then Mazarin, who had been waiting on events at Lillebonne, in Normandy, seized the advantage offered him by circumstance, flew to the Havre, walked, booted and spurred, and in his travelling dress, into the citadel, himself informed the princes they were free, and, asking nothing but their friendship in return, opened their prison doors. Deceived, the princes promised what he asked. Mazarin made them a long speech: he warned Condé to be on his guard against his enemies, enlightened him as to the duplicity of this person and that: Condé assured him of his faithful devotion. When all was done, the Cardinal rode to Dieppe, thence to Doullens, Peronne and Bar-le-Duc, crossed the frontier, and took refuge at Cologne. He knew very well what he was doing when he set the princes free! He had cast them into the midst of the Frondeurs, and soon all the allies would be fighting amongst themselves!

It was Mme. de Chevreuse, according to Mme. de Motteville, who advised Mazarin and the Regent to decide on the Cardinal's departure, for a season at all events: "So," she said, "as to let the storm blow over." The Duchess promised the Queen she would do her best to bring about a reconciliation between the Cardinal and the Duc d'Orléans, and after that it would be easy to persuade the Prince to consent to his return. "Perhaps," adds Mme. de Motteville, "she did this simply for the amusement of the intrigue and the novelty of it!" On the other hand, the Duchesse de Nemours thought that "Mme. de Chevreuse had always asserted in the council of the Fronde that the only thing to be done was to remove the Cardinal from the Queen's neighbourhood, and that, knowing her as she did, she was perfectly certain that once he was removed from Her Majesty's sight, she would forget all about him." Retz, to conclude, was convinced it was Mme. de Chevreuse who, with Châteauneuf's help, had brought about the Cardinal's flight: "A great political move," he considered it, "prepared by Mme. de Chevreuse and the Keeper of the Seals, so as to cause the Cardinal to work his own ruin!" If Mazarin and Anne of Austria had preserved any illusions as to the fiedelity of the Duchess, they must have been thoroughly informed, by this time, as to what they were to expect.

From the Castle of Brühl, near Cologne, where Mazarin had taken refuge, he poured out his rage against Mme. de Chevreuse. "She has broken everything to pieces," he wrote in April, 1651, "and set everything to work, to entice this man and that away from the King's service, to surprise fortresses, raise the Huguenots in revolt, establish them (with the help of Spain), at La Rochelle; she has always been a pensioner of the Spaniards, who paid her for the services she rendered them! She has done all she could for the interests of Spain and of the Duc de Lorraine, at the expense of France, to ruin the Queen, and overthrow the State!"

But though Mme. de Chevreuse had succeeded, though her intrigues had brought about the Cardinal's departure, and the triumph of the Fronde, though she had secured a brilliant marriage for her daughter in the course of the enterprise, the end of the business was not to fulfil the brilliant promise of its opening stages!

The Prince de Condé—"the great Condé"—whose prison doors had just been opened, was then a man of thirty. He was a haughty being, whose scruples were few and far between. As soon as he reached Paris, he went to pay his respects to Mme. de Chevreuse; he was aware of the stipulations made by the Princess Palatine in his name, and that he was bound to accept the marriage of his brother, the Prince de Conti. The interview was of a cordial nature. The Duchesse de Nemours relates that the Prince thanked Mme. de Chevreuse for what she had done, assuring her that he owed her his freedom; according to

THE INTRIGUES OF THE FRONDE

the undertaking made in his name, he requested the hand of her daughter for Conti, Conti himself being present. Mme. de Chevreuse replied that she felt the proposal to be a great honour for her family, but that engagements made in prison might be taken to have been made under compulsion, and she requested the Prince to take back his word, and that any future action he decided on might be perfectly sincere. Condé replied by adhering to his request. Mme. de Chevreuse then granted it, and Conti at once began to pay his court to the young lady.

Preparations for the marriage were forthwith begun. The Hôtel de Chevreuse was hung with tapestries which had belonged to Mazarin: "I am informed from Paris," writes the Cardinal on April 1, "that the Hôtel de Chevreuse is being sumptuously adorned for the wedding solemnities, and that three tapestries which are my property have been hung up there—to wit, the 'Scipio,' the 'Paris,' and one set of forest scenes, touched up with gold threads, which formed part of those pledged to Herwart." To calm his mind, Colbert informed the fallen Minister that the Duchess and Laigue had bought the tapestries for 300,000 *livres* more than they were worth. Just at this juncture, Mme. de Longueville, Condé's haughty and high-spirited sister, reached Paris from Stenay, where she had been detained by business.

Mme. de Chevreuse at once paid her a visit. In the course of the conversation that ensued, the Duchess made no reference whatever to the Conti marriage. This silence boded ill. And, as a matter of fact, Mme. de Longueville had come back to Paris resolved this marriage should be broken off at all hazards. She still nursed her old hatred of Mme. de Chevreuse. She could not forget that it was in the Duchess's house, where all her family had been so detested, that the arrest of the princes her kinsmen had been resolved and plotted, a few short years previously. She could not swallow the idea that Châteauneuf, the

THE DUCHESSE DE CHEVREUSE

murderer of her uncle, the Duc Henry de Montmorency, was to receive the reward of his crime in the shape of honours and greatness. And further, Mlle. de Chevreuse, when she became Princesse de Conti, would take precedence of herself at Court! Even in the houses of the Condé family, Mme. de Longueville would have to give way to this Princess, younger, more admired, than herself! And would not Charlotte end by supplanting her in the good graces of the Prince, over whom she still wielded so much influence?

She decided to act at once. Her first step was to express doubts, in public, as to the morals of Mlle. de Chevreuse: she said openly that Conti's betrothed was "the Coadjutor's mistress," that she had had lovers. This was an objection for which everybody was prepared. "I cannot understand," wrote Mazarin to Lionne, on March 21, 1651, "how Mme. de Longueville and La Rochefoucauld, who have the most complete ascendency over the mind of the Prince de Condé, can put their hands to it (this marriage). As it is a well-known thing in Paris, it is impossible that the people whose interest it is to disgust the Prince de Conti can fail to know that the Coadjutor sees Mlle. de Chevreuse in private every night, and that he has a better understanding with her than can be desired by the man who is going to marry her."

Anne of Austria, on her part, had manifested the most lively dislike of the plan. Mazarin's letters encouraged her feeling in the matter. The opinion of the Government was unanimously hostile. Condé was warned of the feeling of the Court, and the dangers to which such a woman as Mme. de Chevreuse would certainly expose his house, were pointed out to him: "a woman of that character and mind," whose "dangerous cleverness, and whole conduct" were so well known! The Ministers pressed him hard: Lionne and Servien were the go-betweens: the Regent herself made advances, offered governorships to Condé.

THE INTRIGUES OF THE FRONDE

Urged on by Mme. de Longueville, the Prince lent his ear to these suggestions. Quite early in April he had made up his mind to break off the marriage: and this meant a quarrel between the two Frondes, and the reconciliation of the Princes with Anne of Austria, who was making ready for that event.

Advised by Mazarin, so Brühl writes, the Government tried to take advantage of the situation. A sudden blow would reveal the extent of its real power. This blow was to be the dismissal of Châteauneuf, and on April 3, Brienne called on the friend of Mme. de Chevreuse to deliver up the Seals. The Duchess and her daughter were informed of this proceeding, and were further warned that there was a talk of exile for them both. The two ladies, so Guy Joly tells us, "spent a whole night without taking off their clothes, and with all their jewels in a casket, which Mlle. de Chevreuse kept under her arm. The Coadjutor and some of the other Frondeurs also spent the night at the Hôtel de Chevreuse, taking measures to obtain vengeance, when chance should serve them; but the order for their arrest did not arrive, and each person departed to his own home, in rather less alarm."

Next day, they all met again at the Duc d'Orléans' palace of the Luxembourg. Their excitement was extreme. The most extravagant expedients were suggested; there was talk of stirring up the populace, marching on the Palais-Royal, killing the new Keeper of the Seals, throwing all the Ministers out of the windows, and carrying off the King. All these exaggerated threats were really symptoms of weakness. The Prince de Condé would have none of them. Since the beginning of April, he had discontinued his visits to the Rue St. Thomas du Louvre. Some amount of blood relationship between Conti and Mlle. de Chevreuse had been discovered, necessitating a dispensation from Rome; this dispensation was still awaited, and the ceremony had been put off. Mme. de

THE DUCHESSE DE CHEVREUSE

Chevreuse grew anxious. Conti, to whom Condé had repeated everything that was being said about Mlle. de Chevreuse's light behaviour, was now beginning to slacken in his attendance at the Hôtel de Chevreuse. Condé had quite made up his mind to take back his promise; the only difficulty lay in finding a pretext; this was suggested by Anne of Austria: the King, as head of the family, would forbid Conti to make this marriage: the proposal was accepted.

On the morning of April 15, Anne of Austria, in the name of the King, informed Condé of her desire that he should renounce all idea of carrying through the project of marriage he had entertained. "This marriage," she said, "was not at all seasonable." The princes bowed to her will.

It was necessary that their decision should be notified to Mme. de Chevreuse, and the President de Viole was commissioned to perform this duty. Retz has left a description of the scene, at which he was present. Viole made his appearance at the Hôtel de Chevreuse, looking very uncomfortable. He vaguely explained the object of his visit, protesting that "the affair was deferred, not broken off," that the princes were very much annoyed, and hoped that in time they might obtain the consent which the Queen at present refused to grant. Mme. de Chevreuse, who had expected his communication, replied to it calmly and courteously: her daughter, "who was dressing herself beside the fire, burst out laughing."

Five days later, on April 20, Mme. de Chevreuse, beside herself with rage, wrote to Noirmoutier, who was then at Charleville, of which place he was Governor, that he was to let Mazarin know immediately that after the humiliation she had just been forced to undergo, she was entirely at the Cardinal's service. On the receipt of this letter, Mazarin wrote to Lionne as follows: "I have discovered that everything Mme. de Chevreuse and all the others can

THE INTRIGUES OF THE FRONDE

possibly do to avenge themselves on M. le Prince will certainly be done." The Cardinal's advice to the Queen was that she should play off one party against the other, prevent any reconciliation between them, and wait.

Then the Frondeurs, instigated by Mme. de Chevreuse and the Coadjutor, opened their campaign. They cried down Condé, representing him to be a man without faith, or conscience, or honour: the populace followed them. Every kind of calumny was put about concerning the princes. According to Guy Joly, Mme. de Chevreuse even went the length of asking Mazarin to have the Prince rearrested. The Court answered by demanding the Cardinal's recall to Paris as a preliminary condition; negotiations began; the Government's game was to make use of the parties to them. In May and June, Mme. de Chevreuse and the Coadjutor had several interviews with Anne of Austria: the Duchess betrayed the most relentless thirst for vengeance, she clamoured for Condé's arrest even in the open street, and at the risk of sacrificing his life. The Queen made as though she would consent. But Condé, warned of his danger by her intermediaries, left Paris on July 6, and fled hastily to Saint-Maur: the coast was clear.

Then the Queen came to an arrangement with the Frondeurs: Gondi was to have his oft-promised cardinal's hat: Mlle. de Chevreuse was to marry a nephew of Mazarin's, who was to have the Duchy of Réthelois, and governorships as well: the Frondeurs were to accept the Cardinal's return.

And, thereupon, on September 7, 1651, the majority of Louis XIV was proclaimed. This event, a mere formality, as it seemed to be, was in reality a most important fact, which singularly increased the power of Mazarin, and was to hasten his return. Condé, now in open revolt, was organizing his resistance in the provinces, raising troops, and beginning to make war. Mazarin, summoned by the

THE DUCHESSE DE CHEVREUSE

King, drew near the frontier. While the fighting with Condé was going forward in Saintonge, the Cardinal was slowly moving forward on the other side of the country. After various ups and downs of fortune, and some violent opposition on the Parliament's part, he reached Sedan on December 24, and rejoined the Court at Poitiers on January 29, 1652; Mme. de Chevreuse took his side: "I saw Mme. de Chevreuse yesterday," wrote Pennacors to the Cardinal on January 21, "she told me you must absolutely rely on her, and on her friends, and that her daughter is of the same mind." Mazarin sent a reply expressing similar sentiments. These two personages, once more united, gave each other assurances of their reciprocal fidelity. During the war with Condé, in 1652, the Duchess rendered useful service to the Minister: in the month of June, she interposed herself between the French Court and the Duc de Lorraine, who had marched to the help of the princes with a force of five or six thousand men; she won him over to the Queen's side, and induced him to march his troops back again.

To reward her for her trouble, she put forward claims for her friends, and was given due satisfaction. Gondi had at last received his cardinal's hat, in February, 1652; the biretta was bestowed on him on the 11th of the following September, by the King himself, at Compiègne: Mlle. de Chevreuse was shortly to be married to Mazarin's nephew, Mancini. The Duchess was in favour, once more she seemed all-powerful; was there anything in the world for which she dared not hope? This was the last bright flash of her political existence. The majority of Louis XIV had changed the face of all things. This closing scene of the career of Mme. de Chevreuse was a blaze of splendour and good fortune.

She had reached her fifty-second year; she had grown heavy, her face was worn, the gaiety of old days had departed. The young King was growing up, and already

THE INTRIGUES OF THE FRONDE

a few of his sayings, curt, imperious, portended a future lord whose patience was likely to be short-lived. There was no place for such persons as Mme. de Chevreuse under the coming régime. And certain cruel humiliations and sorrows, too, were warning the Duchess that her time was over.

In the course of the events that marked the year 1652, Condé's campaign against the King's troops, the fights at Bléneau and at the Porte Saint-Antoine, Mazarin's second departure, and the return of Louis XIV to Paris, Mme. de Chevreuse, save in the matter of the Duc de Lorraine, had been kept at a distance. She was on such bad terms with the Prince de Condé that there was no reason to fear her coming to any understanding with him; and the Court, having no reason to dread her, simply neglected her. Towards the close of April, negotiations took place between Mazarin and Condé: Mme. de Chevreuse and her associates were not taken into account at all. "We are done for!" cried the Cardinal de Retz, on the 27th, to a friend he happened to meet, "the settlement has been made, and without us, for neither Mme. de Chevreuse, nor M. de Châteauneuf, nor I myself, have had anything to with it!" When the Duchesse de Chevreuse, adds Conrart, asked the King to grant her a passport to go to Saint-Germain, where the Court was settled, it was refused, "which confirmed the opinion that an agreement had been arrived at secretly." No agreement had been reached, nor was the moment of such a conclusion very near, but all these circumstances proved that the position occupied by Mme. de Chevreuse was much less influential than she had imagined; this fact affected her extremely.

And thereupon, early in the morning of November 7, after a very few hours of illness, Mlle. de Chevreuse, her daughter Charlotte, passed suddenly away in her mother's arms! It was a frightful blow! "This death," wrote Guy Joly, "came as a surprise to everybody: it was remarked

THE DUCHESSE DE CHEVREUSE

that the face and body of the dead woman turned quite black, and a report consequently got about that this was the result of poison she had taken herself, or which her mother had administered to her, for secret reasons." Such an insinuation is quite inadmissible. Mme. de Chevreuse was in the deepest grief. Her daughter had been her friend, her counsellor. Satirical, eager-hearted, impulsive and high-spirited, Charlotte de Chevreuse, so like the Duchess in many particulars, had shared all her mother's passions. That mother had seen herself live again in her child, and her sorrow now completely overwhelmed her. This grief, added to all the rest, disheartened her utterly: she made up her mind to quit the world and spend the rest of her life far from the Court.

The idea had already occurred to her in April of that same year. "Perceiving herself to be somewhat left aside in Paris," wrote Retz, "she had come to the decision to leave it, and betake herself to Dampierre." But it had proved no easy matter for her to give up all active employment so quickly, and by the month of October, she was back, and trying to gather up the threads again. Laigue had gone about paying visits. But the result had not been what the Duchess had expected. "She had not," adds Retz, "met with either the consideration or the confidence she had expected, at Court." Her daughter's death settled the question. Worn out and saddened, Mme. de Chevreuse turned her back on Paris, and departed to Dampierre.

CHAPTER X

RETIREMENT AND DEATH

Dampierre—Financial difficulties—Lawsuits with the whole family—Dissensions in the household—Foreclosures, penury, a separate maintenance—The son and daughters of Mme. de Chevreuse—Her final retirement to Gagny—Her death, 1679.

ON her retirement to Dampierre, in the green and smiling valley of Chevreuse, the Duchess made a vow never to touch politics again. When her friend the Cardinal de Retz, whose intrigues Mazarin had not pardoned, and never was to pardon, was arrested, on December 19, 1652, the Duchess did not lift a finger. "Mme. de Chevreuse," writes Guy Joly, on February 3, 1653, "takes no further interest in the business of the Cardinal de Retz." Mazarin had returned in triumph to Paris, and Mme. de Chevreuse, like everybody else, had accepted the situation. Whether by policy or by temperament, the Cardinal, more willing to forget treachery than to take the trouble of punishing it, heaped civilities on every body. "I have seen the persons your Eminence commanded me to see," writes Colbert; "Mme. de Chevreuse expressed her gratitude to your Eminence for the honour of your recollection of her." And the Duchess writes to assure Mazarin of her friendly feeling for him. "It is an extreme satisfaction to me," she says, "to see that you are persuaded of the pleasure I take in rendering you all the services I can, and I protest I will continue to prove to you, whenever your interests are concerned, that they are as dear to me as they ought to be. I wish you all kinds of prosperity, and am, more than any one else in the world,

THE DUCHESSE DE CHEVREUSE

your very humble and obedient servant." Greater deference could not be expressed! Henceforward the Cardinal might depend upon her. He asked her to induce Noirmoutier, who still continued refractory, to yield, and reconcile him to the Government; she consented. Mazarin was always paying her compliments. "I have received, Madame," he writes on October 16, 1653, "two of your letters, the most obliging in the world; and M. de Laigue has said so many things to me in your name, to acquaint me with the good graces with which you have the kindness to honour me, that I confess, Madame, I know not how to express my sense of them as I ought! Therefore I have begged Monsieur l'Abbé Fouquet, who will have the honour of carrying this letter to you, to do it for me, and that in the most expressive terms he can discover." The two found it pleasanter to exchange compliments than to make war upon each other.

And, indeed, if Mme. de Chevreuse had attempted to mix herself up with State affairs, the Government, directed by Mazarin, and no longer dependent on a weak woman like Anne of Austria, but on that strong-willed young Prince, Louis XIV, who had now reached his majority, would soon have put a stop to it. Of this the Duchess was well aware. The utmost she ventured was to intervene in favour of the Duc de Lorraine, her own kinsman, who, having lost his State in the course of the wars between France and the Empire, came to the French Court in 1660, and spent a year pleading for the return of his territory.

She intervened again to plead for the Jansenists. M. du Hamel, parish priest of Saint-Merri, and a friend of the nuns of the Port-Royal, who had been exiled for having defended Retz, begged Mme. de Chevreuse to get him the Cardinal's leave to go and take some waters: Mme. de Chevreuse forwarded his request, and backed it up, and on August 14, 1655, Mazarin replied as follows: "As to

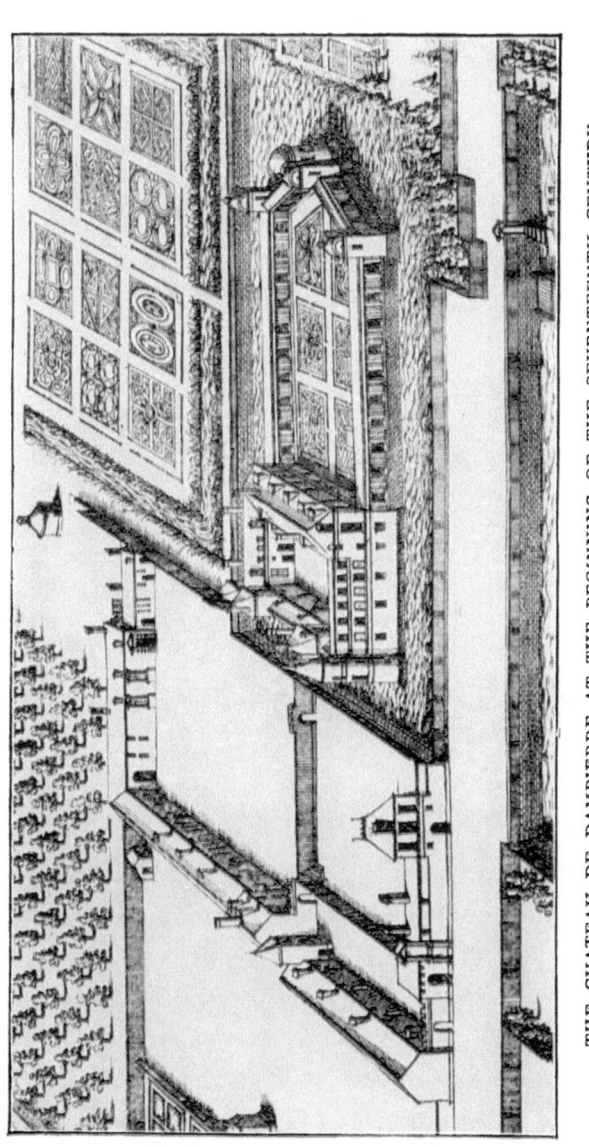

THE CHATEAU DE DAMPIERRE AT THE BEGINNING OF THE SEVENTEENTH CENTURY
(From an engraving by d'Androuet de Cerceau)

RETIREMENT AND DEATH

the permission for which the Sieur du Hamel asks, I am in some difficulty, for the King and Queen are very ill-pleased with his behaviour, and he has, indeed, behaved very badly since his departure from Paris, and this has been the cause of his being sent into Brittany; nevertheless, if you will not relieve me of the necessity of praying their Majesties to give him leave to go to the waters, I will do it, to obey you; but I shall await your further orders on the subject." And when Mme. de Chevreuse pressed her request: "I send you the permission you have asked for the Sieur du Hamel, having besought the King to grant it, out of blind deference to the commands you have been pleased to lay on me."

In 1656 Arnauld d'Andilly appealed to the Duchess, and also to her sister-in-law, the Princesse de Guémené, to use their good offices to prevent his being driven out of Port-Royal-des-Champs, from which place the Government desired to remove all the solitaries—his friends, who had shared his seclusion, had already departed. Mme. de Chevreuse replied that she had seen Anne of Austria and Mazarin, and that the Government insisted on M. d'Andilly's departure, for a time at all events: Andilly was obliged to retire to Pomponne; the Duchess had achieved a partial success only.

Twice again, at most, did Mme. de Chevreuse, in spite of her good resolutions, attempt to mix herself up, though indirectly, with more important matters, such as the choice or dismissal of a Minister. In 1652, when the disgrace of Le Tellier was noised abroad, Laigue took it into his head to get his place for one of his own friends, Jérome de Nouveau, Seigneur de Fromont, who had made himself useful both to the Duchess and to Mazarin. M. de Fromont was ready to pay for his office in hard cash, and 100,000 *livres* of the sum were to pass into Laigue's pocket—hence his zeal! Mme. de Chevreuse asked Retz, who was not yet in prison, to help her in the matter. "I

THE DUCHESSE DE CHEVREUSE

began to smile," writes the Coadjutor, "and said I thought they must take me for a madman! that it was well known I was better aware than anybody that we were not in a position to appoint Secretaries of State; and further, that if we had been, it was not for M. de Nouveau that we should have laboured!" Le Tellier defended his own position, and the whole business came to nothing.

The second instance was connected with the disgrace of Fouquet. Nine years later, towards the end of June 1661, Anne of Austria, in performance of an old promise to visit Mme. de Chevreuse at Dampierre, spent two or three days there with the Duchess. With her she brought her daughter-in-law, Madame (Henrietta of England), then just seventeen. Louis XIV, a man of three-and-twenty, was too much inclined to hang about the young wife, and it was to deliver her from his somewhat alarming attentions that the Queen, to whom they were anything but pleasing, had betaken herself to Dampierre. Laigue suggested that the Duchess should make an attack on Fouquet, the Superintendent of the King's Finances. How his interests were affected by this intrigue we know not. In the course of the long conversations between the two Princesses, the subject came up. Anne of Austria was attached to Fouquet. The efforts made to oust him distressed her; but for a considerable time the King, her son, roused to fury by the Superintendent's exactions, had betrayed his intention to rid himself of him, and strike him a deadly blow.

Mme. de Chevreuse pleaded the public weal, and the issue of events may have led her to believe her intervention had been crowned with success; but it is not credible, as Mme. de Motteville says, that this visit to Dampierre, during which "an important affair was discussed, had any particular effect on the decision of the fate of a Minister whose credit then appeared to stand so high." The business had been settled beforehand, and elsewhere.

RETIREMENT AND DEATH

Louis XIV would never have allowed Mme. de Chevreuse to interfere in such a matter—nor in any other.

In fact, the young monarch, as he grew older, was making his Court aware, in more and more overwhelming fashion, of his own strong-willed and autocratic nature. His haughty mien, imposing and severe, his proud and majestic manner, his habit of using few words, but those few chillingly concise, struck fear into his courtiers' hearts: they dreaded him. Less and less possible had it become for Mme. de Chevreuse to hope for any return to her former dreams of influence and power.

And she made up her mind to it. Nothing but persistent spells of bad weather, or the numerous lawsuits in which she was engaged, could drive her back to Paris: she lived at Dampierre, and entertained there. "Monsieur," she writes to the Duc d'Épernon in October 1657, "after having thanked you a thousand times for your recollection of me, I must tell you in these lines the displeasure I feel at not being able to have the honour of seeing you at Dampierre this year: the bad weather drives me thence to Paris, where I pray you will send me word when I may hope (to see you)."

Once she showed herself willing to live without making plots, the King, who, like his father, was obliged to consider her position as a Princess, to some extent, of a foreign house, was very ready to treat her without any symptom of unfriendliness. Mme. de Chevreuse was free to come to Court whenever she chose; she had not the honour of any close intimacy with the sovereign, but she had the right to hold her own rank as a Duchess. On rare occasions she made her appearance in the King's circle. When the Court proceeded to view the fortifications of the northern towns — one of those magnificent journeys during which Louis XIV exhibited the pomp he so dearly loved—Mme. de Chevreuse accompanied Mlle. de Montpensier.

THE DUCHESSE DE CHEVREUSE

In Paris she went and came as she chose. The Great Mademoiselle records her having been seen out walking, leaning on the arm of Laigue or Noirmoutier. Thus she tells us, once: "I went to see Monceau, because I was told that house was for sale. On my return I heard that Mme. de Chevreuse and Noirmoutier had been there." Was Mme. de Chevreuse thinking of buying the place? It would seem likely. And yet her fortune would hardly have permitted of her doing it. Her whole life, in fact, was occupied with the numberless difficulties arising out of the confusion in her business affairs, and the consequences of the successive bereavements that had befallen her.

On October 16, 1654, her old father, the Duc de Montbazon, had died. His share in her life had not been a large one! In his retirement at Couzières, in Touraine, he had reached his eighty-sixth year—a peaceful old age—without much care for his own kin, as regardless of his family as of his patrimony. Four years previously, Anne of Austria had made him sell his office as Governor of Paris, the duties of which his advanced age rendered him incapable of performing. M. de Montbazon obeyed without a word. Nor did he say a word, either, concerning the endless lawsuits his children brought against him, on account of the disorder into which he had allowed his family affairs to fall.

His son, the Prince de Guéméné, had obtained two Parliamentary decrees against him, one in 1634, and the other in 1638, which ordered M. de Montbazon to give him an account of his wardship, return him a sum of 90,000 *livres* due on a certain property called Briolay, and pay up the arrears of the annual income of 3000 *livres* which the Duke had undertaken to give his son when he married. M. de Montbazon sent no reply. Guéméné appealed to the King in Council, and three decrees, issued in 1639, 1640 and 1654, ordered the whole dispute between

RETIREMENT AND DEATH

father and son to be submitted to Parliament. Thereupon the son had taken possession of the Castle of Rochefort-en-Yveline, which was his father's property.

Then Mme. de Chevreuse, following her brother's example, had called on the old Duke to pay her the dowry promised in her marriage contract, and which she had never received—200,000 *livres*—besides the 10,000 *livres* a year which were to have been taken out of the fortunes left by her mother, a Lenoncourt, and her grandmother, a Laval. If her father, she said, would pay over these 200,000 *livres* at once, as an advance on what she was to inherit at his death, she would not ask him for the accounts of his wardship. M. de Montbazon had agreed. As to the inheritance from the mother and grandmother, which, it had been proved, did not bring in much more than 8000 *livres* in the year, it had been decided under arbitration, in December, 1647, that M. de Montbazon must make up the sum of 10,000 *livres* in question. But he had never paid his daughter either the 10,000 *livres* a year or the 200,000 *livres* down. Once more Mme. de Chevreuse appealed to the Courts of Law. By a decision of the Court of Requests delivered in 1651, the father was ordered to pay the yearly income he owed, and further, to pay the 200,000 *livres*, principal and interest, which, with divers other sums due, amounted in all to 600,000 *livres*. Montbazon appealed against this sentence, and an arrangement was made according to which the father gave his daughter a temporary indemnity, by making over to her certain properties in Anjou and Touraine, and in the neighbourhood of Montbazon, and also Couzières, and the Hôtel de Montbazon in Paris. When Mme. de Chevreuse tried to take possession of these properties, she found they were already in the hands of various creditors. More and more lawsuits ensued, to the joy and delight of the lawyers: one to establish the priority of Marie de Rohan's claim, another for the withdrawal of the seizure, another to have the properties sold, decrees of all kinds, etc. M. de Montbazon was dead before the inextricable tangle of disputes was cleared up.

By his second marriage with the beautiful Mme. de Montbazon, the Duke had had three children, who were joint heirs with Mme. de Chevreuse and the Prince de Guéméné. When the inventory of his property was taken, after his death, it was discovered that the Duchy of Montbazon was in the hands of his creditors, that Rochefort was held by Guéméné, the Hôtel de Montbazon in Paris by more creditors; Couzières and the lands in Anjou were in the hands of the Duchesse de Chevreuse, and the value of all together scarcely reached 200,000 *livres*. There was no ready money at all: 45,000 crowns which had remained over from the sum paid to M. de Montbazon to indemnify him for the loss of his post as Governor of Paris, the jewels, the silver plate, had all disappeared. The family accused Mme. de Montbazon of having stolen them. It had been necessary to sell the furniture to pay the funeral expenses, and those of putting on the seals and having the inventory made.

Each of the heirs—the Prince de Guéméné, the Duchesse de Chevreuse, Mme. de Montbazon and her three children, and some four or five score of creditors—put in a statement of claim: these came to a total of 1,600,000 *livres*, 200,000 of which were owing to the creditors: the debts exceeded the assets.

An attack on Mme. de Montbazon followed: she it was who had squandered her husband's substance! She must be made to "give a true account of all debts incurred since her marriage, and honestly set forth a list of all the title-deeds, documents, precious furniture, jewels, silver plate, and the 45,000 crowns she had made away with!" The Prince de Guéméné demanded the accounts of his wardship from the year 1602; Mme. de Chevreuse was willing to adhere to the arrangement concluded with her father,

RETIREMENT AND DEATH

on condition she was paid the indemnities promised her. The difficulties were not to end here.

M. de Montbazon had left a will by which he desired his son, the Prince de Guéméné, to pay the children of his second marriage a sum of 200,000 *livres*, to be charged on the value of the offices the King had bestowed on M. de Montbazon, and which he had resigned into Guéméné's hands—the government of Nantes, worth 200,000 *livres*; that of the Île de France, which brought in 85,000 crowns; the office of Master of the King's Hunt, 100,000 crowns about 800,000 *livres* in all. Mme. de Chevreuse, perceiving her father's assets would never furnish the 200,000 *livres* and the yearly income to which she was entitled, forthwith cast her eyes on these 800,000 *livres*, and prayed Parliament to order that her claim, too, should be charged upon that sum. She began a lawsuit with her brother, and Guéméné appealed to the King. The King, by a decree of his Council, made answer that he did not intend that offices of honour bestowed by him, in pure kindness, should be reckoned as forming part of any private fortune, "lest," he said, "the division of such benefits should diminish the gratitude felt for them." Mme. de Chevreuse had lost her cause. But Guéméné, furious at the trick his sister had played him, was to take yet another vengeance upon her.

When the Duchess had claimed the yearly income drawn from the fortunes of her mother and grandmother, and promised her by her marriage contract, together with the dowry also specified in that document, an arrangement had been come to, on February 20, 1654, whereby everything was to be settled by the payment by M. de Montbazon of a sum fixed at 440,000 *livres*, and his daughter had at once taken a mortgage for that amount on her father's property. When the settlement of the paternal succession began, she asserted her right to a prior claim over all the other creditors, and demanded full payment out of the assets, before anybody else could touch them.

THE DUCHESSE DE CHEVREUSE

Then Guéméné asserted that he, too, must be allowed to take "his legitimate fortune" out of the assets before anybody else, and even declared that, as the eldest son, he could insist on having it "out of what had been given to the said Lady Duchess of Chevreuse." They went to law again. Mme. de Chevreuse replied that as the Prince, her brother, had received offices worth 800,000 *livres* from their father, he ought to take his "legitimate fortune" out of that sum. "If the value of the said offices and governments did not suffice," she added, "the surplus ought to be taken out of the donations made to the children of the second marriage of the said Duc de Montbazon." But then the children of the second marriage arose in their wrath. By a writ served on March 23, 1655, they called on Guéméné to pay them the 200,000 *livres* left them by M. de Montbazon's will, and to be taken out of the 800,000 *livres* furnished by the offices made over by their late father to the Prince. We have already related that Guéméné had appealed to the King, who would not allow the value of offices conferred by his favour to be reckoned in any succession. Mme. de Chevreuse was to go on bringing lawsuit after lawsuit in every court, and the litigation was to grow more and more complicated.

Meanwhile, Mme. de Montbazon had died. She passed away rather suddenly in April, 1657, killed by an attack of suppressed measles, after barely two days' illness, and in her forty-eighth year. To the very end of her life she was immensely admired. My readers may be acquainted with the story, which has, indeed, been contradicted, according to which M. de Rancé, her last lover, came into the death-chamber, and found the head of the corpse severed from the trunk, because the coffin had been made too small to allow of the body being laid in it intact. So horrified was de Rancé by this unexpected sight that he became a monk, and the ultimate founder of La Trappe. Mme. de Montbazon left a daughter of seventeen, Anne

RETIREMENT AND DEATH

de Rohan, a charming young creature, dearly loved by Mme. de Chevreuse, who took her to live with her: she had practically brought her up. The young girl set her affections on a cloistered life, and became a novice.

The death of Mme. de Montbazon created fresh difficulties. But the affairs of Mme. de Chevreuse were much more seriously affected by the death of her husband, the old Duc de Chevreuse, who had been suddenly carried off three months previously, in January 1657, by an attack of apoplexy.

Up to that time M. de Chevreuse, in spite of his eighty years, had enjoyed fairly good health. He had completely recovered from a first attack, which had left him, so he said, "as well and hearty as if he had been five-and-twenty." His appetite was good, he loved dainty food, and, so Tallemant assures us, he still had a weakness for the fair sex. He was considered rather frivolous. Though he had grown more and more deaf, and was afflicted, in general society, with certain weaknesses which made the young folks laugh, he still led a merry life, and, as Monglat tells us, "thought of nothing but his pleasures." There was a story that even when he had reached his seventieth year he would have "pretty dears" brought to the castle of Dampierre, and that after supper he was in the habit of paying nightly visits to "some creature or other" in the neighbourhood of Saint Thomas du Louvre. He was buried in the Carmelite Church. He had not been a very conspicuous figure when he was alive, and he left no particular void after his death.

If he had not been as horrified as he ought by his wife's ill-conduct, she had certainly suffered a world of vexation on account of his unbusinesslike habits. M. de Chevreuse did not know what order meant. He expected his house to be invariably well kept, his table well served, his stables full of fine horses, and it never occurred to him to consider whether he was in a position to pay for it all or not.

THE DUCHESSE DE CHEVREUSE

Then, every now and then, he would be seized with some ruinously expensive fancy, such as to have fifteen coaches built at once, so as to choose the one that ran the most smoothly!

As a consequence of all this dissipation, he was over head and ears in debt quite early in his life. His whole existence was one long fight with his creditors. His lawsuits were countless. His creditors seized his goods a full score of times. He was in perpetual need of money, and would borrow, and sell anything, at any price, to get the wherewithal to carry on. "You must know," wrote du Dorat to Boispillé on July 9, 1638, "that Monseigneur the Duke is well in health, better provided with ready money at this present moment than when you went away, for he has sold two horses to Mme. de Choisy. It is no news to you, it is true, to hear he has been selling, but the miracle is to hear that Mme. de Choisy has given 600 *livres* for two sorry beasts, and an unheard-of thing that any woman of the Place Royale should have given money to M. de Chevreuse! This leads me to judge that when you come back you will find him very much changed."

Landed properties, pensions, fiefs, the bailiffs laid hands on them all! Then M. de Chevreuse appealed to Richelieu, entreating him to move Parliament, through the Chancellor, to grant him release from these seizures. "Monsieur," he wrote to the Minister, "hearing that the Chancellor is at Rueil, I have seized this moment to come and pray your Eminence to remember my very humble supplication. I am constrained to be importunate, for I am sorely pressed! I beseech you to take pity on me!" But Richelieu replied that M. de Chevreuse must pay what he owed! In 1640, when the Duke offered to go to England and fetch his wife home, he asked the Government to release the mortgages on his pensions as a reward, and even assured the Secretaries of State that the Cardinal had promised him this satisfaction in Boispillé's presence. "I

RETIREMENT AND DEATH

never said one word about the release of his pensions, either to M. de Chevreuse or to his people," wrote the angry Cardinal, sharply, to Chavigny; "on the contrary, I have always said that the King intended him to draw them, but not until the reparation (payment of his debts) had been made. If he wishes to be dishonest, like his wife, he can, but my opinion is that nothing should be given him till his journey is over. I recommend you to speak sharply to Boispillé; after that they can do as they like—that is to say, they can go or stay, just as they choose!"

The Duke was reduced to living on borrowed money. In a humble petition to Richelieu, sent in 1640, he sadly explained that for the last six years more than 80,000 *livres* of his yearly income had been sequestrated. As a result, he avowed himself "extremely inconvenienced and needy." "All his fortune having been actually seized, he had been forced to live on credit and borrowed money almost the whole of that time." And he begged he might have an advance of ten or twelve thousand crowns on the revenues of his offices. He was miserably poor!

So miserably poor, indeed, that Mme. de Chevreuse resolved, in her exasperation, to ask for a separate maintenance! M. de Chevreuse, who declared his wife was as great a spendthrift as himself, was furious. The suit for this separation was begun in the course of the year 1637. Mme. de Chevreuse was then living in exile at Couzières: she had confided the care of her business affairs to Catinat, the Lieutenant-General of Tours; and her correspondence with Paris, for this particular matter, was carried by a man of the name of Mazelle. "Mazelle," confessed La Porte, in the course of one of his cross-examinations, "only went to Paris in secret because M. de Chevreuse had threatened to thrash him for mixing himself up in the lawsuit Mme. de Chevreuse had brought against him." La Porte further said that Mazelle had been commissioned

THE DUCHESSE DE CHEVREUSE

by the Duchess to obtain the Queen's support, so that the judges might be induced to pronounce in her favour; and, as a matter of fact, Anne of Austria did request du Dorat to take the necessary steps in her name.

There was much angry discussion. Mme. de Chevreuse claimed that her husband was bound to pay every penny of their common debts. These were many and various. The Duke and the Duchess both owed money in all directions: money for advances made by, and wages that had never been paid to, their former stewards, Clercelier and Fosse, who had been fain to accept a yearly income instead of the sums they should have received; another annual sum due to Prou, one of their purveyors—the interest of money he had advanced them; 30,000 *livres* to a certain M. Morant; 14,508 to a M. de Montmort; 40,000 *livres* to MM. le Lièvre and Lhuilier; 500 *livres* a year to M. Ménardeau, and ever so many others! Besides all this, Mme. de Chevreuse claimed a fairly long list of sums, which reached a total close on 500,000 *livres*, and two annual payments, one of 10,000 *livres* for herself, and the other of 6000 *livres* for the support of her daughter. And she expected to retain possession of the Hôtel de Chevreuse. M. de Chevreuse sent in statement after statement, fought every claim, poured forth explanations.

Towards the end of 1637, sentence was pronounced. Parliament assigned the Duchess a yearly pension of 8000 *livres* "for her food," 5000 *livres* for the support of her daughter, and possession of the Hôtel de Chevreuse, on condition she paid her husband a reasonable sum to reimburse him for his expenditure on the enlargement and embellishment of the house. As to the debts, the court held the Duchess to be as responsible as the Duke for the confusion in the family finances, and declared the husband and wife to be bound, "jointly and severally," to pay all they owed. It was a heavy charge, and was to cause endless difficulties! As regarded the capital sum, Par-

RETIREMENT AND DEATH

liament gave the Duchess what she had asked—500,000 *livres*.

Quite unmoved, M. de Chevreuse quietly went on living in the Hôtel de Chevreuse—his wife was in England—without paying any rent. The separation had done him one good turn—the expense of upkeep was no longer cast on him. He did not pay the Duchess the 500,000 *livres* he owed her, nor the yearly income of 8000 *livres*, nor the 5000 *livres* for his daughter's expenses. And he was perfectly delighted, because whenever creditors came and worried him for money, he referred them to his wife.

So the howling mob of creditors fell upon Mme. de Chevreuse. She could not pay them any more than her husband; she tried to quiet the most impatient by giving them instalments—11,540 *livres* to M. de Boissise, and a sum to M. Ménardeau which released her from the payment of his 500 *livres* a year. But these were mere palliatives. They all banded themselves together, and the bailiffs laid hands on the Duchess's belongings.

Thus they lived on for years, in the most utter confusion: how, one hardly knows; Mme. de Chevreuse was generally an exile, outside the borders of France, living on borrowed money and subventions sent her by the Spaniards; M. de Chevreuse lived at home, on the small remnants of his income: the Duchy of Chevreuse, which, as he himself had pointed out, brought him in but little—so much of it returned nothing at all, the revenues had been so diminished by the wars, the repairs to buildings, the wages of officials, the upkeep of Dampierre, all made such heavy inroads on what it did return; a pension of 40,000 *livres* a year, charged on the five big farms; some scraps of charges bestowed by the King on the Abbeys of Corbie, Saint-Rémy de Reims and Saint-Denis—precarious all of them, irregularly and incompletely paid, and frequently seized by his creditors into the bargain.

When Mme. de Chevreuse returned to Paris—it was in

THE DUCHESSE DE CHEVREUSE

1652—the husband and wife decided to look into their affairs. They did not know how to find means of support; it was impossible to go on in this fashion. The tradesmen constantly refused supplies, and violent scenes took place, in the course of which M. de Chevreuse used to lose all self-control, and even go so far as to threaten his wife. A letter to Mazarin, dated February 7, 1652, contains the following passage: "Never has the Duchesse de Chevreuse been so much troubled by her husband's outbursts: he falls into perfect furies. He has horrible requests all ready to put forward against her, and claims the power to have her arrested if he chooses, on the authority of the [marriage] sacrament!" After lengthy debate, an agreement was reached in the month of March. Mme. de Chevreuse, "to arrange matters by the ways of gentleness and decorum, and so enjoy peace in the house," so ran the deed, agreed to reduce her claim of 500,000 *livres* to one of 400,000: she even consented to the payment of this sum after the Duke's death—she or her heirs would wait till that occurred. In return, M. de Chevreuse was to give his wife an income of 20,000 *livres* a year, charged on the 40,000 *livres* brought in by the five big farms; and he undertook to be responsible for all debts, including those "jointly incurred since their separation."

M. de Chevreuse did not adhere to this arrangement any more than he had adhered to its predecessors. He paid nothing whatever, save a few notes of hand which never brought in any money at all. Two years later the Duchess, once more in the bailiffs' hands, appealed to Parliament. Between the advances she had made to creditors, and her own income, which was still owing, as well as her daughter's yearly income, over 71,540 *livres* were due to her from her husband. In her formal prayer she feigned, to save the Duke's feelings, to ascribe this state of things to ill-will on the part of some subordinate. "Seeing," she said, "that the Duke's affairs remained in a state of con-

RETIREMENT AND DEATH

fusion which made it impossible to clear up the debts, or the spending of the income, thanks to the dangerous conduct of the person who had the management of them, and who, taking advantage of the weakness of the said Sieur de Chevreuse, had always put off the payment of all these debts, she had found it impossible any longer to endure the embarrassments in which she was left by the said Sieur de Chevreuse, without appealing to the law to force him to carry out the said transaction honestly." And she went on to announce her intention of seizing the duchy of Chevreuse!

Then M. de Chevreuse made a sharp thrust in return. When the agreement had been made in 1652, he asserted, the rents for that year, on which his wife's income of 20,000 *livres* was to be charged, had already been divided amongst his creditors. For the year 1653 he had given her bills on the rents for 1654. At that moment (July, 1654) the Duchess had received the two first quarterly payments, she was to receive the third on July 15, and the fourth when it fell due, in October. The income for 1654 would be supplied by means of bills drawn on the rents to be paid in 1655. Let Mme. de Chevreuse observe, moaned the Duke, that "the said gentleman was giving her and the creditors the bulk of his income, all that remained being the income on benefices which had brought in nothing for the last eight years and more." As for the revenues of the duchy of Chevreuse, these were well known —they were almost *nil*. All these reasons, concluded M. de Chevreuse, made it impossible for him to pay the income due for the year 1654 in any other way.

Then he gave a list of the creditors who were pursuing him, related what he had done to quiet them, set forth what he proposed to do, so as to give them satisfaction. "And here," wrote the person who had drawn up the document, "is the true statement of the pretensions of my said Lady, and the reasons of Monseigneur, according to which there is no appearance leading to the carrying of the matter to such an extremity as to desire to strip Monseigneur of his duchy, and by an absolute execution, to take judicial proceedings as to the small fortune he can now enjoy to pay his expenses, seeing the pensions on the benefices are growing continually less, and as to the rents of his five big farms, the said Lady takes one half, and the rest goes to his creditors."

Mme. de Chevreuse, thus pinched between her own difficulties and her husband's, and sorely puzzled to know what she should do, addressed herself to Séguier, the Chancellor. In September, 1654, she sent him a detailed memorandum, setting forth her state of penury, her extreme poverty, and telling him that instead of the income her husband was bound to pay her, he had sent her bills only payable at dates a long way ahead. Live she must, somehow! She had been forced to borrow from her tradesmen, and give them bills charged on those five big farms! She spoke of the creditors who were always upon her heels, tormenting her, threatening her with executions. Could any woman be in a more miserable position? And she besought the Chancellor to come to her rescue, "because of the necessity to which she was reduced, seeing she had nothing in the world but the 400,000 *livres* M. de Chevreuse owed her that could bring her in any income at all."

Then an idea flashed across the man of business who was in the habit of advising the Duchess. Why should not M. de Chevreuse sell his duchy to his wife? This transaction would solve all the difficulties: the Duke would be relieved of the engagements he had made as to the Duchess; he might, if he chose, continue to enjoy the use of Dampierre, just as he enjoyed the use of the house in the Rue Saint Thomas du Louvre. The causes of disagreement would thus be eliminated. But how, indeed, was Mme. de Chevreuse, who had not a crown to her name, to pay for the duchy? That difficulty might be solved,

RETIREMENT AND DEATH

perhaps, by borrowing the money. Mme. de Chevreuse agreed to the plan, and after a long period of reflection M. de Chevreuse consented as well: so the duchy was sold to Marie de Rohan.

The deed was signed in the presence of the notaries, Ogier and Gallois, on October 15, 1655, at the house in the Rue Saint Thomas du Louvre, in which the couple still lived. The advisers of Mme. de Chevreuse had skilfully secured their client's interests; the Duke's had defended his with much talent.

By the deed, M. de Chevreuse made over the separate ownership of the whole duchy to his wife, with the exception of 550 acres of woodland, sold to M. de Montmort, the castellany of Châteauneuf, its fiefs and dependencies, together with the farm of Oinvilliers and 34 acres of wood, which had been sold to a M. de Montrouillon. The Duke reserved his title of Duke and Peer for life, and likewise his right to exercise justice over the whole of the duchy from which he took his name. After his death, Mme. de Chevreuse was to have power to ask the King to grant her letters-patent either continuing the dukedom, or creating another dukedom and peerage, in favour of her son, the Duc de Luynes, or her grandson, the Marquis d'Albert.

M. de Chevreuse transferred Dampierre to his wife, together with all the furniture in it, but not the silver plate. He was to have the enjoyment, for all the rest of his life, of the castle, "buildings, poultry-yard, edifices, gardens, canals, fountains, ponds and parks of the said place." He was to keep it up at his own expense, and the walls round it as well.

The price Mme. de Chevreuse was to pay comprised certain conditions of a complicated nature. In the first place she was to give her husband 1,030,000 *livres;* then she was to undertake to defray various expenses: to repay to a certain Mlle. Boisset the price of the offices of clerk and tabellion at Chevreuse; to pay all the wages of the forest-

THE DUCHESSE DE CHEVREUSE

wardens, lieutenant, woodmen, bailiff and fiscal attorney of the duchy; to see that 200 *livres* a year were sent to the Augustines in Paris, or to the Dames des Hautes-Bruyères de Port-Royal; 495 *livres* to the parish priest and church at Dampierre; to send the prior of Chevreuse three hogsheads of wine and three *setiers* of wheat yearly; the wood off seven acres of forest to MM. de Montmort and de Méridon, and so forth. M. de Chevreuse was released from all and every obligation to his wife, whether incurred by marriage contract or by any subsequent arrangement.

Then out of the million of *livres* due to the Duke, the notaries took the following sums: the 400,000 *livres* M. de Chevreuse owed his wife, according to the agreement made in March 1652; and 20,000 *livres* representing the interest on that sum for the year 1654; various sums paid out by the Duchess to her husband's creditors: 8720 *livres* to MM. Gratien and Ménardeau; 1500 to a Mme. le Coigneux; sixty to Rémond, a notary; 514 for duties on spices and interest thereupon. The original sum was reduced, one way or another, to 600,000 *livres*. Of these 600,000 *livres* Mme. de Chevreuse was to pay her husband 280,000 within eight days; but so as to have a quiet mind as to the creditors, she made a proviso that this money should "be instantly employed, as Monseigneur the Duke promised and bound himself to do, in the presence of the said lady, or of the person named by her, for the payment and acquitting of the debts he was obliged to pay, as my said lord shall be advised: my said lady being jointly and severally responsible for them with the said lord." A sum of 320,000 *livres* would be left over; and until that was completely paid off—for which the parties would have to wait till better times—Mme. de Chevreuse was to pay the Duke interest on it at the rate of five per cent. Taking it all together, M. de Chevreuse was not to receive a single crown of the purchase money.

But the arrangement, on the whole, was not a bad one for

RETIREMENT AND DEATH

either party. M. de Chevreuse kept his title, he kept the use of Dampierre, he was rid of the disputes with his wife, to whom he no longer owed a *sou;* he could enjoy his income from the five big farms in peace, and need not give the Duchess anything out of it. Mme. de Chevreuse, on her side, had acquired a huge property at a fairly moderate price. Both parties were pleased.

The 280,000 *livres* the Duchess had undertaken to pay down, had to be raised. But with the duchy to raise them on, it was not likely that lenders would be difficult to find. The Duchess's advisers and her son, the Duc de Luynes, looked about them. In consideration of certain yearly payments and mortgages, seven persons agreed to advance the money, M. de Luynes undertaking to share his mother's responsibility, and guaranteeing the payment of interest at the rate of five per cent. In the list of these lenders we find the Port-Royal, and certain adherents of that religious house. "The ladies, abbess, and nuns of Port-Royal" lent 40,000 *livres:* Simond Arnauld de Pomponne, second son of Arnauld d'Andilly, lent 40,000 too : Jean Hamelin, Comptroller-General of Bridges and Highways within the generalship of Paris, who hid Arnauld and Nicole in his house, advanced 60,000 *livres:* then a M. Léger Meunier, a former Master of Accounts, lent 28,000 *livres:* Mme. Antoinette de Beaucler, widow of M. François de Rochechouart, 18,000 : and the House of the Institution of the Oratory of Jesus Christ our Saviour, founded in the Faubourg Saint-Michel by M. Pinet, 22,000 *livres*. All these sums only made up a total of 248,000 *livres*. The difference, 32,000 *livres,* was kept back by Mme. de Chevreuse for interest due to her and the payment of various accounts. On November 22, 1655, the Duke's secretray, Jean Moron, duly provided with his master's power of attorney, received the 248,000 *livres* in his name; he signed the receipt at the Hôtel de Chevreuse in the presence of the two notaries, Ogier and

THE DUCHESSE DE CHEVREUSE

Gallois, and added the promise, already embodied in the deed of purchase, that the money should be forthwith used for the payment of the Duke's debts. Four months later, Mme. de Chevreuse, in accordance with the rights of those times, took the oath of allegiance to the King in the presence of the Chancellor, Séguier: "pour raison du Duché de Chevreuse, ses appartenances et dépendances, circonstantes et annexées, tenues et mouvant de nous," so ran the letters-patent from Louis XIV, "à cause de la grosse tour de notre château du Louvre." The financial difficulties with the Duke were over. Husband and wife were now free to enjoy their hard-won quietness of mind in peace: but this enjoyment was to be of short duration: the very next year, M. de Chevreuse breathed his last!

Widowed, Mme. de Chevreuse found herself in a most difficult position. Her household expenses were too heavy for her, her habits far too lavish and sumptuous. She was forced to cut down her expenditure. Desiring above all things to keep Dampierre, she made up her mind to sell the Hôtel de Chevreuse in Paris. It was a painful thing to do. The house was sold, in 1657, to the Duc de Candale, for his father, the Duc d'Épernon; the price given was 400,000 *livres*. M. de Luynes had bought it for 175,000 *livres:* he had thrown another house, for which he paid 24,000 *livres,* into the larger one, and carried the gardens right down to the ramparts, thanks to Louis XIII, who bestowed a piece of land on him for that purpose. Mme. de Chevreuse had already sold the house once, to her second husband, the Duc de Chevreuse, in 1622, for 180,000 *livres:* and this second time, with all the improvements the Duke had added to the mansion, she was obtaining a price that amounted to more than double that sum. From that time forward, as though fated never to find another place in all the city where she might lay

RETIREMENT AND DEATH

her head, she was destined to wander hither and thither all over Paris. We find her in the Rue de l'Université, in the parish of Saint-Sulpice, in 1658: in the Rue Gît-le-Cœur, in the parish of Saint-André-des-Arts, in 1660: in the Rue Saint-Dominique, in the parish of Saint-Sulpice, again, in 1663. Age, worries, money difficulties, were to weigh heavier on her, year by year.

She still retained indeed, the yearly income of 40,000 *livres* which her husband had received from the five big farms! But this income did not suffice for her wants. By letters-patent, dated March 19, 1658, the King had consented to allow her the enjoyment of the County of Charolais and the Barony of the Mont Saint-Vincent, with their mills and ponds and other appurtenances, which belonged to the King of Spain, to indemnify her for the loss, by Spanish confiscation, of certain properties she had bought in Flanders, at Karpen and Lommerein: even this did not clear her difficulties away.

Then she tried speculation; she dreamt of buying an island in the Antilles, Martinique! In a memorandum addressed to the King, she set forth that a French Company having been formed, in 1626, to colonize the Antilles, St. Kitts, Martinique, Guadaloupe, King Louis XIII had granted it the government and ownership of these islands. But this company had failed, had sold Guadaloupe to a M. Houel, who had been governor of the island, Martinique to a M. Duparquet, and St. Kitts to the Knights of the Order of Malta. Being desirous, now, of buying Martinique from M. Duparquet's heirs, Mme. de Chevreuse prayed His Majesty to grant her the same privileges as those he had allowed the Knights in St. Kitts, that is to say, sovereign rights, except as to the duty of doing homage, and of presenting a crown of gold to each sovereign, on his accession. Louis XIV refused the petition, and nothing more came of the business.

Mme. de Chevreuse still owned the duchy of Chevreuse!

THE DUCHESSE DE CHEVREUSE

But it was a heavy burden on her! She had to reconcile the necessity of keeping up the dignity of her rank with that of meeting the outlay inseparable from the management of so important a property. Once more the Duchess found herself up to her ears in debt, with creditors harrying her on every side. Then it occurred to her that she might sell Chevreuse and Dampierre, and "free herself," as she said, "from the cares the possession of such great domains brought on her, and also provide for the payment of what she owed, so as to live, in future, in greater peace and quietness." But how could she part with this dwelling, to which she was so much attached, in which she had lived for forty years, which teemed with so many memories?

She conceived the idea of simply making over Dampierre and Chevreuse to her son, the Duc de Luynes. In return, M. de Luynes was to pay his mother's debts, and give her an annual income of 20,000 *livres*—the Duchess, like the late Duke, retaining her right to the use of the castle as long as she lived. The Duc de Luynes consented. The deed, which was signed on March 1, 1663, in the presence of MM. le Carron and Gallois, notaries, stated that the gift was made as an instalment on ultimate inheritance, to date from the following Saint John the Baptist's Day: Mme. de Chevreuse reserved herself the use of "lodging for herself and her people," at Dampierre, "whenever she chose to go thither, and the use of her furniture there."

Four months later, on September 9, 1663, M. de Luynes handed over the title and property of Chevreuse, by deed of gift, to his own son, Charles-Honoré d'Albert, reserving to himself, even as his mother and his step-father had done, the enjoyment for life of "the castle, poultry-yards and other lodgings, together with the gardens, flower-lawns, canals, ponds, and all other things enclosed within the park of Dampierre." So fondly did every member of this family cling to the beloved spot! He undertook to

RETIREMENT AND DEATH

keep it all up, plantations, fountains, canals, boundary walls. And to balance this, the grandson, the Marquis d'Albert, was to pay his grandmother's debts—the Duc de Luynes had paid 49,000 *livres* for her already—and give Mme. de Chevreuse her annual income of 20,000 *livres*.

As the Duc de Chevreuse had died without leaving a son, his peerage, according to the letters-patent of 1612, had died with him, and the duchy alone, unless the King were to will it otherwise, could pass to another person. Louis XIV ratified the donation of the duchy, and maintained the ducal title of its new owner; but he did not recreate the peerage.

And thus it came about that in her old age the children Mme. de Chevreuse had borne to Luynes, the only male children she ever had, ensured the peace and quietness of her declining years. She was proud of these children—of her grandson, at least, in whom the brilliant and warlike qualities of his ancestors of the preceding century lived again!

Her son gave her less satisfaction. She considered M. de Luynes, a fervent supporter of the Jansenists, whose wife, a Séguier, was as ardent as he in her friendship for the nuns of Port-Royal, to be over-devout, and "furiously degenerate." He had built a little country-house at Vaumurier, close to the Monastery of Port-Royal-des-Champs, to be near the nuns, and thither he would retire with his wife, and live in isolation and in silence, rising in the middle of the night, saying the prescribed prayers, giving all he had to the poor. "The Jansenists did everything in his house," says Tallemant. He was called the nuns' "Constable." Mme. de Luynes, always a delicate woman, died, on September 13, 1651, at the age of twenty-seven, leaving four children. M. de Luynes returned to the social world. Six years later, he fell in love with his own half-aunt, Anne de Rohan, daughter of Mme. de

THE DUCHESSE DE CHEVREUSE

Montbazon, who lived with Mme. de Chevreuse. His mother was sorely perturbed, for Anne de Rohan desired to enter the religious life, and had already become a novice. "Mme. de Chevreuse," writes Saint-Simon, "who dreaded the idea of her son's returning to his retreat at Vaumurier, had been so afraid his despair at not being able to possess the object of his passion might drive him back into seclusion, that she urged her half-sister to put off her white veil, and by dint of money, with which, at Rome, all things can be done, obtained a dispensation for the marriage, which she arranged in 1661, and which was a very happy one." The couple were to have seven children. When Anne died, in 1684, at the age of forty-four, M. de Luynes married for the third time: his wife was Marguerite d'Aligre. As Sainte-Beuve says, he was a *vir uxorius*, he loved the married state. Bussy-Rabutin tells us that after he had married Anne de Rohan, "Mme. de Chevreuse, whose person, after having been the temple of all delights, had now become their tomb, not being in a position to do anything for herself, put forward Mme. de Luynes, who is one of the most beautiful women in France," in the hope of her supplanting Mlle. de la Vallière in the affections of Louis XIV! The source of this piece of information leads us to suspect its reliability. If correct, it would prove how little Mme. de Chevreuse can have esteemed her own son!

Her grandson was far dearer to her. Though he had been brought up in the Port-Royal atmosphere, and more particularly by Lancelot—the "Logique" of Port-Royal had been specially written for his benefit—the Marquis d'Albert was much less ruled by the Jansenists than his father. He was a man of action, devoted to the career of arms, and had done brilliant service in the Flemish campaigns, during which he had been wounded: in him his grandmother recognized her own natural activity, her longing to attract attention, to display her power, to attain

RETIREMENT AND DEATH

her ends. He was to gratify her most ardent desires by making a splendid and wealthy marriage, with the daughter of Colbert.

There was talk of this alliance as early as in the year 1666. "There is a report of another marriage at Court," wrote Guy Patin, on December 29, "that of the daughter of M. Colbert, who is now τὰ πάντα Cæsaris, with M. le Duc de Chevreuse, who is the son of the Duc de Luynes, and grandson of the Constable. M. Colbert, who is the son of a shopkeeper, has become a great lord, and, though unseen, rules the whole of Europe; at any rate he is, as it were, the master of France!" In a letter to the Duc de Chaulnes, grand-uncle of Charles-Honoré d'Albert, Colbert, as though to excuse the fact that he, the clothworker's heir, should be marrying his daughter to a Duke, grandson of a Constable of France, declares that "the King, who was much more the father of his children than he (Colbert) was himself," had deigned to think of this union. Mme. de Chevreuse, he went on to say, had also been one of the first persons to whom it had occurred, and he concluded as follows: "I assure you that by this means I attach myself to the interests of your house, for which you will always find my feelings most sincere, and most passionate." And this, with a rich dowry, was precisely what Mme. de Chevreuse and her grandson most desired.

In spite of Colbert's assertion, Louis XIV, so Lefèvre d'Ormesson tells us, would seem to have been more or less opposed to the marriage. Colbert, while he fixed his choice on the Duc de Chevreuse as a husband for Marie, his eldest daughter, was thinking of marrying the second, Henriette-Louise, to Paul de Beauvilliers, son of the Duc de Saint-Aignan. This was to set up two very exalted claims at once! However, the King did not persist in his opposition: he even made the first advance to Luynes himself, "which," as d'Ormesson himself acknowledges, "proved how high M. Colbert's credit stood."

THE DUCHESSE DE CHEVREUSE

The wedding ceremony took place on February 1, 1667. The Archbishop of Paris conferred his benediction on the newly married pair in the private chapel in Colbert's house. At the subsequent banquet there were three tables, each accommodating forty-five guests. "It was an entertaining parallel," wrote d'Ormesson again, "all M. de Luynes family on one side, and that of M. Colbert on the other. M. le Brun told me how magnificent the wedding had been; the Chancellor had been present, and went to the supper." Public rumour was already busy with the rich benefits the De Luynes family was likely to reap from this alliance: M. de Luynes to be appointed Governor of Paris, or Guyenne, the Duc de Chevreuse to replace the Duc de Mazarin as Grand Master of the Artillery, the Duc de Chaulnes to be Governor of Brittany! And if the whole family was provided for now and in future, it would all be thanks to the cleverness with which Mme. de Chevreuse had ensured her grandson's prosperity!

She had not troubled herself nearly so much about her daughters. There had been four of them: the eldest by M. de Luynes, the three others, Anne-Marie, Henriette, and Charlotte, by M. de Chevreuse. The only method that had occurred to her, to rid herself of the encumbrance her children were in her troubled and wandering existence, was to make them over to the care of her sister-in-law, the Abbess of Jouarre. The best chance for her girls, she thought, seeing how sorely embarrassed the family finances had become, lay in their being brought up in a convent, where they might discover a vocation, and become nuns. Unluckily, Mme. de Jouarre died, in 1638, when the youngest child was seven, and the eldest twenty. Some other home for them had to be found, and Mme. de Chevreuse, desiring to place them in the Abbey of Saint-Antoine, near Paris, wrote to Richelieu to request the King's permission to make this arrangement. Richelieu,

RETIREMENT AND DEATH

not wishing to have the children of the Duchess so near the Court, refused: the Superior, he said, would not be the mistress of her own house long: the children—the Cardinal concluded them to be as turbulent as their mother—"would very likely upset the minds of numbers of the inhabitants of Saint-Antoine, and they would attract such a flow of visitors that it would be one perpetual procession." Then Mme. de Chevreuse threw her children on their father's hands. M. de Chevreuse did not know what to do with them. As a temporary measure, he settled them, with the nuns from Jouarre who had conducted them to him, at Issy. But here the Archbishop of Paris made difficulties: "Monsieur," wrote the Duke to Chavigny, on August 17, 1640, "I am in such a quandary about my children, that I have been forced, thanks to the violence of Monseigneur de Paris, to remove Mlle de Luynes and my daughters from Issy, and I have sent them to Dampierre until it shall please his Eminence to command what is to be done with them: if it were his pleasure that they should remain on at Issy, and there await his will, it would be a great favour to me. Pray do me the honour of speaking to him and obtaining a letter from him to Monseigneur de Paris, and to the nuns from Jouarre who are with them." But it was impossible for M. de Chevreuse to keep his daughters at Dampierre for ever. He cursed their mother and the worry she caused him. Two, at least, of the girls seemed disposed to enter conventual life, and the Duke, hearing the Superior of the Abbey of Remiremont was far advanced in years, was inspired with the idea of sending one of them to take the veil in that house, if Richelieu would give him a promise that she should be appointed Abbess on the death of the present holder of that dignity. The Cardinal consented. "Ah!" wrote the Duke, "you are lightening the burden of a father whose daughters are a sore hindrance to him! Your Eminence knows wherefore, and all the

THE DUCHESSE DE CHEVREUSE

ingratitude of their mother, the losses and the troubles she has brought upon me!"

The Remiremont plan was destined to fail. The eldest daughter, Anne-Marie, did take the veil and ultimately became Abbess of Pont-aux-Dames, where she died young, in her twenty-eighth year, in 1652: another daughter, Henriette, also became a nun, and Abbess of Jouarre, like her own great aunt; she lived into old age, till 1693, and had several disputes with Bossuet: the youngest, Charlotte, whose tastes were far removed from the monastic, returned to her mother, never left her side again, and played the part in her life which we have already described. As for Mlle. de Luynes, she died of the small-pox at the age of twenty-eight, in September, 1646.

Thus, Mme. de Chevreuse, rid of debts, worries, husband, and children, was free to live at ease. Laigue was still with her. "This petty nobleman from Limoges, with his 5000 *livres* a year," as Mazarin scornfully described him, was her slave, ruled by an influence against which he never essayed to struggle, and so accustomed to her that he never left her side. Yet Mme. de Chevreuse had but little beauty left! She had grown heavy and thick, her face was puffy and wrinkled, her hair was turning grey, her charm was gone! In his *Carte Géographique de la Cour*, published in 1668, Bussy-Rabutin draws a picture of her, not over kind, but which would seem to have been fairly truthful: "Chevreuse," (the Duchess was then a woman of sixty-eight) "is a large fortress, quite ruined now, the quarters in which are all unroofed: notwithstanding this, it is fairly strong outside, but it is very ill-guarded within: in old days it was exceedingly famous and full of traffic; it did business in several kingdoms, and the citadel is now quite in ruins, thanks to the many sieges laid to take it. It is reported to have frequently surrendered at discretion. The natives are very changeable and disagreeable in temper. There have

RETIREMENT AND DEATH

been several governors. At present it is badly provided in that respect, for the man in charge is quite good for nothing!" Laigue, thus accused of being "good for nothing," was fifty-four.

So completely was his life bound up with that of Mme. de Chevreuse, that they were universally believed to be united in one of those private marriages, secret, but not clandestine, which, we are assured, were not uncommon at that period. Saint-Simon has repeated this report. It must surely have been a true one, or the relations between the two persons concerned must at all events have become perfectly irreproachable, for what other explanation can be found of the fact that the gentlemen of Port-Royal, so severe in their views, accepted Laigue and the Duchess as their close friends? Laigue was constantly with the Jansenists, and actively employed about their business. In a conversation with Saint-Evremond, which that writer has set down, Stuart d'Aubigny, one of the intimate associates of the Port-Royal recluses, declared Laigue to be at the head of the "political leaders" who were labouring for the cause. He was one of M. d'Andilly's intimate friends, and when that gentleman was accused to the King of having fomented disturbances, it was to Laigue and the Duchess that he turned to defend him at Court, and they did actually make an appeal to the King. Laigue's pious affection for Port-Royal is proved by his will, drawn up at Dampierre, on July 30, 1658, and still preserved in the office of a notary in the town of Chevreuse, in which he desires he may be buried in the church of the nuns at Port-Royal, bequeaths an income of 3600 *livres* a year to the Convent, and legacies to the Duchesse de Chevreuse, to M. d'Andilly, and his son. It is difficult to believe that so devout a nobleman can have been living in open sin, or that a will of so edifying a nature can have been dated from a house in which his presence amounted to a public scandal!

THE DUCHESSE DE CHEVREUSE

Mme. de Chevreuse and Laigue were never to be parted in this life. He died before her, on May 19, 1674. He was sixty. He was not buried at Port-Royal (circumstances had rendered that impossible), but in the Church of the Jacobins in Paris. A monument was placed there to his memory, it was destroyed during the Revolution.

The death of her old friend afflicted the Duchess deeply. She had reached her seventy-fourth year, life held no further interest for her. She was the survivor of an age that had departed, utterly unlike that in which she was now living. Forsaken, forgotten, without hope or expectation to brighten the future, her only resource was to withdraw herself into a seclusion deeper still, and there devote her remaining days to preparation for the hour of death. She had grown very devout, and found in her religion the consolation for which the weary soul, nearing the close of life's journey, generally hungers. Her choice fell on a deserted Benedictine Priory at Gagny, three leagues and a half from Paris, and not far from Chelles, where some of her Port-Royal friends—the Akakia family—had been Priors since the beginning of the century—the house was called the Priory of Saint-Fiacre, or the Maison Rouge. A quiet village, numbering some two or three hundred inhabitants, clustered round the old church. Thither the Duchess came to end her stormy life. She went nowhere, spent her days in prayer, and waited for the end. That end came to her, in her silence and her solitude, after five long years. She passed away on August 12, 1679.

She was buried, as she had requested, in the simplest fashion. There was no pomp, no funeral oration. Her corpse was laid near the Chapel of the Blessed Virgin, in the southern aisle of the church at Gagny. She had commanded that her epitaph should be modest and brief, there was to be no "princess" nor "très haute et puissante dame," nor were her husband's titles to be mentioned in it. "Here lies," it ran, "Marie de Rohan, Duchesse de Chev-

RETIREMENT AND DEATH

reuse, daughter of Hercule de Rohan, Duc de Montbazon. Humility having long since killed in her heart all the glory of the century, she forbade the slightest mark of the greatness she desired to bury for ever beneath the simplicity of this tomb to be recalled on the occasion of her death."

Beneath that tomb her body rested till towards the middle of the nineteenth century. Since that time, the church has been pulled down, and the Priory as well, and the ashes of Mme. de Chevreuse have been scattered to the winds : the epitaph alone, last remnant of her life-story, has been recovered, and is now piously preserved at the Castle of Dampierre!

INDEX

AARSENS, M., 96
Abbeville, 71
Accounts, Court of, 263
Agen, 184
Aiguillon, Duchesse d', 278
Akakia family, the, 334
Aligre, Marguerite d', 328
Amiens, 30, 46–7; the episode at, 64, 67–75
Andilly, Arnauld d', 305, 323, 333
Anet, 247, 249
Angoulême, castle of, 153, 227, 239, 254
Angoulême, Duc d', the park at Grosbois, 43
Angoulême, Duchesse d', 25
Anjou, Duc d'. *See* Orléans, Gaston d'.
Anne of Austria, portrait of, 12–13; favours bestowed on Marie de Rohan, 13–16; evil influence of Mme. de Luynes, 15–19; coldness of the king, 20–1; renewed friendship with Mme. de Luynes, 23, 53; disappointed of an heir, 24–5; letters from the king, 25, 46; the marriage of Henrietta-Maria, 51–2, 53; the affair of the Earl of Holland, 55–6; and the Duke of Buckingham, 56–8, 61–6, 74–5; the Amiens episode, 67–8, 69–72; servants of, dismissed by the king, 73; attitude towards Richelieu, 87, 88; and the Ornano plot, 91–93, 94, 96, 101, 113; and Chalais, 104, 105; and Gaston d'Orléans, 114–15, 135; on the condemnation of Mme. de Chevreuse, 116; correspondence with Mme. de Chevreuse at Lorraine, 121–2, 125, 127, 128, 131–4; and Montague, 123; intervention on behalf of Mme. de Chevreuse, 134; hostility towards Marie de Médicis, 137; reconciliation with Richelieu, 138, 145; intimacy with Mme. de Chevreuse, 140, 144–5, 147, 154–5; growing hostility towards the Cardinal, 151; the parting with Mme. de Chevreuse, 154–5; intrigues with Mme. de Chevreuse at Couzières, 158–66; the affair of the Val de Grace, 163, 165, 169–71; confessions to Richelieu, 171–2; forbidden to see Mme. de Chevreuse, 174; warning to Mme. de Chevreuse, 177; and the flight of Mme. de Chevreuse, 189; renewed friendship, 194–6; the draft letter, 196–7; and Mme. de Chevreuse, 215; her reply to Mme. de Chevreuse, 220; assumption of the Regency, 226–31; relations with Mazarin, 229–30, 246; exile of Mme. de Chevreuse, 247–9; changed feelings towards her, 231–7; reception of the Duchesse, 237; refuses to sanction the return of Châteauneuf, 238; policy towards Mme. de Chevreuse, 239, 261–2, 269–72; and Mme. de Montbazon, 243–4; letter to, from Tours, 250–1; commands regarding the Duchesse's friends, 252; and the Spanish peace, 259; flight from Paris, 260, 263; loss of power, 272; reception of Mme. de Chevreuse at Compiègne, 273–4;

z

INDEX

and the Prince de Condé, 281-4; favours for Mme. de Chevreuse, 285-9; and the Chevreuse-Conti marriage, 291, 296-8; release of the Princes, 292; and flight of Mazarin, 293; Mazarin's advice from Brühl, 298; and the Frondeurs, 299-300; visit to Dampierre, 306; and the Duc de Montbazon, 308; and Mme. de Chevreuse's debts, 316
Anne, waiting-woman, 179, 180
Annemets, Bois d', Memoirs *quoted*, 67, 96, 99, 102, 105, 107, 111-12, 115
Antilles, the, 325
Ardouin, coachman, 181
Arnolphini, Don Joseph Illesca, 266
Arnoux, Père, 20
Artenay, 165
Aubigny, Stuart d', 333
Auger, Secretary of the English Embassy, 160, 166, 171, 217
Augustines, the, Paris, 322
Aumale, M. d', 279
Auvergne, 89, 122
Avancourt, 245
Ax, waters of, 183

Bagnères, 183, 185-7
Barbastro, 187
Barèges, 185
Bar-le-Duc, 124, 293
Barradas, 225
Barre, La, 246
Barrois, the, 126
Bassompierre, *Journal* cited, 21, 22, 32, 104; intervention on behalf of Mme. de Chevreuse, 43-6; in Guyenne, 45
Bastelica, Sampietro, 90
Bastille, the, 96, 109 *note*, 127, 128, 166-9, 173, 192, 225, 257
Bautru, M. de, *Ozonandre*, 2; sent to England, 85; counsels Mme. de Chevreuse, 110, 116
Bayonne, 178
Beauce, Pont de, 40
Beaucler, Mme. Antoinette de, 323

Beaufort, François, Duc de, plot against Mazarin, 233-4, 236-7, 244-7; and Mme. de Chevreuse, 237, 283; and the Montbazon incident, 242-4; arrest, 247; escape, 249-51; and the Old Fronde, 275, 277; and Mme. de Chevreuse, 278; and the arrest of Condé, 284
Beaufort-Vendôme party named "The Importants," 240
Beaujolais, 89
Beaupuis, M. de, 244
Beauregard, 110, 115
Beauvilliers, Paul de, 329
Becquencourt, château of, 40
Bellegarde, Duc de, and Anne 18; and Claude de Lorraine, 31; and Chalais, 102
Belle-Île, 241
Bellerose, actor, 266
Bellièvre, M. de, French Ambassador in London, 198, 200, 202, 204, 214, 222, 283
Bellièvre, Mme. de, 200
Bentivoglio, Papal nuncio, 19-20
Beringhen, M. de, 249
Bernadets, 185
Bertechères, M., 94
Berulle, reports to Richelieu, 135
Besançon, town of, 169
"Bethizy (Prince de)," name given to Duc de Montbazon, 2
Biron, Maréchal de, 30
Blagny, Captain, 126
Blainville, M. de, French Ambassador in London, 35, 78; warning given to Louis, *quoted*, 95-6
Blaye, 190
Bléneau, 301
Blois, 106, 108
Boislève, M. de, 287
Boispillé, M. de, mission to Tours, 189-90; letter from Mme. de Chevreuse, 193; mission to London, 198-201, 204-12; letter to Richelieu, 210-11, 215; and Mme. de Chevreuse, 235; and the Duc de Chevreuse, 314-15

INDEX

Boisset, Mlle., 321
Boissise, M. de, 317
Bonneuil, M. de, 26
Bordeaux, 125, 190
Bossuet, 332
Bouillon, Duc de, 249, 258
Bouillon, Duchesse de, 137
Boulogne, 71, 75-6
Boulogne, M. de, 128
Bourbonnais, the, 122
Bourbonne, M. de, 126-8
Bourg, Antoine du, 1
Bourgogne, Hôtel de, 266
Bouthillier, Richelieu's reply to, 121; and M. de Bréval, 129-30; and Châteauneuf's correspondence, 153
Boutteville, 176
Bréquigny, M. de, 268
Bretagne, Marie d'Auverjour de. *See* Montbazon, Duchesse de.
Bréval, M. de, envoy of Lorraine, 129-30
Brézé, Duc de, 238
Brienne, M. de, on Buckingham, *quoted*, 65; mission to England, 76; and Buckingham, 83-4; on Mme. de Chevreuse, *quoted*, 120, 123; and Chateauneuf, 238, 297
Brillet, equerry, 245, 249, 284
Briolay, 308
Brion, M. de, Mme. de Chevreuse and, 145-8, 151
Bruges, 221
Brühl *cited*, 297
Brühl, castle of, 294
Brun, M. le, 330
Brussels, intrigues in, 161, 220-2, 235, 257, 259, 264-70
Buckingham, Duke of, and Mme. de Chevreuse, 7, 79; and Anne of Austria, 19, 56-66, 74-5; the secret journey to Spain, 57; letter to Mme. de Chevreuse, 57-8; reason for his going to France, 58-9; account of, 60; entry into Paris, 61; the Amiens episode, 67-72; and Henrietta-Maria, 77; departure of the French Ambassadors, 83-4; offer to return to France, 85; and the Ornano plot, 95; intrigues against Louis XIII, 123-5; departure for Ré, 126; the charge against, 129-30; death, 132
Buffon, 153
Bullion, 98, 127; letter to Richelieu, 164-5
Burgundy, 127
Bussy-Rabutin *quoted*, 328, 332-3

"Cabal, The Ladies," 44
Cahuzac, 182, 183, 184, 186, 188
Calais, 218, 219
Callot, Jacques, 120
Cambrai, 235, 270
Campion, Alexandre de, letters of, *quoted*, 95, 222; advice to Mme. de Chevreuse, 234-5; plans of Mme. de Chevreuse for, 241; the plot against Mazarin, 244-5; news-bearer to Dampierre, 248-9, 251-2
Campion, Henri de, the plot against Mazarin, 244-6; flight to Holland, 249
Candale, Duc de, 279, 324
Cangé, M., spy for Mazarin, 251-2
Canterbury, 77
Cardinal-Infante, the, in Flanders, Anne of Austria's correspondence with, 161, 162-3, 171
Carlisle, Earl of, Ambassador to France, 50-4; and the Buckingham affair, 57-9; and the Ornano plot, 95-6
Carlton, 85
Carmelite Church, the, 313
Carré, spy, 244
Carron, M. le, 326
Castille, Jeannin de, treasurer, 102, 141
Catholics, treatment under Charles I, 78, 84-5
Catinat, M. Georges, and Mme. de Chevreuse, 177-9, 189, 192, 315
Chalais, Mme. de, letter to the king, 112

339

INDEX

Chalais, Marquis de, and Gaston d'Orléans, 30, 88–9, 107, 108, 115; his confessions to Richlieu, 88, 97-9, 103, 104; letters to Richelieu, 90; account of, 101-2; and Mme. de Chevreuse, 101–5; information against the Duc de Vendôme, 104–5; at Blois, 108; arrest at Nantes, 109–11; accusations against Mme. de Chevreuse, 110–11; death, 112-13, 176; letter to Louis XIII, 113

"Chambre de St. Louis," 263

Champagne, Army of, 126, 127

Chancellor, the, search of the Val de Grâce, 169–70; examination of Anne of Austria, 170–1; examination of La Porte, 173; hears of the flight of Mme. de Chevreuse, 191. *See also* Séguier.

Chantilly, 166, 170

Charenton, 266, 269

Charité-sur-Loire, La, Convent of, 170

Charles I of England, court of, 7; and the Duc de Chevreuse, 33–4, 49, 78–80, 219–20; marriage with Henrietta-Maria, 45, 48–53; and Buckingham, 56, 58, 60: the secret journey to Spain, 57; misunderstandings with Henrietta-Maria, 74–85; persecution of the Catholics, 78; and Mme. de Chevreuse, 78–80, 84, 132–5, 174, 187, 195, 197, 209, 217, 219, 249; letters to the Duc de Chevreuse, and to Louis XIII, 82; and the "solemn promise," 84–5; and the Ornano plot, 96; the marriage contract, 123, 128, 134–5; and Montague, 126, 128, 158; and the plot in Lorraine, 127; French policy of, 135; and Marie de Médicis, 203; and the revolution in England, 255–6, 262

Charles IV of Lorraine. *See* Lorraine, Charles IV, Duc de.

Charles IX, and the Duchy of Chevreuse, 40

Charleville, 283, 298

Charny, Charlotte de Castille, Comtesse de, 102

Charny, Comte de, 102

Charolais, County of, 325

Charpentier, M., mission to Verdun, 121

Charpentier, secretary, 143

Chartres, 108

Châteaubriant-Beaufort, M. de, 257

Châteauneuf, castellany of, 321

Châteauneuf, Marquis de, and Mme. de Chevreuse, 55, 134, 142–52; account of, 140-2; disgrace, 153–4; provisions of Louis XIII against his recall, 226–8; return demanded by Mme. de Chevreuse, 238; letter to Chavigny, 239; recall of, 284, 285–7, 290–2; and the flight of Mazarin, 293–4; Mme. de Longueville and, 295–6; dismissal, 297, 301

Châtre, La, *cited*, 237

Chaulnes, Duc de, governor of Amiens, 46–7, 67, 235, 330; Colbert's letter to, 329

Chaulnes, Duchesse de, 235

Chavigny, Comte de, governor of Vincennes, 247

Chavigny, M. de, and Louis XIII, 93; letter from Duc d'Orléans, 158; Richelieu's letters to, 160, 231-2, 315; and M. de Marsillac, 192; and Mme. de Chevreuse, 198, 210, 226; letter from du Dorat, 207; Richelieu's conversation with, 212; M. de Chevreuse and, 219, 221, 331; letter from Châteauneuf, 239

Chelles, 334

Chêne Vert, the, 180

Chennetier, M., 160

Cherbury, Lord Herbert of, 13

Cherré de, secretary, 140

Chevau-légers, the, 126

Chevreuse, Albert, Marquis de

INDEX

(Charles-Honoré d'Albert), 321 ; Dampierre made over to, 326-7 ; personality, 328-9 ; marriage, 329-30

Chevreuse, Anne-Marie de (aft. Abbess of Pont-aux-Dames), 81, 330, 332

Chevreuse, Charlotte, and her mother, 81, 250-1, 254, 316, 317, 330 ; and Anne of Austria, 269 ; returns to Paris with her mother, 270 ; and Paul de Gondi, 271-2, 277-81 ; at Compiègne, 273-4 ; a portrait, 277-8 ; and the Prince de Conti, 289-92, 294-8 ; and the President de Viole, 298 ; and Mancini, 299, 300 ; death, 301-2

Chevreuse, Duc de, marriage with the Duchesse de Luynes, 22, 31-5 ; and Anne of Austria, 26 ; account of, 29-30 ; and Henri IV, 30-1 ; interest in Dampierre, 43 ; effect of his marriage on his position, 44 ; favour of the king, 45-7 ; represents Charles I at his marriage, 48-9, 50-3 ; the Hôtel de Chevreuse, 54 ; and the Earl of Holland, 55 ; and the Buckingham affair, 57-8, 75 ; mission to England, 76-83 ; children of, 81-2, 331 ; return to France, 84 ; blamed for the non-performance of the "solemn promise," 84-5 ; his wife's exile, 116-17, 122, 129-32 ; and M. de Montmorency, 139 ; and Richelieu, 147, 148 ; sent to Couzières with Mme. de Chevreuse, 154 ; despatch from M. de Catinat, 189 ; Mme.'s appeal from London, 198-9 ; Richelieu's appeal to, 204, 216 ; sent to London, 209, 215-17 ; letter to his wife, 217-19, 221 ; letter to Charles I, 219 ; Great Chamberlain to Louis XIV, 228 ; and Mme. de Montbazon, 242 ; entreats Mazarin on behalf of his wife, 260 ; letters from Mme. de Chevreuse, 260-1 ; and the Fronde, 268 ; appeal to the Regent, 269 ; and Gondi, 279 ; death, 313 ; affairs of, 313-24

Chevreuse, Duchesse de (Marie de Rohan, Duchesse de Luynes, aft. Duchesse de Chevreuse), childhood, 4-5 ; "Discourse on Love," 7 ; marriage settlement with M. de Luynes, 9-11 ; evil influences on Anne of Austria, 13-16 ; children of, 14-15, 81-2 ; anger of Louis XIII against, 19-27 ; marriage with the Duc de Chevreuse, 31-5 ; letter to Louis XIII, 35-6 ; the marriage contract, 37-44 ; return to court, 46-7 ; and the English marriage, 50-3 ; friendship with Anne of Austria renewed, 53 ; and the Earl of Holland, 55, 68 ; and the Buckingham affair, 56-75 ; in England, 76-82 ; return to France, 84 ; attitude towards Richelieu, 86 ; and the Ornano plot, 88-100 ; and the Prince de Condé, 93 ; consternation at arrest of Ornano, 101 ; appeal to Chalais, 101-5 ; and the arrest of the Vendôme brothers, 106 ; and Gaston d'Orléans, 107 ; the accusation of Chalais, 110-11 ; the warrant for, 111-13 ; implores Gaston to break with Mlle. de Montpensier, 114-15 ; Richelieu's charge against, 115-16 ; flight to Lorraine, 116-17 ; and Charles IV of Lorraine, 118-27, 135 ; and Montague, 123-5, 127; Montague's charge against, 129 ; Bouthillier and, 129-30 ; correspondence with the Queen, 131-2 ; and death of Buckingham, 132 ; appeal to Charles I, 132-5 ; return to Dampierre, 133 ; and Châteauneuf, 142-52 ; hostility towards Marie de Médicis, 137 ; understanding with the Cardinal, 138-40 ;

341

INDEX

intimacy with Anne of Austria, 140, 144–5, 147, 154–5; growing hostility towards the Cardinal, 151; exiled to Touraine, 153–5; at Couzières, 156; at Tours, 157–60; intrigues with Anne of Austria at Couzières, 158–66; Anne's letter to, 171–2; attempt to prevent her leaving the kingdom, 174–5; flight into Spain, 177–92; in Madrid, 193–4; her negotiations with Richelieu, 197–212; in London, 198–219; flight to Flanders, 219–23, 254–8; return to France, 230–7; the plot against Mazarin, 237–47; in exile, 248–61; pardon after the Fronde, 270; reception at Compiègne, 273–4; the understanding with Mazarin, 274–87; intrigues of the Fronde, 262–302; retirement to Dampierre, 303–8; financial difficulties, 308–27; her sons and daughters, 327–33; Bussy-Rabutin's picture, 332–3; retirement to Gagny, and death, 334–35
Chevreuse, Duchy of, 38–43, 317, 319–21, 326
Chevreuse, Henrietta de, *aft*. Abbess of Jouarre, 81, 330
Chevreuse, Hôtel de, 12, 54–5, 166–7, 271, 278–81, 284, 295, 297, 316, 317, 320, 323–4
Chevreuse, village of, 40, 333
Choiseul, 40, 43
Choisy, Mme. de, 314
Cinq-Mars, 76; plot of, 232
Cinq-Mars, Abbé de, 175, 176
Clercelier, 316
Clèves, Catherine de, 37
Clèves, Hôtel de, 245
Coatquin, Marquis de, and Mme. de Chevreuse, 254–5, 257, 267
Coiffy, fortress of, 127, 128
Coigneux, M. le, 204, 214, 217
Coigneux, Mme. le, 322
Colbert, M., Mazarin's secretary, 286–8, 295, 303; daughters of, 329–30

Colbert, Mlle. Henriette Louise, 329
Colbert, Mlle. Marie, 329–30
Coligny, Admiral de, 1
Coligny, Comte Maurice de, 242–3
Cologne, 293
Combraille, Duchy of, 89
Comminges, Lieut., 284
Compiègne, 66, 137, 273, 274, 275
Concini, 9, 12
Condé, 235
Condé, Duc de, 243
Condé family, 90; hatred of the Duchesse, 241–3
Condé, Prince de, and the Ornano plot, 93; at the Council, 247; and the Spanish plot, 259; victory at Lens, 263, 265; attack on Charenton, 266; and Mlle. de Chevreuse, 274; attack on Mazarin, 281–2; arrest of, 282–4; in Vincennes, 289; release, 292–3; visit to Mme. de Chevreuse, 294–5; and the Conti marriage, 296–8; campaign of the Frondeurs against, 299–300; and Mazarin, 301
Condé, Princess de, cousin of the Duc de Chevreuse, 24, 37; at marriage of Henrietta-Maria, 52; hostility towards Mme. de Chevreuse, 240, 242; and Mme. de Montbazon, 244–4
Condé, Princess de (the Dowager), 37, 282
Condour, 182
Conflans, 189
Conrart, *quoted*, 301
Contarini, Venetian envoy, 20
Conti, Prince de, 16; and the Fronde, 268, 269; and Mlle. de Chevreuse, 278, 289–92, 294–8; arrest, 284; release, 292–3
Conti, Princesse de, 16, 22, 24, 52; and the affair of the Duc de Bellegarde, 18; and Mme. de Chevreuse, 31, 33, 37, 43; and Bassompierre, 44; and the Buckingham affair, 62–63, 72, 75; and the Ornano plot, 92

342

INDEX

Corbeil, 266
Corbie, abbey of, 317
Corneille, 184
Corsini, Papal Nuncio, 17
Cottigny, fief of, 40
Coudren, Père de, 88
Couhé, town of, 180
Council of the Regency, 227-8
Couzières, château of, 3, 5, 154, 156, 164, 177, 179, 189, 192, 207, 215, 248, 249, 250, 308, 310, 315
Craft, Mme. de Chevreuse and, 159-60, 162, 176, 219, 251
Cressi, ensign, 284
Cromwell, 255, 277

Dames-des-Hauts-Bruyères de Port Royal. *See* Port Royal, nuns of.
Dammartin, 267
Dampierre, château of, 37, 38-43, 116, 117, 119, 130, 131, 133, 134, 136, 139, 189, 204, 206, 208, 210, 237, 248, 249, 270, 272-3, 302, 303, 306, 307, 313, 317, 320-7, 331, 335
Damvilliers, manor of, 39
Dartmouth, 254
Datel, 73
Dauphiné, 124, 265
Declaration drawn up by Louis XIII, 227-8
Denmark House, 79
Dieppe, 96-7, 209, 293
Digby, Lord, 194, 198
Dolce, 190
Dombes, duchy of, 89
Dorat, Abbé du, and the Duc de Lorraine, 154; agent of Richelieu, 164; and Mme. de Chevreuse, 175-8, 198-202, 204-14; despatch from M. de Catinat, 189; letter from Mme. de Chevreuse, 208-9; letter to Richelieu, 213-14; and the affair of M. de Chevreuse, 314, 316
Doullens, 293
Douzains, 184
Dover, 255

"Duke," limitation of the title by Parliament, 39
Dulorier, 182
Dumoulins, 81
Dunault, secretary, 94, 98
Dunkirk, 219, 220, 221, 255, 256
Duparquet, M., 325
Dutch, the, and Louis XIII, 127

Effiat, Commissioner d', interviews Chalais, 109
Effiat, Comte d', 76, 83
Elbeuf, Duc d', 241
Elbeuf, Duchesse d', 37, 52, 98
Empire, the plots against French, 124, 127, 153, 161
Enghien, Duc d' 184-5, 251, 291
England, relations with Gaston d'Orléans, 95; treaty of peace (1629), 133; French policy, 249, 251
Épernon, Duc d', 97, 107-8, 238, 259, 307, 324
Eschaux, estate of, 178, 182, 189, 190
Eschaux, Monseigneur Bertrand d', at marriage of Marie de Rohan, 11-12, 157; Mme. de Chevreuse's farewell to, 178-9, 182, 188-90, 192
Eschaux, Vicomte d', 178
Essarts, Mme. des, intervention of, 130-1
Estissac, M. d', 188
Estrade, Sieur de l', 248
Estrées, d', *cited*, 236-7
Estrées, Gabrielle d', 94
Étampes, Achille d', and Chalais, 104-5, 109
Étampes, Duchess d', 39
Étampes, Duc d', 39
Excise, Board of, 263
"Exempts," meaning of the term, 109 *note*

Fargis, Charles d'Angennes du, 161
Fargis, Mme. du, intrigues in Brussels, 161-3, 174
Fervaques, Maréchale de, 31

343

INDEX

Feudal property, revenue from, 39
Flanders, influence of the Duchess in, 160; Mme.'s flight to, 219-23, 254-61
Flavigny, M. de, 121, 126
Flèche, La, 254
Fleury, château of, 100, 115
Folaine, M. de la, 25
Fontainebleau, 3, 67, 73, 100, 165
Fontarabia, 194, 204
Fontenay, Marquis de, 106
Fontenay-Mareuil, Memoirs *quoted*, 7, 35, 60, 92, 101, 105, 107
Fossé, Sieur du, 98
Fosse, steward, 316
Fouquet, Abbé, 127, 304, 306-7
Fourqerolles, Mme. de, 243
Franciscan monastery, Nantes, 111
François I, 28, 38, 39
François II, 28
Fromont, Seigneur de, 305
Fronde, intrigues of the, 240-68, 274, 277; the Old Fronde, 275, 277, 282, 290-1, 297; the New Fronde, 281, 290-1, 297; campaign of the Frondeurs against Condé, 299-300
Fruges, Mme. de, 233
Fuensaldagna, Conde di, 267
Fulton, assassination of Buckingham, 132

Gagny, Benedictine Priory, 334
Gaillon, 42
Galareta, secretary, 264
Galigai, Eleonora, 12
Galland, Mlle., 251
Gallois, le, notary, 321, 324, 326
Ganseville, 245
Garaison, Notre-Dame de, 183, 188
Gardes Françaises, the, 265
Garter, Order of the, bestowed on M. de Chevreuse, 83
Gaudin, letters to Servien *quoted*, 248, 256
Gaultier, Leonard, picture of the Duc de Chevreuse, 29-30
Gazette, the, reports of Mme. de Chevreuse, 236, 274

Gerbier, 129
Giron, Spanish Ambassador, 19-20
Gondi, Paul de. *See* Retz, Cardinal de.
Gondrin, 184
Gonsalvo, Don Domingo di, 194
Gonzague, Charles de, 37
Gordes, M. de, 153
Goring, Lord, English Ambassador in France, 195, 249
Goulard, M., arrest of La Porte, 166-7
Goulas, Nicolas, Memoirs *quoted*, 118, 129, 225, 228, 238, 242, 270, 275
Grancey, Comte de, 268
Gras, Le, 171
Gratien, M., 322
Gravelines, siege of, 265
Greenwich, 195, 198
Grosbois, park of, 43
Guadaloupe, 325
Guéméné, Prince de, 4, 5, 117, 156; lawsuits, 308-9, 310-11
Guéméné, Princesse de, 305
Guise, Cardinal de, 28
Guise, Duc de, 15, 26, 37, 39, 241
Guise, Duchesse de, 37, 52
Guise, Duke François de, 28
Guise, Henri de, "le Balafre," murdered at Blois, 16, 28-9, 39
Guise, Hôtel de, 244
Guise, in the Aisne, 267
Guise Princes, the, 119; position at the French Court, 32-3; influence of, 44; the plot against Mazarin, 244; intervention on behalf of Montrésor, 257
Guitant, M. de, 166, 247, 284
Guitry, M., 94
Guyenne, 124, 222, 290; Huguenots of, 43-5

Haqueville, M. de, 280
Hallier, M. du, 100, 130
Hallot, M., 214
Hamel, M. du, request of, 304-5
Hamelin, Jean, 323
Hampton Court, 77, 81

INDEX

Harcourt, Comte d', 37, 246
Haro, Don Luis de, 238
Hautefort, Mlle. de, 173, 177, 189
Havre, the, 96–7, 289, 293
Henri II, 2, 29, 39, 119
Henri III, 2, 264
Henri IV, 3, 16, 18, 29, 30, 34, 39, 49, 94, 97, 130
Henrietta of England, 306
Henrietta-Maria, and Marie de Rohan, 7; marriage, 44, 48–53; and Buckingham, 59; departure from France, 65–6, 68–71; misunderstandings with Charles I, 74–85; reception in England, 76–7; the marriage contract, 123, 134–5; letters to Châteauneuf, 153; and Mme. de' Chevreuse, 197, 203, 209; in Paris, 253, 259
Hericourt, 245
Herwart, 295
Hilaire, servant, 178, 179, 180, 181, 182, 184, 188
Hocquincourt, Marquis de, 235, 274
Holland, Earl of, Ambassador from Charles I, 50–3; account of, 54; and Mme. de Chevreuse, 55, 68, 76, 79–80, 148; and the Buckingham affair, 57, 59, 68, 71, 75; letter to Richelieu, 84; despatched to Paris, 85
Houel, M., 325
Hugo, *Vie de Charles IV*, 124–5
Huguenots, the, campaign against, 43–5; Richelieu and, 74; Buckingham and, 75; and the Ornano plot, 93; and Gaston d' Orléans, 96; and Mme. de Rohan, 115; Mme. de Chevreuse and the, 122–3, 127, 259, 294; fall of La Rochelle, 132
Humbert, Henri, 120

Île de France, government of, 311
" Importants," the, 240, 244
Ingrandes, 108
Issy, 331

Jacobins, Church of the, Paris, 334
James I, relations with France, 49, 50, 54; and Buckingham, 56, 60
Jansenists, the, 304, 327, 328, 333
Jars, Chevalier de, 143, 153
Jars, M. de, 73
Jeannin of the treasury. *See* Castille.
Jeannin, President, 26, 27, 34, 112
Jean-Paul, M. *See* Malbâti.
Joly, Guy, *quoted*, 243, 284, 290, 297, 299, 301, 302
Jouarre, Abbess of, 160, 330, 331
Jouarre, Abbey of, 81, 130, 131, 332
Joyeuse, M. de, 15, 89
Julien, Abbé de St., 251
Julien, M., 160

Karpen, 325
King's Hunt, mastership of the, 311

La Fère, siege of, 30
La Rochelle, Protestants of, 96, 259; and Gaston, 107; siege of, 122, 124, 132, 133, 294
Laffemas, Richelieu's agent, 173
Laigue, M. de, and Mme. de Chevreuse, 264–7, 275–6, 302, 305–6, 308, 332–3; despatches from Brussels, 267–8; return of, 270–1; account of, 275–6; Mlle. de Chevreuse and, 280, 281; reward for, 283, 285; and the Conti marriage, 290; and the Mazarin tapestries, 295; and the Jansenists, 333–4
Laigue, Marguerite de, 276
Lamont, guard, 112
Lamothe-Houdancourt, M. de, Bishop of Mende, letters to Richelieu, 75–6, 78–81, 96
Lancelot, 328
Lange, 212
Languedoc, 125
Lannoy, Mme. de, 48, 72
Laulne, De, secretary, 275
Laval, 254
Le Cabinet satyrique, 17

345

INDEX

Le Cid, 158, 184
League, the, 29, 264
Lenet *quoted*, 231, 259, 278
Lenoncourt, Madeleine de. *See* Montbazon, Duchesse de.
Lenoncourt, Marquis of, 127
Lens, battle of, 263-5
Leopold, Archduke, 258; attack on Condé, 264; appeal of Mme. de Chevreuse, 266-8
Lescot, work on the Louvre, 55
Lésigny-en-Brie, 12, 38, 268
Lhulier, M. le, 316
Liancourt, M., le, 35, 191
Lie, De, 245
Liège, 255-58
Lièvre, M. le, 316
Ligne, Prince de, 285
Lillebonne, 293
Lionne, secretary, 288; Mazarin's correspondence with, 266, 298-9
"Logique of Port-Royal," 328
Lommerein, 325
London, Mme. de Chevreuse in, 198-219
Longuetille, 22
Longueville, Duc de, governor of Normandy, 94, 96, 259, 284, 292-3
Longueville, Duchesse de, and Mme. de Chevreuse, 37, 240, 282; and M. de Coligny, 242-43; claims for, 281; and the Conti marriage, 292, 295-7
Lorraine, Cardinal de, 28, 39, 40, 41
Lorraine, Charles de. *See* Guise, Duc de.
Lorraine, Claude de, Prince de Joinville. *See* Chevreuse, Duc de.
Lorraine, princes of, position at the French court, 32
Lorraine, Charles IV, Duke of, and Mme. de Chevreuse, 117-23, 134-5, 140, 174-6, 200-2, 205-12, 300, 304; claims advanced by, 122-4, 130; and Buckingham plot, 124-9; demands release of Montague, 127-8; treaty with France, 139;

plots against France, 152-4, 161; Anne's dealings with, 171-2; Mme. de Chevreuse's correspondence with, 210, 258
Louis XIII, birth, 3; and Marie de Rohan, 6, 9-12; favours bestowed on M. de Luynes, 13-15; relations with the Queen, 15-19; and Mme. de Luynes, 19-21; anger against the Duchess, 22-7, 31-2, 35-6; and her second marriage, 38-9; the English marriage, 44-53; reception of Mme. de Chevreuse, 45-7; and the Duchess de Montmorency, 47; and the Buckingham affair, 61, 65, 75, 78, 80; the Amiens episode, 67-74; attitude towards Mme. de Chevreuse, 78, 116; and Charles I, 78; and the Order of the Garter, 83; the articles of the marriage contract, 84-5; appreciation of Richelieu, 87-8, and the Montpensier marriage, 90, 114; and the Ornano plot, 91-9; Gaston's request for admission to the Council, 100; arrest of Ornano, 100-1; the Chalais affair, 101, 105, 111-13; arrest of the Vendôme brothers, 106; at Blois, 108; exile of Mme. de Chevreuse, 116-17, 121, 122, 154-5; and Charles IV of Lorraine, 121-3; starts for the Isle de Ré, 126; and Montague, 127-30; pardons Mme. de Chevreuse, 130-7; impressions of the pardon at Court, 132-5; entry into La Rochelle, 132; and Richelieu, 136-7; disgrace of Châteauneuf, 152-4; at Couzières in 1619, 156; hostility of Mme. de Chevreuse, 158-60; the affair of the Val-de-Grâce, 163-72; forbids Anne to see Mme. de Chevreuse, 174; grant of money to Mme. de Chevreuse, 175-6; hears of Mme. de Chevreuse's flight, 189, 191, 194;

346

INDEX

attitude towards Mme. de Chevreuse in England, 196–7, 199, 200; the " abolition " granted to Mme. de Chevreuse, 201–2, 212–13; Mme. de Chevreuse allowed to return to Dampierre, 208; passports for Mme. de Chevreuse, 217; refuses to reply to Mme. de Chevreuse, 220; revolt of Soissons, 222; influence of Richelieu, 224–5; animosity against Mme. de Chevreuse, 224–230; the declaration, 227–28; death, 228, 231; and the Duc de Luynes, 324; and the colonization of the Antilles, 325

Louis XIV, 2; provisions of the regency, 227–8; Mazarin his godfather, 229; driven out of Paris, 263, 264; Mme. de Chevreuse pays her duty to, 274; attempted flight, 292; forbids the Conti marriage, 298; majority, 299–301, 304; and Mme. de Chevreuse, 301, 307, 324–5, 327; and Fouquet, 306–7; and the Colbert marriage, 329

Louvière, Gaston de la, mission to Sedan, 107

Louvière, M. de la, the warrant for, 111–12

Louvre, the, 11, 22, 57, 61, 166, 225, 237, 246, 247, 261; the Salle Lacaze, 24; chamber of the Duc de Chevreuse, 34; Lescot's work in, 55; Jardin de l'Infante, 63; the Queen's apartments, 63; Galerie d'Apollon, 63–4; Chapel of the, 102–3

Lussan, M. de, of Amboise, 252

Luxembourg, palace of the, 297

Luynes, Antoinette de. See Vernet, Mme. du.

Luynes, Duc de, marriage to Marie de Rohan, 9–11, 157, 324; and Anne of Austria, 13; birth of his son, 15; favours from the king, 19; death, 21–2; and the Duc de Cheuvreuse, 31; moneys belonging to, 46–7

Luynes, Duc de, son of Mme. de Chevreuse, claim for his mother's return, 268–9; income of, 321; affairs of, 323, 326; account of, 327–8; marriage of his son, 330

Luynes, Hôtel de, 15

Luynes, Mlle. de, 331, 332

Luynes, Mme. de, 327

Madeleine, the, Paris, 40

Mademoiselle, the Great, 274, 278, 308

Madrid, 193–4

Maignelay, Marquise de, 131

Maillé, Comte de, 244

Maincourt, manor of, 39

Maine, Duc du, 10, 34

Maine, Mlle. du, 34

Maison Rouge, 334

Maisons, 246

Malbâti (M. Jean-Paul), and Mme. de Chevreuse, 182–6, 190, 192–3

Malherbe, 18

Malta, Knights of, 325

Mancini, nephew of Mazarin, 299, 300

Mandat, 251

Mansard, architect, 41, 169

Marc aux Bois, 40

Marchais, château of, 30

Marcheville, 133

Marcoussis, 289

Marfée, battle of, 222

Marie de Médicis, the regency, 3, 9, 33, 49, 135–6; and the Duchesse de Luynes, 15; reconciled to the king, 23; and Claude de Lorraine, 34; the marriage of Henrietta-Maria, 51, 52, 53, 59; and Buckingham, 61, 65–6, 67, 70–3, 75; correspondence with Mme. de Chevreuse, 80; and the Montpensier marriage, 89; and the Ornano plot, 93, 94; and M. de Bréval, 129; letter from Richelieu, 130–1; Mme. de Chevreuse and, 131, 135; hostility to the Cardinal, 136–7, 141; flight to Flanders,

INDEX

137, 162–3; at Couzières in 1619, 156; visit to England, 203
Marie, Princess, 135, 136
Marillac, Marshal Louis de, Letters to Richelieu, *quoted*, 16, 31, 36, 38, 44; command in Champagne, 126, 141
Marillac, M. de, Keeper of the Seals, disgrace, 141
Marsillac, M. de (La Rochefoucauld), friendship for Mme. de Chevreuse, 160, 232–3, 235–6, 249–50; warning to Mme. de Chevreuse, 176–7; loan of the coach and saddle horses, 180–4, 188, 190–2; and the Havre, 238
────── *quoted*, on Mme de Chevreuse, 9, 85, 90, 240; on the Buckingham affair, 56, 57, 62, 69; on Richelieu, 85; on the Ornano plot, 99; on Chalais, 102–3; on the regency, 226; on return of Mme. de Chevreuse, 235–6; on Gondi's friendship, 278; on the Conti marriage, 296
Marston Moor, 255
Marthon, 182
Martinique, 325
Mary Stuart, 28
Massetière, Hôtel de la, 157, 160, 178
Maugiron, Mlle. de, 19
Maulévrier, M. de, 243
Mauny, Marquis de, 52, 94
Maurepas, manor of, 39
Mazarin, Cardinal, reports of Mme. de Chevreuse, 9, 222, 226, 241; and Rosetti, 215; advice to Anne, 228; Louis XIII's confidence in, 229; policy, 230–33; the plot against, 233–8, 244–7; policy towards the Duchesse, 234–6, 239, 250, 257–8, 261–2; and the demands of the Duchesse, 237–9; attack by the "Importants," 244; reply to the Marquis de Coatquin, 255; England's offer to hand over the Duchesse, 256–7; flight from Paris, 263, 266; the Reuil conferences, 268; and the return of Mme. de Chevreuse, 269–70, 272–5; the understanding with Mme. de Chevreuse, 272–87; and Gondi, 276, 279, 280, 281, 288; and Mme. de Montbazon, 280; and the Hôtel de Chevreuse, 280–1; the arrest of Condé, 281–4; unpopularity, 288–9; Mme. de Chevreuse designs his fall, 290–2; flight, 292–4; letters from Cologne, 294; his tapestries hung in the Hôtel de Chevreuse, 295; letter to Lionne, 296; advice to Anne, 297–8; recall, 299–300, 303; negotiations with Condé, 301; letter from the Duchesse in her retirement, 303–4; replies to the Duchesse's requests, 304–5; on Laigue, *quoted*, 332
Mazarin, Duc de, 330
Mazarinades, 8, 263, 272
Mazelle, 315
Mazuel, 190
Meilleraye, M. de la, 94, 192
Menardeau, M., 316, 317, 322
Mende, Bishop of. See Lamothe-Houdancourt, M. de.
Mercœur, Duchesse de, 37
Mercure, reports of Buckingham's visit, 61, 64
Mercy, Abbé Ernest de, 258, 260, 263, 264
Méré, Poltrot de, 28
Méridon, M. de, 322
Métézeau, Clément, 12, 55
Metz, 107, 121, 126, 191
Meudon, 40, 266
Meunier, M. Léger, 323
Mirabel, Marquis de, Anne of Austria's letters to, 135, 160–2, 166, 168, 171–3
Moissac, 20–1
Molé, First President, and Mme. de Chevreuse, 270–3, 275
Molé, Mathieu, Memoirs, 268
Molière, M. de, 251
Monceau, 308

INDEX

Monceaux, 131
Monglat, Memoirs *quoted*, 8, 171, 269, 282, 288, 289, 313
Monluc, Jeanne de, 101
Monluc, Marshal de, 112
Mons, 235
Monsigot, M., 204, 214, 217
Mont Saint-Vincent, Barony of, 325
Montague, Lord, on Marie de Rohan, *quoted*, 7; and Mme. de Chevreuse, 123–5, 127, 160; return to London, 126; arrest, 126–8; letter to Louis XIII, 128–9; charge against Mme. de Chevreuse, 129; release, 130; letters to Châteauneuf, 153; at Tours, 158; reception of the Duchesse in England, 195; advice to the Duchesse, 198–200; departs for Flanders, 219; and Mazarin, 234; at Roye, 235
Montaigne, 7
Montastruc, 185
Montauban, 20, 125
Montbazon, château de, 3
Montbazon, Duc de, account of, 1–4; marriage of his daughter, 10–11; and the queen, 17; mission to Louis, 26; and the marriage of Mme. de Chevreuse, 37; house of, 252; and the Fronde, 277; death, 308; lawsuits following, 308–12; will of, 311
Montbazon, Duchesse de, account of, 2–4, 242; the incident at her house, 242–3; the collation at the Tuileries, 243–4; exiled, 244; and Beaufort, 275; and Mme. de Chevreuse, 280; rewards for, 291; accusation against, 310–11; death, 312–13
Montbazon, Duchy of, 310
Montbazon, Hôtel de, 1–2, 309–10
Montbéliard, County of, 281
Montdidier, 66
Montguyon, Comte de, 10
Montmorency, Constable de, 4, 14

Montmorency, Duc de, and the Queen, 18–9; takes up his mother's quarrel, 47; and the Ornano plot, 93; and M. de Chevreuse, 139; death, 141, 143, 176, 240, 296
Montmorency, Duchesse de, and Marie de Rohan, 14, 27, 47, 48
Montmort, M. de, 316, 321–2
Montpensier, Duchy of, 89
Montpensier, Mlle. de, 52, 89–91, 94, 106, 108, 114, 135, 307
Montrésor, Comte de, Memoirs, 251–3, 254, 265; arrest, 257
Montreuil, M. de, reports, 214, 217, 222
Montreux, 71
Montrouillon, M. de, 321
Morant, M., 316
Moret, Comtesse de, 30
Moron, Jean, 323
Morosini, M., 288
Mortale, 165
Motteville, Mme. de, Memoirs *quoted*, 8–9, 14, 16–19, 23, 26, 56–8, 64–5, 69, 75, 88, 103, 138, 141, 142, 194, 228, 231, 242, 269, 273, 274, 277, 282, 283, 290, 293, 306
Moulins, 137
Mousseaux, 40
Münster, Congress of, 215, 259
Mussidan, 182

Namur, 260–1
Nancy, Mme. de Chevreuse at, 120–1, 123, 124, 160
Nani, Venetian Ambassador, 252, 260
Nantes, castle of, 108, 109, 115; Franciscan monastery, 111; execution of Chalais at, 112–13; government of, 311
Naseby, 255
Négrepelisse, attack on, 45
Nemours, Duc de, 37
Nemours, Duchesse de, *cited*, 282, 293, 294
Nemours, Hôtel de, 252

349

INDEX

Nevers, Duc de, and the Ornano plot, 93, 94, 135, 289
Newbury, 255
Newport, Lord, 219
Nicole, daughter of Henri II, 119–20
Nogent, M. de, 116
Noirmoutier, Duc de, 265, 267, 270, 280, 283, 290, 298, 304, 308
Normandy, 124, 127
Notre-Dame de Garaison, 183, 188
Notre-Dame de Paris, 51–3
Noyers, Des, Secretary of State, 168

Obazine, Abbé d', 97
Ogier, notary, 321, 323
Oinvilliers, farm of, 321
Olivares, Duque, correspondence with Anne of Austria, 162; and Mme. de Chevreuse, 203, 221–2
Orange, Prince of, 248, 249, 257
Orléans, Duc de, 157–8; and Mazarin, 246, 247; and Mme. de Chevreuse, 275, 285, 288, 291, 293; prevents the queen's flight, 292; and the Frondeurs, 297
Orléans, Gaston d', Duc d'Anjou, on the Duc de Chevreuse, 30; and the English marriage, 52, 66, 71; relations with Anne of Austria, 85; personality, 88–9; marriage with Mlle. de Montpensier, 89–90; influence of d'Ornano, 91, 92; refuses to marry, 92–3; requests admission to the Council, 92, 99–100; accusations against Louis XIII, 95–6, 224; confession to the king, 12 July 1626, 96; and the Ornano plot, 94–6, 98–100, 113; the arrest of Ornano, 101; and the Chalais affair, 101, 103, 105, 106, 107; and the arrest of the Vendôme brothers, 106; proposed flight, 107–8, 125; Louis insists on the marriage,

114; and the king's pardon, 133; and the Princess Marie, 135, 136; flight to Lorraine, 136, 140, 152–4; and the Duc de Montmorency, 143; revolt, 151; and Mme. de Montbazon, 242; Mme. de Chevreuse's proposals to, 283, 286; demands release of the princes, 292
Orleans, meeting at, 165
Ormesson, Lefévre d', 329, 330
Ornano, Alfonso d', 91
Ornano, Marshal d', plot of, 90–101; at Vincennes, 109; death, 113–114
Ozonandre, 2

Palais Royal, the, 261, 283, 292, 297
Palatine, Princess, and the Conti marriage, 289–92; and Condé, 294
Paris, return of Mme. de Chevreuse to, 236, 270, 272, 277; flight of the court from, 263, 264; barricaded, 262, 292
Paris, Archbishop of, 263, 276, 330, 331; search of the Val de Grâce, 169–70
Paris, Parliament of, attitude towards Mazarin, 251; plays the part of States-General, 262–4
Parliamentarians, the, and Mme. de Chevreuse, 255–7
Parliamentary Fronde, the, 282
Passe-volants, des, 84, *and note*
Patin, Guy, *cited*, 261, 329
Paulet, Angélique, 31, 64
Peace, Treaty of, between England and France, 133
Pembrock, 75
Pembroke, Earl of, Mme. de Chevreuse's letter to, 256
Pennacors, letter to the Cardinal, 300
Péronne, 235, 293
Phalsbourg, Princesse de, 258
Philip IV, of Spain, and Mme. de Chevreuse, 194, 221
Piccolomini, General, 258

INDEX

Piedmont, 123
Pinet, M., 323
Piquecos, château of, 20, 21
Plainville, 158
Poitiers, 180, 300
Poitou, 127, 204
Pompignan, 30
Pomponne, Simond Arnauld de, 305, 323
Pons, Mlle. de, 278
Pont-aux-Dames, 81
Pontavert, 267
Pont-de-l'Arche, 281
Porte, La, Memoirs, *quoted*, 54, 60, 68, 69, 73, 123, 128, 154, 160–1, 171; dismissal, 73; sent to Lorraine by Anne, 135; at Tours, 160; defence of Anne, 164; and the intrigues, 165, 166; arrest, 166–7; denials of Mère St. Étienne, 170; examination, 167–9, 171, 172, 173, 315–16; exile, 173
Porte Saint-Antoine, 301
Port-Royal-des-Champs, nuns of, 304, 305, 322, 323, 327, 328, 333, 334
Portsmouth, 132, 194
Poterie, M. le Roy de la, 167
Potet, servant, 182, 183, 184, 185, 187, 188, 191
Praslin, 45
Préaux, M. de, 57
Prince, The, journey of Henrietta-Maria in, 75–6
Prou, surveyor, 316
Provençe, affairs in, 124, 284–5, 290
Puisieux, M. de, 46
Putange, M. de, equerry to the queen, 26, 68, 70, 73
Puylaurens, and Gaston, 96; the warrant for, 111–12

Rambouillet, Hôtel de, 64
Rancé, M. de, 312; Richelieu's correspondence with, 135, 136
Ravaillac, 3
Ré, Île de, 75, 126, 129
Réaux, Tallemant des, *quoted*, 5,
13, 16, 21, 30, 43, 54, 69, 157, 196, 313, 327
Remiremont, Abbey of, 331–2
Rémond, notary, 322
Renard, 243
Renault, man-servant, 178, 179, 180, 182, 184, 188, 216
Rennes, Parliament of, 252
Réthelois, Duchy of, 299
Retz, Cardinal de (Paul de Gondi), Memoirs *quoted*, 8–9, 63–4, 69, 230, 242, 244, 246–7, 263, 276, 278–80, 293–4; appeal to Spain, 265; the despatches from Laigue, 267–8; and Mme. de Chevreuse, 271, 275, 283, 302; and Mlle. de Chevreuse, 271–2, 277–81, 296; account, 276–8; claims of, 283, 288; interview with Anne, 283–4; and the arrest of Condé, 284; Mazarin's distrust of, 285–7; and the Conti marriage, 290, 291, 292; the campaign against Condé, 299; created Cardinal, 300–1; arrest, 303, 305–6
Rhodes, Marquis de, 279
Rhodes, Marquise de, 6, 279–80, 289–9
Richelieu, Cardinal de, and Mme. de Luynes, 6–8, 15–16, 31, 36, 38; and Buckingham, 58–61, 64, 74, 75, 80; correspondence with the Bishop of Mende, 78, 81; language applied to Mme. de Chevreuse, 81; and the articles of the marriage contract, 84–5; personality, 86–7; letters from Chalais, 90; and the Ornano plot, 92–9; the council at Fontainebleau, 100; and Chalais, 103–11; charges against Mme. de Chevreuse, 115, 120, 125, 134–6; reply to Bouthillier, 121; precautions in Lorraine, 121, 126, 127; and M. de Bréval, 130; letter to Marie de Médicis, 130–1; attitude of Mme. de Chevreuse towards, 131, 133; siege of La Rochelle, 132; on

INDEX

the Italian Front er, 135; hostility of Marie de Médicis, 136-7, 141; reconciliation with the queen and Mme. de Chevreuse, 138-40; and the correspondence between Châteauneuf and Mme. de Chevreuse, 143-57; Mme. de Chevreuse exiled to Lorraine, 154-5; uneasiness about the Duchess at Tours, 158; letters to Chavigny, 160; hostility of Mme. de Chevreuse, 160; and the affairs of the Val de Grâce, 164-71; hostility of Anne, 164; examination of La Porte, 167-9; Anne's confession to, 171-2; prevents Mme. de Chevreuse leaving the kingdom, 174-5; her confession, 176; annoyance at Mme. de Chevreuse's flight, 189, 191; letter from Mme. de Chevreuse in Spain, 193; Mme. de Chevreuse's negotiations with, 197-212; and M. de Chevreuse, 204, 216, 219; Mme. de Chevreuse's letters from London, 207-9; money sent to Mme. de Chevreuse, 209; Mme. de Chevreuse's appeal to, unanswered, 220-1; death, 223; influence over Louis XIII, 224-5; policy, 230, 238-9, 244-45, 262; and the monetary affairs of the Duc de Chevreuse, 314-15; and the children of Mme. de Chevreuse, 330-2
Richelieu, Duc de, 278
Richmond Palace, 77, 78, 83
Riquetti, of the King's Bodyguard, message to Mme. de Chevreuse, 253-4
Rivière, M. de la, and La Porte, 173
Rochechouart, M. François de, 323
Rochefort-en-Yveline, castle of, 244, 309, 310
Rochefoucauld, Cardinal de la, marriage of Henrietta-Maria, 53
Rochefoucauld, La. *See* Marsillac, M. de.
Rochefoucauld, M. de la, 160; houses of, 180-2, 252; reports to Richelieu, 191
Rochefoucauld, Mme. de la, 181, 191
Rochevalon, 165
Roger, Louise, 3
Rohan, Anne de, 312-3, 327-8
Rohan, Henri de, 259
Rohan, M. de., 117, 124, 125
Rohan, Mme. de, and the Huguenots, 93, 115
Rohan, Tancred de, 259
Rohan-Guéméné, Marie de, 4
Rossetti, the Nuncio, and Mme. de Chevreuse, 23-4, 214-15; the Ornano plot, 96
Rouen, 209
Roundheads, the, 255
Roussel, arrest, 263
Royan, 45
Roye, 235, 236
Rucellaï, letters to Duc de Chevreuse, 31; letter to Claude de Lorraine, 33
Rueil, 191, 208; conferences at, 267, 268; Peace of, 270, 274
Ruffec, 180, 181, 190

Sablé, Marquise de, and the Duc de Montmorency, 18
Saclay, fief of, 40
Saint-Aignan, Duc de, 329
Saint-Antoine, abbey of, 330-1
Saint-Cloud, 266, 269
Saint-Denis, abbey of, 266, 317
Sainte-Beuve, *quoted*, 328
Sainte-Chapelle, Paris, 175
Saint-Émilion, 45
Saintes, 181, 190, 191
Saint-Étienne, Mère (Louise de Milly), 164, 169-70
Saint-Évremond, *cited*, 259, 333
Saint-Fargeau, duchy of, 89
Saint-Fiacre, priory of, 334
Saint Germain-en-Laye, 153, 215, 224, 225, 233

INDEX

Saint-Ibal, M. de, and Mme. de Chevreuse, 258–9, 263, 264
Saint Kitts, 325
Saint Luc, 30
Saint Magloire, 280
Saint-Maixert, 190
Saint-Malo, 254, 256, 257
Saint-Maur, 299
Saint-Merri, 304
Saintonge, 129, 300
Saint Rémy de Reims, abbey of, 317
Saint-Simon, *quoted*, 8, 328, 333
Saint-Vincent de Connezac, 182
Sant Estaban, 193
Saragossa, Viceroy of, 187, 193
Sarmiento, Don Antonio, and Mme. de Chevreuse, 222, 241
Saumur, 173
Sauval, *cited*, 1
Savoy, Duke of, plots against France, 96, 98, 123, 125, 128, 161
Savoy, Prince Thomas of, 214
Schomberg, 30, 81, 100
Scots, the, and Charles, 255
Sedan, 107, 300
Séguier, M., 168, 285, 320, 324
Séguiran, Père, 23, 73
Senlis, 43
Servien, 248, 256, 296
Sierck, 210
Sipierre, Comtesse de, 76
Soissons, Comte de, and Mlle. de Montpentsier, 90; and the Ornano plot, 93, 94; and Mme. de Chevreuse, 107, 125; revolt, 222
Soissons, Comtesse de, 52, 125
Sommerive, 30
Soubise, and Mme. de Chevreuse, 214, 222
Souvigny, *cited*, 4
Souvré, Commandeur de, 7
Spa, conference at, 264
Spain, Mme. de Chevreuse and, 96, 202–3, 222, 239, 248, 252, 257, 258, 259, 263–4, 294; policy towards France, 123, 161–3, 172, 223, 249, 266–8;

Anne and, 151–2, 226; Mazarin's policy towards, 260
Stains, 66
Stenay, 295
Superintendent of the Queen's Household, office suppressed, 48
Switzerland, 125

Tabouret, privilege of the 11, 200
Talleyrand, Daniel de, 101
Tan, mills of, 40
Tarbes, 185, 186
Tellier, Le, Secretary of State, 270, 273, 284–8, 305
Termes, 30
Terne, La, 182, 192
Thémines, Mme. de, 81
Thibaudière, M. de la, 160, 166, 168–9, 171
Thou, M. de, 141
Thuillin, bodyservant, 181–2, 183, 184
Tillac, M. du, 251
Tillières, Comte Léveneur de, 58–9, 62, 65, 74, 76, 77
Tillières, Comtesse de, 76
Titus, anonymous informant, 214
Tonniens, 182
Toul, garrison, 121
Toulouse, 143
Touraine, Mme. de Chevreuse exiled to, 154–5; plotting in, 252–4
Tours, Archbishop of. *See* Eschaux, Monseigneur Bertrand d'.
Tours, Mme. de Chevreuse in, 108, 157–60, 163–78, 189–92, 249, 251, 253
Trappe, La, 312
Trémoïlle, la, family of, 265
Tresmes, M, de, 109
Tuilerie, La, lands of, 40
Tuileries, the, 55, 243
"Two Angels (The)," 246

Uzés, Duc de, 52

Vadencourt, 267
Val de Grâce, Convent of, Paris, affair of the, 163, 169–71, 259

INDEX

Valette, M. de la, 107–8, 204, 214, 217, 219, 222
Valette, Mme. de La (Mlle. de Verneuil), 16, 24; the king's letter to, 25–6; the Ornano plot, 92
Vallier, Jean, *quoted*, 272
Vallière, Mlle. de la, 328
Vaumorin, M. de, 251
Vaumurier, 327, 328
Veleda, Marquis de, Spanish Ambassador in London, 203, 214, 219, 257
Vendôme, Alexandre de, 94, 98–9
Vendôme, Alexandre and Cæsar de, plot against Richelieu, 100, 104; arrest, 106; Mme. de Chevreuse's negotiations with, 115, 249; indemnity for, 283
Vendôme, Cæsar Duc de, 233, 237, 247, 251; and the Ornano plot, 94–5, 97, 99
Vendôme, Duchesse de, 37
Vendôme, Mlle. de, and Duc de Chevreuse, 10, 34
Venetian Ambassador, *quoted*, 22–3
Venice, 125, 127
Verdun, 121, 127
Verger, Château du, in Poitou, 117
Vernet, Barthélemy du, 16

Vernet, Mme. du, 15, 16, 23
Verneuil, M. de, mission to Louis, 26
Verneuil, Marquise de, 30, 31
Verneuil, Mlle. de. *See* Valette, Mme. de La.
Versailles, 225
Versine, 236
Verteuil, 180–2, 190–2
Vertus, Charles, Comte de, 4
Vic, treaty signed at, 139
Vieuville, Hôtel de la, 12
Vieuville, La, 214, 217, 219
Vigean, Mme. de, 246
Vignier, President, 192, 196
Villars, Mme. de, 31
Ville, M. de la, 140, 210–13, 214, 219
Villelongue, 90
Villepreux, 40
Vincennes fortress, 96, 100, 109, 113, 136, 247, 257, 259, 284, 289
Viole, Président de, 298

Wight, Isle of, Mme. de Chevreuse in, 256–7
Women, Spanish, Mazarin on, 238–9

Zamet, M., 35

THE END

Richard Clay & Sons, Limited, London and Bungay.

www.ingramcontent.com/pod-product-compliance
Lightning Source LLC
Chambersburg PA
CBHW022048160426
43198CB00008B/155